CORPORATE VALUATION FOR PORTFOLIO INVESTMENT

Analyzing Assets, Earnings, Cash Flow, Stock Price, Governance, and Special Situations

Robert A. G. Monks
Alexandra Reed Lajoux

Foreword by Dean LeBaron

BLOOMBERG PRESS
An Imprint of
WILEY

ISBN 978-1-576-60317-8 (cloth); ISBN 978-0-470-88074-6 (ebk);
ISBN 978-0-470-93675-7 (ebk); ISBN 978-0-470-93676-4 (ebk)

10 9 8 7 6 5 4 3 2

*To John P. M. Higgins, who has for a half
century explored with me the challenges
of valuation.—RAGM*

*To Stella Swingle Reed, who taught me the value
of perseverance.—ARL*

Contents

Foreword

A SMALL FRACTION of cohorts who lived through the age of the Nifty 50 still tackle important problems. We don't know that the torch has been passed, as an earlier president reminded us. We forgo shuffleboard and leisure suits for writing and mounting platforms on issues that we believe to be important—where we can bring our personal experiences to bear and where our voices will remind others that we bring personal history, energy, and foresight to vexing problems. Bob Monks is the archetype of the group.

We will get to his capabilities shortly, but let us first examine Bob's courage to tackle a really big topic: the valuation of securities. It is as big a subject as they come, running in multidimensions from qualitative to psychological, from static to dynamic, from one dominant measure to a complex soup, and using measures that range from those that are internal to the observer to those determined by the markets. He categorizes the enduring tussles between momentum speculators and fundamental investors (as they often label themselves) and bravely wades into academe and critically tackles anyone, from Nobels to postdocs. Nothing escapes his attention.

Many investors aspire to universal skills, often proclaiming to be rotating specialized investors in the changing days of one valuation mode to another. In truth, most of us adopt a valuation scheme that is suited to the nature of our psyche. We search for nomenclature that proclaims its wisdom; we quest for indices that illustrate our brilliance; and we market . . . oh, we really market.

In *Corporate Valuation for Portfolio Investment*, Bob and his worthy coauthor (more later) cover the full range of valuation methods. We are reminded how narrow most of our outlooks really are. Our normal style as investors in public securities, usually as fiduciaries investing for others, is to examine, select, implement, measure, and report . . . with some ingredient of hope and justification. But Bob's stamp on this book is clear. As in life, so in this book he goes to a rare and important next step. He adds the active behavior of someone who behaves as if he owns the entire business and sends a message to institutional shareholders who tend to rely on buying or selling to express their views to management.

He and I reached the same conclusion independently at about the same time, he as assistant secretary of labor for ERISA [Employee Retirement Income Security Act], and I while chairing a governance committee at the Securities and Exchange Commission. Back in the private sector we shared valuation insights, models, and spreadsheets. I went the next step in aggressively voting against directors who supported protective measures against shareholders and announced our actions—practices unheard of at the time. Bob started an investment management enterprise, the Lens Fund, to invest in potential target companies, announcing plans for some to improve their accountability to owners. Whereas institutional investors typically vote proxy statements with management, without even knowing the individual positions of directors receiving their endorsement, Bob makes his views known. He lays out a clear program.

He is an active investor in large publicly traded securities that need, but normally fail to get, attention from investors who take a position and then aggressively attempt to change companies in directions of greater value. Thus, his focus on valuation is a natural complement to his governance activities. He has to know how to start at a low enough price to provide a cushion for the time it takes to implement his approach. He is usually attracted to a yield sufficient to finance his efforts. He has to develop a cogent program that has not been adopted by the directors charged with just that job. And, finally, he has to have the credibility to make it work. The list of major companies who have felt his attention looks like a typical high-quality list, but the members of that list are better now in hindsight than when Bob and his staff first visited them.

Rarely do companies welcome the interference from someone who proposes to alter their clubby atmosphere. But his investment record is a clue that his ideas, when implemented, work. From its founding in 1992 until it became part of the Hermes Pensions Management group in 2000, activities of the Lens Fund were followed by such august publications as

Barron's and the *New York Times*. As noted in the *Times*: "Lens's investing style pays. In six years of operation, through Dec. 30, 1998, it returned 25.1 percent a year, on average, compared with 20.5 percent for the Standard & Poor's 500-stock index." Well-known shareholder activists like Boone Pickens and Carl Icahn are disruptive and make their intentions to fire managements well-known. It is not surprising they would be met by vigorous objection. Bob Monks, on the other hand, comes in with a plan that can be implemented by the existing management. His proposal is more about accountability than disruption. He too meets with objection but less so than others storming the corporate gates with devastating firepower.

Bob's colleague in this endeavor, Dr. Alexandra Reed Lajoux, brings her own long history to the quest for better approaches to corporate valuation. Alex, who has served as editor of a variety of influential business periodicals, is the lead author of *The Art of M&A* series of books and, through these and her many other writings, is an ardent proponent of the overarching principle of stewardship and long-term sustainable value creation.

Bob and Alex wrote in the Preface: "We wrote this book to advance world prosperity by explaining how to determine the value of corporate equity securities for the purpose of portfolio investment." Together, with records of success improving corporate accountability in their hip pockets, they are ready to storm—tactfully—the barriers to full understanding of what constitutes sustainable value.

DEAN LEBARON
Adventure Capitalist

BOSTON AND ZURICH
DeanLeBaron.com

Preface

WE WROTE THIS BOOK to advance world prosperity by explaining how to determine the value of corporate equity securities for the purpose of portfolio investment.

A number of recent changes have made this subject lava hot: international accounting conundrums, massive transformations making both forward and backward comparisons meaningless, low inflation with rumors of deflation, and—now—government-created assets and earnings! These volcanic trends have brought equity valuation nearly to a meltdown. Yet certain truths remain.

Equity capital provides two main benefits: a flexible funding option for companies and superior returns to investors compared to debt. But unless an investor can buy every stock and hold all stocks for decades, the long-term, general superiority of equity over debt is of little use. To take advantage of equity's power, investors must learn how to put *a precise value on a specific stock for a specific investment period.*

This book advocates a multidimensional approach to equity value, asserting that value exists only in specific temporal and situational contexts. This said, the "default setting" for investment appropriately remains an intelligent investor considering public equity securities as a choice among alternatives.

Corporate valuation for portfolio investment means determining the present value of future worth. There are two main sources of information about the worth of a stock: financial reports and the stock's current trading price.

Financial reports contain riddles that must be decoded by the valuation-minded investor. The first step in valuation for investment is to bridge the gap between current valuation in financial reports and the future value of the company for investment purposes. Despite the work of numerous groups to reform generally accepted accounting principles (GAAP) and their global equivalent, international financial reporting standards (IFRS), financial reports remain only dim mirrors of company value. Sources of complexity in GAAP/IFRS accounting include variation in accounting models, scope exceptions, mixed attributes, and bright line standards.

All this requires reading between the lines. And the main message is that equity securities are difficult to value in part because both companies and the markets that trade in their equity are living human systems prone to self-deceptive traits that militate against pure valuation logic.

Paradoxically, however, human nature, which makes the valuation of equity so difficult, is also the fundamental reason for the superiority of equity. Value-minded investors can put a financial value on the greatest contributor to securities' value: long-term corporate action based on vision. To do so, however, requires a multifaceted approach to valuation, including both respect for quantitative fundamentals and an appreciation for qualitative complexity.

This book, intended for the professional investor building an investment portfolio that includes equity, takes the reader through a range of approaches, including those primarily based in assets, earnings, cash flow, and securities prices, as well as hybrid approaches. It also discusses the importance of qualitative measures that we call "governance" (going well beyond GAAP/IFRS) and addresses a variety of special situations in the life cycle of businesses, ranging from initial public offerings to bankruptcies.

In the process, the book offers formulas, checklists, and models that we and others have found useful in making equity investments. As long as investors thoughtfully use a variety of tools to make their investments, corporate securities will continue to generate wealth for their owners and for society at large.

Acknowledgments

MANY INDIVIDUALS HELPED us write our tome; the chapter endnotes name them. But special acknowledgment goes to those who corresponded with us and/or consented to be interviewed during the actual writing of this book (January 2008–June 2010).

Matthew Bishop, bureau chief for *The Economist*, New York

Steve Brown, founding partner and chief investment officer, Governance for Owners, London

Paul Druckman, chairman, Executive Board of The Prince's Accounting for Sustainability Project, London, United Kingdom

Robert Ferris, executive managing director, RF|Binder, New York

Phillips Johnston, analyst, Dawson Herman Capital, New York

John P. M. Higgins, president and chief investment officer, Ram Trust Services, Portland, Maine

Dean LeBaron, founder, Batterymarch Financial Services, Geneva, Switzerland

Rocky Lee, partner and head of Asia Venture Capital and Private Equity, DLA Piper, Hong Kong

Colin Meyer, dean, Said School of Business, Oxford University

Deborah Hicks Midanek, principal, Solon Group, New York

Lester Myers, professorial lecturer, Georgetown University

Mark Mills, director, Generation Management, London

Paul Pacter, IASB, Hong Kong and London

Al Rappaport, cofounder, LEK-Alcar Consulting Group, La Jolla, California

Anthony Riha, vice president, Bowne Asia, Beijing
George Soros, founder, Soros Fund Management, New York
Allen Sykes, economist and author, London
Raj Thamotheram, senior adviser, Responsible Investment, AXA Investment Managers (AXA IM), Paris
Simon Thomas, chief executive, Trucost, London
Stephen Young, executive director, Caux Round Table

We would also like to acknowledge the encouragement and guidance that we received from the Bloomberg Press team that launched this project, including JoAnne Kanaval, Stephen Isaacs, Mary Ann McGuigan, and Fred Dahl. We also thank the professionals of John Wiley & Sons, including Bill Falloon, Emilie Herman, Tiffany Charbonier, and Todd Tedesco. Artist Mary Graham (mary@oakinsights .com) helped illustrate some of the concepts we discuss in Exhibits 2.1, 5.1 through 5.11, and 6.1. We are grateful for her unique combination of mathematical, artistic, and technical genius. The contributions of these individuals, as well as many others, prove an important point: published books convey knowledge at a level the blogosphere will never match.

Bob extends special thanks to his colleagues Nell Minow, Ric Marshall, Sylvia Aron, and Christine De Santis for their usual superb help.

Alexandra thanks her family, friends, and colleagues past and present at the National Association of Corporate Directors.

CHAPTER 1

Corporate Valuation for Portfolio Investment
A Philosophical Framework

EQUITY SHARES must be valued—but how? It may seem that sophisticated financiers have taken over valuation. The phrase "equity valuation" may conjure up visions of financial specialists feeding numbers into algorithmic programs, relentlessly making buy, sell, or hold decisions unrelated to the operating realities of businesses or to understandable economic concepts such as replacement value.[1]

A great deal of controversy surrounds the mathematicians and physicists (aka "quant jocks") on Wall Street. Some blame them for the economic problems of the first decade, noting their complex trading programs that, once automated, accelerated doomsday events for markets.[2] Others say that the quant jocks boosted the overall intelligence of the market by introducing new and sensible ways of looking at risk and return, pointing out that they were among the first to warn against the crisis.[3] In fact, sophisticated trading programs do have a role to play, but the programs must be based on sound principles. Sophisticated trading activities are the symptom, not the substance, of stock valuation.

In fact, valuation begins from the hour a company's leaders find equity investors who believe so strongly in the company's economic prospects that they are willing to provide capital for it, no strings attached. This belief in a company's future—in a word, *hope*—is what makes the value of the stock something more than the current value of all its assets, if sold in a fire sale. Combined with the investor's own time horizon for a return, hope is the key to securities valuation. Vision and time are the alpha and omega.

Valuable vision is what propels a company's stock into the marketplace; it is what preserves the value of the stock in spite of market chaos. Understanding this concept requires an integrated theory of valuation that includes consideration of assets offset by liabilities, of income, of cash (liquidity), of securities market dynamics, and of comparable pricing. Understanding also requires consideration of what we call *stories*— meaningful information beyond the financial statements and market prices. This book is structured accordingly.

Of course, not all investors base their trades on such an integrated framework for valuation. Some are index investors, some are algorithmic traders, and some are fund managers who buy assets based on classes of risk. In fact, fewer than half of all investors actually choose an investment based on the quality of a particular company.[4] It is for these happy few volitional, value-minded investors that this book is intended.

Cost/Benefit of Information Gathering

There is also the issue (which I found out in the S&P strat[5]) of the price of gathering data. One of the reasons such simple strats exist is the cost of gathering the information you need to implement them is fairly high compared to the payout. Would I be better off screen scraping all the livelong day to implement some lousy subjective strat with a low Sharpe[6] anyway? Or would I be better off getting a job at a bank, making a lot of money, and buying bonds?"

—Posted by Scott Locklin at the Algorithmic Traders Discussion Board on *LinkedIn.com*, April 19, 2009.

Valuation Defined

Valuation means determining a value for something. This book sets forth all the elements of a company that are to be valued and offers guidance on how to determine those values.

➤ *Corporate valuation* determines the worth of a corporation *today* (its present value); *valuation for portfolio investment* joins that present value with a future value. As Al Rappaport said so succinctly in *Expectations Investing*, the key to successful investing is "to estimate the level of expected performance embedded in the current stock price and then to assess the likelihood of a revision in expectations."[7]

➤ *Expectation* is indeed a fitting word for the process of valuation for investment. "Valuation" comes from the Latin word *valere*—to be worth something in an exchange.[8] "Investment" derives from *vestire*—to clothe. It means exchanging money now for something that may offer more money in the future.

Valuation alone is relatively simple; *corporate valuation for portfolio investment* is complex. Valuation alone says A is worth X today. But valuation *for investment* says A is worth X today and *may be worth Y at a future date*. Valuation for investment means determining the present value of future worth.

Valuation is not a one-time event. It is a process. There is no one set of steps to value the stock of an existing public company, but it is generally agreed that the valuation journey proceeds with the following steps:

1. Select the item to be valued (the security).
2. Identify its current price (e.g., today's closing price).
3. Evaluate whether the current price is low, correct, or high.
4. Make a corresponding buy, hold, or sell decision based on the investor's own circumstances—including liquidity needs and the timing of those needs.

As part of step 3, the investor can adjust the values of price (step 2) based on six valuation matrices:

1. Time—Short term versus long term
2. Place—Market versus nonmarket
3. Slope—Level versus skewed playing field
4. Volition—Degree of willingness or unwillingness of the buyer or seller
5. Utility—Purpose (e.g., wealth versus liability collateral for a fund)
6. Quality—Level of certainty of return (high, medium, or low grade) based on investing standards

To get real value, one needs to pass each valuation through these six lenses. This paradigm appears throughout this book.

The Importance of Equity

Few financial topics matter more than equity valuation. Without the possibility of placing a reasonably accurate value on equity securities, there could be no equity marketplace. And without an equity marketplace, society would not have such a diversity of products and services. Some corporate undertakings are so long term and expensive that *only equity capital*—as opposed to operating capital or debt capital—can fund them.[9] Societal commitments such as payments made out of defined pension plans simply cannot be honored unless the obligated payor (the company or union offering the pension) has access to funding that can beat inflation at the level that equities have achieved historically.[10] It is no coincidence that these financial instruments are nicknamed "stock." For an equity market to function, the economy at large must "put stock" (trust) in equities and continually "take stock of" (measure) their value.

The presence of the federal government as an investor (discussed in Chapter 2) raises new issues in equity valuation: as the holder of the shares, will a government entity's focus be on financial return, as in the past, or on matters of broad social significance, such as jobs? There is some precedent for this concern at the state level. Public pension plans have at times made political rather than economic decisions.[11] In general, however, the equity investment decisions of pension plans are based on universally recognized financial principles. One of the purposes of this book is to articulate those principles so that equity valuation maintains its integrity as a discipline.

Equity Defined

First invented by Dutch and English traders some 500 years ago, the term "equity" or "stock" as a form of corporate financing has been part of the business world for half a millennium.[12] *Equity* is created when companies offer ownership stake to buyers, giving stock certificates in return for cash. The value of a company's equity (the number of shares times the current price per share) is its *market value*.

There is another kind of equity. It's the *accounting* kind, namely the dollar-value number remaining on the balance sheet after liabilities are subtracted from assets. This version of equity is also known as "net worth" or "book value." The accounting number is usually much lower than market value, but it can be used as a check on it because it is far less volatile.[13]

Regulators have done a good deal of hand-wringing over what equity is as opposed to debt. (See Appendix A.) In brief, equity represents ownership with potential for returns, while debt represents a claim entitling the holder to guaranteed payments.[14]

The issuance of equity securities brings two distinct values to an economy. For the company's management, the *sale* of equity securities can bring patient capital—funds that support growth without making fixed demands for return. To the company's investors, the *purchase* of securities can bring returns—a share in a company's total worth that grows in value as the company does.

Growth in share prices does not happen in each and every company, but it is common for all companies' stocks as a net total over any given 10-year period. Based on this general trend, Nobel Prize winners Franco Modigliani and Merton Miller asserted that the payment of dividends does not change the firm's market value: it changes only the mix of elements in the firm's financing. The Modigliani-Miller theorem has been true historically, but is it true today? If investors, over time, cannot count on share price appreciation, then the theorem would not hold; dividends would become indispensable for equity investors.

Articles of Faith Undermined: Securitization at Risk

When markets sustain shocks or experience long declines, it is hard for investors to maintain a reasonable expectation of share price appreciation. Such events not only undermine such expectations, but they also diminish faith in securities markets—and understandably so.

Take, for example, the turn-of-the-millennium scandals of Enron and WorldCom. Their share price decline was so rapid and unexpected that it fooled even fairly sophisticated investors.[15] In the space of half a year, two giants—large in market capitalization, book value, and revenues— lost almost all their value virtually overnight upon declaring surprise bankruptcies in late 2001 and mid-2002, respectively.[16]

A decade later, a new series of giants has fallen, including several Wall Street titans felled by the devaluation of securities backed by weak mortgages that went into default—the so-called subprime mortgage crisis. Following severe financial stress, Bear Stearns became part of JPMorgan Chase, and Merrill Lynch part of BankAmerica. Lehman Brothers Holdings sold off multiple divisions and declared bankruptcy. Even Goldman Sachs got heat from the meltdown when SEC made allegations of fraud in an April 2010 lawsuit, triggering shareholder lawsuits and sparking a subpoena from the Financial Crisis Inquiry Commission (FCIC).[17] By June 2010, Goldman's stock was trading at two-thirds its previous 52-week high, showing the heavy toll that companies pay for scandal.[18]

The events from Enron to Goldman bookend what has been called the "worst decade ever for equities," with an overall negative return of –3.3 percent, according to one study.[19] In this crisis, market prices experienced both artificial inflation and deflation, depending on circumstances. The securities of many companies that appeared to have high levels of capitalization, assets, and revenues should have been trading at *lower* prices, given economic realities. Conversely, in at least one case (Bear Stearns), short seller rumors (bordering on illegal activity) caused the firm's security price to plummet, even though the true value of those securities, absent false rumors, was arguably *higher* than their trading price.[20]

It's a well-known statistic that U.S. equities lost more than a third of their value in 2008.[21] Then, in 2009, the crisis continued for one quarter, dragged down by global financial stocks, and then began a slow recovery that continued into 2010.[22]

But this recovery was punctuated with caution. In a report dated May 7, 2009, four key banking regulators released the results of a "stress test" administered to 19 major banks. The report showed that more than half of them needed additional capital to insulate themselves against adverse scenarios. This news was not as bad as many investors had feared—shares rose in response—but gloom about the financial system persisted, weakening confidence in equity securities, not only those of financial institutions but of other companies as well.[23] In 2010, the European Union followed with the publication of their own banking stress test results.[24]

The subprime crisis and its seemly endless aftermath undermined confidence in equity securities in general. Long an engine of liquidity and growth in free economies, securitization is coming under unprecedented scrutiny today. Structured finance, once the darling of financial economists, is getting a bad name.[25]

Speaking before the Council of Institutional Investors in April 2009, Federal Reserve Board Governor Kevin Warsh called the mortgage banking crisis a classic economic "panic." His riveting speech distinguished between recessions and panics:

> Fear. Breakdown in confidence. Market capitulation. Financial turmoil. These words are . . . indicative of *panic* conditions. In panics, once firmly held truths are no longer relied upon. Articles of faith are upended. And the very foundations of economies and markets are called into question.[26]

A footnote in his prepared remarks elaborated: "A panic involves a more insidious set of events in which risk aversion rapidly displaces confidence and individuals and institutions are forced to reexamine fundamentally their world views."[27]

And in a *Wall Street Journal* op-ed that same month, mutual fund guru John Bogle cast aspersions on securitization by including it in a list of alleged causes of the economic crisis, stating that it "severed the traditional link between borrower and lender."[28] Bogle may not have meant to tar all types of securities with the same brush he intended for mortgage-backed bonds. Nonetheless, his widely read column helped make securitization a taboo 14-letter word.

Whether their concern involves dollars and cents or broader issues of governance, by 2010 investors were still shying away from equities, despite the protections of a massive financial reform bill passed in June of that year.[29]

To be sure, equities did not suffer greatly in some economies. For example, the loss of equity values in Scandinavian countries was less precipitous than in other places. But why? Does a societal element come into play? Are certain social conditions associated with fragile equity values?[30]

This book helps investors ask and answer such questions as they analyze the value of corporate securities—starting with a look, right now, at the very raison d'être for equity securities in the first place.

Benefits of the Equity Marketplace

The issuance of equity securities brings two distinct values to an economy. For the company's management, the *sale* of equity securities can bring patient capital—funds that support growth without making fixed demands for return. To the company's investors, the *purchase* of securities can bring returns—a share in a company's total worth that grows in value as the company does. It may be useful to elaborate on each of these points.

> ➤ *Flexible funding*. Without equity capital, all companies would be forced to operate at a sustained level of profitability or seek debt funding, pledging regular repayment according to the terms of their loans or bond offerings. This type of discipline can be good for companies, but it limits their flexibility. Equity securities markets provide a uniquely flexible source of capital for companies with long-term vision, enabling them to employ and reward people for creating new technologies, products, and services that require a long start-up phase. Thanks to the ability to sell equity to choice-driven (or algorithm-driven), thinking investors,[31] companies can generate the extra funds they need over time and under changing circumstances to pursue long-term goals—goals they might not be able to fund by making a profit on their sales, taking out loans, issuing bonds, or, exceptionally, selling troubled assets to the government.
>
> ➤ *Superior returns to shareholders*. At the same time, equity (or stock) investments represent a special financial opportunity for investors, especially institutional investors that need to generate relatively high returns over long periods of time in order to overcome the ravages of time,[32] especially during periods of high inflation.[33] If institutional funds were limited to investments in debt securities, they would have less of a chance for high returns over time. Although some debt securities have a feature that guarantees a percentage return that exceeds the rate of inflation, not all do, and returns from such vehicles are still relatively low.[34]

The Flexible Nature of Equity Capital

The flexibility of equity capital (compared to the obligations of debt capital) may be taken for granted after more than 500 years of use, but it is a remarkably positive feature from a company's perspective. Consider that companies that sell stock are *under no legal obligation to pay back the capital*, much less offer a return on the stock. In fact, when companies reorganize due to insolvency, shareholders are legally among the last in line to be paid. Indeed, this back-of-the-line creditor status is fundamental to the very definition of equity.[35]

The flexibility that equity offers to issuing companies does not come without strings attached: in many countries, such as the United States, equity issuers must adhere to a rigorous disclosure regime. A myriad of federal and state securities laws, stock listing requirements, and domestic and global accounting standards require U.S. public companies to disclose a great deal of detailed information to investors in order to help them determine the value of the securities they are buying, holding, or selling. There are even accounting standards for disclosing information about "securities within securities," that is, about the market value of other companies' securities held by a company that itself is issuing securities.

Long-Term Superiority of Equity over Debt— with a Caution about Volatility

The flexibility of equity makes it more attractive than debt as a source of funds for companies. If economics were merely a matter of trade-offs, the equity advantage for companies would translate into an equity disadvantage for shareholders. But this is not the case. Paradoxically, equity seems to provide stronger returns over time than debt.

The explanation for this paradox is complex.[36] Obviously, time is a critical dimension. If you can't wait a hundred years for a return on your investment, you won't care about the hundred-year average return. On the other hand, it is absurd to compare a single day's returns from two types of investment and expect to learn anything.

Let's look at the record of equity versus debt over different time periods in different regions. Given the variety of studies available, we can create a kind of patchwork quilt of findings that point to at least one general principle: it makes sense to invest in both debt and equity.

In any given region or period, debt securities may offer equal or superior returns and with less volatility. When in 2008, U.S. equities lost more than one-third of their value, their performance was obviously inferior to the positive 2.2 percent rate paid by one-year Treasury bonds that year.[37] This was not a fluke. There have certainly been periods of time when bonds do as well or better than stocks—without the volatility associated with equity securities.[38]

At the same time, despite the plunge in equity trading prices seen by investors in 2008 and early 2009, there is strong evidence that over the long reach of history, stocks outperform bonds. This is not to say that stocks will beat bonds by "divine right"; this theory is eschewed by even Jeremy Grantham, noted for keeping a level head about the value of equity when others panic.[39] A century-and-decade-long time horizon (for what it may be worth) puts equity in the lead over debt. The *Credit Suisse Global Investment Returns Yearbook 2010* shows that from 1900 through the end of 2009, global stocks averaged an annual real return of 5.4 percent, compared with 1.7 percent for bonds and 0.9 percent for bills.[40] (Australia has been the best performing equity market over the 110 years since 1900, with a real return of 7.5 percent per year, with South Africa and Sweden also performing well, with real returns of 7.2 percent and 6.2, respectively, on average since 1900.)[41] All three markets have outperformed the United States over time; the average real return on U.S. equities since 1900 is 6.2 percent. But you will see mostly U.S. examples in this book, because nearly half of all equities (41 percent) are traded in U.S. markets.[42]

Apparently, a single bad year is a drop in the bucket when it comes to a century. Thus the Credit Suisse 109-year finding is not much lower than studies that ended two years earlier:

➤ From 1900 to 2007, the Cowles Commission index, linked to the Standard and Poor's Composite Index (S&P 500), shows an *average real equity return of 6.0 percent per year*, compared to a real bill return of 1.6 percent per year and a real long-term government bond return of 1.8 percent per year.[43] From the start of 1941 to the end of 2007, equity returns averaged 6.9 percent per year, bill returns 1.4 percent per year, and bond returns 1.1 percent per year. Similar gaps between stock and bond and bill returns have typically existed in other long-term periods.[44]

➤ Research conducted for the authors by a researcher within the Treasury of Sweden indicates that from 1900 to 2007, real returns from the shares of 18 major economies have ranged from 2.5 percent (Belgium and Italy) to 7.9 percent (Australia), with Sweden close behind at 7.8 percent. Also beating the Cowles Commission average were South Africa (7.5 percent), the United States (6.5 percent), Canada (6.3 percent), and the United Kingdom (5.5 percent).[45]

So even if we include the disastrous year 2008, long-term returns for equity look good. The problem is that most investors don't hold stock for a century long—and stocks are volatile over time. Another problem is that the returns include reinvested dividends. If dividends are spent rather than reinvested, returns are much lower—only 1.7 percent.[46]

Caveat on Volatility

Even though returns from equity may be strong, they are not predictable. Recent research has shown the annualized 30-year variance from stocks is 1.5 times greater than the one-year variance, due to various kinds of uncertainty facing investors.[47]

The main engine of volatility may be stock declines due to overleveraging. Recent research shows an economic reason for the negative correlation between volatility and stock returns: Stock return volatility is a function of the level of the stock price, which depends on the value of the firm. As a firm's stock value declines, the firm's leverage ratio increases; hence the equity becomes more risky and its volatility increases.[48]

The Focused Nature of Valuation for Investment

The general superiority of equity over debt is *only a long-term average*, of course, and does not apply to all cases. Obviously, if one buys stocks that perform under the market average, returns will be lower than the market average. The hope of the value-minded investor is to select one or more stocks that will perform better than the market average. A middle course is to buy a random selection of stocks through a fund or index and to at least keep up with the market average.[49] This is the basic idea behind mutual funds or other funds that hold diverse stocks.

Some professional investors use indexes that are random in nature, but others want to exercise choice, selecting specific company stocks with a reasonable prospect of positive return over time—from the present to some specific future. Whether they hand-select stocks based on careful research, as many special purpose funds do,[50] or use an algorithmic program, these volitional investors apply some choice to their purchases.

Two Main Sources of Information about Equity

There are two main sources of information about the worth of a stock: financial reports about the company issuing the stock and the current trading price of the stock. Each poses challenges:

> ➤ *Financial reports* are written using conventional accounting standards—e.g., international accounting standards (IAS) to be required worldwide by 2014), or generally accepted accounting standards (GAAP) allowable currently in the United States). But many of these principles have become arcane; they must be decoded by the valuation-minded investor. (Financial reporting issues are discussed in Chapters 2 through 4.)

> ➤ *Stock prices* show the dollar values of trades at specific points in time, indicating what investors think (or have thought) of the equities at given moments in time. These investor opinions are influenced by many factors, including financial reports. (For more on the valuation of equities, see Chapter 5.)

Financial Reports: Issues with GAAP and IFRS/IAS

Company financial statements are prepared according to U.S. GAAP and its international counterpart, IFRS, or, more globally, IAS. Both are based in principles considered to be universal. (See Appendix B.)

U.S. GAAP standards are formulated by the Financial Accounting Standards Board (FASB) and available at its web site, FASB.org, which is overseen by the Securities and Exchange Commission (SEC) and publicly funded via levies from public companies.[51] FASB standards, recognized as authoritative by the SEC and the American Institute of Certified Public Accountants (AICPA), cover some 90 general areas,[52] such as when a company recognizes revenue or losses. GAAP currently has 2,000 pronouncements, which it has codified to make them easier to use. This codification is making it easier to align GAAP with International Financial Reporting Standards (IFRS) standards as the world moves toward a global standard.

A continual complaint against U.S. GAAP has been that it differs from prevailing standards outside the United States. For example, until the turn of the millennium, U.S. GAAP permitted a special accounting treatment, called "pooling" accounting (different from regular so-called purchase accounting) for certain corporate acquisitions that used stock as a currency. The FASB abolished pooling, and now all transactions must be accounted for as purchases. Still, other differences between U.S. and non-U.S. accounting principles have remained. So the FASB and the International Accounting Standards Boards (IASB) have joined together to harmonize standards.

The FASB and the IASB are working on "an improved common conceptual framework that provides a sound foundation for developing future accounting standards." The organizations want to develop standards that are "principles-based, internally consistent, and internationally converged and that lead to financial reporting that provides the information capital providers need to make decisions in their capacity as capital providers." The Conceptual Framework project has eight phases, including notably measurement—arguably the most important for the purposes of valuation.[53]

As we go to press, the goal of an international accounting standards is being achieved, one standard at a time. (See Appendix C.)

Sources of Complexity in Accounting for Company Value

Sources of complexity in GAAP and IFRS accounting include variation in accounting models, exceptions to rules, mixed attributes, and bright line standards.

Variation in Accounting Models

Accounting models complicate matters—so says an SEC group that studies accounting complexity.[54] Examples of competing models are:

➤ Different models for when to recognize impairment of assets such as inventory, goodwill, long-lived assets, financial instruments, and deferred taxes.
➤ Different likelihood thresholds for recognizing contingent liabilities, such as probability for legal uncertainties versus more-likely-than-not for tax uncertainties.
➤ Different models for revenue recognition such as percentage of completion, completed contract, and pro rata (models also vary based on the nature of the industry, as discussed in other sections).

➤ Various standards for "derecognition" of liabilities (i.e., taking them off the balance sheet).

➤ Different models for determining whether an arrangement is a liability or equity.[55]

Exceptions to Rules, or "Scope Exceptions"

If accounting rules were applied universally, it would be relatively easy to use them. But many rules have important exceptions. The Securities and Exchange Commission's Complexity Subcommittee (yes, there is one) has identified such so-called scope exceptions as problematic. For example, using the FASB's new Accounting Standards Codification (ASC) followed by the pre-codified name of the standard:

➤ ASC 815, *Derivatives and Hedging* (SFAS 133), excludes certain financial guarantee contracts, employee share-based payments, and contingent consideration from a business combination, among others.

➤ ASC 820, *Fair Value Measurements and Disclosures* (SFAS 157), requiring mark-to-market accounting for certain equity holdings by corporations, excludes employee share-based payments and lease classification and measurement, among others.

➤ ASC 810, *Consolidation of Variable Interest Entities* (FIN 46R), excludes employee benefit plans, qualifying special-purpose entities, certain entities for which the company is unable to obtain the information necessary to apply FIN 46R, and certain businesses, among others.[56]

Scope exceptions arise for a number of reasons, including cost-benefit considerations, the need for temporary measures to quickly minimize the effect of unacceptable practices (rather than waiting for a final "perfect" standard to be developed), avoidance of conflicts with standards that would otherwise overlap, and political pressure.

Mixed Attributes

Another accounting conundrum noted by the SEC Complexity Subcommittee stems from mixed accounting attributes. The carrying amounts of some assets and liabilities are measured at historic cost, others at lower of cost or market, and still others at fair value. Several measurement attributes currently coexist in GAAP. They result in combinations and subtotals of amounts that make no real economic sense (or, as the Complexity Subcommittee says more tactfully, "are not intuitively useful"). This complexity is compounded by requirements to record some adjustments (to the value of an asset) in earnings, while others are recorded in equity. In preparing a comprehensive income statement, an issuer may choose among these approaches.[57]

Bright Lines: "Either/Or"

Another complexity introduced by accounting is the notion of strict pass-fail thresholds that achieve an all-or-nothing recognition of an asset. Take, for example, lease accounting. Under current requirements, the lessee accounts for the lease in one of two significantly different ways: Either (1) reflect an asset and a liability on its balance sheet, as if it owns the leased asset, or (2) reflect nothing on its balance sheet. The accounting conclusion depends on the results of two quantitative tests, where a mere 1 percent difference in the results of the quantitative tests leads to very different accounting. The four-part pass-fail standard for recognition of revenue from software in some cases leads to zero recognition when in fact partial revenue is received.

The SEC's Complexity Subcommittee notes that bright lines make financial reports less comparable. The accounting is not "faithful to a transaction's substance." Bright lines produce less comparability because two similar transactions may be accounted for differently.

Reforming GAAP and IFRS

Investors, creditors, auditors, and others all have opportunities to weigh in on standards through a comment process or other means. Since 2005, the FASB has sponsored an Investor Task Force (ITF) made up of the country's largest institutional investors.[58] Task force members assign industry analysts at their firms to advise the FASB on standard-setting initiatives.

Despite the presence of investors in the setting of standards, GAAP is still prone to investor criticism. In recent years, some investors have complained that GAAP standards for reporting fail to capture the information investors need to make investment decisions. The American Institute of Certified Public Accountants, the FASB, and others have been taking steps to correct this gap—along with global standard setters.

Enhanced Business Reporting (EBR)

In 2001, the AICPA launched the Enhanced Business Reporting (EBR) initiative, to propose additions to financial reporting, to be adopted on a voluntary basis by companies. This initiative grew out of work initially done by the AICPA (the so-called "Jenkins report").[59]

The recommendations of this group can help the valuation-minded investor. EBR suggests ways to report important intangible factors such as strategy, innovation, people, customer loyalty, market share, leadership, technological change, R&D, what competitors are doing, brand, patents, reputation risks—all obviously important contributors to the value of a company.

Much of the information envisioned for disclosure under the EBR framework is already required for U.S. SEC registrants in the Management's Discussion and Analysis of Financial Condition and Results of Operations, the "MD&A" required under Regulation S-K. But the EBR framework contains useful classifications—taxonomies—for qualitative information. The disclosure requirements contained within the MD&A categories—liquidity, capital resources, results of operations, off-balance-sheet arrangements, and contractual obligations—do in fact cover many value-critical activities, but this information can get lost in the prose. The EBR initiative creates a reporting framework that organizes both quantitative and qualitative information in rational and consistent structure. In fact, the EBR group has already created a taxonomy for use in the new financial reporting software XBRL (a way of tagging electronic records so that they can be totaled, compared, grouped, and otherwise treated as data).[60] (For more on EBR, see Chapter 7.)

Emerging Issues Task Force (EITF)

The FASB has an Emerging Issues Task Force (EITF) composed of representatives of major accounting firms and corporations. This group strives to keep the FASB in touch with economic reality. If issues arise that do not seem to be receiving proper treatment under GAAP, the

EITF holds meetings to discuss them and publishes the findings. Eventually, EITF findings make their way into rules. Issues undergo debate that often pits accounting theory against real-world concerns. Observers note that some EITF members, as users of the standards, have conflicts of interest. One question is, do these conflicts of interest prevent the standards from being fair for and useful to all users?

The Problem of Fair Market Value: Reporting Values for Securities with No Current Market

Problems with the two main sources of information about a security—financial reports (which can be arcane) and market trading prices (which can be subjective)—increase geometrically when companies have to report the value of the *other* companies' securities they hold. And these problems relate to the dreaded concept of fair market value. During times of extreme market volatility, determining such a value is a difficult task, to say the least.

During the 2008–2009 financial crisis, the federal government took ownership of securities held by troubled financial institutions, under the Troubled Asset Relief Program (TARP) initiated under Public Law 110–343, a multipart piece of legislation that included a $700 billion to repurchase troubled financial assets under the Emergency Economic Stabilization Act of 2008.[61] TARP cast government into the role of a lender and investor, providing capital in the form of $1.5 trillion in loans and purchases of government-sponsored enterprise (GSE) securities. The government wanted to be able to value the securities it was going to hold. So the Congressional Oversight Panel asked Duff & Phelps, a securities rating agency, to value preferred stock and warrants under the program, resulting in a report published in February 2009.[62] Because the TARP preferred stock and the TARP warrants are not publicly traded, Duff & Phelps used data from the public debt, equity, and derivatives markets to estimate discount rates, volatility, and default assumptions. In Chapter 5, on valuation using stock prices, we will present Duff & Phelps' findings on the narrow but important issue of valuing a specific set of securities held by a company. (See also Appendix D.)[63]

The Duff & Phelps valuation work gave the government a useful benchmark to use in its new role as an equity investor. In the end, though, TARP program provided greater proof for equity valuation's difficulty than for its ease. Whereas the government had projected heavy losses from its investments, by mid-2010 it was making gains.[64]

Value

At the end of the investor's 24-hour day, value comes down to whether the buyer wants to buy more than the seller wants to sell.

Robert A. G. Monks

Three Studies

Valuation studies like the Duff & Phelps valuation report are well and good, but an equally important question is how companies are "valuing" themselves on an ongoing basis For example, how do boards of directors define performance when creating long-term incentive pay plans linked to long-term corporate performance? This is an important question, because pay benchmarks reflect values. If a board says to a CEO, "you will receive a bonus if you increase operating profits," this implies (or should imply) a belief that the value of the company stems from its profits.

In 2010, three organizations (an association and two compensation consulting firms) published surveys on metrics used to determine pay. All three studies show *profits* as the dominant financial metric, with variable use of others. Also, all three studies showed that companies reward executives for *more than financial results.*

Here are representative results from one of the studies, the *2010 NACD Public Company Governance Survey* published by the National Association of Corporate Directors.[65] The two lists show what results, financial and nonfinancial, are being rewarded in pay plans (Multiple answers accepted.):

Financial results:

➤ Profits 66 percent
➤ Revenues 41 percent

> Cash flow 36 percent
> Stock prices 31 percent
> Ratios based in earnings or returns 31 percent
> Hybrid formulas (e.g. economic value added) 16 percent
> Assets 10 percent

Nonfinancial results:

> Customer satisfaction 54 percent
> Legal compliance 41 percent
> Employee morale 38 percent
> Product quality 34 percent
> Workplace safety 30 percent
> Employee retention 19 percent
> Workplace diversity 14 percent

The other two surveys showed a similar range of responses.[66]

Investors apparently see corporate value differently. A study of investor views of performance metrics showed that the nearer a measure is to cash flow, the more investors consider it a valid measure of corporate performance.[67]

The Need to Read between the Lines

The cumulative effect of these challenges is to make financial reports less transparent with regard to value. Investors must therefore "read between the lines and conduct additional research to discover the real drivers of and threats to value. One purpose of this book is to show investors how to seek the additional company information they need to determine the true value of a security.

Human Nature Complicates (but Also Informs) Equity Valuation

Equity securities are difficult to value, in part because both companies and the markets that trade in their equity are living human systems prone to self-deceptive traits that militate against pure valuation logic. The human element runs deeper than just the market itself, affecting the instruments the market is valuing all along the value supply chain.

Before an equity security can be valued in a market, the security and the market must come to exist. And for this to happen, a number of people must decide or agree to do a number of things. One or more persons must:

1. Conceive of a product or service (entrepreneurs or management).
2. Expend effort producing, delivering, and/or selling the product or service (management and labor).
3. Provide capital for expanding these activities, including buying and selling securities (banks, investors, and venture capitalists).

These three groups are reminiscent of the classical economic categories of entrepreneurship, labor, and capital. They form a continuum of valuation. At each step along the way, the people involved make a judgment about value. How wise is each judgment? In each case, only time will tell.

It may be helpful to revisit the 1934 edition of *Introduction to Security Analysis* by Benjamin Graham and David Dodd. Like the authors and readers of that classic, the authors of this book had to ponder a crashed stock market. How could people attribute high value to stocks one day and little value the next? Certainly human nature plays an enormous role. We quote two sections from the Introduction to the 1934 text, which could have been written yesterday:

> One of the striking features of the past five years has been the domination of the financial scene by purely psychological elements. . . . The "new era" doctrine—that "good" stocks (or "blue chips") were sound investments regardless of how high the price paid for them—was at bottom only a means of rationalizing under the title of "investment" the well-nigh universal capitulation to gambling fever. We suggest that this psychological phenomenon is closely related to the dominant importance assumed in recent years by intangible factors of value, viz., good-will, management, expected earning power, etc. *Such value factors, while undoubtedly real, are not susceptible to mathematical calculation; hence the standards by which they are measured are to a great extent arbitrary and can suffer the widest variations in accordance with the prevalent psychology.* [Emphasis added.]

Then, in a section aptly titled "No Automatic Relationship between Value and Price," Graham and Dodd opine:

> There are a number of other factors involving human nature in Wall Street to which recent experience should lead us to pay . . . serious attention . . . Investment theory should recognize that the merits of an issue reflect themselves in the market price not by any automatic response or mathematical relationship but through the minds and decisions of buyers and sellers. *Further, the investors' mental attitude not only affects the market price but is strongly affected by it* . . . Hence in selecting an investment . . . reasonable allowance must be made for such purely *market-price elements* as can be ascertained, in addition to the more primary consideration which is paid *to factors of intrinsic value.* [Emphasis added.]

The important point is that the trading price of securities can be affected by investors' attitudes and in turn affect them. Equity values rise and fall with market tides, as every investor knows. The value of a security may be influenced by movements in the stock market in general—well beyond the scope of the company and its industries.[68]

George Soros's Concept of Reflexivity

World-class financier George Soros has a term for the effect of human behavior on valuation: *reflexivity*. He says that investors are inherently biased (not objective) about their investments because they are involved in investing, and their involvement in turn changes the value of what they invest in. More philosophically:

> Thinking participants cannot act on the basis of knowledge. Knowledge presupposes facts which occur independently of the statements which refer to them; but being a participant implies that one's decisions influence the outcome. Therefore, the situation participants have to deal with does not consist of facts independently given but facts which will be shaped by the decision of the participants. . . . Reflexivity is, in effect, a two-way feedback mechanism in which reality helps shape the participants' thinking

and the participants' thinking helps shape reality in an unending process in which thinking and reality may come to approach each other but can never become identical.[69]

Complicating matters is the fact that the company fundamentals that investors may consider in setting a buy, sell, or hold price for stock are themselves complex. Even the formulas investors use to set their expectations for returns are influenced by subjectivity. Soros writes:

> Earnings, dividends, asset value, free cash flow: all these yardsticks are relevant, as well as many others, but the relative weight given to each is subject to investors' judgments and is therefore subject to their bias.[70]

Setting an expectation for return is ultimately subjective, and people can move in packs. Soros attributes boom-bust cycles to a flawed perception of fundamentals that is self-reinforcing until it becomes so out of touch with reality that it must reverse itself.

Other Paradoxes in Equity Investing

Reflexivity is no doubt the greatest paradox haunting equity investment, but it is not the only one. Mathematicians versed in game theory have identified many others. John Paulos, a brilliant mathematician who lost his shirt investing in WorldCom, blames his own human nature as an investor—not WorldCom managers or regulators! We highly recommend his book, *A Mathematician Plays the Stock Market*.[71]

Here are just a few of the paradoxes that made it difficult for this genius to invest profitably:

1. *Keynesian beauty contest*. John Maynard Keynes has said that the short-term investor is like a voter in a beauty contest who will win by picking not the most attractive contestant, but the one selected by most others. Research by W. Brian Arthur at the Santa Fe Institute, using a different experiment, has proven that the beauty contest approach leads to mediocre results.[72]
2. *The winner's curse*. In opening bidding, some buyers will overestimate the value of an item, and some will underestimate it. The

higher bidder will usually be one who overestimated it. Therefore, the winner is more likely to overpay.

3. *Cognitive bias*. People tend to be biased toward information that is available (availability bias). They also tend to pay attention to information that confirms rather than refutes their bias (confirmation bias). They tend to prefer what they already have, rather than a new alternative (status quo bias, and a correlative endowment effect—"It's my stock and I love it"). People take far more risks and spend far more money to avoid losses than to achieve gains.

4. *Loss aversion bias*. This kind of bias relates to the so-called Shubik's auction, named after Yale University Professor Martin Shubik, who auctions dollars for higher amounts in class to prove the point that people would rather risk losing large amounts of money in order to avoid losing than walk away after a small loss.

5. *Factoring out failure (survivorship bias)*. In studying the performance of any group (for example, a group of publicly listed companies), the study may leave out companies that have failed and no longer exist. This inflates the average performance of the group by weeding out failures.[73]

6. *The prisoner's dilemma*. The two players in the game can choose between two moves: either cooperate or defect. Each player gains when both cooperate, but if only one of them cooperates, the one who defects will gain more. This dilemma was discovered by Princeton mathematician John Nash, subject of the book and movie *A Beautiful Mind*. His discoveries apply to stock market investing. Paulos argues that if every investor would cooperate by focusing on fundamentals, we would all be better off. But it is human nature to "defect" from this model by finding and exploiting an edge, even if that edge, by becoming common knowledge, benefits only the first investor who finds it.

All these sources of bias and others lead investors to paint themselves into cognitive corners. At the height of the financial meltdown of 2007–2009, one psychiatrist was able to build a practice working with hedge fund traders to help them stay out of their own way, that is, to avoid loss aversion and other foibles.[74] But the foibles that came out in the meltdown are timeless. Irrational investment behavior is so prevalent and persistent that it has become a branch of economics, called behavioral finance.[75]

When you add it all up, as one theoretical physicist observed, "the economy does not compute." It is no wonder that the greatest minds of our day are urging the use of computer simulations to understand market behavior.[76]

The Observer Effect

There is something very human about all this—to a cosmic degree. We are all familiar with the uncertainty principle of Heisenberg, which sets limits on how precisely we may measure the position and momentum of a particle at the same time. (By increasing the precision in measuring one quantity, one is forced to lose precision in measuring the other.[77])

But a more relevant principle from physics is the so-called observer effect, which states that the act of observation will change the phenomenon being observed. A number of physicists, including John D. Barrow and Frank J. Tipler, Max Tegmark, and the late John Archibald Wheeler, have noted the necessity of observation for the very existence of the universe! (Seeing is not only believing; it is being itself.)[78]

Human Nature as the Key to Equity Value

If stock markets exemplify reflexivity, and reflexivity exemplifies life in the universe, the study of stock market behavior can reveal keys to human prosperity. At the very least, the study of the stock market will tell us a lot about human nature, and vice versa.

Paradoxically, human nature, which makes the valuation of equity so difficult, may also be the fundamental cause of the superiority of equity. Think about it. The financial pundits say that greater risk brings greater returns, but this isn't really a given. Risk is merely the uncertainty of loss, as the insurers say;[79] there's nothing intrinsically rewarding about that. Knowing a risk level—or a proxy for it, such as a ratio out of line with peers—can give you a discount level, but it can't help you assess returns. Assets with similar risk levels can bring dissimilar rewards, as financial economist William Sharpe has noted.[80]

Certainly in a world of unknowables, the equity investor's willingness to accept the risk of open-ended returns or losses *deserves* the higher returns accorded to equities. But, again, this willingness does not necessarily *cause* the returns. Certainly companies may take bold risks to provide generous returns to shareholders, but those risks do not always pay off.

The financial returns from equity are made possible by multiple variables beyond the control of company managers, including stock market trends and macroeconomic factors such as interest rates.[81] But the most important variable is in the hands of management. It's corporate genius in action—or, more explicitly, *long-term asset-enhancing vision realized through informed strategy, effectively implemented.*

But how can the value of vision be expressed in terms of dollars and cents? This leads to the important topic of monetization.

Need for Expression in Currency Values

Everything in financial reporting is expressed in currency amounts (e.g., dollars, euro, or yen). This makes it possible to compare amounts from category to category. Common language solves many problems, but it also creates some. Some values are difficult to express in currency amounts because they do not involve a cash transaction. And even when a cash transaction is involved, the amount recorded belongs to the past rather than to the future. Inevitably, the dollar amounts on company financials only approximate value and sometimes do so poorly. The mark-to-market requirement, mentioned earlier, has attempted to correct this problem with respect to securities on balance sheets, but when markets are in turmoil, this is not always a viable solution. In fact, some have argued that mark-to-market-accounting contributed to the 2007–2009 financial crisis.[82] Being a value-minded investor means being able to think in terms of dollars and asking companies to make a greater effort to quantify elements of value. In the long term, investors want this quantification to occur under GAAP/IFRS. In the short term, investors can and do ask companies to report on it voluntarily—the way firms like General Electric have done (more later).

The valuation of options is a good example of putting a dollar number on an intangible—in effect, monetizing a value that has not previously been expressed in a currency amount. Prior to accounting standards that forced expensing of options, companies did not book options as expenses on the grounds that their value was impossible to quantify. But soon various methods to quantify options came to the fore, such as the Black-Scholes method. Today the quantification of options is a requirement under GAAP.

To some, the concept of expressing values in terms of money may seem like an affront to decency. Who can put a dollar value on the things that really matter, such as life, liberty, or the pursuit of happiness? Yet such values are quantified every day in courts of law.

From Science to Philosophy

For many purposes, value must be expressed as a number. For all important purposes, value is subjective and quantification is ultimately arbitrary. In his later years, Peter Drucker changed his description of the duty of corporate managers from maximizing shareholder value to optimizing shareholder value. This is a change from science to philosophy.

—Robert A. G. Monks

One goal of enhanced business reporting (ERB) and similar movements, such as intellectual capital, social responsibility reporting, and the like, is to quantify information that was previously considered nonquantitative. Because accounting must report everything in money (as discussed), ERB tries to help in this regard.

On Financial Mathematics

Valuation-minded investors who wish to put numbers on information need to know how mathematics are used in valuation. One goal of enhanced business reporting is to provide quantitative financial measures for items that are not traditionally expressed as money amounts, and mathematics can help.

Some believe that the use of advanced mathematics in investing over the last 40 years has gone too far, leaving common sense behind.[83] The phenomenon of securitization has created instruments of wealth that are too distant from the wealth-generating sources underlying them. The rise and fall of securities backed by subprime mortgages is a good example of a departure from common sense.

The Market as a CAS

The market is a complex adaptive system (CAS). One need simply reflect on such homilies as overbought, oversold, momentum, or cyclical to touch on this fertile soil. Indeed, most of what is now being expensively sold by hedge fund managers probably could be described as a subset of CAS. Each mathematical formula, each algorithm, is based on perception or guess as to characteristics of the great beast: the market itself.

———————————
—Robert A. G. Monks

Even the best of formulas fail if the values put into them are flawed. Valuation is more than formulas; it involves human judgment. Nonetheless, it is important to understand how math is used in the equity marketplace, not only by investors but also by traders.

Math matters, even if it is something as simple as a side-by-side comparison of a number or set of numbers—the precursor of a ratio. Not every decision maker wants to make the jump from comparison to ratio, but in the world of investment finance, such a leap is obligatory— at least for professional investors.[84]

Based on our experience in valuation, there seems to be a hierarchy of complexity for mathematical tools used in valuation by an investor, progressing from an informal, intuitive realm into a more formal, mathematical realm.

From lowest to highest complexity, the stages are

➤ *Integers*—Numbers expressing a value—such as $2 billion (in, say, operating earnings).
➤ *Ratios*. Relational comparisons of two or more different items through a single fraction or multiplier—e.g., earnings per share or price to earnings per share.
➤ *Multiples*. Numbers derived from ratios.
➤ *Averages* (of ratios or multiples). Averages of many ratios or multiples.

➤ *Algorithms.* Formulas composed of more than one ratio—often yielding a buy/sell or yes/no decision; sometimes expressed as decisional logic rather than as a formula.

Ratios and multiples weight one element of value against another, and use this comparison to indicate value. A ratio or multiple by itself tells investors little or nothing, but if they compare that same ratio across an industry, they can begin to scope out value.

Knowing these tools is helpful to investors valuing a company as they move from one financial statement to another. Therefore, the discussion of these valuation tools will follow the movement from one financial statement to another. For example, the discussion of the debt-to-equity ratio in Chapter 2 focuses on the assets on the balance sheet, while the interest coverage ratio is introduced in Chapter 3, which discusses earnings and the income statement. And obviously a ratio such as free cash flow to operating cash flow belongs in the discussion of the cash flow statement—all coming up.

Tools that combine attributes from multiple sources—balance sheet, income statement, cash flow statement, and/or market price—appear in Chapter 6.

(For more on the use of math in valuation, see Appendix E.)

In Closing: About This Book

This book is intended primarily for use by institutional investors—professionals who buy and sell equity securities on behalf of institutions. At the same time, we hope that others may find it of interest as well. We would be honored if professors of finance chose to recommend this book along the other classics on valuation we recommend at the end of this book, such as Graham and Dodd's *Security Analysis.* Furthermore, we believe that securities valuation is a broad-based competency needed by all participants in financial markets, including not only those who buy securities but also those whose work gives securities their value—managers and other employees. Indeed, investors and managers speak a common language when it comes to valuation: They both want to know what they will get for what they will give. Risk and reward considerations apply to both.

The coauthors hope to offer a set of valuation tools that combine two equally important aspects of valuation for investing: fundamentals and complexity.

Fundamentals

This book contains all the necessary *fundamentals* for valuation analysis. It takes the reader through the major financial statements of a company and shows how to assess key elements of value within them. Although a certain level of reader sophistication is assumed, the coauthors know that individuals have varied backgrounds. Some readers may be extremely sophisticated in equity instruments but have gaps in their knowledge of debt markets—or vice versa. Others may be financial accountants but lack a grasp of economics, or an investor trained in economics may find pronouncements of the FASB to be nothing short of Greek. Therefore, with apologies to the few readers who may in fact know all the fundamentals, the book is packed with basics. If you already know something, just skip over it.

Complexity

The book should make its greatest contribution by bringing discipline and meaning to the notion of corporate synergy—the undeniable fact that the corporation is more than the sum of its parts. Fundamentals can go only so far in helping investors assess the value of an investment in a security. Investors can calculate the market value of every asset, tangible and intangible, reported and nonreported. They can scrutinize the income statements over time for trends in profitability. And they can make cash flow statements their focus and gain an appreciation for the sustainability of cash flowing into the enterprise. But beyond all these fundamentals (presented chapter by chapter), the investor must be aware of other dimensions of corporate value. That is why this book, in addition to explaining fundamentals, will offer windows of insight—presented as boxed text—enabling investors to stretch beyond logic into other realms of possibility. This visual device is meant to convert experience into intuition for the reader.

The Authors

The senior author, Robert A. G. Monks, has spent a lifetime making sense of valuation for investment—a complex set of moving targets. Many in the business world know Bob Monks best as a shareholder activist who founded Institutional Shareholder Services and the Lens Fund after working on private pension fund issues at the U.S. Department of Labor. In his much earlier years, he was a securities runner for

Paine & Webber in the summer of 1950; served as a principal in his family money management business, Gardner Associates (a money management firm); and eventually became chairman of the Boston Company and Boston Safe Deposit & Trust Co. Many of the windows on valuation come from his vast experience as a direct risk-taking participant in the rough-and-tumble of financial markets.

The book's coauthor, Alexandra Lajoux, has spent three decades making technical financial material understandable to professional audiences through her own books or through books and reports prepared with and for others, including a variety of experts and task forces concerned about questions of corporate value. Her task in this book has been to construct its fundamental framework so that its new windows on valuation can let in the most light.

A Range of Approaches

Investors need to use a full spectrum of valuation approaches. At one end there are the tire-kicking skills of the old-fashioned appraiser—the value investor. At the other end of the valuation spectrum are the gambling instincts of those who can anticipate market moves—the technical investor. The best valuation practices span this full range, for good reason. As noted earlier, stock prices both reflect and influence the value of the securities being priced.

➤ *Tire-kicking*. There is an entire profession of business appraisers who focus on the value of assets and who base valuation estimates largely on those values. These professionals often serve as expert witnesses in cases concerning the value of privately held enterprises for which there is no securities market. Asset-based valuation of this kind is used in valuing natural resource companies. For example, a crude oil producer such as Petrobras (NYSE: PBR) may be valued based on the value of its current proven reserves, minus a discount for the costs and risks of extraction (such as an oil spill), and a forest industry company such as Weyerhauser (NYSE: WY) might be valued based on the value of the timber it controls.[85]

➤ *Gambling*. The notion of an economy that operates like a casino for investors emerged out of the worldwide Great Depression following the 1929 stock market crash. Economist John Maynard

Keynes wrote, "Speculators may do no harm as bubbles on a steady stream of enterprise, but the position is serious when the enterprise becomes the bubble on a whirlpool of speculation. When the capital development of a country becomes a by-product of the activities of a casino, the job is likely to be ill-done."[86]

➤ Value lies somewhere between these two extremes of absolute and relative value—or, if you will, between economic value and market value. Throughout this book, the coauthors steer a middle course. The terrible consequences of valuation extremes have worn on all of us in recent years. May you invest within the golden mean and may this book be a helpful guide along the way.

Notes

1. Tobin's Q ratio is an example. This ratio, invented by the late James Tobin of Yale University, is calculated as the market value of a company divided by the replacement value of the firm's assets. Professor Tobin, a Nobel laureate in economics, theorized that the combined market value of all the companies on the stock market should be approximately equal to the sum of their replacement costs.

2. The role of algorithmic trading was a focus for the Financial Crisis Inquiry Commission (FCIC), chaired by former treasurer of the State of California, Phil Angelides. Formed in late 2009, the Commission has plans to deliver its final report in December 2010. See remarks Chairman Angelides made June 2, 2010, at http://www.fcic.gov/hearings/pdfs/2010-0602-Angelides .pdf. For questions Robert A. G. Monks has posed to the Angelides Commission, see his web site, RAGM.com.

3. For a balanced view on the role of algorithmic trading, including a reading list of books on the subject, see Dennis Overbye, "They Tried to Outsmart Wall Street," *New York Times*, March 9, 2009. Interesting blogging and lively commentary appear at *Discover* magazine's web site: http://blogs.discovermagazine.com/cosmicvariance/2009/03/22/the-physicists-killed-wall-street/.

4. See Robert A. G. Monks, "The Return of the Shareholder," Harvard Law School Forum on Corporate Governance and Financial Regulation, February 2, 2009, http://blogs.law.harvard.edu/corpgov/2009/02/02/the-return-of-the-shareholder/.

5. S&P Strategy indexes.

6. *Sharpe ratio*. In 1966, and later in 1977, Professor William Sharpe introduced a *reward-to-variability ratio* to measure the performance of mutual funds. A low Sharpe ratio means high volatility. In a 1994 article, "The Sharpe

Ratio" (see *Journal of Portfolio Management*, Fall 1994, at http://www
.stanford.edu/~wfsharpe/art/sr/sr.htm), he explained how to use the ratio
before making an investment (ex ante): "Let *Rf* represent the return on
fund F in the forthcoming period and *RB* the return on a benchmark
portfolio or security. In the equations, the tildes over the variables indicate
that the exact values may not be known in advance. Define *d*, the *differential
return*, as:

$$d \equiv R_F - R_B \qquad (1)$$

Let *d*-bar
   be the expected value of *d* and sigma *d* be the predicted standard
deviation of *d*. The ex ante Sharpe Ratio (S) is:

$$S \equiv \frac{\overline{d}}{\sigma_d} \qquad (2)$$

The S ratio indicates the expected differential return per unit of risk associated with the differential return."

    During the 2007–2009 financial crisis, the Sharpe ratio came under
questioning, as some funds with a high Sharpe ratio (low volatility) failed (see
The Economist, http://www.economist.com/business-finance/displaystory
.cfm?story_id=12948575); and SeekingAlpha.com, http://seekingalpha
.com/article/171438-spotlight-on-the-sharpe-ratio-part-i).

7. Alfred Rappaport and Michaell J. Mouboussin, *Expectations Investing:
   Reading Stock Prices for Better Returns* (Boston: Harvard Business School
   Press, 2001), xv.

8. For an interesting discussion of value, see Michael Eldred, "Questioning the Earth's Value—Including a Proposal for a Capitalist Carbon Sink
   Industry," at the Conference on Climate & Philosophy, University of South
   Florida, September 14–16, 2006, industry (http://www.webcom.com/
   artefact/untpltcl/qstnerth.html#one, delivered at 1st International). He notes,
   "The verb 'valere' is linked (via an Indo-European root °ual-) to the German
   'walten' which means 'to prevail,' again from L. prævalere 'to be very able,'
   'to have greater power or worth,' 'to prevail' . . . . [Thus] there is an intimate
   interconnection between the powers of exchange (exchange-value) and
   productive powers/powers in use (use-value)."

9. For a definition of equity securities versus debt securities, see Appendix A.

10. Traditionally, at least half of all corporate funds has been invested in public
    equity. In the last part of the first decade, this proportion has changed,
    with some plans reducing their equity investments from half to a third. See

Mark Anson, "One-Two Punch to Pension Funds," *Pensions & Investments*, January 22, 2009. Also, starting in 2000, pension funds began investing in private equity and hedge funds, as well as in traditional stocks and bonds. See "Defined Benefit Pension Plans," Government Accountability Office, http://www.gao.gov/new.items/d08692.pdf.

11. Steven Malanga. "Public Pension Funds Become Political Playthings," *Real Clear Markets*, April 22, 2009, http://www.realclearmarkets.com/articles/2009/04/public_pension_funds_become_po.html.

12. For commentary on the history of stock-issuing corporations, see the books by Robert A. G. Monks posted at RAGM.com.

13. The growth (or decline) in book-value equity can be measured through the impact of events that have changed the book value of an investor's interest in a business from the start of a financial period to the end of the period. Here is the formula:

> Shareholders' equity at beginning of period (per share)
> + Dividends paid (per share)
> + Shares buybacks (premium over book value per share)
> − Share buybacks (premium over book value per share)
> + Comprehensive income (per share)
> = Shareholders' equity, end of period (per share)

14. Some instruments do not fall neatly into either category, even if they have the name equity or stock. For example, consider preferred stock instruments such as private investment in public equities (PIPES). For a discussion of this type of instrument, see "PIPES: What Issuers Are Thinking About Preferred Stock Investments," Deloitte & Touche, June 2009. http://www.deloitte.com/assets/Dcom-UnitedStates/Local%20Assets/Documents/MA/us_ma_Insights_PIPEs_102309.pdf. See also Appendix A.

15. See John Allen Paulos, *A Mathematician Plays the Stock Market* (New York: MJF Books, 2003).

16. The Enron example from December 2001 is particularly compelling. This was a company with a market capitalization of $70 billion, equity of $11.5 billion on booked assets of $65.5 billion, and revenues of over $100 billion. All these numbers plummeted as soon as Enron declared bankruptcy and investors got the chance to see what was really going on (such as questionable accounting practices that in some instances amounted to fraud). Enron's stock went from $90 to $15 per share in a matter of weeks, and today Enron is a shell corporation with virtually no value by any measure. To realign dollars with value, regulators focused on governance and disclosure reforms. The U.S. Congress passed the Sarbanes-Oxley Act, the Securities and Exchange Commission passed some 50 new rules interpreting this

law, and the major stock exchanges set forth new governance standards for listed companies. The post-Enron era lasted until 2008, when a financial panic brought about a new set of reforms even more comprehensive than Sarbanes-Oxley.

17. For more on the Angelides Commission, see note 2. For insights on the Goldman Sachs matter, see "Goldman Sachs' Role in Crisis at Stake, Defends Valuations that Helped Put AIG in Bind," *Wall Street Journal*, July 2, 2010.

18. At the close of trading June 23, 2010, Goldman Sachs (GS) closed at $135.07, down from its 52-week high of $193.60.

19. Charles Jones, North Carolina State University, cited in Dan Burrows, "After Equities' Worst Decade Ever, the 2010s Gotta Be Better, Right?" *Daily Finance*, http://www.dailyfinance.com/story/investing/after-equities-worst-decade-ever-the-2010s-gotta-get-better-r/19298144/.

20. An April 2008 client letter from Weil, Gotshal & Manges notes: "Spreading false rumors in order to induce others to trade in a company's securities may constitute market manipulation under Sections 9 and 10(b) of the Securities Exchange Act of 1934. On the Self-Regulatory Organization front, NYSE Rule 435(5) and its FINRA corollary prohibit member firms from circulating 'in any manner rumors of a sensational character which might reasonably be expected to affect market conditions on the Exchange'" ("Regulators Announce Investigation and Enforcement Priority with Respect to False Rumor Spreading by Short Sellers, or 'Short and Distort' Activities," Weil, Gotshal & Manges, April 3, 2008, http://www.weil.com/news/pubdetail.aspx?pub=6465).

21. Jonathan Burton, "The Year of Investing Dangerously," *Wall Street Journal*, January 5, 2009, http://www.marketwatch.com/story/after-brutal-2008-beating-stock. *Note*: The most dramatic losses occurred in the fall of 2008. From September 15, 2008, to July 15, 2009, the Dow Jones Industrials suffered a net loss of 3,062.50 points. It closed at 11,421.99 on September 14, 2008, and at 8,359.49 on July 17, 2009, after much volatility and a spring rally that continued throughout 2009.

22. The Dow Jones global index fell 15 percent from January 1, 2009, through March 31, 2009, and global financial institution indexes also fell: the United Kingdom's FTSE 350 bank index (down 27 percent), Japan's Nikkei 500 bank index (down 12 percent), and the Dow Jones Euro Stoxx Banks. Then losses seemed to level off. In the United States during 2009, the Dow Jones Industrial Index started at 8,776, plunged in January and February, but climbed back up to top 10,000 by the end of the year. As of mid-2010, the Dow Jones Industrial Stocks were still at the 10,000 mark.

23. David Enrich, Robin Sidel, and Deborah Solomon, "Fed Sees Up to $599 Billion in Bank Losses: Worst-Case Capital Shortfall of $75 Billion at 10 Banks Is Less Than Many Feared; Some Shares Rise on Hopes Crisis Is

Easing," *Wall Street Journal*, May 8, 2009. See also "Joint Statement by Secretary of the Treasury Timothy F. Geithner; Chairman of the Board of Governors of the Federal Reserve System Ben S. Bernanke; Chairman of the Federal Deposit Insurance Corporation Sheila Bair; and Comptroller of the Currency John C. Dugan: The Treasury Capital Assistance Program and the Supervisory Capital Assessment Program," May 6, 2009, http://www.federalreserve.gov/newsevents/press/bcreg/20090506a.htm.

24. Jan Strupczewski, "EU to Publish Bank Stress Test Results in July," Reuters, June 17, 2010. http://www.reuters.com/article/idUSLDE65G23720100617.

25. Joshua D. Coval, Jakub W. Jurek, and Erik Stafford, "The Economics of Structured Finance," Harvard Business School Finance Working Paper No. 09-060: "The essence of structured finance activities is the pooling of economic assets (e.g. loans, bonds, mortgages) and subsequent issuance of a prioritized capital structure of claims, known as tranches, against these collateral pools. As a result of the prioritization scheme used in structuring claims, many of the manufactured tranches are far safer than the average asset in the underlying pool. We examine how the process of securitization allowed trillions of dollars of risky assets to be transformed into securities that were widely considered to be safe, and argue that two key features of the structured finance machinery fueled its spectacular growth. *At the core of the recent financial market crisis has been the discovery that these securities are actually far riskier than originally advertised.*" [Emphasis added.]

26. Kevin Warsh, governor, Federal Reserve Board, "The Federal Reserve Agenda," Keynote Luncheon Speech of April 6, 2009, at Council of Institutional Investors. http://www.cii.org/events/2009_spring_meeting.

27. Ibid.

28. John Bogle's point is that "[t]he proximate causes of the crisis are usually said to be easy credit, bankers' cavalier attitudes toward risk, 'securitization' (which severed the traditional link between borrower and lender), the extraordinary leverage built into the financial system by complex derivatives, and the failure of our regulators to do their job. But the larger cause was our failure to recognize the sea change in the nature of capitalism that was occurring right before our eyes. That change was the growth of giant business corporations and giant financial institutions controlled not by their owners in the 'ownership society' of yore, but by agents of the owners, which created an 'agency society.'" Robert A. G. Monks has been saying this in books, articles, and speeches for more than 20 years.

29. The Wall Street Reform and Consumer Protection Act of 2010 has been hailed as the most significant piece of financial legislation since the 1933 Securities Act and 1934 Securities Exchange Act, although it does not replace those laws or even modify them to any great extent. The law

would strengthen the regulation of derivative securities, hedge fund advisors, impose stricter oversight of credit rating agencies, and expand SEC enforcement powers and funding.

30. See Carmen M. Reinhart and Kenneth S. Rogoff, "The Aftermath of Financial Crisis," *Money Science*, January 27, 2009, http://www.moneyscience.com/ Finance_Focus/Research_-_The_Aftermath_of_Financial_Crises.html. Professor Reinhart is at the University of Maryland and Professor Rogoff is with Harvard University.

31. The word *thinking* merely emphasizes the fact that investors make choices. It does not suggest that their choices are always correct. See the discussion of irrationality later in this chapter.

32. The U.S. Treasury defines the inflation rate as the percentage change in the Consumer Price Index for all Urban Consumers (CPI-U) over a six-month period ending prior to May 1 and November 1 of each year, http:// www.treasurydirect.gov/forms/savpdp0039.pdf.

33. Inflation rates can be mild (4 percent or less), moderate (5 to 9 percent), or severe (10 percent or more).
As we go to press, the inflation rate in the United States is 3.2 percent, based on the Consumer Price Index, a target measure (http://www.statistics .gov.uk/cci/nugget.asp?ID=19).

34. The U.S. Treasury states that the Long-Term Real Rate Average (the unweighted average of bid real yields on all outstanding TIPS with remaining maturities of more than 10 years) can be a proxy for long-term real rates, http://www.ustreas.gov/offices/domestic-finance/debt-management/ interest-rate/real_ltcompositeindex.shtml.

35. During their deliberations on the Financial Instruments with the Characteristics of Equity in April 2007 and for the following year, the joint meeting of the International Accounting Standards Board (IASB) and Financial Accounting Standards Board (FASB) proposed that "the distinction between equity (risk capital) and liabilities is based exclusively on the ability or inability of capital to absorb losses incurred by the entity with losses being tentatively understood as accounting losses." However, at the joint board meeting in October 2008, the IASB used a new definition of equity based on the perpetual approach (that is, *no settlement feature* and entitlement to pro rata share on liquidation of the issuing entity) and the basic ownership approach (that is, *most subordinated instrument* and entitlement to percentage of net assets), http://www.iasplus.com/agenda/ liabequity.htm. For more details on equity versus debt, see Appendix A.

36. Researchers have found "nonlinearity in the relationship between U.S. excess stock and bond returns and macroeconomic predictor variables, finding evidence of multiple regimes and time varying covariances and

demonstrate the superior out-of-sample predictive accuracy of such a model to a comparable, single-state linear [value at risk]" (Massimo Guidolin, Stuart Hyde, David McMillan, and Sadayuki Ono "Non-Linear Predictability in Stock and Bond Returns: When and Where Is It Exploitable?" Working Paper 2008-010A, April 2008, Federal Reserve Bank of St. Louis, Research Division, http://research.stlouisfed.org/wp/2008/2008-010.pdf).

37. The Dow Jones dropped 36.2 percent, the biggest decline since 1931 when aftershocks from the crash of 1929 sent stocks down 40.6 percent (Joe Bel Bruno, "Wall St. Closes Out on 2008, Year of Record Losses," *Associated Press*, December 28, 2008).

38. In the G7 countries, between 1979 and 2007, bond returns were comparable to stock returns and yet displayed considerably lower volatility—the same bang for a smoother buck. During the 1900–2007 period, U.S. equity returns were subject to a standard deviation of 20 percent, for example, with most major nations having even higher volatility. According to research conducted for the authors by a source within the Treasury of Sweden, standard deviations in that period were United Kingdom, 19.8 percent; United States, 20.0 percent, Italy, 28.9 percent, Japan, 29.8 percent, and Germany 32.3 percent—the last three no doubt affected by losing World War II. According to one study, bonds have lower volatility. See Massimo Guidolin et alia, "Non-linear Predictability in Stock and Bond Returns: When and Where Is It Exploitable?," *International Journal of Forecasting*, 25, Issue 2, April-June 2009. Overall, for the period from 1900 to 2009, volatility of equity investments per year for the average country was 23.5 percent. Credit Suisse Research Institute, *Credit Suisse Global Investment Returns Yearbook 2010*, February 2010, http://www.london.edu/newsandevents/news/2010/02/Credit_Suisse_Global_Investment_Returns_Yearbook_2010_1077.html.

39. Grantham calls the idea that equity automatically returns more than debt "dangerous," dismissing it as no better than the theory of "divine right" that once supported inherited monarchies, http://www.scribd.com/doc/21673022/Jeremy-Grantham-Third-Quarter-2009-Letter.

40. Credit Suisse Research Institute, *Credit Suisse Global Investment Returns Yearbook 2010*, February 2010+p. 47, Figure 3. http://news.morningstar.com/pdfs/CS_Year_Book.pdf. The introduction to this source notes that its indexes "represent the long-run returns on a globally diversified portfolio from the perspective of an investor in a given country. The charts opposite show the returns for a U.S. global investor. The world indexes are expressed in U.S. dollars; real returns are measured relative to U.S. inflation; and the equity premium versus bills is measured relative to U.S. treasury bills."

41. Ibid.

42. Ibid.

43. J. Bradford DeLong and Konstantin Magin, "The U.S. Equity Return Premium: Past, Present and Future," Coleman Fung Risk Management Research Center, Paper CFRMRC07-010, February 1, 2008, http://repositories.cdlib.org/iber/cfrmrc/CFRMRC07-010 or http://www.j-bradford-delong.net/2008_pdf/20080228_jep_submit.pdf.

44. DeLong and Magin (see note 41), citing Ranjish Mehra (2003reports an annual equity return premium of 4.6 percent in post–World War II Britain, 3.3 percent in Japan since 1970, and 6.6 percent and 6.3 percent respectively in Germany and Britain since the mid-1970s. Mehra's paper, "The Equity Premium: Why Is It a Puzzle?" *Financial Analysts Journal*, January/February 2003, pp. 54–69, received a Financial Analysts Foundation Graham and Dodd Scroll for excellence in financial writing.

45. *Credit Suisse Global Investment Returns Yearbook 2010.*

46. *Credit Suisse Global Investment Returns Yearbook 2010.*

47. "Conventional wisdom views stocks as less volatile over long horizons than over short horizons due to mean reversion induced by return predictability. In contrast, we find stocks are substantially more volatile over long horizons from an investor's perspective. This perspective recognizes that parameters are uncertain, even with two centuries of data, and that observable predictors imperfectly deliver the conditional expected return. We decompose return variance into five components, which include mean reversion and various uncertainties faced by the investor. Although mean reversion makes a strong negative contribution to long-horizon variance, it is more than offset by the other components. Using a predictive system, we estimate annualized 30-year variance to be nearly 1.5 times the 1-year variance" (Lubos Pastor and Robert F. Stambaough, "Are Stocks Really Less Volatile in the Long Run?" Social Science Research Network, May 22, 2009, http://papers.ssrn.com/sol3/papers.cfm?abstract_id=1136847. *Note*: Pastor is with University of Chicago–Booth School of Business, the Centre for Economic Policy Research [CEPR], and the National Bureau of Economic Research (NBER). Stambaugh is with the University of Pennsylvania–The Wharton School and the National Bureau of Economic Research [NBER].).

48. See Robert Geske and Yi Shou, "Capital Structure Effects on Prices of Firm Stock Options: Tests Using Implied Market Values of Corporate Debt," Social Science Research Network, November 2007, revised January 2009, http://papers.ssrn.com/sol3/papers.cfm?abstract_id=1341993.

49. It is not easy to get a random sample of stock, as noted by Eugene Fama, in "Random Walks in Stock-Market Prices," Graduate School of Business, University of Chicago, http://www.chicagogsb.edu/faculty/selectedpapers/sp16.pdf. The classic article by Fisher and Lorie on equity stock returns

was not from a random sample; they actually measured the rate of return for each and every stock in their sample (common stocks listed on the New York Stock Exchange for various time periods from 1926 to 1960). The basic assumption in all their computations is that at the beginning of each period studied, the investor puts an equal amount of money into each common stock listed at that time on the Exchange. This amounts to random sampling where the sampling is, of course, exhaustive. (L. Fisher and J. H. Lorie, "Rates of Return on Investments in Common Stocks," *Journal of Business* 37, no. 1 (January 1964): 1–21, http://www.crsp.com/50/images/rates%20of%20return%20paper.pdf.)

50. The authors interviewed representatives from several funds that put extensive research into stock selections. For a complete list of interview subjects, please see the Acknowledgments.

51. The Sarbanes-Oxley Act requires public companies to pay mandatory fees to fund the FASB. Prior to this federally mandated funding, FASB was funded by voluntary contributions, making it prone to special interests. For this history and its implications for accounting rules, see Jack Coffee, *Gatekeepers: The Professions and Corporate Governance* (Oxford: Oxford University Press, 2006). There is some concern that IASB will be prone to the same conflicts, since the IASB is not publicly funded. See William W. Bratton and Lawrence A. Cunningham, "Treatment Differences and Political Realities in the GAAP-IFRS," April 28, 2009, Accepted Paper Series, http://papers.ssrn.com/sol3/papers.cfm?abstract_id=1375617.

52. The principles have developed over time as needed. Now they are being organized into a codified scheme for easier use. The subjects in the codification scheme will become tags for data management under XBRL language, discussed elsewhere in this chapter and in Chapter 7. For more about the GAAP codification, see http://www.fasb.org/project/codification&retrieval_project.shtml.

53. The phases of the project are A: Objectives and Qualitative Characteristics; B: Elements and Recognition; C: Measurement; D: Reporting Entity; E: Presentation and Disclosure; F: Purpose and Status; G: Application to Not-for-Profit Entities; and H: Remaining Issues. As of late 2009, Phases A through D have begun, whereas phases E through H are pending, http://www.fasb.org/project/conceptual_framework.shtml and http://www.iasplus.com/agenda/agenda.htm.

54. http://edocket.access.gpo.gov/2008/E8-11276.htm.

55. Source for discussion of competing models: http://sec.gov/rules/other/2008/acifr-scsupdate-050208.pdf. For more about equity versus debt securities, see Appendix A.

56. The FASB Accounting Standards Codification (ASC or the "Codification"), which organizes U.S. GAAP into 90 general topics. Each topic contains at least one subtopic; subtopics have sections and sections have paragraphs. Full FASB citation style requires topic, subtopic, section, and paragraph. However in this book we are using a short form of citation, namely the new name (topic only) followed by the old name. Note: Effective July 1, 2009, changes to the source of authoritative U.S. GAAP, the *FASB Accounting Standards Codification™* (FASB Codification), are communicated through an Accounting Standards Update (ASU). As of June 25, 2010, the FASB had issued 36 updates. Note: This new nomenclature does not affect the numbering of FASB *Statements*. Although the American Institute of Certified Public Accountants has codified them (Codification of Statements on Auditing Standards, February 2010), their names remains the same. See   http://www.cpa2biz.com/AST/Main/CPA2BIZ_Primary/AuditAttest/ AuditPreprationandPlanning/PRDOVR~PC-057205/PC-057205.jspA number of organizations have prepared charts juxtaposing the new and old nomenclature. See, for example, this one from the GBQ audit firm, http:// www.gbq.com/SiteObjects/2C7663414A9BA0AC4EBFA488512D857C/ Codification%20Quick%20Reference%20092009.pdf.

57. Comprehensive income is defined by the FASB as "the change in equity [net assets] of a business enterprise during a period from transactions and other events and circumstances from nonowner sources. It includes all changes in equity during a period except those resulting from investments by owners and distributions to owners." (FASB Statement 130, *Reporting Comprehensive Income*, June 1997.) In other words, comprehensive income is the sum of net income, and other items that cannot be included in the income statement because they have not been realized. They unrealized holding gains or losses from available-for-sale securities or foreign currency translation gains or losses. According to ASC 220 (SFAS 130), Comprehensive Income, three alternative formats are allowed for presenting OCI and total comprehensive income:

➤ Below the line for net income in a traditional income statement (as a combined statement of net income and comprehensive income).

➤ In a separate statement of comprehensive income that begins with the amount of net income for the year.

➤ In a statement of changes in stockholders' equity.

Under ASC 220, FASB encourages reporting entities to display the components of OCI and total comprehensive income using the first or second of these formats. Cumulative total OCI for the period should be presented on the balance sheet as a component of stockholders' equity, separate from additional paid-in capital and retained earnings. See Ganesh J. Panditt and Jeffrey J. Phillips, "Comprehensive Income: Reporting Preferences of Public Companies," *CPA Journal*, November 4, 2004, http://www.nysscpa.org/cpajournal/2004/1104/essentials/p40.htm.

58. Current task force members are The Capital Group Companies, Fidelity Investments, General Electric Asset Management, Mellon Financial Corporation, Putnam Investments, T. Rowe Price, and Wellington Management.

59. See http://www.aicpa.org/Professional+Resources/Accounting+and+Auditing/BRAAS/EBR.html and http://www.aicpa.org/Professional+Resources/Accounting+and+Auditing/Accounting+Standards/ibr/chap1.htm.

60. For the SEC's new rule, see http://www.sec.gov/rules/final/2009/33-9002.pdf.

61. Emergency Economic Stabilization Act of 2008 (Division A of Pub. L. 110-343, enacted October 3, 2008). http://www.gpo.gov/fdsys/pkg/PLAW-110publ343/content-detail.html.

62. *Valuation Report: Congressional Oversight Panel*, Duff and Phelps, February 4, 2009. http://cop.senate.gov/documents/cop-020609-report-dpvaluation.pdf

63. See Appendix D, "Duff & Phelps February 2009 Report to the Congressional Oversight Panel."

64. "Total bank investments of $245 billion in FY2009 that were initially projected to cost $76 billion are now projected to bring a profit. Taxpayers have already received over $16 billion in profits from all TARP programs and that profit could be considerably higher as Treasury sells additional warrants in the weeks ahead." ("Treasury Receives $45 Billion in Repayments from Wells Fargo and Citigroup —Tarp Payments Now Total $165 Billion," December 22, 2009, http://www.financialstability.gov/latest/pr_12232009b.html.)

    For 2010 performance, see "Secretary of the Treasury Timothy F. Geithner Written Testimony before the Congressional Oversight Panel," June 22, 2010 (TG754). http://www.treas.gov/press/releases/tg754.htm.

65. Surveys by the National Association of Corporate Directors (NACD), an association of 10,000 corporate directors and board advisors, show that boards are concerned about corporate financial performance, which ranks along with strategy as a top board concern year after year. In 2010, NACD included a question about corporate performance definition in its annual survey. The NACD also convened a Blue Ribbon Commission on performance metrics that year. See *Report of the NACD Blue Ribbon Commission on Corporate Performance Metrics* (Washington, DC: NACD, 2010).

66. The findings from the other two surveys, regarding long-term performance measures, were as follows:

    PM&P On Point: 2010 Executive Pay-for-Performance Survey, Pearl Meyer & Partners, 2010.

➤ Profits or earnings ratios 62 percent

➤ Revenues 48 percent

➤ Ratios showing returns 45 percent

➤ Profit ratios 31 percent

This survey also specified customer satisfaction/experience as a criterion, cited by more than one quarter of respondents.

Study of 2008 Performance Metrics Among Top 200 S&P Companies, James Reda and Associates, February 2010.

➤ Profits or profit ratios 49 percent

➤ Total shareholder return 44 percent

➤ Return ratios 29 percent

➤ Revenue 15 percent

➤ Cash flow 8 percent

This survey also cited quality assurance and customer satisfaction as metrics.

67. Jan Barton, Bow Hanson, and Grace Pownall, "Which Performance Measures Do Investors Value the Most—and Why?" "A factor capturing nearness to cash flows is positively associated with a performance measure's value relevance; a factor reflecting the measure's persistence, predictability, smoothness and conservatism is negatively associated." January 23, 2009. http://ssrn.com/abstract=1230562.

68. For an advanced mathematical discussion of this fact, see Per Frederiksen, Frank S. Nielsen, and Morten Orregaard Nielsen, "Local Polynomial Whittle Estimation of Perturbed Fractional Processes," Center for Research of Econometric Studies of Time Series, CREATES Research Paper 2008-29, ftp://ftp.econ.au.dk/creates/rp/08/rp08_29.pdf.

69. George Soros, "The Theory of Reflexivity," lecture delivered April 26, 1994, MIT Department of Economics World Economy Laboratory Conference, Washington, D.C.

70. Soros, note 60.

71. John Allen Paulos, *A Mathematician Plays the Stock Market* (New York: MJF Books, 2003).

72. W. Brian Arthur, "Inductive Reasoning and Bounded Rationality (The El Farol Problem)," Stanford University and Santa Fe Institute. Paper given at the American Economic Association Annual Meetings, 1994 Session: Complexity in Economic Theory, chaired by Paul Krugman and published in *American Economic Review* (Papers and Proceedings), 84 (1994), 406–411.

73. Sometimes, to avoid survivorship bias, analysts can overcorrect, leading to reverse survivorship bias, argues Juanni T. Linnainmaa in "Reverse Survivorship Bias," November 26, 2009, http://faculty.chicagobooth.edu/workshops/finance/pdf/RSB20091126.pdf.

74. Joseph A. Giannone, "Hedge Fund Shrink Says Success Is All in Your Head [profiling psychiatrist Ari Kiev]," *Reuters*, March 19, 2009.

75. See, for example, Andrew Lo, "Reconciling Efficient Markets with Behavioral Finance: The Adaptive Markets Hypothesis," http://web.mit.edu/alo/www/Papers/JIC2005_Final.pdf.

76. See Mark Buchanan, "This Economy Does Not Compute," *New York Times*, October 1, 2008. Mark Buchanan, a theoretical physicist, wrote this from Notre-Dame-de-Courson, France.

77. The uncertainty principle says that you can't measure position and motion at the same time. The amount by which a measurement errs is called the observer effect; the lower limit to that error is called the uncertainty principle. A mathematical statement of the uncertainty principle is that every quantum state has the property that the root-mean-square (RMS) deviation of the position from its mean (the standard deviation of the X-distribution)

$$\Delta X = \sqrt{\left\langle \left(X - \left\langle X \right\rangle \right)^2 \right\rangle}$$

times the RMS deviation of the momentum from its mean (the standard deviation of P)

$$\Delta P = \sqrt{\left\langle \left(P - \left\langle P \right\rangle \right)^2 \right\rangle}$$

can never be smaller than a small fixed fraction of Planck's constant:

$$\Delta X \Delta P \geq \frac{\hbar}{2}$$

Any measurement of the position with accuracy ΔX collapses (reduces to a single state) the quantum state, making the standard deviation of the momentum ΔP larger than $\hbar/2\Delta x$.

See W. Heisenberg, "Über den anschaulichen Inhalt der quantentheoretischen Kinematik und Mechanik [On the actual contents of quantum theoretical kinematics and mechanics]," *Zeitschrift für Physik*, 43 (1927): 172–198, and W. Heisenberg, *The Physical Principles of Quantum Theory* [translation of *Physikalische Prinzipien der Quantentheorie*] (Chicago: University of Chicago Press, 1930).

78. One way to assert the relationship between life and observation is to imagine life without observation. According to Max Tegmark: "Abstract: Some superstring theories have more than one effective low-energy limit corresponding to classical spacetimes with different dimensionalities. We argue that all but

the (3 + 1)-dimensional one might correspond to 'dead worlds,' devoid of observers, in which case all such ensemble theories would actually predict that we should find ourselves inhabiting a (3 + 1)-dimensional spacetime. With more or less than one time dimension, the partial differential equations of nature would lack the hyperbolicity property that enables observers to make predictions. In a space with more than three dimensions, there can be no traditional atoms and perhaps no stable structures. A space with less than three dimensions allows no gravitational force and may be too simple and barren to contain observers." (Max Tegmark, "On the Dimensionality of Spacetime," *Class. Quantum Grav.* 14 (1997): L69–L75.)

79. This definition has been around for at least 40 years. See Robert I. Mehr and Emerson Cammack, *Principles of Insurance* (Homewood, Ill.: Richard D. Irwin, Inc., 1961).

80. The Sharpe ratio, or reward-to-variability ratio, is named after financial economist William Sharpe. It measures excess return (or risk premium) per unit of risk in an investment. The simplest version of it is

$$S = \frac{E\left[R - R_f\right]}{\sigma} = \frac{E\left[R - R_f\right]}{\sqrt{\mathrm{var}\left[R - R_f\right]}}$$

where R is the return on the target investment, Rf is the return on a benchmark asset, such as the risk-free rate of return (such as a T-bill), $E[R - Rf]$ is the expected value of excess of the asset return over the benchmark return, and p is the standard deviation of the asset excess return. The Sharpe ratio shows how well the return of an asset is expected to compensate the investor for the risk taken by investing in the asset. When comparing two assets, each with the expected return $E[R]$, against the same benchmark with return Rf, the asset with the higher Sharpe ratio gives more return for the same risk. Investors are often advised to pick investments with high Sharpe ratios.

81. When it comes to macroeconomic variables, "interest rates are the most consistent and reliable predictors of stock returns," say researchers. See Massimo Guidolin, Stuart Hyde, David McMillan, and Sadayuki Ono, "Non-Linear Predictability in Stock and Bond Returns: When and Where Is It Exploitable?" Federal Reserve Bank of St. Louis, Research Division, Working Paper 2008-010A, April 2008, http://research.stlouisfed.org/wp/2008/2008-010.pdf.

82. See Chris Chiovacco, "Pet Rocks and Mark-to-Market Accounting," March 13, 2009, http://www.ciovaccocapital.com/sys-tmpl/petrocks/.

83. "The once 'gentlemanly' business of finance has become a game for 'players.' These players are increasingly technically sophisticated, typically having PhDs in a numerate discipline. The roots of this transformation

have their foundation in the 1970s. Since then the financial world has become more and more complex. Unfortunately, as the mathematics of finance reaches higher levels so the level of common sense seems to drop. There have been some well-publicized cases of large losses sustained by companies because of their lack of understanding of financial instruments. In this article we look at the history of financial modeling, the current state of the subject and possible future directions. It is clear that a major rethink is desperately required if the world is to avoid a mathematician-led market meltdown." (Paul Wilmott, "The Use, Misuse and Abuse of Mathematics in Finance," *Philosophical Transactions: Mathematical, Physical and Engineering Sciences* 358, no. 1765 (2000): 63–73.)

84. This very simple approach is favored by many decision makers. See Shih-Kung Lai, "An Empirical Study of Equivalence Judgments vs. Ratio Judgments in Decision Analysis," *Decision Sciences* (April 2001): "Two commonly used elicitation modes on strength of preference, equivalence and ratio judgments, were compared in an experiment. The result from the experiment showed that ratio judgments were less effective than equivalence judgments. Based on an iterative design for eliciting multi-attribute preference structures, equivalence judgments outperformed ratio judgments in estimating single-attribute measurable value functions, while being nearly more effective than ratio judgments in assessing multi-attribute preference structures. The implications of the results from the experiment are that multi-attribute decision-making techniques should take advantage of the decision maker's inclination of making effective equivalence trade-off judgments, and that useful techniques should be devised to incorporate different commonly used techniques, such as multi-attribute utility theory and the Analytic Hierarchy Process, to elicit and consolidate equivalence trade-off judgments." Lai's hypothesis: "Ratio judgments on attribute gains are more difficult to express than equivalence judgments because the former presumably require the decision maker first to transform the attribute levels into strength of preference values in a transformed attribute space, and then make ratio judgments based on the transformed scale, which needs more cognitive effort than the latter that require only trade-off judgments in the original attribute space." Further, "strength of preference judgments within attributes are easier to make than those among attributes because no trade-off judgments across attributes are needed in the former case." For these two reasons, investors don't always use rigid ratios or formulas to make their decisions.

85. This example is based on one given in John D. Stowe, *Equity Asset Valuation* (Hoboken, New Jersey: John Wiley & Sons, 2007), 20.

86. John Maynard Keynes, *The General Theory of Employment, Interest, and Money* (New York: Harcourt, Brace & Jovanovich, 1936).

CHAPTER 2

Valuation Based on Assets

Buying a house is not the same as buying a house on fire.
—James Dimon, chief executive officer, JPMorgan Chase,
testifying before the Senate Banking Committee April 3,
2008, about Morgan's purchase of Bear Stearns with
support from the federal government

CORPORATE VALUATION BEGINS with an understanding of assets held by the corporation being valued. This is the most straightforward way of valuing a corporation and in some regions, such as Asia, the most widely accepted way.[1]

To be sure, few investors or corporate leaders consider assets to be a primary indicator of corporate value. However, this does not diminish the importance of this corporate element. If accounting standards could recognize the full extent of true assets, then balance sheets would become a more important point of focus for investors—and for corporate boards.[2]

Asset values are shrouded in mystery. Some assets are reported on the balance sheet; many are not. Still, astute investors strive to understand how key assets drive the value of the equities they buy. In theory, a proper valuation of all assets, including the value of unreported items such as corporate reputation and culture, equals the value of the company. Dividing that value into total shares outstanding should yield the maximum price to pay per share. But the question is, how much time and money would it take to study all assets in order to determine that price? The cost of analysis cannot exceed the investment returns it makes possible.

To save the analyst time and to set sensible boundaries on analysis, this chapter provides a primer on asset fundamentals. It identifies the location of assets in the balance sheet, then moves on to a caveat and cautionary tale. After suggesting a working definition of assets, the valuation of assets is reviewed in a going concern versus a liquidation. Other topics in this chapter include the role of the appraiser in valuing assets and how to value securities and other intangibles on and off the balance sheet, using international standards. Closing the chapter is a discussion of special issues in asset valuations, especially those that are industry specific.

The goals are to increase the investors' understanding of the asset values embedded in securities, to offer rules of thumb for assessing those values, and to provide tools to improve analysis when the investor's time and funds permit.

Wise Words

Yes, we could collect the gold at the bottom of the ocean. But that would cost more than the gold is worth!

———————————
—Stanley Foster Reed (1917–2007), ca. 1957

Overview of Assets as a Unit of Valuation

The valuation of assets or of any other elements reported on a financial statement begins with an understanding of the accounting standard used to record the value. For ratios focused on asset values, see Appendix 2.1 at the end of this chapter. For guidance on when to use an asset-based approach, see Appendix 2.2.

Currently, global businesses are coping with the convergence of two dominant systems for accounting (see Appendix C). The valuation-minded investor needs to understand what standard is being used to value an asset—including assets not reflected in the balance sheet.

The classic accounting formula for the balance sheet is

$$\text{Assets} - \text{Liabilities} = \text{Equity}$$

The value of assets is offset by liabilities; the remaining value is equity (also known as "net worth"). Here are the definitions:

➤ The most authoritative global definition of *assets*—from a 2008 joint task force of the Financial Accounting Standards Board (FASB) and the International Accounting Standards Board (IASB)—says that an asset is a "present economic resource to which an entity has a present right or other privileged access."[3]

➤ According to the same global standard, "a *liability* of an entity is a present economic obligation for which the entity is the obligor."[4]

➤ Finally, the global standard says that *equity* is "the residual interest in the assets of the entity after deducting all its liabilities."[5]

These definitions of assets, liabilities, and equity, along with the basic equation for the balance sheet, have an internal logic. Accounting theoreticians call this "primacy of assets" (as opposed to earnings) as a valuation concept.[6]

Right Questions, Right Order

The result of applying the asset and liability view is an internally consistent, well-defined system of elements . . . that make it clear that in accounting for a transaction or other event, these are the right questions to ask, and this is the right order in which to ask them:

- What is the asset?
- What is the liability?
- Did an asset or liability change, or did its value change?
- Increase or decrease?
- By how much?

(Continued)

(Continued)

Did the change result from:
- An investment by owners?
- A distribution to owners?
- If not, the change must be comprehensive income.
- Was the source of comprehensive income what we call:
- Revenue?
- Expense?
- Gain?
- Loss?

To start at the bottom and work up the list will not work.

—Reed K. Storey and Sylvia Storey, FASB Special Report, "The Framework of Financial Accounting Concepts and Standards," January 1998

The asset/liability approach, emphasizing the balance sheet over other statements, presents two challenges. One is temporal, the other spatial.

➤ The *temporal* challenge with the balance sheet is twofold:
  ➤ First, a balance sheet in its totality is only one moment in time—close of business the last day of the financial year. This freeze-frame clashes with the inherently protean nature of asset values, which change over time. How can companies and their investors stay current with the changes? The mark-to-market mandate has met with mixed success and some backlash.[7] The very notion of the market value of assets is fraught with difficulty.
  ➤ Second, each of the values reported on the balance sheet is based on valuations conducted prior to the point in time studied. Even though the securities held on the balance sheet are marked to market (however imperfectly), *other assets are not.* So the balance sheet is forever out of date.
➤ The *spatial* challenge with the balance sheet is even more fundamental. The purpose of financial reports, by the standard setters' own admission, is *not to report values.* Rather, it is to *report*

economic transactions according to a consistent methodology that may illuminate value. Thus the location of those transaction valuations is not where the entity is operating now as a going concern, but rather all the places it has been when engaging in economic transactions.

In summary, the balance sheet presents a universe that is parallel to, but not identical with, securities value. The time and space of what the balance sheet describes are fundamentally different from what the company is. Value-minded investors need to know how to interpret information from accounting numbers—as a consistently applied system—into revenue-producing values for the future.

Therefore, this chapter begins with a caveat and a cautionary tale.

Accounting Antiquity

One can understand financial statements only by imagining that the figures are in Roman numerals and the footnotes in classic Greek.

—Robert A. G. Monks

An Opening Caveat: The Limitations of Accounting Numbers

In the two lifetimes of experience in equity markets (as an investor and researcher respectively), the coauthors have seen dirt-floor basement operations grow to become skyscraping multinationals, and they have seen those same giant multinationals implode to dust. Either phenomenon exemplifies the limitations of accounting numbers, which, when looked back upon for a certain day or period, can underreport rising worth and/or overreport declining worth. In many cases, the price investors paid for a company's securities gives a better indication of a company's present asset values than do accounting numbers. Yet there's no escaping reported asset values because security prices often factor them in. This is the chicken-and-egg situation. One must consider both.

Asset values reported in the balance sheet provide clues to company value. Indeed, assets are featured in many popular financial ratios (see Appendix 2.1). But investors need to understand the nature of accounting numbers, as well as the information they contain about the value of the company as a going concern and the value of its assets.

Step one in this understanding is to realize that reported assets and the ratios based on them should be viewed with caution. The gap between accounting numbers and market values is great, no matter what consistently applied system is applied. The system may be U.S. generally accepted accounting principles (GAAP) as determined by the FASB. Or the system may be international financial reporting standards (IFRS) as determined by the IASB.[8] Last but not least, the system could be the integrated global standard the IASB is devising now as we go to press.

Whatever system is chosen, it is bound to miss value by a mile; the challenge is to measure that mile.

The values assigned to a corporation's assets by accountants usually err on the side of pessimism. By professional oath, accountants must be conservative. They record the actual cost of purchase of an asset and do not mark it up to higher market value except under certain conditions (e.g., securities held). Also, they must abide by certain accounting concepts and conventions that tend to depress net income.[9]

But conservatism in reporting assets is more than a worst-case calculation. It's a state of mind.[10] Accountants stand in the present, looking toward the past; therefore, they always fall short of capturing all the true value of the company for investors, who by nature look to the future.[11] Intangible values—such as brand values—not associated with a particular recordable transaction do not get reflected on the balance sheet under accounting rules.

Accounting Numbers: Why Assets as a Starting Point?

Assets are not the be-all and end-all of valuation, not even in asset-intensive industries (as described at the end of this chapter). If any element has that distinction, it would have to be cash flow. Yet *what is cash but an asset?* And how does an enterprise attract cash if not through its assets, both those recognized in financial statements and those reflected (or ignored) in stock prices? Given their teleological importance, assets provide our starting point.

Another reason to start with assets is that they are fundamental to the recognition of revenues. In fact, as of mid-2010, the FASB and IASB are working on a joint project to adopt a new "assets and liabilities approach" to revenue recognition. A major project is in process to provide revised standard for revenue recognition based on balance sheet changes.[12]

And there is yet another reason that a book on valuation for investment should begin with assets. Shareholders own shares in a corporation, but *they do not own its assets*, which are owned by the corporation. It is a well established principle of corporation law that only the board of directors has the authority to direct the corporation to sell all or part of the assets it owns.[13] So, one important reason shareholders value and use their voting rights is for control of assets. They want to vote for new policies or vote in new board members in order get the greatest possible benefit out of those assets.

Cash Conundrum

I have long pondered the unresolved conundrum of the lack of value of cash in the largest companies. Focusing on the importance of P/E (price-earnings ratio), what does $1 billion more or $1 billion less mean to Exxon's market value? The Delaware Chancery Court in the Disney decision held that the $150 million payment to former CEO Michael Ovitz was not "material." Could it be that in the largest companies, cash has no real value?

———————
—Robert A. G. Monks

Definition of an Asset

What exactly is an asset? As stated earlier, according to the current definition from the IASB, an *asset* is a "present economic resource to which an entity has a present right or other privileged access."[14]

According to the IASB, an asset of an entity has three essential characteristics:

1. There is an economic resource.
2. The entity has rights or other privileged access to the economic resource.
3. The economic resource and the rights or other privileged access exist at the financial statement date.

In theory, if managers could access all the economic resources owned by their company, and if assets were valued accordingly, then the total value of the assets would approximate the true value of the corporation.

The problem is that managers do not always access all their assets and (as emphasized earlier) cannot always recognize them in financial statements. Nonetheless, the notion of asset value is an *important check against other methods of valuation* that are more susceptible to manipulation than the simple truth of historic transaction price. In the case of income, for example, the relevant formula is Revenues − Expenses = Income. Managers have some discretion in how they recognize revenues, report expenses, and calculate income; this is called "earnings management." (See Chapter 3 for more on earnings-based valuation.)

Compared to the rules for reporting earnings, the rules for valuing assets leave little room for creative accounting. Assets are rarely reported as *exceeding* their true value, except in the rare situation of liquidation; generally, their reported value is lower than their real value. Particularly when valuing fixed assets, or assets with long depreciable lives such as aircraft, the realities of inflation make it certain that carrying values will be below market.

Companies can do only so much to "talk up" their assets, for fear of running afoul of accounting principles, notably the conservatism concept. Also, following the crash of the stock market in 1929 due to inflated stock values, securities exchanges around the world have put forth rules discouraging any kind of forward-looking statement without a disclaimer. Thus, although the value of any asset really does lie in its future use, a company can say only so much about that use without looking like it's selling snake oil.

Two Kinds of Assets

There are two kinds of assets: accounting assets and real assets. In their totality, real assets approximate market value, but they do not equal it. The changes in market value do not correlate exactly to the changing value of real assets. Also, nothing is more "real" than cash, yet items like cash really don't influence market value.

————————————

—Robert A. G. Monks

Flow-Dominant vs. Value-Dominant Assets

The IASB is currently working on a new standard that, if approved, will distinguish between *two types of assets* for the purpose of valuation. The distinction is slightly different from the old distinction between intangible and tangible assets or even between soft and hard assets. Rather, this new definition is based on differing correlations to cash flow: indirect for flow dominant and direct for value dominant.

➤ *Flow-dominant assets.* For these assets, the current value is less important than the cash flows they generate. Such assets are often used in conjunction with others to benefit the entity. If these assets are measured at current values, the cash flows and value changes attributable to them need to be separated in the statement of comprehensive income.[15]

➤ *Value-dominant assets.* These assets produce cash flows by being collected or sold; the flows produced are directly related to the value of those assets in market exchanges. Most liabilities are value dominant because their values are directly related to the cash flows required to extinguish them.[16]

The new accounting treatment of the assets will depend not only on the asset itself but also on how it is used. A machine that is being used in production is a flow-dominant asset. A machine that is boxed up and waiting to be sold is a value-dominant asset. Flow-dominant assets can be valued at a level higher than their market value.[17]

The Market Premium and Nonmarket Discount

The notion of flow-dominant versus value-dominant assets may lead to better value capture. At present, however, values reported are typically low; as professionals, accountants have done a good job of keeping a lid of value—perhaps too good a job. The primary proof of this is the market premium, which is the gap between accounting numbers (balance sheet equity) and market value (Price of shares times number of shares outstanding = Market equity). A secondary proof is in the converse, called the nonmarket discount.

Market Premium

At the height of the most recent bull market, intellectual capital made up around 80 percent of the value of a Standard & Poor's (S&P) 500 company.[18] That is, the reported equity value on the company's balance sheet was worth on average only 20 percent of market capitalization.[19] With a $10 value on every $2, this was a premium of 500 percent, or a multiple of 5!

This premium/multiple dropped with the halving of market prices during the bear market period prior to the publication of this book. Here's how it worked. Stocks with a $1 book value can trade for $5 in a bull market; so 80 percent of the value of such a stock is in intellectual capital ($4 out of every $5). But when those same stocks, with the same book values, are trading for $2 rather than $5, the percentage of the intellectual capital component must be recalculated. Assuming that the book value stays the same (and does not get discounted), the premium drops from 80 percent to 50 percent ($1 out of every $2). Sometimes, when the market value is actually trading *below* book value, there is no premium. Clearly, the typical market premium paid over book value reflects general market conditions, which fluctuate.

The Enhanced Business Reporting (ERB) initiative (see Chapter 1) features this checklist of assets and competencies:

➤ Key processes
➤ Customer satisfaction
➤ People
➤ Innovation

- ➤ Supply chain
- ➤ Intellectual property
- ➤ Information and technology
- ➤ Financial assets
- ➤ Physical assets

Value-minded investors can and should consider these elements, even though they do not appear on the balance sheet. These can help explain the discrepancy between market price per share and book value per share. (See Chapter 7 for the entire ERB framework.)

Nonmarket Discounts

Nonmarket discounts are the converse of the market premium: they focus on the lesser of the two values (discounts), rather than on the higher one (premiums). But they are not a perfect converse: They are making a different point.

Whereas the people who talk about market premiums attribute the difference between book and market equity to intellectual capital, the people who talk about market discounts attribute the difference to the existence of an active market—in other words, liquidity.

There are two common ways to generate market discount data. One way is to compare before and after in an initial public offering (IPO), when one sees the value of shares for a company rise once they are in the marketplace. Another is to study the difference in value between shares with and without trading restrictions (restricted versus nonrestricted shares).

Tax court rulings on valuations focus on nonmarket discounts—with the IRS trying to give a relatively low discount (and so collect more taxes). Taxpayers have used expert witnesses to establish higher discounts, and have generally prevailed, with discounts ranging from 30 percent to 50 percent.[20]

Empirical studies have shown even steeper discounts for lack of marketability.[21] In going-private cases, the buyer and seller have to determine a value of the company in order to take it out of public markets at a price that is fair to all shareholders. There is a great deal of useful information in Securities and Exchange Commission (SEC) filings on going-private issuers.[22]

The Message in the Premium or Discount

The message of market premium and nonmarket discount is the same. When shares are sold to the public, they gain value, both from the valuation provided by investors (the value they see in the company over and above what accountants have booked) and from liquidity (it is simply more valuable to own shares that people will buy or sell on an open market).

But neither the market capitalization theory nor the nonmarket discount theory really gets at the true value of securities. Each is merely a rule of thumb, which is useful if time and funds are scarce. But if an investor can afford doing so, researching the complex reality of a company is always preferable.[23]

Analysts need to get away from rules of thumb and analyze the actual company, as much as time and money allow. At the very least, the assessment of assets helps to determine liquidation value, which can be important as collateral and thus as a safety net. Liquidation value tends to be lower than book value, just as market value tends to be higher than book value—and for the same reason: The whole of a business is greater than the sum of its parts. But how much greater? This is the challenge of valuation.

Neologism

To date, intellectual capital (IC) measurement has relied heavily on "accountingisation" [but] alternate methods to understand IC need to be developed.

———————
—John Dumay "Intellectual Capital Measurement: A Critical Approach," *Intellectual Capital Journal* 10, no. 2 (2009)

Bear Stearns: A Cautionary Tale

In 2008, at the dawn of the financial crisis (or "Panic," per Federal Reserve Board Governor Kevin Warsh[24]), one major financial firm— Bear Stearns—died a quick death due to a lack of liquidity. Valuation of assets was at the root of that problem.

In prepared testimony before the House Financial Services Committee, Alan Schwartz, president and chief executive officer of Bear Stearns, explained what hit the firm: "Even though the firm was adequately capitalized and had a substantial liquidity cushion, unfounded rumors and attendant speculation began circulating in the market that Bear Stearns was in the midst of a liquidity crisis. . . . Due to the stressed condition of the credit market as a whole and the unprecedented speed at which rumors and speculation travel and echo through the modern financial media environment, the rumors and speculation became a self-fulfilling prophecy. . . . There was, simply put, a run on the bank."

In fact, before this "run on the bank," Bear Stearns had a book value of some $12 billion. When asked whether some assets (such as mortgage-backed securities) might be carried at artificially high values, Mr. Schwartz readily agreed, but he also pointed out that *other* assets were in fact worth *more* than their book value, citing the firm's real estate holdings.[25]

In plain English, asset valuation can be all over the map. In the case of mortgage-backed securities, valuations were too high, despite the clear guidance of multitiered accounting rules that guided companies on asset valuation (as discussed later in this chapter). On the other hand, the street valuation of Bear Stearns shares before the fire-sale merger was too low, based on Schwartz's testimony.

As then SEC Chairman Christopher Cox said in the hindsight of December 2008, "These events illustrate just how critical not just capital, but liquidity is to the viability of financial firms and how the evaporation of market confidence can lead to liquidity being impaired."[26]

It is up to investors to conduct their own valuations, so that they are not vulnerable to market panic. Developing a strong understanding of the value and liquidity of firm assets can help slow or even prevent any "run on the bank" that may occur to the detriment of all.

The Asset-Focused Investor

Most valuations for investment give assets only a small role in their valuation approaches. For example, as discussed later in this book, earnings, cash flow, and stock price play larger roles in many methods.

Yet assets should not be neglected; indeed, some investors consider them more important than any other single financial indicator. Although most investors see stock prices as the main indicator of value, a contrarian school, called "value investing," finds more clues in financial statements than in stock price.[27] And one corporate philosopher, Adrian Slywotsky, has said that assets, considered in their fullest sense, are the ultimate expression of value. The "modern value chain" begins with customer priorities, moves through channels, and, ultimately, produces nothing more or less than "assets and core competencies."[28]

So-called asset-based financing usually refers to securities based on financial instruments such as loans or leases. The recent credit crisis tainted the word "asset" because in those loans, the underlying assets (defaulted mortgages) had low value. But in a broader sense, asset-based financing really means any financing grounded in collateral. It has been said that Islamic financing, based in Sharia law, is asset-based, as opposed to currency based.[29]

When a company has a concentration of salable, tangible assets, such as car fleets[30] or plants and equipment, it is a superior candidate for a going private transaction funded by debt—aka leveraged buyout. For a partial investor in equity, this asset concentration is not paramount, but it is a consideration as a fallback value. Behind the asset intensity is liquidation value.

Current Asset Value

In their classic work on *Security Analysis*, Benjamin Graham and David Dodd write about the "Significance of Current-Asset Value." They define *current-asset value* as the sum of all current assets (including cash, worth 100 percent of its book value; receivables, worth 70 to 90 percent of their book value; and inventories, worth 50 to 75 percent of their book value), plus all fixed and miscellaneous assets (generally worth 1 to 50 percent of their book value). From there, with the lessons of the 1929 stock market crash in mind, they make these three points:

1. The current-asset value is equivalent to the liquidation value.
2. Sometimes company stocks sell for less than their current asset value.
3. This is illogical and indicates an error in the judgment of the stock market, the policies of company management, and/or the attitude of stockholders toward their property.[31]

Of course, liquidation value is the last thing an investor wants to contemplate because it is typically much lower than market value except in extremely depressed markets (the illogic Graham and Dodd criticized).

Graham and Dodd note that cash and cash equivalents have a liquidation value identical to what is carried on a company's books. But notably, especially in the aftermath of the meltdown in the auction markets, fewer and fewer noncash items can safely be called cash equivalents! To qualify, they must be short-term, highly liquid investments that are both readily convertible to known amounts of cash and that are near their maturity (three months or less), so that their value can't change greatly due to shifts of interest rates. This includes generally Treasury bills, commercial paper, money market funds, and federal funds sold (for an entity with banking operations).[32]

Noncash assets may have a lower value than book in a liquidation. Once the going concern *stops* going, its inventory *drops* in value. On the other hand, when a business *is* operating (not liquidating), assets are typically worth *more* than their historic value recorded on the balance sheet. And the more dynamic the company's synergy is, the higher the true value will be of those assets.

Fateful Choices

In the mid-1970s, the boards of General Electric Company and Westinghouse Electric needed to find new CEOs. GE picked Jack Welch, who led the company to greatness, and Westinghouse made a series of leadership choices that turned out to be disastrous. The difference between a company with the highest market value in the world and a liquidated enterprise was the selection of the right CEO. Is that hyperbole? Yes, but important to our understanding of value.

———————
—Robert A. G. Monks

Taking Clues from Assets

There are just nine basic kinds of assets to report:[33]

1. Cash and cash equivalents
2. Receivables
3. Investments—debt and equity securities
4. Investments—equity method and joint ventures
5. Investments—other
6. Inventory
7. Deferred costs and other assets
8. Intangibles—goodwill and other
9. Property, plant, and equipment

The standard setters have extensive rules on how to account for each. The job of the investor is to understand those rules and to be able to see the whole picture as well because all these types of assets interact with one other.

So here is how to read between the lines of reports on these elements. Commentary is based in part on IAS standards.

Cash and Cash Equivalents

"Cash and cash equivalents" generally means cash on hand and demand deposits, together with short-term, highly liquid investments that are readily convertible to a known amount of cash and that are subject to an insignificant risk of changes in value. An investment normally meets the definition of a cash equivalent when it has a maturity of three months or less from the date of acquisition. Equity investments are normally excluded.[34]

Money market securities no longer have automatic status as cash. This standard changed when Reserve Management Company's Primary Fund "broke the buck," causing the fund's share price to be worth less than $1.[35] The chilling announcement read as follows:

> The value of the debt securities issued by Lehman Brothers Holdings, Inc. (face value $785 million) and held by the Primary Fund has been valued at zero effective as of 4:00PM New York time

today. As a result, the NAV of the Primary Fund, effective as of 4:00PM, is $0.97 per share.

This zero valuation came the day after Lehman Brothers, which had sold debt securities to the Reserve Management Company's Primary Fund, announced that it would file for bankruptcy.[36] In 2009, the SEC sued the Reserve Management Company, alleging that its managers had known about this and other vulnerabilities before its September 16 break-the-buck announcement. Today, given this event, money market securities are no longer considered as good as cash.

Receivables

Receivables and payables are recorded initially at fair value.[37] Subsequent measurement is stated at amortized cost.[38] In most cases, trade receivables and trade payables can be stated at the amount expected to be received or paid, but payables with long credit periods should be discounted.[39] If a receivable is delayed, its carrying amount is written down to its recoverable amount, which is the higher of value in use and its fair value, less costs to sell). *Value in use* is the present value of cash flows expected to be derived from the receivable.[40]

Investments—Debt and Equity Securities

Companies and funds invest in debt and equity securities and must report on the value of these investments, and reporting becomes difficult when markets change. (For a discussion by Norges Bank, see "Norges Bank on Valuation of Bank Investments.") The definition of financial instrument under IAS 39 encompasses investments in both equity and debt instruments, as well as loans and receivables. ASC 320 (SFAS 115) also deals with investments in debt and equity securities, classified in the same way as IAS 39 except that it puts loans and receivables in a separate standard.[41]

Investments—Equity Method and Joint Ventures

Under proportionate consolidation, the balance sheet of the venturer includes its share of the assets that it controls jointly and its share of the liabilities for which it is jointly responsible. The income statement of

Norges Bank on Valuation of Bank Investments

The following is the footnote explanation for the carrying values of assets without a clear market value during the financial turmoil of 2008:

> Equity investments are considered relatively easy to value, as there are official and observable market prices based on an active transaction market for almost all positions in the portfolio. When it comes to holdings of bonds, the price uncertainty picture is somewhat more complex. The pricing of government bonds and liquid government-guaranteed bonds is based on observable market prices in an active market with quotes and frequent transactions. Corporate bonds, covered bonds and some government-guaranteed and government-related bonds, however, are priced using models with observable data points.
>
> Exposure is considered particularly uncertain in terms of pricing totaled 74.2 billion Norwegian kroners [NOK] at the end of the year. This consisted almost exclusively of asset-backed securities not guaranteed by U.S. federal agencies such as Fannie Mae, Freddie Mac and Ginnie Mae. This represented a decrease in exposure of NOK 29.1 billion since the end of 2007, when there was exposure of NOK 92.5 billion to asset-backed securities and NOK 10.8 billion to structured investment vehicles (SIVs). The decrease was due primarily to falling prices for asset-backed securities, but also to instruments maturing and repayments of principal. When it comes to the remaining exposure to SIVs, only exposure of NOK 0.4 billion was considered particularly difficult to price at the end of 2008. An additional NOK 2.1 billion of SIV exposure was reclassified into the category for model pricing with observable data points. The remainder of the decrease in exposure to SIVs in 2008 was due primarily to repayments on maturity.
>
> Following a number of analyses and discussions with various players in the market (price providers, brokers and external managers), simple valuation methods have been developed to take account of this additional uncertainty. These methods mean that the value of some types of instrument has been adjusted downwards by means of a liquidity deduction from

the value reported from the ordinary price sources. The size of this liquidity adjustment depends on the estimated uncertainty related to the price from the price source.

The liquidity adjustment for accounting purposes over and above the prices from ordinary sources totaled NOK 3,424 million at the end of 2008, as against NOK 2,134 million a year earlier. Of this figure, NOK 975 million relates to cash collateral re-invested in bonds (see Note 3).

—Norges Bank Investment Management's Annual Report for 2008

the venturer includes its share of the income and expenses of the jointly controlled entity.[42]

Investments—Other

For noncontrolling investments (of 20 percent or less), the cost method is used. That is, the value of the asset is written as the purchase price (cost method).

Inventory

The value of inventory is covered in IAS 2 (see Appendix C). Inventories include:

➤ Assets held for sale in the ordinary course of business (finished goods).
➤ Assets in the production process for sale in the ordinary course of business (work in process).
➤ Materials and supplies that are consumed in production (raw materials).

However, IAS 2 does not include:

➤ Work in process arising under construction contracts (covered under IAS 11, *Construction Contracts*).

➤ Financial instruments (covered under IAS 39, *Financial Instruments*).
➤ Biological assets related to agricultural activity and agricultural produce at the point of harvest (covered under IAS 41, *Agriculture*).

Deferred Costs and Other Assets

Deferred acquisition costs are a type of deferred asset common in an industry that has large up-front costs in obtaining new business, such as insurance. IAS 39 allows a company to defer the cost of acquiring a new customer over the duration of the insurance contract. It allows only direct, incremental costs to be deferred rather than all acquisition costs. The deferred cost is considered an asset.

Intangibles—Goodwill and Other

An intangible asset (covered under IAS 38.12) is identifiable when it:

➤ Is separable (capable of being separated and sold, transferred, licensed, rented, or exchanged, either individually or as part of a package); or
➤ Arises from contractual or other legal rights, regardless of whether those rights are transferable or separable from the entity or from other rights and obligations.

Examples of intangible assets are computer software, patents, copyrights, motion picture films, customer lists, mortgage servicing rights (of questionable value in 2009), licenses, import quotas, franchises, customer and supplier relationships, and marketing rights.

Property, Plant, and Equipment

These assets (covered under IAS 16) are acquired for use in normal business operations, are long-term in nature, and possess physical substance.

The Sykes Model

The authors met with Allen Sykes in London for an extended conversation about valuation. His wisdom extends broadly throughout this book.

Exhibit 2.1 Classic Economic Valuation Theory

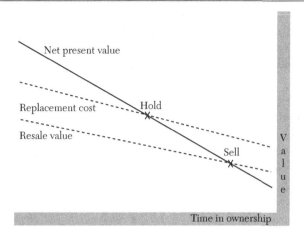

But the great treasure from the meeting was a simple chart on three methods for valuation (see **Exhibit 2.1**). It showed that there are three main ways to value an asset:

1. Calculate the present value of its future economic benefits.
2. Calculate the cost (and inconvenience) of replacing it.
3. Calculate the net resale value (proceeds less costs of disposing).

In the example shown in Exhibit 2.1, net present value has the highest value on day 1 but quickly declines over time as the asset depreciates. Replacement cost also declines, but not as steeply. The flattest curve comes with resale value. As time goes on, the most advantageous strategy for our investor changes. At first, the highest value is net present value, but, at the end of the line, replacement value is the highest.

Beyond Assets: Clues from Liabilities and Equity on the Balance Sheet

To this point in this chapter, we have been focusing on the left side of the balance sheet—assets. Everything reported must have a corresponding entry on the other side, either as a liability or as equity.

Exhibit 2.2 Display of Equity Instruments That May Be Settled with Cash or Other Assets

	Period 1	Period 2
Total assets	$ 1,300	$ 1,600
Total liabilities	$ 450	$ 450
Equity		
Mandatorily redeemable basic ownership interests	$ 200	$ 200
Cumulative change in current redemption amount	—	$ 50
Redeemable equity	$ 200	$ 250
Nonredeemable basic ownership interests	$ 500	$ 500
Retained earnings[a]	$ 150	$ 400
Nonredeemable equity	$ 650	$ 900
	—	—
Total liabilities and equity	$ 1,300	$ 1,600

[a]Retained earnings increased by $250, which is $300 in net income less the $50 change in the current redemption amount.
Source: "Financial Instruments with Characteristics of Equity," Novmeber 2008. http://www.fasb.org/draft/pv_liab_and_equity.pdf.

Let's recap the FASB-IASB definitions:

➤ An asset is a "present economic resource to which an entity has a present right or other privileged access."[43]

➤ A *liability* of an entity is a present economic obligation for which the entity is the obligor."[44]

➤ An *equity* is "the residual interest in the assets of the entity after deducting all its liabilities."[45]

The FASB has produced some 60 studies on this issue and has recently consolidated those views.[46] **Exhibit 2.2** presents an example of how equity should be broken out. This is a display, in the equity section of the statement of financial position, of equity instruments that may be settled with cash or other assets. The assumptions are as follows:

➤ Mandatorily redeemable basic ownership interests were issued at the end of period 1 at a transaction price of $200 (the market price on that date).

➤ The mandatorily redeemable basic ownership interests are redeemable at fair value on the redemption date.

➤ Redemption will not occur until after the end of period 2.

➤ The entity's net income for period 2 was $300.

➤ The fair value of the mandatorily redeemable basic ownership interests (the current redemption amount) increased by $50 during period 2.

Although this chapter focuses on *assets* as reported in the traditional balance sheet, there remain, of course, the equally important and necessary topics of *liabilities* and *equity*. (Those subjects are treated in Chapter 8 and in Appendix F.)

The Role of the Appraiser and Appraisal Standards in Valuing Assets

An entire profession has grown up around the appraisal of assets, especially assessing the value of collateral for loans. Asset appraisers follow Uniform Standards of Professional Appraisal Practice (USPAP), published by an independent Appraisal Foundation composed of some 80 appraisal organizations. The Financial Institutions Reform Recovery and Enforcement Act of 1989 (FIRREA), passed after the savings and loan lending crisis in the 1980s, requires USPAP to be used in the appraisal of real estate in federally related transactions.

So how is this useful in the valuation of a publicly held company? Surprisingly, the standard can be useful. Take, for example, the notion of highest and best use for an asset. The USPAP standard sets as a valuation standard a certain level of use for an asset: "The reasonably probable and legal use of a property that is physically possible appropriately supported, and financially feasible, and that results in the highest value."[47]

To be valued accurately (listing the tests in order), the use of the asset must be:

➤ Legally permissible
➤ Physically possible

➤ Financially feasible
➤ Maximally productive

This definition, interpreted broadly, could well be applied to the job of the corporate board and management, which should in fact be looking for the highest and best use of the assets of the corporation on behalf of investors. The value of the company can be seen as the amount of money one would have to spend to reproduce the same company from scratch, and that approach assumes putting assets to best use.

Fair Market Value Treatment Assets

One very important kind of asset for the investor to analyze is the financial asset. For many years, financial assets and financial liabilities were carried on company books at their original values when booked. In recent years, there has been a movement to account for them using fair market value. The two main applicable standards are ASC 820 (SFAS 157) and 825–10 (SFAS 159).[48]

ASC, *Fair Value Measurements and Disclosures* covers any financial asset not covered under 825–10, *The Fair Value Option for Financial Assets and Financial Liabilities* (described in the next section). The ASC 820 standard is parallel to the more stringent one in IAS 39, *Financial Instruments: Recognition and Measurement.*[49]

Fair Value of Assets Under FASB (GAAP) and IASB (IFRS)

Both FASB and the IASB have put forward pronouncements on the fair value of assets.

ASC 820 and ASC 825–10

The *Fair Value Measurements* standard explains how a corporation should value financial assets for which there is no clear market. It sets forth a hierarchy based on valuation inputs, rather than methods. It gives the highest priority (Level 1) to quoted prices in active markets and the lowest priority (Level 3) to what are called "unobservable inputs."[50]

Level 2 inputs are between these two levels and include, for example, quoted prices for similar assets in an active market or identical assets in nonactive markets.[51]

The standard for *The Fair Value Option for Financial Assets and Financial Liabilities* elaborates on this for the most liquid financial assets. It permits companies to measure the financial assets on their books (cash and cash-like instruments) at fair value. The statement applies to most recognized financial assets and financial liabilities, with some exceptions.[52] A financial asset is defined as:

➤ Cash;

➤ Evidence of an ownership interest in an entity; or

➤ A contract that conveys to one entity a right to receive cash or another financial instrument from a second entity or to exchange other financial instruments on potentially favorable terms with the second entity.[53]

This is like a story within a story. The valuation-minded investor looks at a company and tries to value that company's equities. The investor is mentally securitizing the assets of the company. Conversely, though, when looking at the equities held by that company, the investor does just the opposite mentally. The investor *de*securitizes the equity in an effort to see what assets are really behind the paper.

A Bold Decision

The decision to invest in equities might have seemed bold at the time. But was it really so? I have already demonstrated that equities much more so than petroleum safeguard the capital saved. Moreover, equities are real assets in that we acquire a stake in the world's production capacity.[54]

—Knut N. Kjaer, executive director of the Norwegian Pension Fund–Global at the Norwegian Polytechnic Society, November 2, 2006

Standard IAS 39 and Beyond

The IASB has been developing guidance on fair value, looking forward to a global standard. In a preliminary paper, IAASB Chair Sir David Tweedie noted:

> The use of fair value in financial reporting is of great interest to preparers, auditors, users and regulators. We believe that an essential ground-clearing step in the debate is to establish a *clear international definition of fair value and a consistent framework for measuring it*. [Emphasis added.]

The IASB, he says, wants to codify, clarify, and simplify the guidance that is at present dispersed widely in IFRSs (including IASs that have not been repealed).[55]

There are two international standards for fair value: IAS 39 and IFRS 7. In early 2009, the IASB voted to use the existing fair value hierarchy in IAS 39, which represents what some entities are doing in practice to comply with both IAS 39 and IFRS 7's disclosure requirements.

Valuing Intangible Assets on the Balance Sheet

The FASB has formed the Valuation Resource Group to address issues relating to valuation for financial reporting. The group has been meeting periodically since October 1, 2007, to discuss a variety of issues surrounding the implementation of fair value accounting in the United States and globally.[56]

The issues discussed in meetings include:

➤ Definition of an active market
➤ Assets and liabilities without markets
➤ Definition of "legally permissible"
➤ Valuation of intangible assets using "current replacement cost"
➤ Accounting for an asset that an entity does not intend to use or intends to use defensively—not "highest and best use" for valuation

Most intangible assets have to be acquired to be recognized, although the acquisition need not be in the form of a business combination. Sometimes intangible assets that are acquired individually or with a group of assets in a transaction other than a business combination may wind up on the books.[57]

Valuing Intangible Assets That Are Not on the Balance Sheet

A significant percentage of the value of some companies resides in the brand value of the name of the company or its products (such as an associated color, sound, shape, or design, including logos).

In 2002, the FASB began a project to value intangibles "to establish standards that will improve disclosure of information about intangible assets that are not recognized in financial statements." The project was going to consider assets that are developed internally (such as brand names and customer relationships), as well as those that are acquired and written off immediately (acquired in-process research and development). In January 2004, the FASB removed this project from its agenda, apparently frustrated by the classic challenge of reconciling high relevance and low reliability.

About Brands

The term "brand" has no accounting or legal definition. Rather, a *brand* is made up of many components, including:

➤ Name (protected by service mark)
➤ Logo (protected by trademark)
➤ Design and color, shape, sound, and other attributes (protected by design right)
➤ Trade secrets, such as a recipe (protected by contract law, common law, and codes of practice)

The value of the brand or components is usually higher than the booked value of the legal instrument protecting the brand (e.g., trademark). GAAP sets standards for when an intangible assets should be separately measured and when they should be recognized as a group.[58]

Specifically, at the date of acquisition, the acquirer must allocate the cost of the business combination by recognizing the acquired company's identifiable assets, liabilities, and contingent liabilities at their fair market value. This requires the disclosure of specific categories of intangible assets that are *separately identifiable as sources of future economic benefits that can be reliably measured*. Assets may be artistic, marketing related, customer related, contract based, or technology based.[59]

The journal *Brand Finance* conducted a Global Intangibles Study of all companies quoted on the world's major stock markets.[60] The study showed that on average almost 70 percent of total enterprise value (as reflected in the company's market value) was represented by unreported intangible assets. The proportion of intangible asset value varied from sector to sector. Over 90 percent of global technology company valuations were intangible, and most sectors displayed intangible values in excess of 50 percent of enterprise value. The dominant intangible asset class also varies from industry to industry. The following is a list from *Brand Finance*:

➤ Consumer goods—brand trademarks
➤ Film industry—creative copyrights
➤ IT industry—software intellectual property rights
➤ Pharmaceuticals—molecular patents

Valuing the brand name for a company or product means assessing the revenue-generating ability of these names.

A good brand name affects cash flow by increasing sales volume. It compels more consumers to buy the branded items and to pay a higher price per item. (The same multiplier effect applies to the volume and price of the company's securities. Indeed, certain blue-chip stocks have a brand appeal among investors that is in addition to the brand appeal that their companies' products may have.) A strong brand can also create new sources of revenues if the company extends the brand to new items or licenses it.

In sending out stock offering prospectuses to the general, companies have to disclose risks. One commonly disclosed risk is that the company's name brand, or the brands the company owns, may become impaired. As San West Inc. noted in its June 2010 prospectus,

> Promotion and enhancement of our online store will also depend on our success in consistently providing high-quality products to our customers. Since we rely on suppliers to directly ship products purchased to our customers, if our suppliers do not ship

quickly, or if our consumers do not perceive the products we offer as superior, the value of the our San West brand could be harmed. Any brand impairment or dilution could decrease the attractiveness of San West to one or more of these groups, which could harm our business, results of operations and financial condition.[61]

Case Lesson: Be Sure the Company Owns the Brand

When VW bought Rolls Royce Motor Cars from Vickers in 1998, it paid £493 million for the business—three times the company's book value. So it booked two-thirds of the sum as goodwill (the difference between acquisition purchase price and book value). But it turns out that another company, Rolls Royce PLC, owned the trademarks and sold them to another automobile company (BMW) for a mere $40 million.

At this point, the value hunter needs to add another element to the equation for determining the true value of all assets: management. For a brand to have value, it needs to be protected and mined. This requires strong management of intellectual property.

Case Lesson: Anticipate Write-Offs for Goodwill

Companies carry goodwill on their books as an asset. It used to be amortized over time, but now under ASC 350 (SFAS 142) it is carried at full value. Sometimes, following an acquisition, the carried goodwill amount roughly equals the value of the company's brands (to the extent that the above-book premium paid by the acquirer is paid in recognition of the value of the brand. But depending on how well an acquirer manages brands after a deal, the value of the brands can erode and the goodwill can lose value.

Under GAAP and IAS standards, acquirers must estimate the useful life of all tangible assets. If no life span is given, the owner must put the asset through an annual impairment text. If a brand loses value after a merger, this may trigger a write-off.

A straightforward description of this process appears in a recent proxy, specifically in management's discussion and analysis of financial condition and results of operations MD&A) of American Superconductor Corp.[62]

Goodwill. Goodwill represents the excess of cost over net assets of acquired businesses that are consolidated. In accordance with

[ASC 350] SFAS 142, "Goodwill and Other Intangible Assets," goodwill is not amortized. In lieu of amortization, we perform an impairment review of our goodwill at least annually or when events and changes in circumstances indicate the need for such a detailed impairment analysis. Goodwill is considered impaired when the carrying value of a reporting unit exceeds its estimated fair value. In assessing the recoverability of goodwill, we make assumptions regarding estimated future cash flows and other factors to determine the fair value of the reporting unit. To date, we have determined that goodwill is not impaired, but we could in the future determine that goodwill is impaired, which would result in a charge to earnings.

This approach is consistent with IFRS 3, issued by the IASB. Companies may elect to apply IFRS 3 from any chosen date, but they must apply it consistently to all business combinations after that date. IAS 36, *Impairment of Assets*, and IAS 38, *Intangible Assets*, must both be applied from the same date as IFRS 3. The adoption process must, of course, be audited.

The most famous example of brand impairment was Quaker Oats Company's Snapple. In 1993, Quaker paid $1.7 billion for the Snapple brand. Over the next four years, the brand lost value. In 1997, Quaker sold Snapple to Triarc Beverage for $300 million, and then the brand gained value. In 2000, Triarc sold the brand to Cadbury Schweppes for $1 billion.

Impairments charges can occur for a variety of reasons. Observers have cited brand impairment as a likely outcome of the BP oil spill in 2010.[63] But brand impairment can come from less catastrophic events, as the following examples show:

➤ Gannett reported an impairment charge of $72.0 million (pretax) in 2007 to reduce the value of certain mastheads "due to the current business environment and expected operating results for some recent acquisitions in the U.S. and in the UK."

➤ American Italian Pasta reported impairment of $89.2 million for 2005, noting that "in the course of completing its financial statements for its fiscal year ending September 30, 2005, the company performed its annual impairment analysis of its brands as of the fourth quarter of fiscal 2005. The review showed that some of the company's pasta brands continued to experience declines in sales volume and related revenues resulting in corresponding declines in market share and profitability, and operating trends and the forecasted future performance for these brands differed significantly from company's earlier expectations."

➤ British American Tobacco (BAT) reported brand impairment in 2005 of £49 million (net of tax) "following the implementation of a review of brand strategies resulting from the combination of R.J. Reynolds and Brown & Williamson."[64] BAT, a public company, sold the American part of its Brown & Williamson subsidiary to R.J. Reynolds, which at this time is privately owned (following a varied ownership history).

Using the MD&A for Insights on Assets

As these examples show, brands are assets of great value, even though they are not on a balance sheet. Fortunately, companies are not limited to standard accounting reports in communicating to investors. Many companies go beyond these requirements, and investors need to be attuned to these important messages. For example, management's discussion and analysis of financial conditions and results of operations in the proxy statement often contains a useful description of the company's main assets and the risks to them. Although there is no absolute requirement to list key assets, many companies do—particularly companies in the mining or exploration industries, which list their drilling sites. In assessing a company's value, investors need to be on the lookout for these obvious MD&A clues.

Here is an example from the 2008 annual report of Fortsum:

Key assets
- A critical mass of more than 24,000 clients, primarily in Québec with others spread across Canada;
- A team of accomplished professionals;
- The strategic positioning of Acomba in the Québec market place;
- An unparalleled structure of highly efficient technical support and business office help desks;
- Multi-platform accounting technology and expertise in secure and automated data transmission;

- Existing partnerships with Microsoft, Sage Accpac and SAP Business One;
- Proven expertise with major industry partners, government agencies and accounting firms.[65]

Note that the MD&A uses the term "assets" to describe these elements, even though they do not appear on a balance sheet. According to the accounting concept of money measurement, an asset needs to be expressed in currency (money) to be recorded. This should be no problem.[66] Professional appraisers can put a dollar value on *any* assets. (See Appendix G for the ground rules they use.) The problem is not so much the money measurement concept as the totality of all the concepts and conventions of accounting that favor a tangibles-oriented approach to value.[67] The point is that, in valuing a company, the asset-minded investor can identify and value all assets, including assets like these.

Improvements in Fair Value Disclosures: A Checklist for Investors

Among a company's many assets, securities held for investment rank high in importance, but ascertaining their value is not always easy. MD&As also include assessments of securities' fair value. The SEC has issued guidance to companies in a series of "Dear CFO" letters.[68] Among other tips, the guidance urges companies to:

- ➤ Provide a sensitivity analysis for how their valuations may vary.[69]
- ➤ Explain their alternative valuation techniques for securities.[70]
- ➤ Give more detail on the collateral underlying mortgage-backed securities, collateralized debt obligations, collateralized loan obligations, and the like.
- ➤ Disclose (with numbers) the effects of the company's own credit risk and counterparty credit risk—e.g., effects of credit risk on derivatives' fair value.[71]
- ➤ Disclose more about how illiquidity was taken into account.

As this level of disclosure detail becomes more common, it will become easier for investors to assess the value of the securities on the balance sheets of companies they have chosen as investment targets.

Asset-Based Valuation by Industry

Taken by itself, a balance sheet does not contain a lot of useful information. Compared to many other balance sheets in its industry, however, it can provide a lot of information. The value-minded investor analyzes financial statements differently, based on the company's industry.

A general sense of industry orientation can help in the assessment of any company. The Global Industry Classification Standard (GICS) recognizes ten basic industry groups.[72] Of these, the most asset intensive are energy, materials, industrials, consumer discretionary (e.g., automobiles), and consumer staples (e.g., consumer goods retail). The remaining industries (health care, financials, information technology, telecommunication services, and utilities) derive more value from services and/or ideas; so they are less dependent on asset values. (For a list of GIC Classifications, see Appendix H.)

One research organization (ICON Group International) prepares vertical analyses by pooling statistics on tens of thousands of companies across more than forty countries and applies a seven-stage methodology: (1) identification of industry classifications, (2) firm-level data collection and aggregation, (3) standardization of raw statistics, (4) filtering outliers, (5) calculation of global norms, (6) projection of deviations and gaps, and (7) projection of ranks and percentiles. So far, the project has focused on chemical companies, but the approach can be used in other sectors. With such a ready source available, it may not make sense for investors to conduct their own research.

Valuation precision improves as analysis becomes more specialized, focusing, for example, not just on materials (overly broad) but on chemicals, or even more narrowly on fertilizers and agricultural chemicals. The investor wishing to analyze the value of an agricultural chemicals company, such as Archer Daniels Midland or Bunge Limited, would read with interest an analyst report that predicts a rise in the price of agricultural chemicals. So let's take a quick look at asset-based valuations in a few industries, starting with chemicals.

Chemicals

The demand for various types of chemicals depends on economic conditions. Therefore, the valuation of chemicals companies varies greatly. As of late 2009, for example, there was strong demand from the U.S.

agricultural sector but weak demand from the construction and industry sectors—offset by some demand overseas.[73] Companies with a variety of chemicals do better in such an environment than those with a single chemical product that is aligned with a weak economic sector. A good example of a recession-proof chemical company is Dupont, which operates in a number of areas, including agriculture, biology, chemistry, industrial biotechnology, materials science, and manufacturing. Interestingly, though, the relatively strong performance of Dupont stock can be attributed in part to strong management at the company, rather than merely to its product portfolio strategy. See Chapter 7 for our observations on management as a factor in equity valuation.

Ideally, an investor should compare a chemical company's balance sheet structure with global benchmarks. Does the company hold more cash and short-term assets, or does it concentrate its assets in physical plant and equipment? Does it have a higher percentage of payables compared to the benchmarks? Does it hold a higher concentration of long-term debt? Does it have a relatively higher cost of goods sold, operating costs, income taxes, or profit margins compared to global benchmarks? Fortunately, there is a resource for this level of study, a series of reports from a professor at INSEAD.[74]

Tip

When analyzing the balance sheet of a chemicals company, be sure to consider how the type of chemical/s produced by the company fit into the general economy.

Energy (Oil and Gas Exploration and Production)

Companies involved in oil and gas exploration and production (E&P) offer a solid investment opportunity for investors drawn to the security of commodities. As noted by JPMorgan Chase analysts, E&P stocks represent a "pure play" investment on oil and gas prices.[75] Such "resource play producers" have value rooted in tangible assets. As the JPMorgan study notes, much as falling interest rates push up the value of long-duration bonds, rising commodity prices and lower discount rates have driven up the value of long-lived unconventional assets.

In oil and gas companies, cash flow is based on an asset: proven reserves. The SEC requires E&P producers to provide a standardized measure of discounted future net cash flows, known as the SEC PV-10 calculation, or PV-10 for short. As the JPMorgan study notes, the calculation measures the present value of estimated future cash flows (revenues less development costs, production costs, and taxes) from the companies proved reserves, discounted at 10 percent.

The JPMorgan study notes that "[t]he PV-10 calculation is somewhat subjective in that companies provide their own assumptions regarding future development costs, future production costs, how fast the production base is declining, and other variables. Furthermore, companies must take whatever the prevailing commodity prices and costs were at the end of a reporting period and assume these levels are held constant throughout the life of the reserves. This variability leads to significant volatility in the PV-10 calculation from one year to another simply because of fluctuating commodity prices. The PV-10 value is often referred to as the 'liquidation value,'" and it can be more significant than earnings in the typical E&P. (For more on E&P Valuation, see Chapters 3 and 6.)

Tip

In valuing an E&P company, consider making your own PV-10 calculation based on your sense of future costs and other trends.

Banks

The hot issue now for bank valuation pertains to assets, specifically *loan loss reserves*. This is a key issue in SEC cases in the aftermath of the 2008–2009 financial meltdowns in the mortgage banking sector.[76]

More generally, in assessing the balance sheet of any bank, the valuation-minded investor can benefit from using some of the stress test techniques from the U.S. Federal Resource Board's Supervisory Capital Assessment Program (SCAP), a test administered to 19 major bank holding companies (BHCs). The focus would be on the allowance for loan and lease losses (ALLL), which appears on the balance sheet.[77]

In a what-if exercise, the BHCs had to estimate their potential losses on loans, securities, and trading positions, as well as preprovision net revenue (PPNR) and the resources available from the ALLL under two alternative macroeconomic scenarios. Each participating firm had to project potential losses on its loan, investment, and trading securities portfolios, including off-balance-sheet commitments and contingent liabilities and exposures over the two-year horizon beginning with year-end 2008 financial statement data.

Firms used a common set of indicative loss rate ranges (provided by the Federal Reserve Board [FRB]) for specific loan categories under conditions of the baseline and the more adverse economic scenarios. (Firms could diverge from the indicative loss rates when they could show that others were appropriate.) In addition, the largest firms had to estimate potential trading-related market and counterparty credit losses under a provided market stress scenario (which was simulated and based on market shocks that occurred in the second half of 2008). The test asked the banks to project the resources they would have available to absorb losses over the two-year horizon under each scenario. These resources consist of PPNR—net interest income, fees, and other noninterest income, net of noncredit-related expenses—and reserves already established for probable incurred losses at December 31, 2008. PPNR and the ALLL, combined with existing capital over the amount sufficient to exceed minimum regulatory capital standards, are resources that the firm would have available to absorb some of their estimated losses under the scenarios.[78]

Tip

Administer a do-it-yourself stress test. As you analyze the balance sheets of banks and look at those reserves, ask what if?

Insurance

In May 2008, the FASB issued a new rule on Accounting for Financial Guarantee Insurance Contracts. Statement 163 requires that an insurance enterprise recognize a claim liability prior to a default (insured event) when there is evidence that credit deterioration has occurred in an insured financial obligation. It also requires that the insurer disclose what it is doing to foresee such an event, including its risk-management activities and any "watch list" it may have.

Tip

When analyzing the balance sheet of an insurance company, make sure the company is up-to-date on the creditworthiness of its insureds.[79]

Special Topics in Asset Valuations: Valuing Assets in Pension Plans

Valuation-mind investors looking for asset values need to understand some fundamental facts about pension plans. Robert A. G. Monks, coauthor of this book, served as founding trustee of the Federal Employees' Retirement System by appointment of President Ronald Reagan, and as administrator of the Office of Pension and Welfare Benefits Administration, Department of Labor, in charge of the private pension system in the United States.[80]

Retirement plans set up by companies are usually defined benefit plans or defined contributions plans.

A defined *benefit* plan gives fixed monthly retirement benefits starting at retirement age (e.g., age 65). Benefits are based on a formula reflecting a participant's total compensation and years employed. The company's contribution to the plan is the amount actuarially required to fund expected plan benefits. These amounts are carried on the company's books as liabilities, and the assets of the plans themselves are carried as assets. When assets exceed liabilities, plans are funded. When they fall below liabilities, they are underfunded or unfunded.

A defined *contribution* plan contributes fixed monthly amounts into a retirement account starting from the date of employee eligibility. The company does not guarantee any particular ending value for the retirement account, which may be directed by the employee (a 401(k), for example).

In December 2008, the FASB amended SFAS 132, creating SFAS 132R, now codified within ASC 715. The new ASC 715 guidance includes a section on *Postretirement Benefit Plan Assets* that guidance requires employers to disclose information about how they make investment allocation decisions. The guidance also asks companies to disclose asset categories within a portfolio based on the risks and expected long-term rate of return for each asset category—e.g., allocations in debt securities by federal, state, and local governments, as well as corporate debt and mortgage-backed securities and derivatives.[81]

Lens Check

Here is some guidance on how to incorporate our valuation lenses into a consideration of asset quality:

➤ *Time: Short term versus long term.* An investor interpreting the assets portion of a balance sheet needs to consider the value of the assets during an appropriate time frame. For example, what is the value of timberland held by an endowment? Harvard University's endowment fund was known for its diversified assets, including blue chip stocks and bonds, emerging market equities, hedge funds, and private equity partnerships, as well as commodities and, significantly, timberland. This last investment choice seems to show a degree of performance complacency, because timberland is highly illiquid. One must have a very long time frame to make such an investment. This long play did little to help Harvard weather the economic storms of the twenty-first century's first decade.[82]

➤ *Place: Market versus nonmarket.* The presence or absence of an active market for securities makes a tremendous difference in their valuation. Issues traded on major stock markets have an automatic scorekeeper for day-to-day value in the closing prices. Investors require additional analysis to make their buy, sell, and hold decisions, but at least trading price provides a point of departure. But what if there is no market for a security, such as the securities of a closely held private company that is not traded on an exchange? Useful guidance appears in Accounting Series Release (ASR)118, which recommends utilizing the following methodologies to determine fair value:

1. A multiple of earnings
2. A discount from market of a similar freely traded security
3. Yield to maturity with respect to debt issues
4. Or a combination of these, as well as other methods

   In determining which methods to apply, ASR 118 suggests taking into account the following factors to the extent applicable:

1. The fundamental analytical data relating to the investment
2. The nature and duration of restrictions on disposition of the securities
3. An evaluation of the forces that influence the market in which these securities are purchased and sold[83]

➤ *Slope: Level versus skewed playing field.* The value of assets is extremely sensitive to events. This is a well-known fact of portfolio theory,[84] but it can also apply in a corporate setting.

➤ *Volition: Willing versus unwilling buyer or seller.* One of the most fundamental investment decisions any individual or company can make is to keep cash or to spend it on an asset. The risk in purchasing an asset is that no one ever wants it again at a comparable or higher price; the risk in holding onto cash is that it will lose value through inflation. As the IASB says, there are two questions: can an investor make money with this asset (flow-dominant), and will anyone want to buy it (value dominant)?

➤ *Quality: Level of certainty of return (high, medium, or low) based on investing standards.* Assets are particularly amenable to quality analysis, but, like stocks themselves, asset quality can change over time, particularly when it comes to financial assets held by a company. Accountants have known this since the dawn of standards and have created concepts such as depreciation (for the gradual loss of quality) and impairment (for the less predictable loss of quality).

➤ *Purpose: Private versus public.* Why do investors want to own corporations? Traditionally, corporate ownership has focused on producing private wealth, but recent events have added a new dimension: the public good. We will close with comments on this new theme.

Conclusion: Asset Values in Bailouts

Financial asset valuation made headlines on October 3, 2008, when President George W. Bush signed Public Law 110–343, the Emergency Economic Stabilization Act of 2008, a multipart piece of legislation that included the $700 billion Troubled Assets Relief Program. As we go to press, this program is well under way.[85] As of late 2009, taxpayers owned even more of these troubled assets, thanks to the Public-Private Partnership Investment Program announced by Treasury Secretary Timothy Geithner in March 2009.[86] The 2008 bailout bill and the 2009 program gave the government temporary power to affect the management—and in some cases the fate—of a number of major firms.

Some believe that government ownership of securities will change the nature of securities valuation, moving it from classical market-based economic notions, such as asset-based valuation (the subject of this chapter), to a more politicized notion of value based in social values. Only time will tell. Meanwhile, valuation continues.

Our next chapter will discuss earnings-based valuation approaches.

Appendix 2.1: Common Ratios, Multiples, Averages, and Algorithms Based on Assets— and Examples of Their Use

Ratios that are based on *assets* can give an idea of management efficiency, financial liquidity, and financial solvency. (For an idea of profitability, the investor needs to look at ratios based on income, discussed in Chapter 3.) This appendix lists common ratios based on assets and examples of their use. These include efficiency ratios such as return on equity, liquidity ratios such as the current ratio (also called the acid ratio), and leverage ratios such as debt-to-equity.

The astute investor has to be able to recognize the quality of assets and not base a judgment on a ratio alone. A ratio is only as good as the numbers that make it up, and that applies to ratios based on total assets.

Three types of ratios (or other mathematical tools) use assets: They focus on *efficiency, liquidity,* and *leverage.*[87]

Efficiency Indicators Using Assets

These numbers say something about how the business is being managed.

The *accounting rate of return* (ARR) shows the undiscounted *average earnings after taxes and depreciation* divided by the average *book value of the investment during its life.* The ratio then identifies projects with an accounting return greater than a cutoff rate.[88]

Multiple of Average Book Value per Share to Market Price per Share

	BV per Share	MP per Share	Multiple
Comparable A	$40	$80	2.0
Comparable B	20	30	1.5
Comparable C	30	75	2.5
Comparable D	30	45	1.5
Comparable E	20	50	2.5
Average			2.0

By comparing this ratio from company to company, the investor can derive an average multiple to use. So, for example, if the book value of the target is $15 per share, then the proper price per share to offer would be $30 per share.

Return on assets (ROA) shows how management is using the company's resources compared to others in their industry. To calculate ROA, *divide net profit before taxes by total assets.* Industries with a lot of bookable assets, such as plants, equipment, and inventory—all recorded, or booked, on the balance sheet as assets—have a relatively low ROA. Service companies have a high ROA because they require minimal bookable assets to operate.

Return on assets tells an investor about the company's sustainable growth—how it is able to create a return on the capital investments of the company. It is measured as net income divided by total assets. An ROA of 1 says that for every dollar invested in assets, the company makes $1 in profit. ROA can vary greatly from industry to industry.

The *DuPont formula for return on equity* (ROE) includes assets: ROE = (Net income ÷ Sales) × (Sales ÷ Total assets) × (Total assets ÷ Average stockholders' equity). The DuPont formula shows how much cash is created from the existing assets. If the return on equity is 15 percent, then 15¢ of assets are created for each dollar originally invested as equity.[89]

Inventory turnover tells an investor how quickly a company is selling its goods—an important ratio for companies with tangible products (not service companies). It is calculated by dividing total purchases by average inventory. Here are some examples:

> Inventory levels are in good shape as we enter 2008, as we recorded *record high inventory turnover levels* at the end of 2007.[90]

Average collection period (also known as *days sales outstanding*) is calculated by dividing net accounts receivable by total credit sales for the past four quarters and multiplying by 365. Managers and investors alike use this figure to assess the quality of accounts receivable and to predict cash flows (i.e., the expected time to collect). For example:

> The level of both net and gross DSO at June 30, 2009 is slightly lower than the Company's expectation that DSO will be in the 60 to 70 day range based on 60 day payment terms for most customers due to significantly higher average daily sales in the fourth quarter of Fiscal 2009 which were collected by June 30, 2009.[91]

Liquidity Indicators Using Assets

Some ratios measure liquidity. They give investors a good idea of whether a company has enough cash or similarly liquid (easily salable) assets. Here are some of the most common liquidity ratios, followed by examples of how Wall Street analysts are using them in their analysis of publicly traded companies.

The *current ratio*, also called acid ratio, is calculated by dividing current assets (minus inventory) by current liabilities (except the current portion of long-term debts). One looks for a ratio of about 1. A ratio that is lower than 1 may mean the company is flirting with insolvency. Conversely, a ratio higher than 1 could mean that the company's capital is not being used extensively enough. It is putting its gold in a mattress, so to speak. Usually, companies with a current ratio above 1 are proud of the fact. For example:

> Regarding our balance sheet, our balance sheet is very clean. At the end of the quarter, we remained very strong with cash and marketable securities of 56 million. We had no debt. We have

working capital of 149 million. We have a *current ratio* at 3.2, which is pretty strong.[92]

The *working capital ratio* is calculated by dividing a company's current assets (including cash, inventory, and accounts receivable) by current liabilities (including drawdowns on line of credit balances, long-term debts falling due in 30 days, and accounts payable). It is often expressed as a percentage of sales. Although having a high working capital to sales ratio (for example, 20 percent) can be good, it can indicate that the company is carrying too much inventory. For example:

Our *working capital ratio* for the trailing 12 month average in 2007 of 18.3% . . . reflects the impact of carrying higher inventory levels than anticipated through much of the year. However, our year-end working capital ratio at 16.4%, which is roughly equal to the 2006 year end position, reflects the significant progress for the company in managing these issues through the latter part of the year.[93]

Leverage Indicators Using Assets

Certain asset-based ratios, called *leverage ratios*, help the value-minded investor assess the long-term solvency of a company. They are important for investors who plan to take and hold major investment positions in a company.

The *debt-to-equity ratio* can be calculated as:

Total liabilities ÷ Shareholders' equity
or
Total interest-bearing, long-term debt ÷ Shareholders' equity

The meaning of the debt-to-equity ratio depends on the industry in which the company operates. For example, capital-intensive industries such as auto manufacturing tend to have a debt-to-equity ratio above 2, and personal computer companies have a debt-to-equity of under 0.5.

High debt-to-equity ratios (75 percent, according to U.S. federal banking standards) make a company highly leveraged. So does a transaction that doubles liability, even if it only brings the debt-to-asset ratio to 50 percent.

The *total debt-to-total asset ratio* is measured as total liabilities divided by total assets. It shows the proportion of a company's assets that are financed through debt. If the ratio is at 0.5, it shows that the company balances debt and equity as its source of funding. If it is greater than 0.5, most of the company's assets are financed through debt. If the ratio is less than 0.5, most of the company's assets are financed through equity.

Appendix 2.2: Asset-Based Approach to Business Valuation (American Society of Appraisers)[94]

I. Preamble

A. This Standard must be followed in all valuations of businesses, business ownership interests, securities and intangible assets developed by all members of the American Society of Appraisers, be they candidates, Accredited Members (AM), Accredited Senior Appraisers (ASA), or Fellows (FASA).

B. The purpose of this Standard is to define and describe the requirements for the use of the asset-based approach (and the circumstances in which it is appropriate) in the valuation of businesses, business ownership interests, securities and intangible assets, but not the reporting thereof.

C. This Standard applies to appraisals and may not necessarily apply to limited appraisals and calculations as defined in BVS-I General Requirements for Developing a Business Valuation, Section II.C.

D. This Standard incorporates the General Preamble to the ASA Business Valuation Standards.

II. The Asset-Based Approach

A. The asset-based approach is a general way of determining a value indication of a business, business ownership interest, security, or intangible asset using one or more methods based on the value of the assets net of liabilities.

B. In business valuation, the asset-based approach may be analogous to the cost approach of other appraisal disciplines.

C. Assets, liabilities and equity relate to a business that is an operating company, a holding company, or a combination thereof (a mixed business).

1. An operating company is a business that conducts an economic activity by generating and selling, or trading in a product or service.

2. A holding company is a business that derives its revenues from a return on its assets, which may include operating companies and/or other businesses.

3. The asset-based approach should be considered in valuations conducted at the enterprise level and involving:

   a. An investment or real estate holding company.

   b. A business appraised on a basis other than as a going concern.

   Valuations of particular ownership interests in an enterprise may or may not require the use of the asset-based approach.

D. The asset-based approach should not be the sole appraisal approach used in assignments relating to operating companies appraised as going concerns unless this approach is customarily used by sellers and buyers. In such cases, the appraiser must support the selection of this approach.

Notes

1. Interview with Rocky Lee, partner, DLA Piper, Beijing, China, July 30, 2009. DLA Piper is the world's largest law firm, and Mr. Lee is their private equity transactions leader.

2. As mentioned in Chapter 1, note 65, the *2010 NACD Public Company Governance Survey* showed that only 10 percent of the public company directors responding consider assets to be an important indicator of company value. The low ranking and regard of assets as an indicator of value may change in time as accounting standards find better ways to capture the value of assets. Stephen Young, executive director of the Caux Roundtable, has remarked in conversation June 22, 2010, that if it is management's job to increase earnings, it is the board's job to enhance the balance sheet.

3. This definition is from the ongoing work of the Conceptual Framework: Joint Project of the International Accounting Standards Board and the Financial Accounting Standards Board. See "Asset Definition" at http://www.fasb.org/project/cf_phase-b.shtml. The IASB Framework—approved by the IASC board in April 1989 for publication in July 1989, and adopted by the IASB in April 2001, and still current with the IASB—states that "an

asset is a resource controlled by the entity as a results of past events and from which future economic benefits are expected to flow to the entity."

The elements directly related to the measurement of financial position are assets, liabilities, and equity. These are defined as follows:

(1) An asset is a resource controlled by the entity as a result of past events and from which future economic benefits are expected to flow to the entity.

(2) A liability is a present obligation of the entity arising from past events, the settlement of which is expected to result in an outflow from the entity of resources embodying economic benefits.

(3) Equity is the residual interest in the assets of the entity after deducting all its liabilities.

See "Framework for the Preparation and Presentation of Financial Statements," January 1, 2009, http://www.iasb.org/NR/rdonlyres/4CF78A7B-B237-402A-A031-709A687508A6/0/Framework.pdf.

4. Ibid.

5. Ibid.

6. For a discussion of the primacy of assets in accounting theory, see Halsey G. Bullen (FASB) and Kimberley Crook (IASB), "A New Conceptual Framework Project" (May 2005), and a responsive discussion paper by Michael Bromwich et al., "FASB/IASB Revisiting the Concepts: A Comment on Hicks and the Concept of 'Income' in the Conceptual Framework," white paper, July 24, 2005. See Chapter 3 (especially note 7) for more on the subject of asset-based valuations versus income-based valuations.

7. See letter of October 27, 2008, entitled "Further Issues Related to IAS 39," from Jorgen Holmquist, Internal Market and Services Director, European Commission, to Sir David Tweedie, head of the IASB, http://ec.europa.eu/internal_market/accounting/docs/letter-iasb-ias39_en.pdf.

8. The terminology on this can be somewhat confusing because of a shift in standard setters. There used to be an International Accounting Standards Committee (IASC), founded in 1973 by accountancy bodies in several countries: Australia, Canada, France, Germany, Japan, Mexico, the Netherlands, the United Kingdom and Ireland, and the United States of America. It issued several International Accounting Standards (IAS). Then the IASC was replaced with the IASB and stopped issuing IASs. Instead of accounting, it decided to focus on financial reporting. So it began issuing International Financial Reporting Standards (IFRSs). Now "IFRSs" is the term used to indicate the whole body of IASB authoritative literature; it includes:

➤ IFRSs issued by the IASB.

➤ International Accounting Standards (IASs) issued by the IASC, or revisions thereof issued by the IASB.

➤ Interpretations of IFRSs and IASs developed by the IFRIC and approved for issue by the IASB.

➤ Interpretations of IASs developed by the SIC and approved for issue by the IASB or IASC.

9. The basic concepts of accounting are business entity, money measurement, double entry (debt/credit), historic cost, going concern, accrual, realism, periods, and matching (income and expense). The conventions are consistency, disclosure, materiality, and conservatism. Historic cost, realism, and conservatism all tend to encourage worst-case valuation. For good summaries of accounting concepts, see New York Society of Certified Public Accountants, "Accounting Terminology Guide," http://www.nysscpa.org/prof_library/guide.htm#.

10. "Conservatism is not a justification for deliberate understatement. It is rather a quality of judgment to be exercised in evaluating the uncertainties and risks present in a business entity to assure that reasonable provisions are made for potential losses in the realization of recorded assets and in the settlement of actual and contingent liabilities." (Paul Grady. "Inventory of Generally Accepted Accounting Principles for Business Enterprises, Accounting Research Study No. 7," [New York: AICPA, 1965], p. 35.)

11. For a discussion of how the accounting principle of conservatism can distort valuations, see Dr. Niclas Hellman, "Accounting Conservatism Under IFRS," paper of May 2007, Stockholm School of Economics, http://www.essec-kpmg.net/us/eufin/pdf/papers/Hellman.pdf.

12. Barry J. Epstein and Eva K. Jermankowitz, *IFRS 2009: Interpretation and Application of International Financial Reporting Standards* (New York: John Wiley & Sons, 2009).

13. Model Business Corporation Act, Section 12.01, Disposition of Assets not Requiring Shareholder Approval (http://www.abanet.org/buslaw/library/onlinepublications/mbca2002.pdf), states, "No approval of the shareholders of a corporation is required, unless the articles of incorporation otherwise provide:

   1. to sell, lease, exchange, or otherwise dispose of any or all of the corporation's assets in the usual and regular course of business;

   2. to mortgage, pledge, dedicate to the repayment of indebtedness (whether with or without recourse), or otherwise encumber any or all of the corporation's assets, whether or not in the usual and regular course of business;

   3. to transfer any or all of the corporation's assets to one or more corporations or other entities all of the shares or interests of which are owned by the corporation; or

   4. to distribute assets pro rata to the holders of one or more classes or series of the corporation's shares."

14. See note 2.

15. As noted in Chapter 1, note 51, comprehensive income is defined by the FASB, as "the change in equity [net assets] of a business enterprise during a period from transactions and other events and circumstances from non-owner sources. It includes all changes in equity during a period except those resulting from investments by owners and distributions to owners" (FASB Statement 130, *Reporting Comprehensive Income*. June 1997).

16. IASB Agenda Project: Conceptual Framework Phase C—Measurement, http://www.iasplus.com/agenda/framework-c.htm. See also IASB, "Factors to Consider in Selecting a Basis for Measurement after Initial Recognition (Agenda paper 3)," November 2008, http://www.iasb.org/NR/rdonlyres/3B6EA216-3B1B-4CEC-8A77-68A1176275E4/0/CF0811b03obs.pdf.

17. As noted by acquisition broker Jay Whitney of Alpharetta, Georgia, on his company web site (http://www.bizacquisition.com/Company_Profile.html), a company's assets are an important factor in determining value. For example, Company A has a new state-of-the-art equipment and does not need capital purchases to continue to produce its profits. Company B is just as profitable but has old, obsolete equipment that needs to be replaced soon.

18. Nermien Al-Ali, *Comprehensive Intellectual Capital Management: Step-by-Step* (New York: John Wiley & Sons, 2003). Mr. Al-Ali gives the example of Microsoft: To arrive at an approximation of the value of a company's intellectual capital, subtract the book value of a company (the total of its tangible and capital resources) from its market value. For example, Microsoft's book value (total assets minus total liabilities) on March 31, 2001, was $54.3 billion. This included $1.4 billion in goodwill and $277 million in intangible assets. Its market capitalization (number of outstanding shares multiplied by stock price), however, amounted to approximately $301 billion. Subtracting the net book value and that of reported intangible assets results in . . . $248.4 billion. If we agree that this is the value of Microsoft's intellectual capital, then it makes 82.4 percent of the company's total assets.

19. Nermien Al-Ali, *Comprehensive Intellectual Capital Management: Step by Step* (New York: John Wiley & Sons, 2002), 6. The Enhanced Business Reporting Initiative puts the figure at 25 percent.

20. In chronological order, the cases (and *discount* verdicts) are as follows: *Gallo v. Commissioner*, 50 TCM (CCH) 470 TCM (RIA) 85363 July 22, 1985 (36 percent); *Howard v. Shay* 100 F 3d 1934 (9th Circ.), November 22, 1996 (50 percent); *Mandelbaum v. Commissioner* 69 TCM (CCH) 2852, TCM (RIA), I95, 255, June 12, 1995 (30 percent); *Davis v. Commissioner*, 110 TC 530, June 30, 1998 (32 percent). For a discussion of these cases,

see Shannon P. Pratt, *The Market Approach to Valuing a Business*, 2nd ed. (New York: John Wiley& Sons, 2005). Just prior to 2003, there were tax court cases that implied acceptance of discounts ranging from 7.5 percent up to 25 percent with an average marketability discount of 17.5 percent and a median of 20 percent. These tax court cases are based on situations that were strongly contested by the IRS and thus on the low end of the spectrum. (Thomson Reuters *Federal Tax Valuation Digest* 2009.) Expert witnesses in valuation cases often cite federal tax court cases. For example, Exhibit F in the "Valuation of Valrico Bancorp, Inc. in Amendment to Tender-Offer Statement—Going-Private Transaction," Schedule 13E-3, includes a summary of valuation cases accumulated by the Thomson Reuters *Federal Tax Valuation Digest* for 2003 and 2004. The range of discounts for lack of marketability ranges from 0 to 45 percent with an average and median discount of 25.4 and 25.0 percent, respectively, for the 42 cases identified.

21. To measure the converse of a premium, a discount, in a study of 173 IPO transactions during a fairly bullish market, one researcher saw significant marketability discounts applied to restricted stock of companies that later went public. The average discount ranged from 40 percent to 66 percent, with an average marketability discount of 47 percent.

22. The buyer and seller are required under Rule 13e-3(b)(2)(i) to complete, file, and disseminate a Schedule 13E-3. Each person filing the schedule must state whether it "reasonably believes that the Rule 13e-3 transaction is fair or unfair to unaffiliated security holders." Each must evaluate the going-private transaction from the standpoint of fairness to the issuer's unaffiliated shareholders and appropriately disclose the results of such evaluation. (Going Private Transactions, Exchange Act Rule 13e-3 and Schedule 13E-3. Securities and Exchange Commission. January 26, 2009, http://www.sec .gov/divisions/corpfin/guidance/13e-3-interps.htm.)

23. As we will discuss in Chapter 7, complexity theory can be of help in getting away from "accountingization" of values—to quote a term from philosopher John Dumay (see also the feature box "Neologism," which quotes Dumay.

24. See Chapter 1 for the words of Mr. Warsh on the Panic of 2008.

25. "Turmoil in U.S. Credit Markets: Examining Recent Actions of Federal Financial Regulators," April 3, 2008, 10 AM, SD-G50 Dirksen Senate Office Building, http://banking.senate.gov/public/index.cfm? FuseAction =Hearings.Hearing&Hearing_ID=ec013d8f-fe1e-4fb6-a514-ab93be32ad38 and http://banking.senate.gov/public/index.cfm?FuseAction =Hearings.Testimony&Hearing_ID=ec013d8f-fe1e-4fb6-a514-ab93be32ad38&Witness_ID=db6646b2-a778-453d-a5e3-05b538a1c66e.

26. "Chairman Cox Letter to Basel Committee in Support of New Guidance on Liquidity Management," March 20, 2008, http://sec.gov/news/press/2008/2008-48.htm.

27. See, for example, David Dreman, *Contrary Investment Strategies: the Next Generation* (New York: Simon & Schuster, 1998).

28. Adrian J. Slywotsky, *The Profit Zone* (New York: Random House/Time Books, 1997), quoted in Alfred Rappaport and Michael J. Mauboussin, *Expectations Investing* (Boston: Harvard Business School Press, 2001).

29 "Under Islam, interest is banned. Sharia-compliant products are often asset based, sharing profits rather than paying interest" (Stella Dawson et al., "UBS sees Growth in Islamic Finance," Reuters, April 16, 2009).

30. Fleet management companies are an example of an asset-intensive industry. For commentary, see Diaswati Mardiasmo, et al., "Asset Management and Governance—An Analysis of Fleet Management Process Issues in an Asset-Intensive Organization," a paper delivered at the International Conference on Infrastructure Systems, November 10–12, 2008, Rotterdam, Holland. This paper tries to reconcile two different ways of looking at asset values: one focused on an engineering model, the other on a governance model.

31. Benjamin Dodd and David Graham, *Security Analysis* (New York: McGraw-Hill, 1934), 495 ff.

32. The relevant standard is ASC 230 *Statement of Cash Flows* (FAS 95). For the text of this standard, along with links to other standards impacting it, see http://www.fasb.org/pdf/aop_FAS95.pdf and "The Fair Value Option for Financial Assets and Financial Liabilities—Including an Amendment of FASB Statement No. 115," http://www.fasb.org/st/summary/stsum159.shtml.

33. The FASB listed these nine categories as a part of its new codification scheme under the category Assets (Topic 300). (http://72.3.243.42/project/B-Topics_and_subtopics.pdf). This is not a reporting requirement.

34. This is per IAS 7.7-8, which is currently undergoing review. The International Financial Reporting Interpretations Committee (IFRIC) met at the IASB's offices in London on Thursday, March 5, 2009. Here are notes from the meeting: "IAS 7 *Statement of Cash Flows*—Determination of cash equivalents": "The staff presented the IFRIC with an issue about the definition of cash equivalent in IAS 7. The submission asked whether money market funds that are readily convertible and subject to only an insignificant risk qualify as cash equivalents. It was clear that the question was whether an entity had to look through the investment and make sure that all underlying investments meet the definition of a cash equivalent to conclude that the money market fund was a cash equivalent." (Deloitte &

Touche observers, http://www.iasplus.com/pastnews/2009mar.htm.) Note from the authors: IAS may undergo a revision that will bring it closer to a GAAP standard, which does factor in such analysis.

35. Reserve Funds press release of September 16, 2008, http://www .reservefunds.com/pdfs/Press%20Release%202008_0916.pdf?scp= 2&sq=eric%20dash&st=cse.

36. Lehman Brothers' press release of September 15, 2008 read, "Lehman Brothers Holdings Inc. Announces It Intends to File Chapter 11 Bankruptcy Protection," http://www.lehman.com/press/pdf_2008/091508_lbhi_ chapter11_announce.pdf.

37. IAS 39.43.

38. IAS 39.46 and 47.

39. See, for example, IAS18.11 for accounting for revenue.

40. IAS 36.9 and 59.

41. For an explanation of our accounting standard citation style, see Chapter 1, note 54. For additional comparative commentary, see http://www.icai.org/ resource_file/11643p592-595.pdf.

42. IAS 31 applies. See http://www.iasplus.com/standard/ias31.htm.

43. See note 2.

44. Ibid., note 2.

45. Ibid., note 2.

46. "There are currently more than 60 pieces of [FASB] literature that address various aspects of accounting for instruments that are within the scope of this Preliminary Views. Most of the literature addresses specific narrow issues and was developed as the issues arose. As a result, the current literature is inconsistent, subject to structuring, or difficult to understand and apply. The complexity has caused many questions and numerous restatements over the past few years." ("Financial Instruments with Characteristics of Equity," FASB, May 2007, http://www.fasb.org/draft/pv_liab_ and_equity.pdf.)

47. For an example of how one state applied this principle, see "Highest and Best Use Example, 09/03/02," posted without name of an author at. http://files .dnr.state.mn.us/lands_minerals/appraisal_mgmt/bestuseexample.pdf. For a thoughtful commentary on this topic, see Joseph S. Rabianski, "Comments on the Concept and Definition of Highest and Best Use," *Real Estate Issues*, Spring 2007, http://findarticles .com/p/articles/mi_qa3681/is_200704/ai_n 19433077.

48. In addition, under ASC 825, *Disclosures about Fair Value of Financial Instruments* (SFAS 107), there is increased "comparability of information about certain financial assets that have related economic characteristics but have different measurement attributes." According to a description of

the standard announced by FASB, it applies to certain financial assets such as (a) debt securities classified as held-to-maturity and available-for-sale and (b) loans and long-term receivables that are not measured at fair value with changes in the fair value recognized through earnings. The required disclosures include (a) a comparison of common measurement attributes for financial assets and (b) the pro forma income from continuing operations (before taxes) under the different measurement scenarios. "These disclosures were developed jointly with the International Accounting Standards Board (IASB), which issued an exposure draft proposing a similar set of disclosures. See "On the Horizon Grant Thornton, February 9, 2010, http://www.grantthorton.com/staticfiles/GTCom/Audit/Assurancepublications/OntheHorizon/2010/OTH_2_9_10.pdf.

49. The IASB has published two papers on the subject of fair value: http://www.iasb.org/NR/rdonlyres/6C8AF291-EB14-4034-84F1-54305F72024D/0/DDFairValue.pdfandhttp://www.iasb.org/NR/rdonlyres/5D20E453-26D3-4E0A-AB08-FC391917FD89/0/DDFairValue2.pdf.

50. In ASC 820 (SFAS 157) the FASB acknowledges that some Level 3 inputs may be of such a hypothetical nature that they "would seem to be of questionable relevance to users of financial statements."

51. In January 2010, the FASB issued an update: "Improving Disclosures About Fair Value Measurements." Fair Value Measurements and Disclosures (Topic 821), No. 2010-06, An Amendment of the FASB Accounting Standards Codification. To see any standard or update under Accounting Standards Codificiation, go to http://asc.fasb.org/. Note: registration required; basic registration is free.

52. For exceptions and other details, see ASC 825 *The Fair Value Option for Financial Assets and Financial Liabilities* (SFAS 159) at fasb.org.

53. ASC 825 guidance on fair value applies only if companies already use fair value accounting to report the earnings from the financial instruments, per ASC 820, the general standard for Fair Value Measurements. The statement defines a financial liability as a contract that imposes on one entity an obligation to deliver cash or another financial instrument to a second entity or to exchange other financial instruments on potentially unfavorable terms with the second entity.

54. For additional insights from the Norwegian Global Pension Fund, see Appendix S.

55. "Discussion Paper on Fair Value Measurement," November 2006, cited at http://www.iasb.org/News/Press+Releases/IASB+publishes+Discussion+Paper+on+fair+value+measurements.htm.

56. See http://www.fasb.org/jsp/FASB/Page/SectionPage&cid=11761544934444#issues.

57. The asset must meet recognition criteria in FASB Concepts Statement No. 5, *Recognition and Measurement in Financial Statements of Business Enterprises*, even though they do not meet either the contractual-legal criterion or the separability criterion (for example, specially trained employees or a unique manufacturing process related to an acquired manufacturing plant). Such transactions commonly are bargained exchange transactions that are conducted at arm's length, which provides reliable evidence about the existence and fair value of those assets. See Accounting Standards Codification at http://asc.fasb.org/section&trid=2144481%26nav_type=subtopic_page.

58. "If intangible assets are complementary and could not be separately sold, then they should be recognized as a group of assets. On the other hand, if the individual fair values of the complementary assets can be reliably measured they should be separately recognized, unless they have similar useful lives." Since the introduction of IFRS, trademarks and other acquired intangible assets have to be separately recognized on the balance sheet. (Tim Heberden and David Haigh, "The Role of Trademarks in M&A," *Intellectual Asset Management*, June/July 2006, p. 37.)

59. See ASC 805 *Business Combinations* (SFAS 141), (limiting the scope to intangible assets that are either grounded in contracts or other legal rights or are separable from the business) and ASC 350 *Goodwill and Other Intangible Assets* (SFAS 142). Under FASB Interpretation No. 4, *Applicability of FASB Statement No. 2 to Business Combinations Accounted for by the Purchase Method*, in-process research and development assets are written off to expense on the day they are acquired.

60. Tim Heberden and David Haigh, "The Role of Trademarks in M&A," *Intellectual Asset Management*, June/July 2006, pp. 37–41.

61. Source: San West, Inc., Form S-1/A, June 18, 2010. http://www.faqs .org/sec-filings/100618/san-west-inc_s-1.A/#IXZZ0RLJ85LS0.

62. From the proxy filing of August 9, 2007.

63. Anand Chokkavelu "Better Bet: Goldman or BP?" posted on the popular financial website, The Motley Fool, June 7, 2010. www.fool.com/ investing/high-growth/2010/06/07/better.

64. British American Tobacco PLC, May 4, 2005.

65. Fortsum 2008 Annual Financial Report, http://www.fortsum.com/ Portals/ 0/pdf/Rapport_annuel_2008_EN.pdf.

66. Expressing a value in terms of currency prepares the way for actual true monetization—the practice of selling or leasing an asset to a third party and obtaining money from its sale or use.

67. See note 7 re basic accounting concepts and conventions.

68. The authors acknowledge the Center for Audit Quality for bringing these letter to our attention. See http://www.thecaq.org/members/alerts/CAQ

Alert2009_13_02062009.pdf (citing http://www.sec.gov/divisions/corpfin/guidance/fairvalueltr0308.htm and http://www.sec.gov/divisions/corpfin/guidance/fairvalueltr0908.htm).

69. Suggestions for guidance on a sensitivity analysis in these circumstances include FR-72, Section 5—(Release 33-8350), *Commission Guidance Regarding Management's Discussion and Analysis of Financial Condition and Results of Operations;* IFRS No. 7, *Financial Instruments: Disclosures,* Par. 27(c). Sensitivity disclosure best practices include the following: base the sensitivity on other reasonably likely inputs to the model and effects on the value, and use reasonably likely assumptions—not a default to one assumption for all transactions. See http://sec.gov/news/speech/2008/spch120908wc-slides.pdf.

70. The SEC wants companies to quantify whether alternative valuation techniques for illiquid instruments would result in materially different fair values or amounts realized based on current sales to the extent possible; discuss strengths and weaknesses of the technique that was used (and possibly other techniques considered); and disclose how the values ultimately used in the financial statements sync up with accounting rules. (ASC 820 *Fair Value Measurements* (SFAS 157), described at http://sec.gov/news/speech/2008/spch120908wc-slides.pdf.)

71. Derivatives can be affected by credit risk when an underlying security depends on creditworthiness. The accounting issues here are complex. See ASC 820: *The Fair Value Option for Financial Assets and Financial Liabilities* (SFAS 159), at fasb.org.

72. The GICS structure consists of 10 sectors, 24 industry groups, 67 industries, and 147 subindustries. Developed by two financial information companies, MSCI and Standard & Poor's (S&P), the GICS classifications "aim to enhance the investment research and asset management process for financial professionals worldwide. It is the result of numerous discussions with asset owners, portfolio managers and investment analysts around the world and is designed to respond to the global financial community's need for an accurate, complete and standard industry definition."

73. Andrew Dolback, "Valuation of the Chemical and Drug Industry," Weekly Corporate Growth Report, Monday, January 28 2008, http://www.allbusiness.com/energy-utilities/renewable-energy-biomass/8893246-1.html.

74. See, for example, Professor Philip M. Parker, *Dongbu Hannong Chemical Co. Ltd.: International Competitive Benchmarks and Financial Gap Analysis* (http://www.icongrouponline.com/pr/Dongbu_Hannong_Chemical_Co__Ltd_KR/PR.html). There are 35 reports in this series.

75. Shannon Nome, Phillips Johnston, Scott Arndt, and Rodney C Clayton, "E&P 101: A Primer Oil and Gas Exploration & Production," November 2005.

76. The SEC is "looking into whether Countrywide set aside the right level of loan-loss reserves, a barometer of the health of a mortgage firm's portfolio" ("SEC Poised to Charge Mozilo with Fraud," May 14, 2009, http://online .wsj.com/article/SB124224647957816523.html.html).

77. For a guide to ALLL on the balance sheet, see http://www.federalreserve .gov/BoardDocs/srletters/2006/SR0617a1.pdf.

78. Board of Governors of the Federal Reserve System, "The Supervisory Capital Assessment Program: Design and Implementation," April 24, 2009, http://www.federalreserve.gov/newsevents/press/bcreg/bcreg20090424a1 .pdf. For results of the tests, see http://www.federalreserve.gov/newsev- ents/press/bcreg/bcreg20090507a1.pdf. Note: for more about scenario planning in general, see Douglas W. Hubbard, *The Failure of Risk Man- agement: Why It's Broken and How to Fix It* (Hoboken, N.J.: John Wiley & Sons, 2009), especially the notion of "common mode failure," where a single event causes failure of multiple components in a system. When common mode failure can be traced to human error, the probability of its occurrence rises.

79. For parallel standards under IAS, see http://ec.europa.eu/internal_ market/insurance/docs/markt-2531-03/markt-2531-03_en.pdf.

80. The job he held is now called assistant secretary of labor due to an upgrade in the status of the position.

81. See Norma Cohen and Jennifer Hughes, "Call for Change in Pension Deficit Reporting, *Financial Times*, December 31, 2008.

82. "Harvard's endowment fell nearly 30 percent in the fiscal year ended June 30, 2009, to $25.7 billion. Source: "Endowment Leads Others Down," *The Boston Globe*, January 20, 2010.

83. ASR 113 and ASR 118: Accounting Series Release No. 113, Inv. Co. Act Rel. No. 5847 (1937–1982 Accounting Series Release Transfer Binder), Fed. Sec. l. Rep. (CCH) 72,135 (October 21, 1969) (hereinafter ASR 113); and Accounting Series Release No. 118, Inv. Co. Act Rel. No. 6295, (1937–1982 Accounting Series Release Transfer Binder), Fed. Sec. L. Rep. (CCH) 72,140 (December 23, 1970) (hereinafter ASR 118). See also Joan Sweeney, chief operating officer, and Penni Roll, chief financial officer, Allied Capital Corporation, "Valuation of Illiquid Securities Held by Business Development Companies: A White Paper" (undated white paper), http://www.foolingsomepeople.com/main/Valua- tion WhitePaper.pdf.

84. See Svetlozar T. Rachev et al., *Fat-Tailed and Skewed Asset Return Dis- tributions: Implications for Risk Management, Portfolio Selection, and Option Pricing* (Hoboken, N.J.: John Wiley & Sons, 2005).

85. See Chapter 1, note 58.

86. U.S. Department of the Treasury, "Treasury Department Releases Details on Public Private Partnership Investment Program," http://www.treas.gov/press/releases/tg65.htm.

87. Sources of ratio information are Dun & Bradstreet's Industry Norms and Key Business Ratios, the Risk Management Association's Annual Statement Studies, and Stanley Foster Reed, Alexandra Reed Lajoux, and H. Peter Nesvold, *The Art of M&A*, 4th ed. (New York: McGraw-Hill, 2007).

88. Example: "Your investment philosophy requires an average AAR of at least 15 percent on all fixed asset purchases. Currently, you are considering some new equipment costing $96,000. This equipment will have a 3-year life over which time it will be depreciated on a straight line basis to a zero book value. The annual net income from this project is estimated at $5,500, $12,400, and $17,600 for the 3 years."
Analysis:

The average net income is (5,500 + 12,400 + 17,600)/2 = 11,833.33.
The average investment is (96,000 + 0)/2 = 48,000.
AAR = 11,833.33/48,000 = 24.6%.

This is higher than 15%; the project should be accepted."

89. As additional cash investments increase the asset side of the balance sheet, this number ensures that additional dollars invested do not appear to be dollars of return from previous investments.

90. "Canon, Inc. Q4 2007 Earnings Call Transcript," *Seeking Alpha*, January 31, 2008, http://seekingalpha.com/article/62612-canon-inc-q4-2007-earnings-call-transcript.http://www.marketwatch.com/story/10-k-lannett-co-inc-2009-09-28.

92. "Datascrop Corporation Q2 2008 Earnings Call Transcript," *Seeking Alpha*, February 8, 2008, http://seekingalpha.com/article/63827-datascope-corporation-q2-2008-earnings-call-transcript?page=3.

93. Lennox International, Inc. Q4 2007 Earnings Call Transcript February 6, 2008. The company maintained an 18 percent level the following year. ("Lennox International, Inc. Q3 2009 Earnings Call Transcript," *Seeking Alpha*, http://seekingalpha.com/article/167940-lennox-international-inc-q3-2009-earnings-call-transcript?page=4.)

94. American Society of Appraisers, ASA Business Valuation Standards, BVS-III.

CHAPTER 3

Valuation Based on Earnings (Income)

A penny saved is a penny earned.

—Benjamin Franklin, *Poor Richard's Almanac*

EARNINGS—THE DIFFERENCE between revenues and expenses during a specific period—provide an important clue to the investment value of a company. As noted in a foundational U.S. accounting pronouncement, earnings are "the basic source of compensation to owners for providing equity or risk capital to an enterprise."[1]

As mentioned in Chapter 1, corporate leaders tend to favor earnings as a measure for corporate performance, while shareholders tend to favor cash flow, since it seems more closely related to returns to shareholders.[2]

But although the relationship between earnings and returns to shareholders is not always easy to see, it does exist. Profitable operations generate the resources companies need to pay dividends to owners and/ or to make further investments in the company.[3] Furthermore, investors' expectations about these company actions affect stock prices and thus investors' returns.

The previous chapter covered assets as a fundamental indicator of value. The focus of this chapter is on earnings, as well as ratios that include this value.

Earnings Defined

This value is called "earnings" rather than "income" or "profit." Professional investors tend to use the word *earnings* (as in "earnings per share," "earnings calls," and the like)[4] for good reason. The term *income* without a modifier has too many potential meanings, especially when a company uses a multistep approach to reporting earnings. (Financial statements may use a single-step or a multistep approach. In the single-step approach, companies show a figure for revenues, minus all expenses, equaling net income. But most large public companies use a multistep approach, breaking out different kinds of revenues, expenses, and especially income.)

This chapter guides investors in the analysis of earnings, offering guidance on how they can assess the quality of earnings. Also discussed are common earnings-based methods of valuation such as average rate of return (ARR) and internal rate of return (IRR). Finally, the chapter appendices list key ratios that include earnings, such as earnings per share (EPS), currently undergoing redefinition as a global standard. Appendix 3.1 (from Hoovers) gives a plain vanilla list of earnings-based ratios. Appendix 3.2 (from this book's authors) provides additional descriptions of these ratios, along with other formulas. Appendix 3.3 (from the Federal Deposit Insurance Corporation) shows earnings analysis in a bank.

Unintended Consequences

From your perspective, where has general-purpose financial reporting helped identify issues of concern during the financial crisis?

Accounting has real-world effects. For example, despite no change in the economics of the business and because of the overemphasis on earnings statements by banks, credit markets can be impacted by accounting changes as companies can be in violation of bank covenants simply because of accounting changes.

———
—"Summary of Written Submissions from the Public," The Financial Crisis Advisory Group (April 14, 2009), http://www.fasb.org/fcag/fcag_written_submissions.shtml.

Types of Earnings

Companies that break out types of earnings show several categories of income:

➤ *Gross profit* (or gross earnings) equals revenue minus cost of goods sold. It identifies the amount available to cover other operating expenses. These are typically positive, even when a company is in distressed financial condition.[5]

➤ *Operating income* (or operating earnings) equals gross profit minus selling, general, and administrative expenses. It is the income from current operations.

➤ *Nonoperating income* is a residual category in which a company can net miscellaneous nonoperating revenues and expenses. Nonoperating income can be from investment income, lease income, special settlements, and the like.

➤ *Earnings (or income) before taxes* is earnings (or income from total operations) before interest, taxes, depreciation, and amortization.

➤ *Net income after taxes* is the income from total operations (continuing and discontinued) after taxes have been taken out.

➤ *Net income from continuing operations* includes income taken after taxes and before the following: preferred dividends, extraordinary gains and losses, income from accumulative effects of accounting change, nonrecurring items, income from tax loss carryforward, and other gains or losses.

➤ *Net income from discontinued operations* represents the net gain or loss resulting from the selling or closing of discontinued operations of the company. This excludes income from extraordinary gains or losses.

➤ *Net income from total operations* is the income from the total operations (continuing and discontinued operations) after taxes and minority interest and before extraordinary gains or losses.

➤ *Total net income* is the income after accounting for all corporate actions:

    Income from continuing operations
    + Income from discontinued opertations
    + Income from extraordinary items
    + Income from accumulative effect of accounting changes
    + Income from tax loss carryforward
    + Income from other gains/losses

The value-mind investor should be able to see all these numbers and consider what they mean in relation to other financial and nonfinancial metrics. In a sense, the value-minded investor can tell the "personality" of a company's earnings. In a typical earnings call, investors don't quibble much over accounting treatments. They focus on the value drivers of the business: How does the company make its money, what is the outlook for these activities, and what risks might be in store? Significantly, these calls have the name of "earnings calls." The terminology shows that, when earnings patterns are analyzed in the larger context of other indicators (found on other financial statements or in other company disclosures such as management's discussion and analysis, or MD&A), they can have significant meaning. Earnings are not just a line or three on the income statement; they are the very thing that makes a commercial activity viable: over time, no matter how a company reports its earnings, it cannot spend more money than it makes and survive.[6]

Fully Loaded

To make a long story short, most transactions and events make their way through the income statement. As a result, it can be said that the income statement is "all-inclusive." Once upon a time, this was not the case; only operational items were included in the income statement. Nonrecurring or nonoperating related transactions and events were charged or credited directly to equity, bypassing the income statement entirely.

———————————

—Larry Walther, PhD, CPA, CMA, professor and head of the School of Accountancy at Utah State University

---

Operating Earnings Are Key to Value

When a value-minded investor looks at operating earnings, the investor is looking at a number with a relatively high chance of persisting, compared to total earnings. (The same applies to earnings per share, which, because it is calculated using total earnings, like operating earnings, has a short-term meaning.)[7]

Operating income contributes significantly to a company's long-term prospects. It counts only the money coming in from the company's ongoing business and does not include windfalls. In calculating operating income, management has to leave out nonrecurring items such as gains or losses from accounting changes, divestures, or write-offs. So the operating income figure gives a more accurate picture of financial health than does net income.

The operating income measure can be expanded by adding depreciation and amortization expenses back to it, as earnings before interest, taxes, depreciation, and amortization (EBITDA). GAAP does not require or define doing this, but it is permissible to report it, and many companies do. The metric is sometimes used as a multiple in merger transactions.[8]

The "B" in EBITDA is for "before," meaning it does not subtract the ITDA items. So earnings are increased by the corresponding amount. This helps investors compare companies with different tax, interest, depreciation, and amortization situations side by side—that is, the core profitability of the actual business. Assuming a close ratio of reported

---

Whatever Happened to EBITDA?

Valuation concepts come and go, but nothing ever changes. Back in 1987, when I was working at Lane & Edson, LP, a premier law firm involved in leveraged buyouts, everyone was talking about cash flow, cash flow, cash flow—a concept made popular by legendary valuation philosophers Alfred Rappaport and Joel Stern. One day, in one of the meetings, one of the L&E partners asked, "Whatever happened to EBITDA?" In the conversation that followed, the attorneys agreed that it was still a useful measure of value, and began using it again for some transactions.

Today, as the business world heads for global convergence of accounting (slated for 2014), similar conversations may be taking place in global valuation circles.

—Alexandra R. Lajoux

earnings and free cash flow, EBITDA can also show what money will be available to make long-term payments. Although it should not be used as an exclusive metric for financial health, it is a good way to eliminate some of the "noise" surrounding value. (EBITDA is discussed again at the end of the following section on valuation methodologies using earnings.)

Earnings Are Relative to Revenues and Expenses

Unlike assets, which have an intrinsic existence of their own, earnings are relative. In a statement of earnings (also called "income statement") earnings (also called "income") is the line that shows a monetary amount representing the difference between revenues and expenses—in other words, revenues minus expenses equals earnings, or income. So clearly, investors, the primary users of financial statements, need to study revenues and expenses to understand earnings. They can also benefit from understanding how all these items (revenues, expenses, and earnings) relate to underlying assets and liabilities.

Earnings Are Ultimately Based on Assets

Accountancy guru Robert Anthony once observed, "single most fundamental issue in financial reporting" is the relationship between the "asset and liability" model (seen best in the balance sheet), on the one hand, and the "revenue and expense" model (seen best in the income statement), on the other.[9]

Currently, the accounting standard setters are using an *asset-based model*. That is, current thinking entails a hierarchy in which the assets and liabilities are the drivers of value and the source of changes in income.

The relationship between assets and earnings can be viewed as fundamental parts of a dynamic corporate system. As one systems philosopher has noted, "a dynamical system is characterized by a set of state variables and a dynamical law that governs how the values of those state variables change with time."[10] In systems language, assets constitute the state of the corporate system, and earnings represent change to that state.

Choosing the Right Valuation Model Includes Consideration of Earnings

This decision tree can help investors choose the right model for valuation.

Earnings

- Are earnings positive? Yes/No

If earnings are normal, enter the following:

- Expected inflation rate
- Expected real growth rate
- Expected growth rate in earnings for this firm
- Does firm have significant and sustainable advantage over competitors? Yes/No

If earnings are negative, please enter the cause:

- Firm in cyclical business? Yes/No
- One-time or temporary occurrence? Yes/No
- Too much debt? Yes/No
- Risk of bankruptcy? Yes/No
- Startup? Yes/No

Financial Leverage

- What is the current debt ratio (in percent)?
- Is this debt ratio expected to change significantly? Yes/No

Dividend Policy

What did the firm pay as dividends in the current year?

Estimate free cash flow to equity (FCFE) = Net income − (Captital spending − Depreciation) × (1 − Debt ratio) − Change in working captial (1 − Debt ratio)

(Continued)

(Continued)

> Output from model: The answer generated = the type of model that should be used to value the firm!
>
> _____
>
> *Source*: Aswath Damodaran, who has posted a variety of models on his web site (http://pages.stern.nyu.edu/~adamodar/New_Home_Page/spreadsh .htm#troubledfirms). For guidance on models, see Appendix I, "Damodaran's Spreadsheets for Valuation."

Hard Times Reveal Earnings-Asset Connection

The connection of earnings to assets can be seen when times are hard. It is relatively rare for major companies to declare losses, but it does happen, typically in a situation of insolvency preceding a bankruptcy filing. This declaration tends to shift the focus to the balance sheet, which makes good fiduciary sense as well as financial sense. As explained in Chapter 8, when a company is in the zone of insolvency, the obligations of directors move from shareholders to bondholders.

In *Security Analysis*, Graham and Dodd addressed the very real question that arises in a depressed or recessionary economy: how to find the value in losses. Substituting a recent bad year (such as 2009) for 1932 makes these words strangely contemporary:

> The analyst must approach a year like 1932 in the spirit of common sense rather than narrow exactitude. No doubt the efforts of many concerns to avoid too harrowing an income exhibit resulted in some highly questionable uses of the surplus account. But in the typical case there seems to be little point in any endeavor to arrive at a precise restatement of the year's operating results. For since prevailing business conditions were thoroughly abnormal, and themselves presumably *nonrecurring*, there is but slight advantage in knowing the exact amount of the operating losses as distinguished from the extraordinary losses. Such a figure would have not value as a guide to future results, and it is doubtful

whether its use as a component of a long-term average would be especially instructive. The real significance of most 1932 reports is to be looked for in the balance sheet, particularly in the extent to which working capital was maintained or impaired, and also in certain contradictory effects following from the drastic write-downs of fixed assets.[11]

Sistine Chapel

To help the valuation-minded investor, all we can do is try to paint a Sistine Chapel showing a struggle with the "angels"—international accounting brouhahas, massive transformations making both forward and backward comparisons meaningless, inflation—and now, government-created assets and earnings.

———————

—Robert A. G. Monks

It may seem that negative earnings, much like the number zero, throw off valuation models by introducing a negative number. But the valuation experts have worked around this difficulty. There are even spreadsheets customized to the valuation of companies that are losing money.[12]

How the Standard Setters Currently Define Earnings

Following 2008, a year almost as bad as 1932, the Financial Accounting Standards Board (FASB) and the International Accounting Standards Board (IASB) proposed similar definitions of the term "earnings."

Earnings (Comprehensive Income)

Comprehensive income, says the FASB, is the "change in equity of a business enterprise during a period from transactions and other events and circumstances from non-owner sources. It includes all changes in equity during a period except those resulting from investments by owners and distributions to owners."[13] Comprehensive income yields a gain if the change is positive, a loss of the change is negative. These terms, too, have technical definitions linked to assets.

The global standard from IASB is similar to that of the FASB. It defines comprehensive income as "increases in economic benefits during the accounting period in the form of inflows or enhancements of assets or decreases of liabilities that result in increases in equity, other than those relating to contributions from equity participants."[14]

The income represents an increase in the owners' potential claim against the assets. As one popular educational site explains, "Income is NOT a cash asset." Through the equity and income accounts, "the balance sheet and income statement reflect the total financial picture of the entity."[15]

So what about the equation—revenues minus expenses equals earnings (or income)? The following definitions of revenues and expenses explain the connection.

Revenues

The FASB defines revenues as "*inflows* or other enhancements of assets of an entity or settlements of its liabilities (or a combination of both) from delivering or producing goods, rendering services, or other activities that constitute the entity's ongoing major or central operations" (FASB Statement 6).

The IASB's global standard mirrors this concept: "Revenue is the *gross inflow* of economic benefits during the period arising in the course of the ordinary activities of an entity when those inflows result in increases in equity, other than increases relating to contributions from equity participants" (IAS 18).

Expenses

"Expenses are *outflows* or other using up of assets or incurrences of liabilities (or a combination of both) from delivering or producing goods, rendering services, or carrying out other activities that constitute the entity's ongoing major or central operations."

Comments to the International Standards Accounting Board Regarding the Discussion Paper Entitled "Preliminary Views on Financial Statement Presentation"[16]

Should an entity present comprehensive income in a single statement of comprehensive income as proposed?

A single statement approach does not adequately reflect an entity's performance. The bottom line in a single statement would be a mixture of realized gains and losses and unrealized fair values changes. These are based on external circumstances and are mainly out of the control of the entity's management.

Due to this uncertainty and unpredictability it is likely that the comprehensive income varies from year to year. The result is that a comparison from year to year is not possible and conclusions based on these figures might be misleading. On the contrary, net income is directly influenced by management and shows the development and performance over the years. It indicates positive as well as negative trends and is easier to explain because of the missing random influences.

To see this comment letter, go to http://www.fasb.org/jsp/FASB/CommentLetter_C/CommentLetterPage&cid=1218220137090&project_id=1630-100 and click on the letter by Brucks (number 52).

We are not concerned whether the statement of comprehensive income has a page break but welcome the acknowledgement of the need for a net income subtotal—investors want to be able to identify the elements that represent operating performance and the underlying operating income and expense. They want to know what management has generated from its operation and the resources allocated to it, and be able to distinguish this from the distortions that arise from remeasurement and on-off gains and losses. An earnings subtotal is particularly useful in this context.

—Investment Management Association, excerpted from a letter dated April 30, 2009, http://www.investmentuk.org/news/research/2009/topic/corporate_governance/imaresponsetoiasbdponfspapril2009.pdf

A Brief Pause to Look at Our Compass

At this point, some readers may feel that the discussion is far too focused on what the accounting standard setters are saying. Why not just get straight to the business of valuation? Unless investors understand what the numbers on the financial statements mean, they can't value them.

The next question is, is it worth poring over financial statements before making an investment? The answer is yes, to a degree. As explained in Chapter 2, securities valuation involves a trade-off. On the one hand, investors may spend the time studying a company to make a good investment decision that will yield a return. On the other hand, there is the value of the investors' time. By crunching through these accounting pronouncements for our readers, the authors hope to save investors' time. Also the accounting theorists are arguing about matters that can have very practical meaning to any investor, such as discussions of what should be presented in an earnings number.

The Other Side of the Equation: Revenues Minus Expenses

When investors see a number for revenues on an income statement, they may take it as an indication of the money a company has made during the period measured, such as a financial quarter or year. But because of the accrual method of accounting, revenue is measured when a sale is made and the money owed, not necessarily when the payment is received (unless it's a cash transaction).[17] (Accrual accounting is required under both GAAP and IFRS.[18]) So part of the challenge for companies booking revenue is to write down that amount of money owed. Revenue is actually not the money that has physically arrived at the entity, but the money that the entity either received or became owed during the period measured.

The FASB and the IASB have had different views on the timing of revenue recognition, but these views are converging. The two organizations initiated a joint project on revenue in late 2008. Since then, the boards have been studying comments and holding meetings.[19] Under U.S. GAAP, there are more than one hundred standards for revenue recognition. Many of these are industry specific, and some can produce contradictory results for economically similar transactions. Ongoing updates to standards are adding clarity.[20] In International Financial

Reporting Standards (IFRSs), the principles underlying the two main revenue recognition standards (IAS 18, *Revenue*, and IAS 11, *Construction Contracts*) are broad and contradictory, and designed for simple transactions, not for transactions involving multiple components or multiple deliverables.

The new approach of the FASB and IASB, called "global accounting" in this book, says *revenue should be recognized on the basis of increases in an entity's net position in a contract with a customer.* The proposed global accounting standard says that when a company enters into a contract with a customer, the combination of the rights and the obligations in that contract gives rise to a "net contract position." In the proposed global accounting model, revenue will be recognized whenever a contract asset increases or a contract liability decreases (or some combination of the two occurs). That will occur when a company "performs" by satisfying an obligation in the contract. Companies will estimate the selling prices of the undelivered goods and services and recognize revenue when goods and services are actually delivered to the customer.

The current process has some challenges. In some cases, companies are not supposed to recognize revenue for a delivered item if there is no objective and reliable evidence of the selling price of the undelivered items. On the one hand, companies have wide discretion in how they report income from projects in process. Overall, the tendency may be positive to revenues.[21] On the other hand, in the proposed model, costs will be capitalized only if they meet certain standards for capitalization.

The upshot of this new global accounting approach may be a slight decline in reported revenues compared to current approaches. Investors should adjust their analysis of global compliance reports accordingly. For industry-related effects, see the end of this chapter.

The FASB and IASB based this new global principle on the existing definitions of revenue. In both definitions, revenue is an increase in assets, a decrease in liabilities, or some combination of the two. Using those definitions, the new global accounting proposes to focus the earnings recognition principle on changes in assets and liabilities. This focus does not mean financial statement preparers and users will no longer use the earnings definition of revenues minus expenses. Rather, the accounting standard setters hope that it will bring discipline to the earnings process approach so that entities can recognize revenue more consistently, thereby reducing the risk of fraud.[22]

How XBRL Can Connect the Dots between Earnings and Assets

Clearly, the world's leading authorities on financial reporting believe that earnings are directly related to changes in asset values. (They are not simply a matter of cash.) This might have only theoretical meaning, but it is becoming very real with the advent of XBRL (extensible business reporting language). XBRL, which operates like a bar code for bits of financial information, is a way of comparing data not only across companies,[23] but also *within* companies. Nearly 120 have adopted XBRL as of mid-2010.

A research company in India called IRIS Business Services (myiris.com), using a taxonomy approved by the Institute of Chartered Accountants in India, has shown that at least 209 out of 1,400 listed Indian companies have discrepancies in their annual audited financial results. (The study has so far covered only companies in manufacturing and services; banks and financial services companies will be covered in the next round.)

The numbers in the XBRL schedules should tally with the total reported for the corresponding item in the main balance sheet or the income statement. For 209 of the companies studied, the numbers don't add up, based on the XBRL tags of supposedly equivalent values.[24] One hundred and nine companies had errors in the balance sheet, 34 had errors in their income statements, and 66 had errors in their cash flow statements. In some cases, the magnitude of the errors is enormous—in one case, a discrepancy of 2.16 billion rupees. Textiles with 27 errant companies accounted for the most discrepancies, followed by IT (18),

---

Good-Bye XBRL Bogeyman

I must state unequivocally that the purpose of introduction of XBRL is not to catch errant companies. In fact, with XBRL, companies will be far less likely to make errors in their reporting if they are able to implement XBRL within the organization effectively.

—S. Swaminathan, founder and CEO of IRIS Business Services and India's leading XBRL evangelist steel (10), and pharmaceuticals (9). The founder and CEO of IRIS is contacting companies to advise them of the discovery, so that by the time they comply with XBRL, the discrepancies will be reconciled.

Earnings Management and Fraud

As is now clear, calculating or interpreting earnings for a large and complex corporation is not a simple matter. There is still considerable discussion in global accountancy about what exactly constitutes revenue, what an expense consists of, and what income is. Using XBRL to tag financial items can help with comparability, but it is not a *deus ex machina*.

For one thing, earnings are subject to manipulation—or, in kinder terms, earnings management. Common occasions for earnings management include restructuring charges and the costs of employee pensions and stock options. Some variations are honest attempts to be true to value, but others can border on (or be) fraud. So, unfortunately, earnings statements can be misleading, and the reporting of earnings (revenue recognition and expenses) is the one most prone to fraud, accounting for over half of all frauds. Investors are well aware of this, and so they need to make sure boards have strong and independent audit committees and auditors. But investors can also flag issues and have been known to save the day by complaining when things don't seem right.

Here are the problem areas in their order of priority based on SEC enforcement releases in the first decade of the current millennium. Note, however, that they vary in frequency by industry, and can change over time:

➤ Improper revenue recognition (41 percent)[25]
➤ Improper disclosures (12 percent)
➤ Manipulation of expenses (11 percent)
➤ Manipulation of assets (8 percent)
➤ Manipulation of liabilities (7 percent)
➤ Manipulation of reserves (7 percent)
➤ Asset misappropriation (4 percent)
➤ Bribery and kickbacks (3 percent)
➤ Manipulation of accounts receivable (3 percent)
➤ Investments (1 percent)
➤ Goodwill (1 percent)

The first three items all pertain to earnings because the improper disclosures include failure to report deterioration in these indicators, among others. Simple math shows that most SEC crackdowns focus on shenanigans affecting the income statement. Investors should read income statements with these problems in mind.

Earnings Caveat from a Sage

Although earnings offer clues to value, these clues must be interpreted carefully. A timely warning about the pitfalls of earnings came from valuation philosopher Alfred Rappaport in a landmark article entitled "The Economics of Short-Term Performance Obsession."[26] Rappaport says that *earnings data are not well suited for use in valuation*. Because investors have less information about a company's operations and prospects than managers do, investors focus on short-term performance. This sets up a vicious circle, as CEOs and other senior corporate executives, in turn, focus on reported short-term performance measures, particularly earnings. Rappaport calls this phenomenon a "mutually reinforcing obsession with short-term performance," with earnings as the key metric.

Yet earnings do not fully capture value and are not intended to, says Rappaport, quoting this FASB's *Statement of Financial Accounting Concept No. 1*: "Financial accounting is not designed to measure directly the value of a business enterprise, but the information it provides may be helpful to those who wish to estimate its value." He explains that earnings are an amalgam of facts and assumptions about future outcomes. The facts are the realized cash flows, and the assumptions are the accruals. The cash flow portion of earnings consists of the cash a company receives for current-period sales, minus the cash it disburses for products and services used during the period. Revenue and expense accruals (excluding arbitrary depreciation and amortization charges) reflect the company's estimates of subsequent-period cash receipts and payments, respectively, that will arise from the most recent period's sales and purchase transactions.

Now here is the significant part: *current contracts determine the amounts that companies record*, but accruals encompass only *existing*, incomplete contracts and the majority of a company's value derives from cash flows attributable to *future* sales and purchase contracts. Speaking metaphorically, we might say that the "ghost" of an as-yet-unsubstantiated future is haunting the earnings figures. This ghost will be busted to some degree by the pending changes to revenue recognition (regarding construction contracts), but only in some industries.

Earnings can rise even when a company is receiving investment returns that are inferior to its cost of capital (as in borrowing at $x + y$ percent for a return of x percent). By contrast, shareholder value increases only if a company earns a rate of return on its new investments that is superior to its cost of capital.

In another blow to the supremacy of earnings as a measure of value, Rappaport points out that investors must go beyond income statements and other financial statements (including even the cash flow statement, though it may be preferable to the income statement) to weigh industry growth potential, the competitive position, technological change, and quality of management.

Rappaport's caveat about earnings is entirely true. (See Chapter 7 for more on this point.) Still, the reported numbers for earnings, if understood for their expectation element, can be analyzed for quality.

The Quality of Earnings

Before valuing a company based on earnings, investors must assess the quality of earnings. There are a variety of approaches. One researcher applied three types of analysis to earnings analysis for a random sample of 90 companies listed in the New York Stock Exchange and found that different approaches led to different assessments. Under one method, a company might appear to have strong earnings, but under another the same company might appear to be weak. The three approaches are:[27]

1. Accruals versus cash—cash gap analysis
2. Variability
3. Low surprise factor

1. Accruals vs. Cash—Cash Gap Analysis

As explained, the accrual method recognizes earnings at the time a sale is made, whereas the cash method recognizes a sale only when the company collects the payment. Since income statements don't emphasize cash, which is important, companies also produce cash flow statements (the subject of Chapter 4).

So one quick way to assess earnings quality is to compare trends between net income and free cash flow. The closer the ratio is to 1:1, or 100 percent, the higher the quality of earnings. Free cash flow is the same as what net income would be if revenues were recognized when they were received (as a payment is made), instead of when the sale is made, as in the accrual approach. When free cash flow approximates accrual net income for a short-term period, people are paying close to the time of sale. When the two are equal over a long-term period, people are paying eventually. But when net income over time is consistently lower than free cash flow, the company has problems with collections or has other earnings quality problems. It can also mean that management has (intentionally or unintentionally) overstated earnings relative to cash flow.

Here are some of the steps investors can take to assess the quality of earnings based on accruals versus cash:

➤ *Calculate the ratio of cash-flow-from-operations to income (the higher the better).* Generally speaking, a higher cash component in earnings strengthens them. To calculate this ratio, at least two approaches are possible.

  ➤ One is to divide cash flow from all transactions (including extra-ordinary items) by net income. The result shows the impact of any transactions that are not related to operations.

  ➤ The other is to divide operational cash flow by income from operations. This offers a more accurate view of the proportion of cash being spun off from ongoing operations).

Now it is true that cash flow can be manipulated. (For example, management may decide to securitize receivables to accelerate cash collections, possibly creating a number that does not reflect the entire truth.[28]) Still, this is one rule of thumb to use.

➤ *Estimate the impact of changes in working capital on cash flow (the lower the better).* This result indicates accruals estimation error and can be a red flag for earnings quality.

➤ *Calculate changes in accruals (the lower the better).* Accruals include estimates and judgments so that they can be manipulated. Dramatic changes in total accruals (or changes in the annual pattern of change) from quarter to quarter may point to manipulations, and they should reduce confidence in reported earnings.

2. Variability

Research shows that managers tend to smooth income streams because they think shareholders want that. Volatility is associated with the perception of lower-quality earnings. (Commentary on the average rate of return in Appendix 3.1 notes this.)

Hour to Hour

Profit is so very fluctuating that the person who carries on a particular trade cannot always tell you himself what is the average of his annual profit. It is affected not only by every variation of price in the commodities which he deals in, but by the good or bad fortune both of his rivals and of his customers, and by a thousand other accidents to which goods when carried either by sea or by land, or even when stored in a warehouse, are liable. It varies, therefore, not only from year to year, but from day to day, and almost from hour to hour.

—Adam Smith, "Of the Profits of Stock," in *Wealth of Nations* (1776)

Some very sharp minds have made some distinctions with regard to volatility. There's more to earnings than mere volatility. There's a greater or lesser degree of persistence, predictability, and variability.

➤ *Persistence* is very trendy because it goes to the entire subject of sustainability that is of such interest in social responsibility and governance (SRG) circles.
➤ *Predictability* is a Catch-22 for some companies with earnings that really are difficult to predict, due to the kind of business they are in. In fact, as one study has noted, trying to meet analysts' forecast or to avoid reporting surprising losses may decrease the quality of earnings. Chapter 7 addresses sustainability.
➤ *Stability (low variability).* To measure variability (instability) of earnings, the investor can calculate the ratio of the standard deviation of operating earnings to the standard deviation of cash from operations. (Smaller ratios imply more income smoothing.)

3. Low Surprise Factor

The third approach is simply the absence of negative market surprises. Research shows that firms with a large beginning balance of net operating assets relative to sales are less likely to report earnings that surprise the market by coming in lower than estimates or guidance.[29]

Conclusion: no single industry or company could be labeled as having a low or high quality of earnings based on the result of any single approach. Clearly, investors have to use more than one approach.[30]

Models to Assess Earnings

The New York State Society of CPAs has identified a variety of sources for earnings quality assessment.[31] Here is our updated version of their list:

Empirical Research Partners (empirical-research.com)

➤ Three components: (1) net working-capital growth rate, net non-current assets, deferred taxes; (2) incremental earnings and free cash flow production relative to each new dollar of revenue or book value; and (3) nine financial indicators, put together for a single gauge of fundamentals.

➤ Items viewed favorably: positive return on assets and operating cash flow; increases in return on assets, current ratio, gross margin, asset turnover; operating cash flow that exceeds net income.

➤ Items viewed unfavorably: increases in long-term debt-to-assets; presence of equity offerings.

➤ Each indicator given a 1 if favorable, a 0 if not; scores aggregated on a 0 to 9 scale.

Ford Equity Research (fordinv.com)

➤ Earnings variability is the minimum standard error of earnings for the past eight years, fitted to an exponential curve.

➤ Growth persistence considers earnings growth consistency over 10 years; projected earnings growth rate is applied to normal earnings to derive long-term value.

➤ Operating earnings are calculated by excluding unusual items, such as restructuring charges and asset write-downs; earnings trend analysis is done on the adjusted figure.

➤ Repurchases of an entity's own shares are analyzed to determine if results are favorable.

Krensavage Partners[32] (krensavage.com)

➤ A rating of 1 (worst) to 10 (best) is assigned for each of 10 proprietary benchmarks; equally weighted ratings are combined to determine the earnings quality score.

➤ Indicators of low earnings quality: increases in receivables; earnings growth due to decreased tax rate; capitalization of interest; high frequency or magnitude of one-time items. (Large acquisitions made in recent periods are penalized.)

➤ Indicators of high earnings quality: practicing conservative pension fund management and increasing research and development budget faster than revenues; cash flow that grows along with net income and increases in gross margin positively impact earnings quality.

Risk Metrics—Center for Financial Research and Analysis (riskmetrics.com/accounting)

➤ Criteria to uncover methods used to manipulate earnings

➤ Financial summary, accounting policy analysis, discussion of areas of concern

S&P—Core Earnings Metric (www2.standardandpoors.com)

➤ The metric focuses on a company's after-tax earnings generated from its principal businesses. Examination of the S&P 500 data showed that pension incomes and stock option grant expenses are largely responsible for the differential between Standard & Poor's core earnings and as-reported earnings.

➤ Items included in core earnings: employee stock option grant expenses; restructuring charges from ongoing operations; write-downs of depreciable or amortizable operating assets; pension costs; purchased R&D expenses.

➤ Items excluded: goodwill impairment charges; gains (losses) from sales of assets; pension gains; litigation or insurance settlements; and reversal of prior-year charges and provisions; merger and acquisition expenses; and unrealized hedging gains and losses.

Standard & Poor's core earnings can be compared to as-reported earnings. Sometimes the discrepancy can be great. For example, on average for Fortune 500 companies in one study, it amounted to $6.54 per share and most heavily impacted companies in the telecommunications and industrials sectors.[33]

UBS—David Bianco (ubs.com)

➤ Compares comprehensive income to operating earnings; difference represents net one-time criteria.

➤ Deducts employee stock option expenses from operating earnings.

➤ Assumes pension asset returns are adjusted to market value.

➤ Times interest or discount rate.

➤ Health-care costs are inflation-adjusted if reported to be 300 basis points higher than weighted average forecasted by S&P 500 companies.

Earnings Guidance: A Waning Trend?

With the help of various approaches to assessing earnings quality, investors can get a good sense of what past earnings are contributing to the company. But what about future earnings—and the so-called earnings guidance? Investors seem to value this guidance, but some believe that this practice makes the market myopic. Several years ago, the Commission on Public Trust and Private Enterprise stated:

> While corporations cannot dictate how investors make their decisions, they can provide them with information that is focused more on long-term strategies, financial goals, and intrinsic values, and less on transitory short-term factors. Corporations should reevaluate the implications of providing short-term "earnings guidance," as well as the advisability of meeting financial targets through aggressive accounting techniques.[34]

Over the past decade (with occasionally yearly upticks), fewer corporations are issuing guidance, and investors do not seem to miss it. Guidance is not a crystal ball. Information a company gives about earnings prospects may or may not match future performance.[35]

Consensus Earnings Programs

The Aspen Institute, a leading think tank, has been concerned about earnings guidance for some time. The Aspen Principles are as follows:

In pursuit of long-term value creation, companies and investors should . . .

2.1 Communicate on a frequent and regular basis about business strategy, the outlook for sustainable growth and performance against metrics of long-term success.
2.2 Avoid both the provision of, and response to, estimates of quarterly earnings and other overly short-term financial targets.
2.3 Neither support nor collaborate with consensus earnings programs that encourage an overly short-term outlook.[36]

Stocks with high capitalization attract coverage by multiple analysts, who give varying earnings projections. The consensus earnings number is an average or median of all those projections. It is usually published after annual earnings are disclosed, and it is periodically updated. Consensus earnings forecasts do indeed encourage a short-term outlook because institutions may base buy decisions on positive earnings forecasts, rather than considering the long-term prospects for the company. As such, the forecasts cause investors to reward companies that will have earnings growth within the next several months, and punish those that won't—even if the reason for lower earnings is a growth in company value (through investment in research and development, for example). But the popularity of such numbers makes sense. In the context of the trade-off between the cost of analysis and the potential gains from it, reading a consensus number saves a lot of time.

A Microsoft Reporting Decision

Due to the volatility of market conditions going forward, Microsoft is no longer able to offer quantitative revenue and EPS guidance for the balance of this fiscal year.

—"Microsoft Reports Second Quarter Results," Redmond, WA, January 22, 2009, http://www.microsoft.com/msft/earnings/FY09/earn_rel_q2_09.mspx.

Earnings Examples

Earnings Deterioration vs. Improvement

As an example of an earnings deterioration, consider General Electric. At the end of 2008, General Electric reported a 12 percent drop in third-quarter earnings. Close analysis of the company shows that the drop was not due simply to lower earnings by its financial unit, GE Capital, but to a variety of factors ranging from overleverage to the credit crisis impacting its finance unit.[37] The point is that analysis of earnings quality needs

Exhibit 3.1 Todd Shipyards in 10K Filing

Todd Shipyards Corporation Audited Consolidated Statements of Income (Loss) Periods ended March 28, 2010, and March 29, 2009 (in Thousands of Dollars, Except per Share Data)

	Quarter Ended		Year Ended	
	2010	2009	2010	2009
Revenues	$ 48,688	$ 33,232	$ 180,023	$ 113,518
Operating expenses				
Cost of revenues	33,952	21,337	131,377	76,554
Administrative and manufacturing overhead	11,183	9,699	38,248	33,545
Other insurance settlements	(49)	(24)	(112)	(90)
Total operating expenses	45,086	31,012	169,513	110,009
Operating income	3,602	2,220	10,510	3,509
Total investment and other income	729	792	1,630	4,248
Income before income taxes	4,331	3,012	12,140	7,757
Income tax expense	(1,696)	(1,370)	(4,331)	(2,975)
Net income	$ 2,635	$ 1,642	$ 7,809	$ 4,782
Net income per common share:				
Diluted	$ 0.46	$ 0.28	$ 1.35	$ 0.83
Number of shares used in calculation of earnings per share (in thousands):	5,776	5,786	5,787	5,780

to refer to a variety of sources (such as the balance sheet), not just the income statement.

Todd Shipyards Corporation provides a contrary example of an upswing in earnings because of a decline in expenses and a rise in revenues, a trend the company believes is now a permanent part of operations. In a press release accompanying the report shown in **Exhibit 3.1**, Todd states: "The increase in operating income in the second quarter of fiscal 2008 versus the second quarter of the prior year primarily results from increased ship repair volumes, cost containment measures, and *improved profitability on ship repair projects.*" This last statement gets at the essence of what investors want to see in earnings—not something temporary, such as a windfall that can never come again, but something of lasting value.

A Test

We came across a web site with the following:

ENTER VALUES AND PRESS BUTTON
In today's fast-moving stock market, many of the more popular stocks do not yet have earnings. This online calculator evaluates individual stocks by projecting future returns based on sales growth and profit margins.
Current stock price $ _____
Earnings per share $ _____
Growth in Earnings per share during the next 10 years
Year 1–3 _____
Year 4–6 _____
Year 7–10 _____
Discount rate (This is the interest rate used to compute present values; 12 percent for typical stocks; 15 percent for riskier stocks.)
Results

(Continued)

(Continued)

> Based on your assumptions, over the next 10 years, the stock is projected to earn:
>
> _____% per year and be worth $_____ in 10 years (this amount includes reinvested dividends).
>
> The stock's current intrinsic value is $_____.
>
> We typed in the following values:
>
> Current stock price $63.23
> Earnings per share $0.80
> Growth in Earnings per share during the next 10 years
> Year 1–3   0 percent
> Year 4–6   6 percent
> Year 7–10 12 percent
> Discount rate
> (This is the interest rate used to compute present values; 12 percent for typical stocks.)
> Results
>
> Based on your assumptions, over the next 10 years, the stock is projected to earn:
>
> –4% per year and be worth $41 in 10 years (this amount includes reinvested dividends).
>
> The stock's current intrinsic value is $10.56.
>
> This is probably not a good investment. You may want to check your assumptions and compare the stock price to its intrinsic value.

EPS: An Emerging Standard

The FASB has issued proposed changes to its EPS standard, in Statement 128.[38] This standard will be closer to the IAS 33, which will result in the same EPS denominator reported under U.S. GAAP and IFRS, with limited exceptions.

The IASB says basic EPS is calculated by dividing profit or loss attributable to ordinary equity holders of the parent entity (the numerator) by the weighted average number of ordinary shares outstanding (the denominator) during the period.[39]

➤ The earnings numerators (profit or loss from continuing operations and net profit or loss) used for the calculation should be after deducting all expenses, including taxes, minority interests, and preference dividends.[40]

➤ The denominator is calculated by adjusting the shares in issue at the beginning of the period by the number of shares bought back or issued during the period, multiplied by a time-weighting factor.[41]

The next frontier will be to focus on the EPS numerator, to make sure that earnings do not include the effect of securities that lack a market.[42]

Earnings-Based Valuation by Industry

Like assets, earnings become more understandable when considered by industry.[43] Financial statements in isolation are not particularly informative, but when an investor can compare many financial statements, useful information emerges.

It goes without saying that investors want a return on their investment. It also goes without saying that this rate of return must be higher than the prevailing risk-free rate (which, unless and until the world changes even more drastically than it has, is still captured by three-month Treasury bonds). What may be less obvious is that the rate of return must be realistic for the industry.

Estimating Industry Rates of Return

To estimate a desired rate of return for any investment, take the risk-free rate and add some target amount that is higher. Then compare actual historical rates of return for specific investments and adjust them for changing circumstances. The adjustments should be appropriate to the industry as well as other factors (exchange rate risk, country political risk, and the like).

One approach to calculating an industry rate of return, recommended by valuation experts Frank K. Reilly and Keith C. Brown, is to take a two-step P/E ratio approach:

1. Establish an expected P/E value at the end of the investment horizon.
2. Compute the expected dividend return during the period.

The formula is

$$P_1 = \frac{D_1}{k - g}$$

where

P_1 = the price per share of the industry at time t

D_1 = the expected dividend per share for industry in period 1 equal to $D_0 (1 + g)$

k = the required rate of return on the equity for industry

g = the expected long-run growth rate of earnings and dividend for industry[44]

Banks

To analyze the earnings of a bank, the classic regulatory approach is found in the Uniform Bank Performance Report (UBPR), which is available at the Federal Financial Institutions Examination Council's (FFIEC) web site (ffiec.gov).[45] Regulators typically refer to the so-called earnings analysis trail, focusing on the five items found on the summary ratios page of the UBPR under earnings and profitability.[46]

➤ *Net income* is also known as "return on assets" (ROA). The ratio is calculated by dividing net income (after all expenses and taxes) by average assets.

➤ *Net interest income*, the second step on this earnings analysis trail, is calculated by subtracting total interest expense from total interest income and dividing the result by average assets.

➤ *Noninterest income* mainly consists of service charges and miscellaneous account fees and is usually the second major type of bank income. Like the other ratios, this is measured as a percentage of average assets.

➤ *Overhead expenses* are accounted for as noninterest expense on the UBPR. This item includes all operating expenses except for interest expense and provisions for loan losses. This line item includes expenses such as salaries, depreciation, consulting fees, and supplies.

➤ *Provision for loan losses*—the main concern is whether the provisions are adequate to maintain the allowance for loan losses at an appropriate level. If the allowance is too low relative to risk in the loan portfolio, additional provisions are necessary, and they must be taken out of earnings.

To set up a grading system, investors wishing to analyze banks can take a clue from the Federal Deposit Insurance Corporation (FDIC)'s Stress Test ratings, which are actually nothing new. (They have been a part of the UBPR for years.) See **Exhibit 3.2**, which is an example of earnings analysis for a bank. (See also Appendix 3.3.)

Energy

Earnings are not of great concern to exploration and production companies, compared to assets. JPMorgan Chase analysts explain:

- *Successful Efforts Versus Full Cost Accounting*: Companies are given a choice between two methods to account for dry holes

Exhibit 3.2 FDIC Stress Test Ratings

Investors should be able to stress test earnings in every industry, using appropriate metrics for the sector.

1. *Earnings are strong.* Earnings are more than sufficient to support operations and maintain adequate capital and allowance levels after consideration is given to asset quality, growth, and other factors affecting the quality, quantity, and trend of earnings.
2. *Earnings are satisfactory.* Earnings are sufficient to support operations and maintain adequate capital and allowance levels after consideration is given to asset quality, growth, and other factors affecting the quality, quantity, and trend of earnings. Earnings that are relatively static or even experiencing a slight decline may receive a "2" rating provided the institution's level of earnings is adequate in view of the listed assessment factors.
3. *Earnings need to be improved.* Earnings may not fully support operations and provide for the accretion of capital and allowance levels in relation to the institution's overall condition, growth, and other factors affecting the quality, quantity, and trend of earnings.
4. *Earnings are deficient.* Earnings are insufficient to support operations and maintain appropriate capital and allowance levels. Institutions so rated may be characterized by erratic fluctuations in net income or net interest margin, the development of significant negative trends, nominal or unsustainable earnings, intermittent losses, or a substantive drop in earnings from the previous years.
5. *Earnings that are critically deficient.* A financial institution with earnings rated "5" is experiencing losses that represent a distinct threat to its viability through the erosion of capital.

Source: Federal Deposit Insurance Corporation, "How do examiners evaluate and rate earnings?" http://www.fdic.gov/regulations/resources/directors college/sfcbleamings.pdf.[47]

(unsuccessful exploration wells). Companies that employ the *successful efforts* method of accounting must expense the cost of the well immediately through the income statement. By contrast, companies that use the *full cost* method of accounting must capitalize the cost of the dry hole onto the balance sheet, and eventually amortize it through depreciation, depletion, and amortization (DD&A) expense. Therefore, earnings from successful efforts companies can be very erratic, compared to those of full cost companies. The two accounting methods produce apples and oranges when looking at relative P/E ratios within the sector.

- *Negative Earnings Are Common in Years of Low Commodity Prices*: The fortunes of E&P companies are largely tied to oil and gas prices, which are cyclical. In times of weak prices, many E&P companies have negative earnings, making P/E ratios not meaningful. The integrated oil companies and majors have other businesses that usually do well when oil and gas prices are weak (like refining, marketing, and chemicals businesses).[48]

Impact on Industries of New Global Accounting Standards for Revenue Recognition

The proposed new global approach of separating and defining performance obligations will have important implications for recognizing revenue for a number of industries.[49]

Construction

Construction companies[50] recognize revenue following a percentage-of-completion method. When a job that might last six months or a year is 10 percent complete, the company recognizes 10 percent of the total expected revenue. It recognizes additional incremental revenue at milestones further along the way.[51] Under the new global accounting standard, a construction company would recognize revenue when it transfers control of the asset to its customer. So for a shipbuilder or an airplane manufacturer, then, revenue on a custom item, built over a period of time, would not be recognized until the item is handed over to the customer.

Software

The new proposed new global approach affects companies with multiple deliverables, such as software companies.[52] Distinguishing performance obligations is a significant issue for technology companies, which often bundle follow-up support with the initial sale of software. The proposed new concept for recognizing revenue would require companies to identify things like warranties or loyalty rewards as performance obligations separate from the initial product or service sold to a customer. Under this proposed guidance, a company would allocate some revenue to the product or service and some to the warranty.

Is a New Earnings Measure Needed?

The convergence of U.S. and international accounting standards into a single global standard provides an opportunity for reexamination of earnings. Fischer Black, codeveloper of the famous Black-Scholes option-valuation formula, once wrote:

> Users of financial statements—analysts, stockholders, creditors, managers, tax authorities and even economists—really want an earnings figure that measures value, not the change in value. Analysts, for example, want an earnings number they can multiply by a standard price-earnings ratio to arrive at an estimate of the firm's value.[53]

The authors of this book agree. In Monks's book *The Emperor's Nightingale*, the concept of profits loses out, metaphorically, to the concept of value. In the story, an emperor does well when he listens to a natural bird. But he replaces it with an artificial bird, which breaks. He brings the natural bird back from exile, and all is well.

Short-term profits are like the artificial bird in the story; they may hold sway temporarily, but they eventually fail. This concept is explored in greater depth in Chapter 9.

Lens Check

To conclude this discussion of earnings, here is some brief guidance on how to incorporate the valuation lenses into a consideration of earnings quality.

➤ *Time: Short term versus long term.* Investors need to focus on operating earnings rather than on comprehensive income.

➤ *Place: Market versus nonmarket.* In analyzing earnings, it is important to ask, is the revenue-generating market for the products and services going to persist?

➤ *Slope: Level versus skewed playing field.* Analysis of changes in earnings and use of ratios that remove windfalls can show the quality of earnings.

➤ *Volition: Willing versus unwilling buyer or seller.* This aspect is key to the tolerance of poor earnings. If investors believe in the fundamental value of a company, they can overlook a period of low or even negative earnings.

➤ *Quality: Level of certainty of return (high, medium, or low) based on investing standards.* Investors' goals for returns determine what kind of earnings they want to see. Clearly, a fund with a short-term horizon doesn't care for a company that has low earnings because it is building for long-term value. Conversely, a pension fund with a 10-year horizon for returns is very interested in such a company.

➤ *Purpose: Private versus public.* Investors with long-term value horizons place less emphasis on the mere number that earnings are achieving for its current owners, and more emphasis on the *meaning* of that number to future owners. To the extent that the value created is sustainable, the good it brings will be public as well as private.

Conclusion

Investors should not let company managers and their auditors do all the thinking for them when it comes to earnings analysis. Instead, they should become earnings experts themselves. Although earnings do not tell the whole story, these figures do contain meaning. Despite its complexity and potential corruptibility, the basic concept of earnings is valid and subject to meaningful definition and analysis.

Appendix 3.1: Hoover's Definitions of Basic Income Statement Terms[54]

Revenue
Revenue equals total sales from operations.

Cost of Goods Sold

Cost of Goods Sold includes all expenses directly associated with the production of goods or services the company sells (such as material, labor, overhead, and depreciation). It does not include SG&A.

Gross Profit

Gross Profit equals Revenue minus Cost of Goods Sold. It identifies the amount available to cover other operating expenses.

Gross Profit Margin

Gross Profit Margin equals Gross Profit divided by Revenue, expressed as a percentage. The percentage represents the amount of each dollar of Revenue that results in Gross Profit.

SG&A Expenses

Selling, General, and Administrative (SG&A) Expenses include all salaries, indirect production, marketing, and general corporate expenses.

Operating Income

Operating Income equals Gross Profit minus SG&A Expenses. It is the income from current operations.

Operating Margin

Operating Margin equals Operating Income divided by Revenue, expressed as a percentage. The percentage represents the amount of each dollar of Revenue that results in Operating Income.

Nonoperating Income

Nonoperating Income is a residual category into which miscellaneous Nonoperating revenues and expenses are netted.

Nonoperating Expenses

Nonoperating Expenses is the combination of "Other Taxes and Interest Expense. Other Taxes, also known as other operating expenses, for most companies includes taxes other than income taxes (except excise taxes, which the company does not actually pay, but only collects on behalf of the government). For financial companies, all expenses other than interest expense and income taxes are included in Other Taxes. Interest Expense is all fixed interest expenses net of capitalized interest. This category also includes dividends on preferred stock of unconsolidated subsidiaries.

Income before Taxes

Income before Taxes is the income from total operations (Continuing + Discontinued operations).

Income Taxes

Income Taxes include any taxes on income, net of any investment tax credits.

Net Income after Taxes

Net Income after Taxes is the income from total operations (Continuing + Discontinued) after taxes have been taken out.

Net Income from Continuing Operations

Net Income from Continuing Operations includes income taken after taxes and before the following: Preferred Dividends, Extraordinary Gains and Losses, Income from Accumulative Effects of Accounting Change, Non-Recurring Items, Income from Tax Loss Carryforward, and Other Gains/Losses.

Net Income from Discontinued Operations

Net Income from Discontinued Operations represents the net (gain or loss) resulting from the selling or closing of discontinued operations of the company. This excludes income from extraordinary gains/losses.

Net Income from Total Operations

Net Income from Total Operations is the income from the total operations (Continuing + Discontinued operations) after taxes and minority interest and before extraordinary gains/losses.

Total Net Income

Total Net Income is the income after accounting for all corporate actions: Income from Continuing Operations + Income from Discontinued Operations + Income from Extraordinary Items + Income from Accumulative Effect of Accounting Changes + Income from Tax Loss Carryforward + Income from Other Gains/Losses.

Net Profit Margin

Net Profit Margin equals the Total Net Income divided by Revenue, expressed as a percentage. The percentage represents the amount of each dollar of Revenue that results in Total Net Income.

Diluted EPS from Continuing Operations

Diluted EPS from Continuing Operations equals the earnings from Continuing Operations divided by the Shares Outstanding, assuming full dilution.

Diluted EPS from Discontinued Operations

Diluted EPS from Discontinued Operations equals the earnings from Discontinued Operations divided by Shares Outstanding, assuming full dilution. This excludes income from extraordinary gains/losses.

Diluted EPS from Total Operations

Diluted EPS from Total Operations equals Diluted EPS from Continuing Operations plus Diluted EPS from Discontinued Operations.

Diluted EPS from Total Net Income

Diluted EPS from Total Net Income is the Diluted EPS after accounting for all corporate actions: EPS from Continuing Operations + EPS from Discontinued Operations + EPS from Extraordinary Items + EPS from Accumulative Effect of Accounting Changes + EPS from Tax Loss Carryforward + EPS from Other Gains/Losses.

Dividends per Share

Dividends per Share is the cash payment, per share, made by the company to its shareholders. Payment is usually made quarterly, but can be paid biannually (ADRs).

Appendix 3.2: Ratios and Other Valuation Indicators Using Earnings

Earnings per Share (EPS)

Earnings per Share is the earnings per the number of shares issued (found in balance sheet).

The FASB is adjusting EPS.[55] Among other changes, the proposed new statement will clarify that the computation of basic EPS should include outstanding common shares and instruments that the holder has the right to share in current-period earnings with common shareholders. This proposed statement, together with the proposed amendments to IAS 33, should enhance the comparability of EPS by reducing the differences between the EPS denominator reported under U.S. GAAP and IFRS, as well as by simplifying the application of Statement 128.[56]

Average Rate of Return

Average Rate of Return is the basic rate of return method measuring profitability.

Total net earnings are divided by the number of years the investment will be held, then by the investment's initial acquisition cost, to derive the annual income rate.

Example

An investment's initial cost was $250,000. It paid a $5,000 annual dividend and can be sold after five years for $375,000. The total return is $150,000 ($25,000 in dividends plus $125,000 in gain). The $150,000 earned over five years represents $30,000 per year, which is a 12 percent *average rate of return*.

This method allows several potential investments to be compared and, as a result, makes it easier to identify opportunity cost. However, the average rate of return does not take into account the value effects of time or variability or the level of risk involved in an investment decision.[57]

Example

Let's assume that you are offered your choice of buying a controlling interest in two different companies, with a plan to exit in six years. Which should you buy?

	Cash Price		Company A—$60,000	Company B—$72,000
Year	After-Tax Profit	Sales	After-Tax Profit	Sales
1	$10,000	$20,000	$33,000	$45,000
2	10,000	20,000	10,000	22,000
3	10,000	20,000	8,000	20,000
4	10,000	20,000	1,000	13,000
5	10,000	20,000	1,000	13,000
6	10,000	20,000	1,000	13,000
Average	$10,000	$20,000	$9,000	$21,000

The averaging process assumes that straight-line depreciation is used over the six-year life of each investment and that no salvage value is taken at the end. We can assume that the amount invested is 50 percent of the purchase price. Dividing the initial investment by two gives this figure. For investment A, that is $30,000; for investment B, $36,000. The average rate of return for investment A is thus 33.33 percent ($10,000 ÷ $30,000), while that for investment B is only 25 percent ($9,000 ÷ $36,000). Investment A is obviously a better investment than investment B.

A variation on this method is to use the full original investment. The average rates of return for Company A and Company B would then be 16.67 and 12.50 percent, respectively; again, the Company A deal looks better.

Average rate of return should not be confused with the accounting rate of return (ARR), which is used for fixed-asset purchases. For this ratio, see Appendix 2.1.

Example

The original investment in Company A would be "paid back" in exactly three years ($20,000 × 3 = $60,000). Company B presents some problems in analysis because it is based on what is known as a *mixed stream* of returns. At the end of the third year, $87,000 will have been paid back. This is more than required if the firm has established a three-year payback hurdle for such acquisitions. The payback period is therefore 2.25 years. For many managers this would be a better buy because the payback period to fully recover the original investment is significantly shorter. For many, this means less risk and is preferred, even though the return on investment (ROI) is lower than it is for Company A.

Internal Rate of Return (IRR)

Internal Rate of Return (IRR) is the discount rate that makes the net present value of an investment equal to zero.

This is typically used with discounted cash flow calculations, but it can also be used with earning-based formulas. The formula is

$$PV = A_1 \div (1 + r)^n_1 + A_2 \div (1 + r)^n_2 + A_3 \div (1 + r)^n_3 + \ldots$$

where

PV	is the present value of the investment.
A_1, A_2, A_3	are the interest or payments received periodically.
r	is the rate of return the investor needs to determine.
n_1, n_2	are the time periods of receipt from the date of investment.

Example

Company A wants to buy a competing firm and would like to fully recover its investment in four years, when it expects to get $120,000 for it as the firm merges into a larger company. Its hurdle rate on all investments has been established at 10 percent. Company A has projected that it will have after-tax profits of $7,000, $8,000, and $8,000 on the acquisition in years 2, 3, and 4. Will this investment meet their objectives? The answer is yes. The IRR for the investment is 10.29 percent.

Note: A modified internal rate of return (MIRR) allows you to set two different rates of return: one from the stream in income and one from reinvestment of that earning stream. The latter is usually lower; so the MIRR is a conservative adjustment.

Price-to-Earnings-per-Share (P/E) Ratio

Price-to-Earnings-per-Share (P/E) Ratio is the is the price of a share of stock divided by earnings per share.

Earnings is an historic number, whereas the price of shares looks forward. Some say this is a fatal flaw in this ratio.

This common method of analysis has been the standard for investment bankers for many years and is still used in due-diligence inquiries and fairness opinions. The *price-to-earnings-per-share* (P/E) ratio relies on the notion that a low PE implies a high expected rate of return, supporting a buy recommendation. (See the "Example" feature box.)

This approach contains useful information:

➤ A company with an earnings growth rate of 12 percent a year and a P/E ratio of 6 is an attractive prospect, but a company with a growth rate of 6 percent a year and a P/E ratio of 12 is an unattractive one.

➤ The P/E ratio of any company that is fairly priced will equal its earnings growth rate.[58] A P/E ratio that is half the growth rate is very positive, and one that is twice the growth rate is very negative. This is a common approach to analyze stocks for mutual funds.[59]

Example

The Market Value Method: Price-to-Earnings-per-Share Ratio

	Price	Earnings per Share	P/E
Comparable A	$40.00	$2.00	20
Comparable B	62.50	2.50	25
Comparable C	45.00	3.00	15
Comparable D	20.00	1.00	20
Comparable E	30.00	1.50	20
Average			20

An up-and-coming ratio is the *price/earnings-to-growth (PEG) ratio*. A stock is considered to be priced fairly if its PEG ratio is equal to 1. A PEG ratio considerably less than 1 supports a buy recommendation. A low PEG implies that the P/E ratio is low relative to the expected rate of growth in earnings, suggesting that the future prospects are expected to improve; implicitly, the expected rate of return is high, supporting a buy recommendation.

Replacement Value

Replacement Value is the price of replacing a company's assets.

If a company appears to be profitable, but the investor doesn't know what is producing the profit, an alternative method of pricing is replacement cost. The investor would ask what it would cost to build a similar company (compensating talent, paying leases or mortgages, purchasing equipment, and so forth) and use that as a proxy value for the enterprise. Once replacement cost has been established, the buyer's cost of capital is used to discover what kinds of earnings must justify the internal rate of return—or what kind of cash flows must be achieved to justify the discounted cash flow (discussed in Chapter 4).

Enterprise Value (EV) to Earnings before Interest, Taxes, Depreciation, and Amortization (EBITDA)

Enterprise Value (EV) to Earnings before Interest, Taxes, Depreciation, and Amortization (EBITDA) is EV divided by EBITDA.

Enterprise value is defined as market capitalization plus total debt minus total cash.[60]

$$EV = M_{cap} + \text{Debt} - \text{Cash}$$

By dividing EBITDA into this, an investor gets a good handle on how well the company is doing in the market. The ratio is similar to P/E, but without some of the adjustments. It is considered best for cash-based businesses and for industry averages for use as a benchmark. The flipped multiple, EBITDA/EV, is used to calculate return on investment.

Example: Videocon Appliances

Shankar Nath supplied this example, referencing Indian currency.[61]

$$EV = M_{cap} + \text{Debt} - \text{Cash}$$

A cursory analysis of the firm's financials makes for good reading:

1. The stock is available at a P/E of just 5.67. Its nearest competitors are priced much higher (Whirlpool at 20.6, BlueStar at 29.4).

2. The M_{cap}/sales is at just 7 percent.

3. The company is profitable and is expected to earn about Rs 17 crores of profits for the year. The operating profit is a huge Rs 160 crores.

Although the stock seems smartly placed for an investor, the EV tells a different story. The EV for Videocon Appliances is about 10 times its market capitalization because of the almost 840 crores of debt it carries on its books. If someone were to purchase 100 percent of the business, the purchaser would be paying 96 crores (M_{cap}) + 841 crores (debt) − 6 crores (cash) = Rs 931 crores (EV).

The most used metric is EV/EBIT. At 931 crores of EV and an estimated EBIT of 77 crores, the EV/EBIT comes to 12.10. Compare this with Whirlpool, which, in spite of a P/E ratio of 20, comes at an EV/EBIT of 8.25.

As a buyer of a business, you have two options:

1. Videocon Appliances: Available at 931 crores; EBIT of 77 crores; P/E of 5.6.

2. Whirlpool India: Available at 773 crores; EBIT of 84 crores; P/E of 20.

Which one would you pick? (How useful is the P/E ratio in this case?)

Interest Coverage Ratio

Interest Coverage Ratio is the ratio of earnings before interest and taxes (EBIT) to annual interest expense. (See Exhibit 3.3 for Exxon's 2008 EBIT.)

This ratio measures a company's ability to pay interest, obviously a critical factor in the valuation of a highly leveraged firm. Inability to make interest payments can lead to insolvency and loss of equity values. A simple analysis of this ratio could have tipped investors off to the

Exhibit 3.3 Sample Annual Income Statement, Including Non-GAAP Measures
Income Statement for Exxon, 2008

View: Annual Data		All numbers in thousands	
Period Ending	31-Dec-08	31-Dec-07	31-Dec-06
Total Revenue	477,359,000	404,552,000	377,635,000
Cost of Revenue	288,810,000	232,852,000	213,255,000
Gross Profit	**188,549,000**	**171,700,000**	**164,380,000**
Operating Expenses			
Research Development	–	–	–
Selling General and Administrative	92,100,000	87,571,000	83,857,000
Non-recurring	–	–	–
Others	12,379,000	12,250,000	11,416,000
Total Operating Expenses	–	–	–

(Continued)

Exhibit 3.3 (*Continued*)

View: Annual Data	All numbers in thousands		
Period Ending	**31-Dec-08**	**31-Dec-07**	**31-Dec-06**
Operating Income or Loss	**84,070,000**	**71,879,000**	**69,107,000**
Income from Continuing Operations			
Total Other Income/ Expenses Net	–	–	–
Earnings Before Interest and Taxes	82,423,000	70,874,000	68,056,000
Interest Expense	673,000	400,000	654,000
Income Before Tax	81,750,000	70,474,000	67,402,000
Income Tax Expense	36,530,000	29,864,000	27,902,000
Minority Interest	(1,647,000)	(1,005,000)	(1,051,000)
Net Income from Continuing Ops	45,220,000	40,610,000	39,500,000
Non-recurring Events	–	–	–
Discontinued Operations	–	–	–
Extraordinary Items	–	–	–
Effect of Accounting Changes	–	–	–
Other Items	–	–	–
Net Income	**45,220,000**	**40,610,000**	**39,500,000**
Preferred Stock and Other Adjustments	–	–	–
Net Income Applicable to Common Shares	**$45,220,000**	**$40,610,000**	**$39,500,000**

Source: Exxon Mobil Corp. Income Statement, 2008, http://finance.yahoo.com/q/is?s=XOM&annual.

precipitous declines in equity value that occurred to some of the major overleveraged financial firms in the recession of 2007–2009.

Appendix 3.3: Net Income Example[62]

What has caused the decline in net income shown in Exhibit 3.4?

Net income declined noticeably over the last 12 months, from 1.39 percent to 1.14 percent and is now below the peer average. The largest

Exhibit 3.4 An Exercise in Reading a Statement

	12/31/2004			12/31/2003			12/31/2002		
AVERAGE ASSETS ($000)	182,836			145,180			143,139		
NET INCOME ($000)	2,084			2,018			1,961		
	BANK	PEER	PCT	BANK	PEER	PCT	BANK	PEER	PCT
EARNINGS AND PROFITABILITY:				*EARNINGS*					
PERCENT OF AVERAGE ASSETS:									
INTEREST INCOME (TE)	8.28	7.79	65	7.74	7.56	62	7.67	7.49	66
− INTEREST EXPENSE	3.63	3.55	69	3.36	3.33	51	3.34	3.31	51
NET INTEREST INCOME (TE)	4.65	4.24	66	4.38	4.24	58	4.33	4.18	61
+ NONINTEREST INCOME	0.52	0.75	38	0.58	0.74	35	0.50	0.72	38
− NON-INTEREST EXPENSE	2.89	2.92	46	2.64	2.95	34	2.53	2.87	33
− PROVISION-LOAN & LEASE LOSSES	0.37	0.16	61	0.16	0.17	49	0.16	0.14	51
= PRETAX OPERATING INCOME (TE)	2.01	1.90	63	2.16	1.85	75	2.14	1.87	81
NET INCOME	1.14	1.26	49	1.39	1.23	63	1.37	1.24	59
MARGIN ANALYSIS:									
NET INTINC-TE TO AV EARN ASSET	4.89	4.53	67	4.51	4.55	53	4.44	4.48	45
LOAN & LEASE ANALYSIS:				*ASSET QUALITY*					
NET LOSS/AVERAGE TOTAL LN&LS	0.22	0.12	84	0.14	0.12	56	0.16	0.14	56
LN&LS ALLOWANCE/TOTAL LN&LS	1.13	1.28	43	1.30	1.29	55	1.26	1.3	48
NON-CURRENT LN&LS/GROSS LN&LS	3.11	0.81	89	1.01	0.83	62	1.02	0.79	63
LIQUIDITY				*LIQUIDITY*					
NET NONCORE FUND DEPENDENCE	21.76	15.22	68	15.25	15.09	53	15.05	14.72	54
NET LOANS & LEASES TO ASSETS	76.94	65.74	76	65.01	64.04	55	63.23	66.18	47
CAPITALIZATION:				*CAPITAL*					
TIER ONE LEVERAGE CAPITAL	8.08	9.11	41	9.61	9.09	56	9.18	9.14	54
CASH DIVIDENDS TO NET INCOME	60.55	40.04	88	59.61	40.54	89	55.69	40.35	89
GROWTH RATES:									
ASSETS	33.60	8.58	78	2.77	7.23	14	1.63	8.68	15
TIER ONE CAPITAL	5.89	12.81	42	6.21	12.78	38	7.51	12.45	37
NET LOANS & LEASES	62.56	12.92	69	6.59	11.71	32	1.13	9.72	20
SHORT TERM INVESTMENTS	−50.88	11.28	15	2.37	13.61	35	5.58	11.03	41
SHORT TERM NON CORE FUNDING	35.43	8.16	78	1.91	8.14	37	2.33	12.14	36

contributor to this decline was a rise in the *noninterest expense (overhead)*, coupled with a rise in *provision expense*. Partially offsetting these rising expenses was the rise in *net interest income*. However, the increase in *interest expense* is noteworthy because it suggests that the bank may lack access to core deposits and is now required to pay more to fund its rapid growth. The increase in *noninterest expense* totaled 25 basis points over the last 12 months.

Notes

1. Statement of Financial Accounting Concepts No. 6, Elements of Financial Statements (a replacement of FASB Concepts Statement No. 3, incorporating an amendment of FASB Concepts Statement No. 2 (Copyright FASB 2008, http://www.fasb.org/pdf/aop_CON6.pdf)).

    The statement goes on to say that "[e]xpectations that owners will be adequately compensated—that they will receive returns on their investments commensurate with their risks—are as necessary to attract equity capital to an enterprise as are expectations of wages and salaries to attract employees' services, expectations of repayments of borrowing with interest to attract borrowed funds, or expectations of payments on account to attract raw materials or merchandise."

2. For a summary of studies on corporate performance metrics, including earnings and cash flow, see Chapter 1, at notes 65–66.

3. Strength of earnings and the payment of dividends are not always strictly correlated. (See Varouj A. Aivazian, Laurence Booth, and Sean Cleary, "Dividend Smoothing and Debt Ratings," *Journal of Financial and Quantitative Analysis* 41, no. 2 (June 2006), http://depts.washington.edu/jfqa/abstr/abs0606.html.) The authors find that "firms that regularly access public debt (bond) markets are more likely to pay a dividend and subsequently follow a dividend smoothing policy than firms that rely exclusively on private (bank) debt. In particular, firms with bond ratings follow a traditional Lintner (1956)–style dividend smoothing policy, where the influence of the prior dividend payment is very strong and the current dividend is relatively insensitive to current earnings. In contrast, firms without bond ratings flow through more of their earnings as dividends and display very little dividend smoothing behavior. In effect, they seem to follow a residual dividend policy."

4. Surveys of shareholders show that the average investor understands the term *earnings* or *profit* more clearly than *income* (T. R. Dyckman, R. E. Dukes, C. J. Davis, and G. A. Welsch, *Intermediate Accounting*, rev. ed. (Homewood, Ill.: Irwin, 1992), 134).

5. For an example of an income statement with positive gross profit and negative net income, see General Motors for 2008. http://www.sec.gov/Archives/edgar/data/40730/000119312509045144/d10k.htm.

6. For good examples of an earnings calls that go well beyond earnings, see "Priceline.com Q1 2009 Earnings Call Transcript," *Seeking Alpha*, http://seekingalpha.com/article/136960-priceline-com-q1-2009-earnings-call-transcript?page=1; "General Electric Earnings Call, First Quarter, 2009," *123 Jump*, http://www.123jump.com/earnings-calls/General-Electric/32586/21.

7. "In general, the growth rate in operating income should be lower than the growth rate in earnings per share. Thus, even if you decide to use analysts' forecasts [of EPS], you have to adjust them [downward] to reflect the need to forecast operating income growth." (Source: Aswath Damodoran, *Investment Valuation: Tools and Techniques for Determining the Value of Any Asset* (Hoboken, N.J.: John Wiley, 2002), 282.

8. "In an email Simon Archer of the bank's equity sales team detailed a one-hour meeting with Cadbury discussing Kraft's offer. Mr. Archer's note says Cadbury CEO Todd Stitzer 'seemed to admit' that a multiple of 15 times EBITDA would be a fair price, but it was 'his job to get as much value as

possible.' The next day Mr Archer clarified his comments: 'In my reference to a 15 × EBIDDA multiple, it is worth noting that Todd's comments were only in the context of comparable transactions being in the mid-teens— he was not implying a fair value for the business.'" "Overheard," *The Wall Street Journal*: Heard on the Street, September 26, 2009

9. Robert N. Anthony, "We Don't Have the Accounting Concepts We Need," *Harvard Business Review* (January–February 1987), pp. 75–83. Currently, accounting theory rests on the assets and liability model, rather than the earnings model. FASB Concepts Statement No. 6, *Elements of Financial Statements*, notes that the revenues are inflows or other enhancements of assets of an entity or settlements of its liabilities (or a combination of both) from delivering or producing goods, rendering services, or other activities that constitute the entity's ongoing major or central operations (FASB Concepts Statement No. 6, *Elements of Financial Statements*, par. 78, http://www.fasb.org/draft/DP_Revenue_Recognition.pdf). Revenue is the gross inflow of economic benefits during the period arising in the course of the ordinary activities of an entity when those inflows result in increases in equity, other than increases relating to contributions from equity participants. (Source: IAS 18, par. 7.) "1. In both definitions, revenue is an increase in assets, a decrease in liabilities, or some combination of the two. 2 Using those definitions, the Boards propose to focus the recognition principle on changes in assets and liabilities. By focusing on changes in assets and liabilities, the Boards do not intend to abandon the earnings process approach. On the contrary, the Boards think that focusing on changes in assets and liabilities will bring discipline to the earnings process approach so that entities can recognize revenue more consistently. In other words, the Boards think there will be more agreement on whether an asset has increased or a liability has decreased than there is currently on what an earnings process is and whether it is complete. This does not mean that judgments will be easy; however, a focus on assets and liabilities provides a clearer objective for making those judgments."

10. "The Dynamical System Approach," undated white paper by G. Vicariu, University of Bucharest, Department of Philosophy, http://www.ub-filosofie .ro/gvacariu/dynamical%20system%20approach.pdf.

11. Benjamin Dodd and David Graham, *Security Analysis* (New York: McGraw-Hill, 1934), 364.

12. See Chapter 8 for more on the valuation of troubled firms. See the "Troubled Firms" and "High Growth" categories at Spreadsheet Programs, http://pages .stern.nyu.edu/~adamodar/New_Home_Page/spreadsh.htm#troubledfirms.

13. The source of the income definition is the FASB's Statement of Financial Accounting Standards 6 (SFAS No. 6), which identifies and defines 10 key

accounting terms. This statement also defines gains and losses in relation to
the balance sheet: "Gains are increases in equity (net assets) from peripheral
or incidental transactions of an entity and from all other transactions and
other events and circumstances affecting the entity except those that result
from revenues or investments by owners. Losses are decreases in equity
(net assets) from peripheral or incidental transactions of an entity and
from all other transactions and other events and circumstances affecting
the entity except those that result from expenses or distributions to owners.
See http://www.fasb.org/pdf/con6.pdf.

14. IASB's Framework par. 70 (a).

15. "The income statement and balance sheet of a company are linked through
the net income for a period and the subsequent increase, or decrease, in
equity that results. The income that an entity earns over a period of time
is transcribed to the equity portion of the balance sheet." ("Accounting
Relationship: Linking the Income Statement and Balance Sheet," *Money
Instructor*, http://www.moneyinstructor.com/lesson/linkincomebal.asp.)

16. The current IASB Standard, adopted in 2007, is intended to give preparers of financial statements the option of presenting items of income
and expense and components of other comprehensive income either in a
single statement of comprehensive income with subtotals, or in two separate
statements (a separate income statement followed by a statement of comprehensive income) (International Accounting Standards Board, "IASB
Issues Revised Standard on the Presentation of Financial Statements,"
September 6, 2007, http://www.iasb.org/NR/rdonlyres/C835C8CF-7C4E-
4F28-8013-EFE0BDD7125D/0/IASBissuesrevisedIAS1.pdf). The standard
proposed in 2009 may be a step back, if it requires a single statement, which
could lead to a combining of operating oranges with nonrecurring apples.

17. Here is what the FASB says: "Accrual accounting attempts to record the
financial effects on an entity of transactions and other events and circumstances that have cash consequences for the entity in the periods in which
those transactions, events, and circumstances occur rather than only in the
periods in which cash is received or paid by the entity." Also: "Realization in
the most precise sense means the process of converting noncash resources
and rights into money and is most precisely used in accounting and financial reporting to refer to sales of assets for cash or claims to cash" (FASB
No. 6, http://www.fasb.org/pdf/aop_CON6.pdf). And here is what the IASB
says: "An entity shall prepare its financial statements, except for cash flow
information, using the accrual basis of accounting" (IAS, par. 27, http://eifrs
.iasb.org/eifrs/bnstandards/en/ias1.pdf).

18. International standards acknowledge the importance of cash accounting
(IASB International Accounting Standard 1, par. 8).

19. "Preliminary Views on Revenue Recognition in Contracts with Customers FASB. Issued December 19, 2008. Comments Due by June 19, 2009." See also "Revenue Recognition: Measurement of Rights Cover Note, Agenda Paper 6, including Agenda Paper 6A: Effects of the Time Value of Money, Agenda Paper 6B: Effects of Uncertain Consideration, and Agenda Paper 6C: Noncash Consideration." See also International Accounting Standards Board, "Information for Observers," March 9, 2009, http://www.iasb .org/NR/rdonlyres/2BF7826F-AE50-49BE-AADA-12418280BA99/0/ RR0903b06obs.pdf; and Financial Accounting Series, "Preliminary Views on Revenue Recognition in Contracts with Customers," http://www.fasb .org/draft/DP_Revenue_Recognition.pdf.

20. In April 2010, the FASB issued an update: "Milestone Method of Revenue Recognition a consensus of the FASB Emerging Issues Task Force (Topic 605), No. 2010-17, An Amendment of the FASB Accounting Standards Codification. To see any standard or update under Accounting Standards Codificiation, go to http://asc.fasb.org/. Note: registration required; basic registration is free.

21. See EITF Issue No. 00-21, "Revenue Arrangements with Multiple Deliverables," and AICPA Statement of Position 97-2, *Software Revenue Recognition*.

22. Management manipulation of how revenue is reported can enable fraud, according to FASB Statement 99, which lists sources of fraud ("Statement on Auditing Standards No. 99, Consideration of Fraud in a Financial Statement Audit Summary," http://www.aicpa.org/download/auditstd/ SummarySAS99 .doc).

23. "[T]he computer language provides a standard vehicle for regulators to track . . . financial positions accruing across many banks and market segments" (Todd Neff, *Compliance Week*, April 7, 2009).

24. For the XBRL's technical explanation of how XBRL content works, see http://www.xbrl.org/Specification/versioning-report-content/PWD-2009- 05-27/versioning-report-content-PWD-2009-05-27.html#eg-normative. For syntax, see http://www.xbrl.org/Specification/versioning-report-syntax/ PWD-2009-05-27/versioning-report-syntax-PWD-2009-05-27.html. For SEC frequently asked questions (very nitty gritty) from filers, see http://sec.gov/ spotlight/xbrl/xbrltechfaq.htm.

25. These include:
    ➤ Recording of fictitious revenue.
    ➤ Recognizing inappropriate amount of revenue from swaps, roundtripping, or barter arrangements.
    ➤ Recognition of revenue from sales transactions billed, but not shipped ("bill and hold").

➤ Recognition of revenue where contingencies associated with the transaction have not yet been resolved.

➤ Improper accounting for or failure to establish appropriate reserves for rights to refunds or exchange, liberal cancellation or refusal rights, or liberal or unconditional rights of return granted through undisclosed oral or written side agreements.

➤ Recognition of revenue when products or services are not delivered, delivery is incomplete, or delivered without customer acceptance.

(Deloitte & Touche, "Ten Things About Financial Statement Fraud: A Review of SEC Enforcement Releases 2000–2006," June 2007, http://www.deloitte.com/dtt/cda/doc/content/us_forensic_tenthings_fraud01072008.pdf.)

26. Alfred Rappaport, "The Economics of Short-Term Performance Obsession," [CFA Institute] *Financial Analysts Journal* 61 no. 3 (2005).

27. The authors acknowledge two main sources for this section. The first is Khaled ElMoatasem Abdelghany, "Measuring the Quality of Earnings," *Managerial Auditing Journal* 20, no. 9 (2005): 1001–1005. Professor Khaled is with the accounting department, College of Business and Economics, Qatar University, Doha, Qatar. Second, Katherine Schipper was an important source for this section of the chapter. For her more detailed and scholarly discussion, see Katherine Schipper, "Earnings Quality," *Accounting Horizons*, January 1, 2003; and Jennifer Francis, Ryan LaFond, Per Olsson, and Katherine Schipper, "The Market Pricing of Accruals Quality," dated March 15, 2004, Paper 22 in the Swedish Institute for Financial Research." See also an excellent report by Gradient Analytics, "Earnings Quality Analytics," April 2005, http://www.gradientanalytics.com/whitepapers/EQRS%20White%20Paper.pdf.

28. "Cash Flow Hocus Pocus," *BusinessWeek*, July 15, 2002, http://www.businessweek.com/magazine/content/02_28/b3791114.htm.

29. Khaled ElMoatasem Abdelghany, see note 24.

30. Ibid.

31. This is based on work by the New York State Society of CPAs (NYSSCPA) but updated to 2010. We retained only the models associated with an active web site as of late 2010, http://www.nysscpa.org/cpajournal/2005/1105/images/p36.pdf.

32. This model was developed by Michael Krensavage, who now has his own company, Krensavage Partners, at Krensavage.com (client intranet). He developed it while he was with Raymond James & Associates, raymondjames.com.

33. Standard & Poor's, "Measures of Corporate Earnings," May 14, 2002, http://www2.standardandpoors.com/spf/pdf/index/Core_Measuringof CorpEarnings_2nd_Ed-v6.pdf.

34. The Conference Board Commission on Public Trust and Private Enterprise, January 9, 2003.

35. Peter A. McKay, "Numbers Game: Why 'Guidance' May Not Matter: Issuing Profit Forecasts Bears Little on Chances of an Upside Surprise," *Wall Street Journal*, July 23, 2007.

36. The Aspen Institute, http://www.shareholderforum.com/op/Library/20070600_ Aspen-Principles.pdf.

37. Elizabeth MacDonald, "GE's Quality of Earnings Problems," *Fox Business*, http://emac.blogs.foxbusiness.com/2008/10/10/ges-quality-of-earnings-problems.

38. "Exposure Draft (Revised): Proposed Statement of Financial Accounting Standards Earnings per Share August 7, 2008," http://www.fasb.org/jsp/ FASB/Page/nr080708.shtml. Comments were due December 5, 2008. The standard is still pending as of late 2010.

39. IAS 33.10.

40. IAS 33.11.

41. This standard is undergoing change. A joint FASB-IASB group is attempting to "[p]rovide a clear principle to determine which shares and other instruments should be included in the EPS calculation. Under that principle, the weighted average number of ordinary shares includes only those instruments that give their holder the right to share currently in profit or loss of the period (Deloitte Touche, "IASB Agenda Project," http://www .iasplus.com/agenda/converge-ias33.htm). See http://www.iasplus.com/usa/ headsup/headsup0808eps.pdf.

42. "The boards reasoned that the changes in fair value recognized in earnings (and hence affecting the numerator) are a better reflection of the benefits received or the detriments incurred by the current shareholders during the period than any of the existing methods to capture dilution (each of which primarily focuses on the number of shares included in the denominator of EPS). Therefore, rather than requiring the treasury stock, the if-converted, or the two-class method...the boards decided to exclude such instruments from the computation of EPS other than for their changes in fair value recorded in net income or earnings available to common shareholders (i.e., the numerator of EPS)."

43. The Global Industry Classification Standard (GICS) recognizes 10 basic industry groups. See Chapter 2, note 66.

44. Frank K. Reilly and Keith C. Brown, *Investment Analysis and Portfolio Management*, 6th ed. (New York: Harcourt Brace, 2000). For a very thorough discussion of earnings analysis, see http://fhyu.mis.cycu.edu.tw/%E 6%8A%95%E8%B3%87%E5%AD%8%E8%8B%B1%E6%96%87%E7 %89%88Power%20Point(Reilly%20&%20Brown)/CH19.PPT.

45. See Federal Financial Institutions Examination Council, http://www.ffiec.gov/ UBPR.htm.
46. http://www.fdic.gov/regulations/resources/directors_college/sfcb/earnings.pdf.
47. See also Thomas Tan, "How Much of Banks' Earnings Are Real?"GoldSeek .com, May 5, 2009, http://news.goldseek.com/GoldSeekl1241503440.php. Tan sees five sources of distortion for bank earnings: sudden increase of financing activities on residential mortgages, a rolling recession by asset class, postponing charges to earnings for loan and credit losses, changing the mark-to-market accounting principle, and booking earnings while debt is losing value. "A good case here is Citigroup, which took advantage of an accounting rule that allows companies to record declines in the market value of their own debt as an unrealized gain. That turned a $900 million loss into a $1.6 billion gain."
48. JPMorgan Chase, "E&P 101: A Primer Oil and Gas Exploration & Production, North American Equity Research," November 2005. The authors thank Phillip Johnston for suggesting this resource, which he helped write when he was at JPMorgan Chase.
49. Industry terms used confirm to the Global Industry Classification Structure (GICS). See Chapter 1, note 66, and Appendix H.
50. Construction companies fall within the Capital Goods Industry Group (2010). See Appendix H.
51. Compliance Week, http://www.complianceweek.com/article/5368/fasb-iasb-begin-l ong-march-on-revenue-standard.
52. Software companies fall within the Software and Services Industry Group (4510). See Appendix H.
53. Fischer Black, "The Magic in Earnings: Economic Earnings Versus Accounting Earnings," *Financial Analysts Journal* 36 (1980): 19–24.
54. Hoover's 2010, http://www-2.hoovers.com/global/msn/index.xhtml?pageid =1968.
55. Earnings Per Share—FASB news release, dated August 7, 2008, http://www.fasb.org/news/nr080708.shtml.
56. Proposed FASB Statement 128, August 7, 2008, http://www.fasb.org/draft/rev_ed_eps_amend_st128.pdf.
57. See Chris Sells, program manager in the Distributed Systems Group at Microsoft, "The Average Return Myth," http://www.sellsbrothers.com/money/ #The_Average_Return_Myth. According to Sells, "As the variability increases, the annualized rate of return gets further away and lower than the simple average rate. On the other hand, as the variability decreases, the annualized rate approaches the maximum value of a fixed rate of return, i.e. zero variability. . . . [S]o long as your investment doesn't go to zero, it doesn't matter when the highs and lows come. [But] the *annualized rate of*

return will always be lower than the average rate as variability increases."
[Emphasis added.]

58. Peter Lynch and John Rothchild, *One Up on Wall Street: How to Use What You Already Know to Make Money in the Market* (New York: Simon & Schuster, 2000), 199.

59. Lynch and Rothchild. See also Peter D. Easton, "PE Ratios, PEG Ratios, and Estimating the Implied Expected Rate of Return on Equity Capital," *Accounting Review*, January 1, 2004.

60. This approach is suggested by one investor commenting on the web site motleyfool.com with a blog under the pen name "olikea" (http://boards. fool.co.uk/Profile.asp?uid=208767628). He explains: "One of the reasons it is useful to consider the 'enterprise value' as opposed to simple 'market capitalization' is that if company A wished to purchase company B outright, it would not only have to buy up all the shares at the current price (market cap) but it would also have to assume the companies [sic] debt. If company B had any cash on hand, this would effectively be an 'instant rebate,' so it gets subtracted from the cost of acquisition."

61. Shankar Nath "Enterprise Value and Stock Valuations," *Ezine@rticles*, April 24, 2008, http://ezinearticles.com/?Enterprise-Value-And-Stock-Valuations& id=1132144.

62. Adapted from FDIC, http://www.fdic.gov/regulations/resources/directors_ college/sfcb/earnings.pdf.

CHAPTER 4

Valuation Based on Cash Flow

"Happiness is positive cash flow."
—Frederick R. Adler, venture capitalist

IN VALUING A company, an investor wants to know what the company owns, owes, and earns. That's why this book has discussed assets/liabilities and earnings in such depth. But another way to analyze the value of a company—some say the only reliable way—is to focus on the movement of its cash.

Like the balance sheet and income statement, the cash flow statement gives clues to company value. But the cash flow statement tells only part of the cash story. The real story is in *future* cash flow, discounted back to the present. Future cash flow is generally considered an economic measure of value, as opposed to the more bounded accounting measures. Indeed, research has shown that in a choice among various valuation indicators, investors around the world tend to associate cash flow with equity value.[1]

Cash puts every enterprise on an equal basis for purposes of valuation. It reveals the grain of truth in Karl Marx's extremist observation that "all social rules and all relations between individuals are eroded by a *cash* economy."[2] Cash flow analysis does indeed strip away the pieties of position and preeminence. Of all the valuation methods out there, it is the most existential: cash is what it is. Philosophy aside, it is certainly a valuable addition to the investor's valuation tool kit.

Cash flow is a kind of ultimate integer of value, but understanding what cash flow actually means is complex and changing, and understanding how to convert future cash flows into present cash flows ultimately means taking a gamble.

To predict future cash flows, investors must do more than look at recent cash flow statements and project a linear trend. Rather, they must use a variety of sources, including *all* the company's financial statements—not just the cash flow statement—to sense where the company, its industry, and the economy are going. This approach enables investors to see what they should pay now to benefit from cash flows later—an especially important issue to any investors who hope to take a controlling position in the company being valued.

Investors can use this chapter to refresh themselves on current standards for cash flow statements and to sharpen their ability to estimate and discount a company's future cash flows. The chapter also explains another economic (nonaccounting) measure: current and anticipated future stock prices.

Cash Flow Statements—Something Old, Something New for Investors

In the long history of financial statements, the cash flow statement is a relatively recent arrival. Although insurance actuaries have been calculating cash flow for generations, the use of cash flow analysis for operating companies is distinctly modern. Unlike the balance sheet, in use before the fifteenth century,[3] or the income statement, which emerged in the nineteenth century,[4] the cash flow statement as we know it is a twentieth-century invention.[5] Moreover, it is not accepted worldwide. For example, in China, where investments tend to be based on assets, investors rarely use future cash flows as an arbiter of value.[6]

Historians associate cash flow statements with the rise of modern equity investors, especially in public companies with widely dispersed ownership.[7] Unlike traditional providers of capital, equity investors in widely held public companies cannot rely on collateral as a backup for their returns. In cases of insolvency, shareholder claims rank lowest on the list. So equity investors rightly see incoming cash as their only sure way of getting a return on their investment, whether directly via dividends or indirectly via increases in stock price.

Therefore, when setting a value for equity securities, investors want to know the company's cash situation today and tomorrow. They want to predict the amount of cash the company will be able to take in based on its future products and services and then to decide what that money is worth now—through discounted cash flow (DCF) analysis.

Value and Liquidity

To see the value of cash, step back and consider its intrinsic characteristics. By definition, cash has both value and liquidity.

➤ The *value* of cash is clear: all other values are given in terms of cash, in whatever currency. One can say, X is "worth" $5. But $5 is not merely "worth" $5; it *is* $5.

➤ Equally clear is the *liquidity* of cash. Barring a total lack of faith in the authority printing the cash, cash is the one and only element that can be spent to obtain other items of value. Few items are as persuasive as cash in an economic exchange. Everything else requires some measure of trust (perhaps the message behind Marx's gloomy assessment of a cash economy).

Cash Flow: What the Global Standard Setters Say

Not surprisingly, the Financial Accounting Standards Board (FASB) and the International Accounting Standards Board (IASB), as global accounting standard setters, have identified the cash flow statement as preeminent among the sources of financial information.

In an essay boldly titled "The Objective of Financial Reporting," the IASB depicts equity investors as particularly cash oriented:

Equity investors. Equity investors include holders of equity securities, holders of partnership interests, and other equity owners. Equity investors generally invest economic resources (usually cash) in an entity with the expectation of receiving a return *on*, as well as a return *of*, the cash provided; in other words, they expect to receive more cash than they provided in the form of cash distributions and increases in the prices of shares or other ownership interests. Therefore, equity investors are *directly interested in the amount, timing and uncertainty of an entity's future cash flows and also in how the perception of an entity's ability to generate those cash flows affects the prices of their equity interests.* Equity investors often have the right to vote on management actions and therefore are interested in how well the directors and management of the entity have discharged their responsibility to make efficient and profitable use of the assets entrusted to them.[8]

Currently, both U.S. generally accepted accounting principles (GAAP, ASC 230 [SFAS 95]) and international financial reporting standards (IFRS, IAS107) require cash flow statements. (See Appendixes 4.2 and 4.3.)

IFRS IAS 7 says (using British spelling), "All enterprises that prepare financial statements in conformity with IFRS are required to present a statement of cash flows."

The statement of cash flows analyses changes in cash and cash equivalents during a period. Cash and cash equivalents comprise cash on hand and demand deposits, together with short-term, highly liquid investments that are readily convertible to a known amount of cash, and that are subject to an insignificant risk of changes in value. Guidance notes indicate that an investment normally meets the definition of a cash equivalent when it has a maturity of three months or less from the date of acquisition. Equity investments are normally excluded, unless they are in substance a cash equivalent (e.g. preferred shares acquired within three months of their specified redemption date). Bank overdrafts which are repayable on demand and which form an integral part of an enterprise's cash management are also included as a component of cash and cash equivalents.

What the Cash Flow Statement Shows

The cash flow statement shows the sources and uses of cash. (In fact, Sources and Uses Statement was the old name for this statement before it rose to prominence in the 1970s.) Statements are typically divided into three components:

1. Operating cash flow
2. Investing cash flow
3. Financing cash flow

Operating Cash Flow

Also called "working capital," the source of this cash flow is internal operations. It comes from and gets spent back on *sales of products and services*, and it is under the direct control of management. Operating cash flow is considered to be better than reported earnings to see how much cash a company is generating because it includes *changes in working capital* (such as changes in receivables and payables). Earnings ultimately also reflect these changes, but the connection is not as direct. Focusing only on assets and earnings, investors can miss a clue that the company might be running out of cash to pay its bills.

Here is the formula for calculating operating cash flow:

Sales $\times$ Operating profit margin (%) = Operating profit $-$ Cash taxes
$$= \text{Net operating profit after taxes (NOPAT)}$$
$$- \text{ Incremental working capital investes}$$
$$- \text{ Incremental fixed capital invested}$$
$$= \textbf{Free Cash Flow from Operations}$$

Investing Cash Flow

Investing cash flow is also generated internally, but it is from nonoperating activities, such as returns from and expenditures on *investments in plant and equipment or other fixed assets*, nonrecurring gains or losses (windfalls, catastrophes), or other sources of cash other than normal operations.

IFRS includes some research and development (R&D) expenditures (the ones that can be itemized on a balance sheet) as investing activities. Under U.S. GAAP companies R&D costs must be immediately expensed on the income statement and appear as a cash outflow for that accounting period.

Negative numbers are usually bad news, but not in this case for long-term investors. Negative cash flows from investing activities are not necessarily bad (unless the company has a severe liquidity problem), and positive cash flows from investing activities aren't necessarily good. Negative flows may mean the company is making long-term investments for the future health of the company, whereas positive cash flows from investing activities may mean the company has sold off investments (even perhaps at a loss) to generate cash in the short term.

Here is the formula for calculating investment cash flow:

Cash received from investments (e.g., dividend payment, sale of property)
− Funds paid to make investments (e.g., buying stock or property)
_____
= Free cash flow from investing activities

Interestingly, some firms define free cash flow as operating cash flow minus investment cash flow.

Financing Cash Flow

Financing cash flow is the cash coming from and going back to *external financing sources*, such as lenders, investors, and shareholders. A new loan, the repayment of a loan, the issuance of stock, and the payment of dividend are some of the activities included in this section of the cash flow statement.

Here is the formula for cash flow from financing activities:

Cash received from issuing stock or debt
− Cash paid as dividends and for reacquisition of debt or stock
_____
= Free cash flow from financing activities

GAAP and IAS 7 rules for cash flow statements have some key differences:[9]

> ➤ GAAP permits a statement showing changes in cash alone or changes in cash and cash equivalents. IAS 7 requires showing changes in both cash and cash equivalents.
> ➤ GAAP and IAS 7 have slightly different definitions of cash equivalents.
> ➤ GAAP requires that interest paid be included in operating activities. IAS 7 allows interest paid to be included in operating activities or financing activities.
> ➤ GAAP and IAS 7 differ on the subject of direct versus indirect, as explained in the next section.

Accounting Note: Converting an Indirect Method Statement of Cash Flows to a Direct Method

One challenge with cash flow analysis is that companies use two different techniques for reporting it. (The analogy to Latin text with Greek footnotes is particularly apt here.) In the *indirect method*, the cash flow statement is usually presented using recorded net income rather than cash. The indirect method is compatible with accrual accounting, as required under GAAP/IFRS. Under the accrual method of accounting, net income is recorded based on a sale transaction, not on the arrival of cash. It is not as factual as the *direct method*, which is based on the actual receipt of cash. A cash flow statement, using *the indirect method*, is presented in **Exhibit 4.1**. For a more complete example of the indirect method, see Appendix 4.1, featuring an analysis of cash flow statements from AT&T.

The direct cash flow statement depicts an actual process. Little or no interpretation is involved: cash is cash. The problem is that most companies use the indirect method, which is more consistent with accrual accounting. It is true that direct statements would be more factual, but so what? Investors rarely use the past as a gauge for the future.

Exhibit 4.1 Illustrative Cash Flow Statement Using the Indirect Method

Cash Flow Statement Month Ended January 31, 2010, Indirect Method Operating Activities (in thousands)	
Net income	XXXXXX
Plus depreciation expense	XXXXX
Less gain on sale of stock	(XXXX)
Less increase in accounts receivable	(XXXX)
Less increase in inventory	(XXXX)
Plus increase in accounts payable	XXXXX
Cash flow from operating activities (may be positive or negative)	XXXXX
Investing Activities	
Purchase of equipment	(XXX)
Purchase of securities	(XXX)
Sale of securities	XXXX
Cash flow from investing activities (may be positive or negative)	XXXX

Source: Adapted from Thomas Robinson, http://tom-robinson.us/Publications.html.

GAAP and IFRS permit both, and may soon permit only direct, despite objections from companies such as IBM, which believe this requirement would be burdensome. According to Gregg L. Nelson, the company's vice president of accounting policy and financial reporting, quoted in an April 2009 issue of *CFO* magazine, "IBM is aware that limited academic research supports the hypothesis that the direct method of cash flow provides better predictive value to future operating cash flows than either the indirect method or the income statement." But Nelson disagrees, based on IBM experience. "To state the obvious, future cash flow is largely driven by future transactions. Historical data is of limited predictive value." He goes on, "IBM believes that revenue, days sales outstanding, changes in accrual balances and company information should be sufficient for investors to make their decisions."

IASB Open Question

Would a direct method of presenting operating cash flows provide information that is decision-useful?

We acknowledge that a direct method of presenting operating cash flows leads to a clear presentation with respect to information about payment and receipt of cash as compared with an indirect method. Therefore, as it enables the users of financial statements to understand the operating cash flow more easily, we believe such method provides users with decision usefulness. However, since it is expected that preparation of cash flow statements based on a direct method would be very costly due to systems development and other circumstances, in practice, entities would often be forced to use a simplified method in preparing their cash flow statements based on a direct method. In order to address such cases, we believe that the final standard should include an example that illustrates the use of a simplified method in the preparation of cash flow statements based on a direct method.

Kiyoshi Ichimura, executive board member, Accounting Standards, Japanese Institute of Certified Public Accountants (in a letter to the FASB dated April 14, 2009)

The current global requirement says that when the direct method is presented on the face of the cash flow statement, the notes to the statement must include a reconciliation of accrual accounting net income to cash from operating activities. *This reconciliation constitutes the indirect method format.*

DCF: Projecting Future Cash Flow

Looking at current cash flow statements can prepare the investor to see what is happening with cash in a company. But there is no substitute for discounted cash flow analysis—looking into the future to predict how flows will be in the future.

In its simplest form, the DCF process proceeds as follows:

Step 1. Set aside the value of all assets—current and fixed—not used in the business to produce the estimated future earnings stream that is to be discounted.

Step 2. Estimate future sales year by year over a preselected time horizon. (This is the period of time the investor intends to hold the investment until selling.)

Step 3. Estimate the gross margins year by year, including depreciation expenses.

Step 4. Estimate earnings before interest and taxes (EBIT) year by year.

Step 5. Subtract interest and estimated taxes year by year.

Step 6. Compute and subtract the average marginal incremental working capital costs required to put on each additional dollar of sales year by year. (Reverse the process for downsizing.)

Step 7. Compute and subtract the average marginal incremental fixed capital costs of putting on each additional dollar of sales year by year (the reverse for asset sales).

Step 8. Add back depreciation (the reverse for recaptures).

Step 9. Compute the residual value of the company after the end of the horizon period by capitalizing last year's projected earnings at the reciprocal of the selected discount rate.

Step 10. Discount all values, including residual to present value, using a risk-adjusted cost of capital for the discount rate.[10]

Step 11. Add back all set-aside values (step 1) for current and fixed assets not used to produce revenues. The total is the net present value (NPV) value of the business based on its anticipated future cash flows.[11]

This is only one approach. A number of professors of finance have developed spreadsheets for calculating DCF.[12]

Crystal Ball: Two Kinds of Questions

The most challenging aspect of doing discounted cash flow is, of course, the very fact of peering into the future. To predict how much net cash a company will be realizing in a future period requires understanding what a company does and how it does it. So there are two levels of inquiry: future strategy and future liquidity. Questions about strategy get at how the company will generate cash. Questions about liquidity get at how the company will manage it.

Strategy Questions

Here is a short list of questions investors might ask about strategy in order to get a feeling for future cash flow:

➤ When do they want their returns? How many hours, days, months, or years from now will be their ideal "exit"? This could be two hours for a day trader or twenty years for a pension fund.
➤ What earnings does the company project for that time period?
➤ How does the company intend to meet those projections?
➤ Are the growth plans reasonable?
➤ Is the company in a cyclical or seasonal industry?
➤ Do projections take this cyclicality into account?
➤ Does the company have a good track record of meeting its projections?
➤ Does the company have any excess assets or divisions that can or should be sold?
➤ How long would it take to make these sales, and how much money would they generate?
➤ Are there any other potential sources of cash?

➤ What can go wrong in all this, and does the company have any contingency plans?

➤ How big is the company's key industry, what is its growth rate, and what is its future outlook?

➤ Does the company have the basic competencies and culture it needs to change its core industry, if necessary?

➤ How well is the company anticipating and responding to competitive threats?

➤ What other risks could affect the projected results?

The complete list of questions is potentially endless. Any investor with knowledge of any industry can customize it to the company at hand. (For some ideas, see "Cash Flow Patterns in Industries" in this chapter.)

Ideally, investors can pose these questions directly to the company, either to management (for example, the investor relations professional) or to the board (by sending a request to the director presiding over meetings of the independent directors). In the United States, under Rule Fair Disclosure (FD), companies are not supposed to make what are called "selective disclosures" of any material nonpublic information to groups of investors. For a while, this requirement put a chill on direct communications. But companies have learned that it's not so bad to have to put out a press release or make a Web posting following a talk. It has become a common practice to post transcripts of earnings calls. So direct communications are still feasible.

If there is no opportunity to talk directly, the best source for information about a company's strategy (and related risks) may be the part of the 10K called "management's discussion and analysis of financial condition and results of operations (MD&A). This section is required by the U.S. Securities and Exchange Commission (SEC) under Item 303 of Regulation SK.

A good introduction or overview in an MD&A statement:

➤ Includes economic or industry-wide factors relevant to the company.

➤ Informs the reader about how the company earns revenues and income and generates cash.

➤ Discusses the company's lines of business, location or locations of operations, and principal products and services.

➤ Provides insight into material opportunities, challenges and risks, such as those presented by known material trends and uncertainties, on which the company's executives are most focused for both the short and long term, as well as the actions they are taking to address these opportunities, challenges, and risks.[13]

Liquidity Questions

In addition to asking questions about a company's strategy to predict its future cash flows, the investor can ask questions about its current liquidity and about its cash management habits. Although it's never good for a company to hoard cash, a company must retain a certain level of liquidity in anticipation of a harsh and extreme "cash economy" (to reference again the haunting imagery of Marx), with its brutal stripping away of economic and personal relations.

If cash flow is positive and high, and if this level is sustainable, then the company has high liquidity. A greatly positive cash flow, if sustainable, means that a company has high liquidity and won't, as they say, "run out of cash." Low cash flow is obviously a problem for companies in recessionary times.

A good source of information for U.S. public companies is in the 10-K statement, again in the MD&A).[14] Liquidity discussions in the MD&A, however, are often too general, using expressions like "adequate cash resources to finance future foreseeable capacity expansions." In a credit crunch, investors want to see more specifics. The SEC has therefore urged companies to be forthcoming about liquidity and capital resources in their MD&A disclosures. The SEC has made three key points:

1. Companies should consider enhanced analysis and explanation of the sources and uses of cash and material changes in particular items underlying the major captions reported in their financial statements, rather than reciting the items in the cash flow statements.

2. Companies using the indirect method in preparing their cash flow statements should pay particular attention to disclosure and analysis of matters that are not readily apparent from their cash flow statements.

3. Companies also should consider including enhanced disclosure regarding debt instruments, guarantees, and related covenants.

In addition to the SEC, the Chartered Accountants of Canada (CAC) has published some recommendations. The CAC is a particularly interesting group at this time because Canada is one of the countries that is most actively reconciling GAAP with IFRS and is thus in tune with the future of economic reporting. Value-minded investors who want to get a good feel for the current and near-term cash flow situation should value the group's checklist, developed during the recent recession. In a recent bulletin, the group recommends that companies tell (and that investors ask) more about the following areas:

Cash-Generating Potential

➤ Adequacy of available credit facilities to finance operations and the cost of that credit, particularly if operating cash flows are negative or declining, including a discussion of the extent of unused facilities at the date of reporting, and the timing of their renegotiation.
➤ Restrictions on the ability to transfer a subsidiary's cash to the parent, including the impact on available cash resources nature of short-term investments and creditworthiness of the counterparty and its ability to provide cash on maturity.

Cash Utilization Requirements

➤ The cash needed to fund operations and how the amount varies depending on the level of activity.
➤ Fixed and variable elements of cash outflows.
➤ The terms of debt or lease agreements that could trigger additional or accelerated payments.
➤ Circumstances under which off-balance-sheet arrangements could result in funding requirements for the entity, including the amounts involved and any plan the entity has to fund or mitigate such requirements (including, for example, sales currently financed through a variable-interest entity).
➤ Arrangements to fund committed capital expenditures; the timing for payments, if known; circumstances that could negate or cancel such financing requirements; and sensitivity to rate, cost of capital, or financial market liquidity fluctuations.

Working Capital Requirements

➤ The reasons for changes in the components in working capital from the previous quarter and for the year as a whole, such as changes in the terms of supplier or customer contracts, changes in policy regarding inventory levels to be maintained, or changes in the period for receivables collection.

➤ Analysis of how changes in activity levels affect working capital components and alternatives for funding any anticipated increase in working capital. The liquidity discussion should also report any defaults or significant risk of default in the terms of a debt covenant or other agreement, the consequences of the default, and steps being taken to remedy the situation.[15]

Some General Methodologies for Considering Cash Flow

Going beyond the futurism and the cash stewardship of strategy, let's now focus on some very general methodologies for thinking about the cash flows to a company. This is classic project management.

Net Present Value of Cash from a Project or a Company[16]

To estimate the future cash flows of a project, set aside accounting conventions and just think about what's happening. Consider any cost saving or incremental revenues to the organization as inflows, and consider all costs outflows.

Here are a series of formulas for net present value from a Lithuanian company called InvestSign, for short. InvestSign uses a formula that says P indicates inflows, IC indicates outflows, along with other standard mathematical symbols. (For the meaning of the abbreviations in this formula, see Appendix E.)[17]

$$NPV = \sum_{k=1}^{n} \frac{P_k}{(1+i)^k} - IC$$

or

$$NPV = \sum_{k=1}^{n} \frac{P_k}{(1+i)^k} - \sum_{j=1}^{m} \frac{IC_j}{(1+i)^j}$$

The following hypothetical examples assume that the life cycle of the project is five years. Numeric cost savings assumptions were made as well. *NPV* for project without external sponsorship is €43,104.[18]

Internal Rate of Return (IRR)

IRR is the discount rate that makes the NPV of a project equal to zero. For purposes of these calculations, any cost saving or incremental revenue to the organization as a result is considered an inflow (*CF*) and a positive number. All costs are considered outflows (I_0) and are negative numbers. IRR is found by solving the following expression:

$$I_0 = \sum_{t=1}^{t} \frac{(CF_t)}{(1+irr)^t}$$

IRR provides us with a single rate of return that summarizes the merits of the project. For our example, when you set the NPV to zero, the IRR is 16.32 percent, which is well over our required rate. This tells investors that they should undertake the project.

Just one quick word of caution about IRR calculations: They work for conventional project cash flows, meaning that the first cash flow (initial investment at time zero) is negative and all of the remaining cash flows are positive. If the cash flows are not conventional, then investors will have multiple rates of return where *NPV* is zero. In the case of nonconventional cash flows, use the *NPV* method only. If the cash flows for multiple projects are conventional, then the *IRR* method is a great way to compare projects because you can talk in terms of rates of return instead of euro amounts (NPV).

Payback Period (PB) Method

The payback period is the amount of time needed for an investment to generate cash flows to recover its initial costs. The payback period method has some serious shortcomings, though. It is calculated by simply adding up the future cash flows. Because there is no discounting of cash flows, the time value of money is ignored. Without discounting the future cash flows, your project will look much more attractive than it really is. Not only will the project look more attractive, but because no required rate of return is used, the risk level of the project is never captured. So a very risky project is treated in the same way as a low-risk project. The biggest shortcoming with the payback method is that there is no economic rationale for determining the correct cutoff period. An arbitrary cutoff period must be chosen; so you need to decide whether two years is acceptable, or four years, or five, and so on. The payback period also tends to bias the user toward short-term investments because it ignores cash flows beyond the cutoff. A project that takes a few years to get up to speed and then creates phenomenal returns would be rejected strictly on its cash flow profile.

With all of the shortcomings of the payback period method, it is easy to see why investors should put very little weight on the analysis results other than as a very general guide when looking at two fairly comparable projects. If payback period is a valuation metric that an organization tends to look at, they can and should perform—before doing the payback analysis—a discounted payback period analysis to determine the discount rate and to discount the future cash flows. This step eliminates some of the method's shortcomings, but very few individuals ever perform such an analysis in practice. Use the discounted payback method only as a quick and dirty valuation method to value a project on the "back of an envelope" and as just another valuation metric in conjunction with the others mentioned here. Do not base your accept/reject decision on it. The payback period for the project is 4.19 years.

Profitability Index

The profitability index (PI) is a slightly different calculation. It is the present value of future cash flows divided by the initial investment. The present value of future cash flows is for the same as the discounted cash flows calculated exactly as shown in the NPV section:

$$|PI = \left(\sum_{k=1}^{n} \frac{P_k}{(1+i)^k} \right) / IC,$$

or

$$PI = \left(\sum_{k=1}^{n} \frac{P_k}{(1+i)^k} \right) / \sum_{t=i}^{m} \frac{IC_t}{(1+i)^t},$$

PI would be larger than 1 for positive-NPV projects and less than 1 for negative-NPV projects. For the preceding example, PI would be 1.0139. As the InvestSign discussion notes, PI measures "bang for the buck." It tells us that for each euro invested, the organization receives $1.01 in value.

PI and the IRR valuation methods are obviously very similar to the NPV method. They just present the results in a different fashion. An attractive NPV project also looks attractive on an IRR or PI basis and vice versa. IRR and PI allow you compare multiple projects on a level playing field. Just be careful because it might make more sense for your organization to pursue a high-NPV project even though it carries a lower IRR and PI than another comparable project. Earning a 50 percent return on a $20,000 project might not add much value to your organization, whereas earning 22 percent on a $5 million project would add considerable value.

Modified Internal Rate of Return (MIRR)
The modified internal rate of return (MIRR) is used to correct a significant inherent problem with the IRR calculation. The IRR formula assumes that you are reinvesting the cash flow at the same rate as calculated by the IRR. As a result, when you have a property that generates significant cash flow, the calculated IRR overstates the likely financial return of the property. MIRR allows you to enter a different rate that is applied to the property's cash flow. Using MIRR more closely mimics the real rate of return because operating cash flow is rarely invested at a higher rate than a bank savings rate. MIRR is 12.45 percent.

Discounted Payback Period (DPB)
The discounted payback period (DPB) is the amount of time needed for an investment to generate cash flows that are discounted to recover its initial costs. The discounted payback period is 4.94 per year. It is calculated by simply adding up the discounted future cash flows.

The biggest shortcoming with this method is that there is no economic rationale for determining the correct cutoff period. An arbitrary cutoff period must be chosen; so you need to decide whether two years is acceptable, or four years, or five, and so on. The discounted payback period also tends to bias the user toward short-term investments because it ignores cash flows beyond the cutoff. A project that takes a few years to get up to speed and then creates phenomenal returns is rejected strictly on its cash flow profile.

Average Accounting Returns (ARR)

The average accounting return (ARR) is the (undiscounted) average project earnings after taxes and depreciation, divided by the average book value of the investment during its life. The rule then accepts projects with an accounting return greater than a cutoff rate. ARR is 47.38 percent.

➤ The first problem with this rule is that it is based on net income figures and the book value of investments. Both of these measures are contaminated by arbitrary decisions about the depreciate rate of assets that are intrinsically irrelevant to the investment process. By contrast the NPV rule uses cash flows.

➤ The second problem is that, like the payback period rule, it ignores discounting and therefore does not take into account the opportunity costs of investing funds in the project.

➤ Third, since the rule is not related to NPV in any obvious way, there is again no rational basis for choosing the cutoff rate of return.

Cash Flow from Projects: What Investors Should Know

The potential application of DCF, used by actuaries to value deferred annuity and pension benefits, is wide. The real value of DCF was perhaps best expressed back in its pioneering days by William Phillips, a British actuary writing a review of *The Finance and Analysis of Capital Projects*, the classic project finance work by A. J. Merrett and Allen Sykes. In Phillips' apt phrase, "cash flow analysis is in essence discounting a series of known or estimated payments and receipts, ranged over a time scale, at interest either to obtain a present value (positive or negative) at a given interest rate, or valuing them at various rates to derive a yield that equates the present values of payments and receipts."[19] As this description implies, then, cash flow is really a way of looking at value—a particularly dynamic way that can unlock many mysteries, more than mere balance sheet or income statement analysis.

In their pioneering work on cash flow for projects, Merrett and Sykes join the use of net present value and yield, equating the present value of payments and receipts. They thus link depreciation (a concept centered in assets) to profit (a concept centered in net income). The substantial cash receipts that arise in the early years of a project qualifying for depreciation allowances impact the yield. As Phillips noted in his review, "This combination of both profit and depreciation provision as a cash receipt (analogous to an annuity payment) will seem less strange to actuaries than to accountants accustomed to rigid distinctions between profit and depreciation."[20]

As explained in Chapter 2 (according to Allen Sykes), there are three main ways to value an asset:

1. Calculate the present value of its future economic benefits.
2. Calculate the cost (and inconvenience) it would take to replace it.
3. Calculate the net resale value (proceeds less costs of disposing).

As shown in Figure 2.1 in Chapter 2, net present value has the highest value on day 1 but quickly declines over time as the asset depreciates. Replacement cost also declines but not as steeply. The flattest curve comes with resale value. As time goes on, the most advantageous strategy for the investor changes. At first, the highest value accorded is net present value, but at the end of the line, replacement value is the highest.

If an entire company is viewed as a kind of asset to value, the approach represented by cash flow is the first method in the list: calculate the present value of future economic benefits, defining those benefits as cash inflows. But this is not the only approach. Remember the old question, buy versus build? That question—ever so relevant to an investor who desires to gain control of an operating company—is very interested in this question, and it is expressed as the second method in the list. Finally, anyone involved in valuing the securities of a distressed company is intensely interested in scrap value, which is reflected in the third method.

Sykes warns that companies are more complex than assets; so he demurs on the value of his chart for corporate securities valuation. We, however, believe that it is an extremely useful reality check on any model for valuation.

For another approach used by a popular analyst of securities and mutual funds: Morningstar, see the box, "The Morningstar Approach: Determining Fair Value."

The Morningstar Approach: Determining Fair Value

This philosophy of fundamental research is the foundation for our valuation model. We believe that:

- How much capital a company invests and what it earns on that capital drive shareholder value.
- Free cash flow—not reported earnings—is what counts.
- As Warren Buffett has said, "Growth is always a component in the calculation of value—sometimes a positive, often a negative." If a company can't earn its cost of capital, growth destroys value instead of creating it.
- Competitive advantages disappear over time.
- It's dangerous to assume that the future will be better than the past.

These core beliefs guide our stock analysts as they estimate future cash flow, using their in-depth knowledge of each company and its competitive position within its industry. Our analysts forecast revenue growth, profit margins, and capital investment (and all of the numbers that go into them) for each firm they cover.

Their forecasts for each company populate our discounted cash flow model, which calculates the present value of the company's future discretionary cash flow based on its cost of capital, as determined by our analysts.

Source: Morningstar Equity Analysts, "Morningstar's Equity Research," November, 6, 2009, http://news.morningstar.com/articlenet/article.aspx?id=83572.

The Work of Alfred Rappaport

Alfred Rappaport has done more than any other individual to popularize discounted cash flow as a method of valuation, and in recent years he has discovered a significant twist to this approach.

When the discounted cash flow approach first rose in prominence, investors used it to discern an appropriate stock price. Rappaport flips the approach. He makes an excellent point in his book, *Expectations Investing*.[21] He says stock price expresses current investor expectations; the job of the investor is to correct them: "If you've got a fix on current expectations, then you can figure out where they are likely to go."

According to Rappaport, you can estimate the current value of a stock by forecasting future free cash flows and discounting them back to the present. He reverses the classic approach, which uses cash flow to predict the value of a stock. Instead, he uses the current value of a stock to predict future cash flow.

Exhibit 4.2 shows an example of a model to yield NPV for a target company, and it was developed by a team at ALCAR, a financial advisory firm cofounded by Rappaport.[22] The printout is only for the most likely scenario. The most optimistic and the most pessimistic scenarios, normally an integral part of a DCF analysis, do not appear.

Using Monte Carlo Simulations for Future Cash Flow Estimates

The Monte Carlo method uses statistical sampling to solve a quantifiable problem in any arena, ranging from biology to business and including cash flow. This technique, developed by philosopher Karl Popper, who referred to games played in the famed principality, simulates the underlying physical process and calculates the average result of the process.

Analysts can use Monte Carlo methods to estimate future cash flow. They construct stochastic (i.e., probability-based) financial models as opposed to the traditional linear models. Different cash flow components get different values and weights, based on their levels of uncertainty, thus reflecting their random characteristics.

Exhibit 4.2 Model to Yield NPV for a Target Company

Income Statement for Sample Company: Most Likely Scenario

($ in millions)	Y1	Y2	Y3	Y4	Y5	Y6	Y7
Sales	$1,934.5	$2,032.0	$2,235.2	$2,414.0	$2,558.9	$2,712.4	$2,875.1
Cost of Goods Sold	1,435.2	1,529.9	1,698.8	1,834.7	1,842.4	1,844.4	1,955.1
Gross Profit	499.3	502.1	536.4	579.4	716.5	868.0	920.0
Salary Expense	156.2	169.3	109.5	118.3	125.4	132.9	140.9
Selling Expense	54.3	57.8	55.9	60.4	64.0	67.8	71.9
Administrative Expenses	87.2	93.5	148.2	125.2	251.0	365.7	377.8
Total SG & A Expense	297.7	320.6	313.6	303.8	440.4	566.4	590.6
Other Operating Income	0.5	1.2	0.9	0.9	0.9	0.9	0.9
Depreciation Expense	49.3	55.1	57.5	61.0	64.0	66.1	68.1
Operating Profit	$ 152.8	$127.6	$166.3	$ 215.4	$ 213.1	$ 236.3	$ 262.3
Interest Income	0.0	0.0	8.7	20.5	33.0	47.4	64.2
Interest Expense: Sched. Debt	N/A	N/A	16.0	16.0	16.0	16.0	16.0
Total Interest Expense	15.4	17.6	16.0	16.0	16.0	16.0	16.0
Less: Interest Capitalized	3.0	3.0	3.0	3.0	3.0	3.0	3.0
Interest Expense	12.4	14.6	13.0	13.0	13.0	13.0	13.0
Gain on Sale of Assets	6.5	7.3	0.0	0.0	0.0	0.0	0.0
Other Non-operating Income	32.4	36.3	40.2	43.1	45.0	45.0	45.0
Earnings before Taxes	$179.3	$156.6	$202.2	$266.1	$278.0	$315.7	358.5
Provision for Income Taxes	67.1	23.4	70.2	92.9	91.8	102.5	114.4

($ in millions)	Y1	Y2	Y3	Y4	Y5	Y6	Y7
Extraordinary Items	0.0	(2.8)	0.0	0.0	0.0	0.0	0.0
Net Income	$112.2	$130.4	$131.9	$173.2	$186.3	$213.3	$244.1
Preferred Dividends	4.1	4.3	4.5	4.7	5.1	5.1	5.1
Income Available for Common	$108.1	$126.1	$127.4	$168.5	$181.2	$208.2	$239.0
Common Dividends	$12.5	$13.4	$14.1	$57.2	$61.5	$70.4	$80.6

Source: Developed by ALCAR and now sold by Hyperion Financial Management/Oracle (cited in Reed, Lajoux, and Nesvold).

Balance Sheet for Sample Company: Most Likely Scenario

($ in millions)	Y1	Y2	Y3	Y4	Y5	Y6	Y7
Cash	$ 4.3	$ 17.8	$ 24.3	$ 30.0	$ 34.7	$ 39.6	$ 44.8
Marketable Securities	4.1	70.9	166.9	268.2	385.3	522.3	673.1
Accounts Receivable	357.9	397.6	420.4	440.4	456.6	473.8	492.0
Raw Materials	73.0	75.7	78.3	80.7	82.5	84.5	86.7
Work in Progress	182.6	189.2	200.2	209.8	217.7	225.9	234.7
Finished Goods	109.5	113.4	120.5	126.7	131.7	137.1	142.7
Total Inventories	365.1	378.3	399.0	417.2	431.9	447.6	464.1
Other Current Assets	43.7	43.7	43.7	43.7	43.7	43.7	43.7
Total Current Assets	$775.1	$908.3	$1,054.3	$1,199.5	$1,352.2	$1,527.0	$1,717.7
Gross PP & E excl. int. Cap.	769.8	798.1	844.2	882.7	910.4	934.9	955.6

(Continued)

($ in millions)	Y1	Y2	Y3	Y4	Y5	Y6	Y7
Cum. Forecast Interest Cap.	N/A	N/A	3.0	5.8	8.4	10.8	13.0
Less: Accum. Depreciation	276.5	269.9	293.7	312.3	329.2	341.2	341.3
Net Property, Plant & Equip.	493.3	528.2	553.5	576.1	589.5	604.5	627.4
Goodwill	52.9	46.5	46.5	46.5	46.5	46.5	46.5
Other Intangibles	4.5	3.3	3.3	3.3	3.3	3.3	3.3
Other Assets	22.6	42.3	42.3	42.3	42.3	42.3	42.3
Total Assets	$ 1,348.4	$ 1,528.6	$ 1,699.9	$1,867.7	$2,033.9	$2,223.5	$2,437.2
Accounts Payable	$ 145.9	$ 192.7	$ 221.1	$ 246.2	$ 266.5	$ 288.0	$ 310.7
Current Portion L-T Debt	12.4	11.8	24.9	25.2	25.9	26.6	27.4
Income Taxes Payable	17.3	17.5	16.4	21.7	21.5	24.0	26.8
Other Current Liabilities	71.6	71.6	71.6	71.6	71.6	71.6	71.6
Total Current Liabilities	$ 247.2	$ 293.6	$ 334.0	$ 364.7	$ 385.4	$ 410.2	$ 436.5
Total L-T Debt	323.7	335.9	340.0	350.0	360.0	370.0	380.0
Deferred Income Taxes	87.3	98.2	108.9	122.7	136.4	151.5	168.4
Other Liabilities	22.6	14.2	15.0	15.0	15.0	15.0	15.0
Total Liabilities	$ 680.8	$ 741.9	$ 797.9	$ 852.4	$ 896.8	$ 946.7	$ 999.9
Preferred Stock	37.9	39.4	41.4	43.4	45.4	47.4	49.4
Common Stock and Paid-in Cap	612.4	620.3	620.3	620.3	620.3	620.3	620.3

($ in millions)	Y1	Y2	Y3	Y4	Y5	Y6	Y7
Retained Earnings	17.3	127.0	240.3	351.7	471.4	609.1	767.6
Total Liabilities and Equity	$1,348.4	$1,528.6	$1,699.9	$1,867.7	$2,033.9	$2,223.5	$2,437.2
Unused Debt Capacity (UDC)	$ 35.3	$ 98.6	$ 153.1	$ 213.2	$ 278.3	$ 355.1	$ 445.4
UDC plus Mkt. Securities	$ 39.4	$ 169.5	$ 320.1	$ 481.4	$ 663.6	$ 877.4	$1,118.4

Funds Flow Statement for Sample Company: Most Likely Scenario

($ in millions)	Y1	Y2	Y3	Y4	Y5	Y6
Net Income	$130.4	$131.9	$173.2	$186.3	$213.3	$244.1
Depr. Exp. excl. Int. Cap.	55.1	57.5	60.8	63.6	65.5	67.3
Depr. Exp. on Cum. Int. Cap.	N/A	N/A	0.2	0.4	0.6	0.8
Less: Interest Capitalized	3.0	3.0	3.0	3.0	3.0	3.0
Incr. in Deferred Inc. Taxes	10.9	10.7	13.8	13.7	15.2	16.8
Incr. in Other Liabilities	(8.4)	0.8	0.0	0.0	0.0	0.0
Incr. in Debt: Scheduled	12.2	4.1	10.0	10.0	10.0	10.0
Net Bk. Value of Ret. Assets	8.1	20.9	18.3	20.0	20.2	14.0
Incr. in Accounts Payable	46.8	28.4	25.0	20.3	21.5	22.8
Incr. in Curr. Port. L-T Debt	(0.6)	13.1	0.3	0.7	0.7	0.7
Incr. in Income Tax Payable	0.2	(1.1)	5.3	(0.3)	2.5	2.8
Proceeds *from* Sale of Common	7.9	0.0	0.0	0.0	0.0	0.0
Proceeds from Sale of Pf. Stk.	1.5	2.0	2.0	2.0	2.0	2.0

(Continued)

($ in millions)	Y1	Y2	Y3	Y4	Y5	Y6
Total Sources of Funds	$261.1	$265.3	$306.0	$313.7	$348.5	$378.4
Fixed Capital Investment	$ 98.1	$100.7	$ 98.9	$ 94.4	$ 98.2	$102.0
Additions to Goodwill	(6.4)	0.0	0.0	0.0	0.0	0.0
Additions to Intangibles	(1.2)	0.0	0.0	0.0	0.0	0.0
Incr. in Other Assets	19.7	0.0	0.0	0.0	0.0	0.0
Incr. in Cash	13.5	6.5	5.7	4.6	4.9	5.2
Incr. in Mkt. Securities	66.8	96.0	101.3	117.1	137.0	150.7
Incr. in Accts. Receivable	39.7	22.8	20.0	16.2	17.2	18.2
Incr. in Raw Materials	2.7	2.6	2.3	1.9	2.0	2.1
Incr. in Work in Progress	6.6	11.0	9.7	7.8	8.3	8.8
Incr. in Finished Goods	3.9	7.1	6.2	5.0	5.3	5.7
Total Incr. in Inventories	13.2	20.7	18.2	14.7	15.6	16.6
Preferred Dividends	4.3	4.5	4.7	5.1	5.1	5.1
Common Dividends	13.4	14.1	57.2	61.5	70.4	80.6
Total Uses of Funds	$261.1	$265.3	$306.0	$313.7	$348.5	$378.4

Cash Flow Statement for Sample Company: Most Likely Scenario

($ in millions)	Y1	Y2	Y3	Y4	Y5	Y6
Sales	$2,032.0	$2,235.2	$2,414.0	$2,558.9	$2,712.4	$2,875.1
Cost of Goods Sold	1,529.9	1,698.8	1,834.7	1842.4	1,844.4	1,955.1
Gross Profit	502.1	536.4	579.4	716.5	868.0	920.0
Salary Expense	169.3	109.5	118.3	125.4	132.9	140.9
Selling Expense	57.8	55.9	60.4	64.0	67.8	71.9
Administrative Expenses	93.5	148.2	125.2	251.0	365.7	377.8

($ in millions)	Y1	Y2	Y3	Y4	Y5	Y6
Total SG & A Expense	320.6	313.6	303.8	440.4	566.4	590.6
Other Operating Income	1.2	0.9	0.9	0.9	0.9	0.9
Depreciation Expense	55.1	57.5	61.0	64.0	66.1	68.1
Operating Profit	127.6	166.3	215.4	213.1	236.3	262.3
Depr. Exp. excl. Int. Cap.	55.1	57.5	60.8	63.6	65.5	67.3
Depr. Exp. on Cum. Int. Cap.	N/A	N/A	0.2	0.4	0.6	0.8
Funds from Opers. Before Tax	182.7	223.7	276.4	277.0	302.4	330.4
Cash Income Taxes	19.5	65.8	85.3	84.3	93.5	103.8
Funds from Opers. After Tax	$163.2	$157.9	$191.2	$192.7	$208.9	$226.6
Increm. Working Cap. Invest.	19.4	22.6	13.6	15.6	13.7	14.4
Fixed Capital Investment	98.1	100.7	98.9	94.4	98.2	102.0
Additions to Goodwill	(6.4)	0.0	0.0	0.0	0.0	0.0
Additions to Intangibles	(1.2)	0.0	0.0	0.0	0.0	0.0
Proceeds (af. tax) Asset Sale	15.4	20.9	18.3	20.0	20.2	14.0
Cash Flow from Operations	$ 68.7	$ 55.5	$ 97.0	$102.7	$ 117.1	$124.2
Cash Flow from Operations	$ 68.7	$ 55.5	$ 97.0	$102.7	$ 117.1	$124.2
Interest Expense: Sched. Debt	N/A	16.0	16.0	16.0	16.0	16.0
Total Interest Expense	17.6	16.0	16.0	16.0	16.0	16.0
Interest Expense (af. tax)	10.6	9.8	9.8	9.8	9.8	9.8
Nonoperating Inc. (af. tax)	33.5	48.9	63.6	78.0	92.4	109.2

(Continued)

($ in millions)	Y1	Y2	Y3	Y4	Y5	Y6
Nonoperating Sources	(8.4)	0.8	0.0	0.0	0.0	0.0
Nonoperating Uses	19.7	0.0	0.0	0.0	0.0	0.0
Proceeds from Sale of Common	7.9	0.0	0.0	0.0	0.0	0.0
Preferred Dividends	4.3	4.5	4.7	5.1	5.1	5.1
Net Cash Provided	$67.1	$91.0	$146.1	$165.8	$194.7	$218.5
Common Dividends	13.4	14.1	57.2	61.5	70.4	80.6
Funding Surplus/(Deficit)	$53.7	$76.9	$ 89.0	$104.4	$124.3	$138.0
Funding Surplus/(Deficit)	$53.7	$76.9	$ 89.0	$104.4	$124.3	$138.0
Incr. in Curr. Port. L-T Debt	(0.6)	13.1	0.3	0.7	0.7	0.7
Incr. in Debt: Scheduled	12.2	4.1	10.0	10.0	10.0	10.0

Cash Analysis Statement for Sample Company: Most Likely Scenario

($in millions)	Y1	Y2	Y3	Y4	Y5	Y6
Net Income	$130.4	$131.9	$173.2	$186.3	$213.3	$244.1
Plus: Depr. Exp. excl. Int. Cap.	55.1	57.5	60.8	63.6	65.5	67.3
Depr. Exp. on Cum. Int. Cap.	N/A	N/A	0.2	0.4	0.6	0.8
Extraordinary Items	(2.8)	0.0	0.0	0.0	0.0	0.0
Interest Expense	14.6	13.0	13.0	13.0	13.0	13.0
Provision for Income Taxes	23.4	70.2	92.9	91.8	102.5	114.4
Less: Nonoperating Profit	36.3	48.9	63.6	78.0	92.4	109.2
Gain on Sale of Assets	7.3	0.0	0.0	0.0	0.0	0.0
Cash Income Taxes	19.5	64.8	85.3	84.3	93.5	103.8

($in millions)	Y1	Y2	Y3	Y4	Y5	Y6
Funds from Opers. After Tax	$163.2	$157.9	$191.2	$192.7	$208.9	$226.6
Plus: Incr. in Accounts Payable	46.8	28.4	25.0	20.3	21.5	22.8
Incr. in Income Tax Payable	0.2	(1.1)	5.3	(0.3)	2.5	2.8
Less: Incr. in Cash	13.5	6.5	5.7	4.6	4.9	5.2
Incr. in Accts Receivable	39.7	22.8	20.0	16.2	17.2	18.2
Incr. in Raw Materials	2.7	2.6	2.3	1.9	2.0	2.1
Incr. in Work in Progress	6.6	11.0	9.7	7.8	8.3	8.8
Incr. in Finished Goods	3.9	7.1	6.2	5.0	5.3	5.7
Total Incr. in Inventories	13.2	20.7	18.2	14.7	15.6	16.6
Cash from Operating Cycle	$143.8	$135.4	$177.5	$177.1	$195.2	$212.1
Less: Fixed Capital Investment	98.1	100.7	98.9	94.4	98.2	102.0
Additions to Goodwill	(6.4)	0.0	0.0	0.0	0.0	0.0
Additions to Intangibles	(1.2)	0.0	0.0	0.0	0.0	0.0
Plus: Proceeds (af. tax) Asset Sale	15.4	20.9	18.3	20.0	20.2	14.0
Cash Flow from Operations	$68.7	$55.5	$97.0	$102.7	$117.1	$124.2
Less: Nonoperating Uses	19.7	0.0	0.0	0.0	0.0	0.0
Plus: Nonoperating Sources	(8.4)	0.8	0.0	0.0	0.0	0.0
Nonoperating Inc. (af. tax)	33.5	48.9	63.6	78.0	92.4	109.2
Cash bef. Fin. Cost & Ext. Fin.	$74.1	$105.2	$160.6	$180.7	$209.5	$233.4

(Continued)

($in millions)	Y1	Y2	Y3	Y4	Y5	Y6
Less: Interest Expense (af. tax)	10.6	9.8	9.8	9.8	9.8	9.8
Preferred Dividends	4.3	4.5	4.7	5.1	5.1	5.1
Common Dividends	13.4	14.1	57.2	61.5	70.4	80.6
Cash bef. External Financing	$45.8	$76.9	$ 89.0	$104.4	$124.3	$138.0
Plus: incr. in Curr. Port. L-T Debt	(0.6)	13.1	0.3	0.7	0.7	0.7
Incr. in Debt: Scheduled	12.2	4.1	10.0	10.0	10.0	10.0
Proceeds from Sale of Pf. Stk.	1.5	2.0	2.0	2.0	2.0	2.0
Proceeds from Sale of Common	7.9	0.0	0.0	0.0	0.0	0.0
Incr. in Mkt. Securities	$66.8	$96.0	$101.3	$ 117.1	$137.0	$150.7
Proceeds from Sale of Pf. Stk.	1.5	2.0	2.0	2.0	2.0	2.0
Incr. in Mkt. Securities	$66.8	$96.0	$101.3	$ 117.1	$137.0	$150.7

Financial Ratios for Sample Company: Most Likely Scenario

	Y1	Y2	Y3	Y4	Y5	Y6	Y7
Profit Performance Ratios							
Gross Profit Margin (%)	25.810	24.710	24.000	24.000	28.000	32.000	32.000
Change in Net Income (%)	N/A	16.221	1.153	31.317	7.538	14.497	14.467
Return on Sales (%)	5.800	6.417	5.901	7.175	7.279	7.863	8.491
Return on Equity (%)	17.818	17.449	15.327	17.821	17.063	17.347	17.589
Return on Assets or Inv. (%)	9.022	9.407	8.334	9.796	9.638	10.030	10.417

	Y1	Y2	Y3	Y4	Y5	Y6	Y7
Return on Net Assets (%)	11.047	11.643	10.372	12.173	11.892	12.299	12.690
Leverage Ratios							
Debt/Equity Ratio (%)	59.393	51.800	47.206	43.064	39.509	36.117	32.911
Debt/Total Capital (%)	37.262	34.124	32.068	30.101	28.320	26.534	24.762
Equity Ratio (%)	46.700	48.888	50.626	52.040	53.674	55.292	56.948
Times Interest Earned	12.448	9.727	13.447	17.442	18.190	20.546	23.221
Activity Ratios							
Days in Receivables	N/A	67.854	66.785	65.072	63.974	62.602	61.307
Days in Payables	N/A	40.391	44.460	46.487	50.781	54.858	55.886
Inventory Turnover	N/A	4.116	4.371	4.496	4.339	4.194	4.289
Fixed Asset Turnover	N/A	3.847	4.038	4.190	4.340	4.487	4.583
Total Asset Turnover	N/A	1.329	1.315	1.292	1.258	1.220	1.180
Liquidity Ratios							
Quick Ratio	1.482	1.656	1.831	2.025	2.274	2.525	2.772
Current Ratio	3.136	3.094	3.156	3.289	3.508	3.723	3.935
Per-Share Data							
Earnings Per Share	8.07	9.41	9.51	12.58	13.52	15.54	17.84
Change in EPS (%)	N/A	16.65	1.03	32.27	7.51	14.91	14.82
Primary EPS	8.07	9.41	9.51	12.58	13.52	15.54	17.84
Fully Diluted EPS	8.07	9.41	9.51	12.58	13.52	15.54	17.84
Dividends per Share	0.93	1.00	1.05	4.27	4.59	5.25	6.01
Cash Flow per Share	N/A	5.13	4.14	7.24	7.66	8.74	9.27
Book Value per Share	47.70	56.61	65.20	73.63	82.70	93.14	105.14

(Continued)

	Y1	Y2	Y3	Y4	Y5	Y6	Y7
Valuation Ratios							
Change in Share. Val./Share	N/A	N/A	7.93	10.12	(0.86)	3.66	3.33
Share. Value per Share (PV)	N/A	N/A	40.11	50.23	49.37	53.03	56.36
Oper. Profit Margin (P) (%)	7.899	6.280	7.439	8.924	8.326	8.712	9.123
Threshold Margin (%)	N/A	7.664	6.325	7.278	8.695	8.118	8.472
Threshold Spread (%)	N/A	(1.384)	1.115	1.646	(0.369)	0.594	0.650
Incremental Profit Margin(%)	N/A	(25.846)	19.035	27.486	(1.638)	15.139	15.971
Increm. Threshold Margin (%)	N/A	2.999	6.774	5.270	4.881	4.639	4.482
Increm. Threshold Spread (%)	N/A	(28.846)	12.261	22.216	(6.519)	10.500	11.490
Value Drivers							
Sales Growth Rate (G) (%)	N/A	5.04	10.00	8.00	6.00	6.00	6.00
Oper. Profit Margin (P) (%)	7.90	6.28	7.44	8.92	8.33	8.71	9.12
Inc. Fixed Cap. Inv. (F) (%)	N/A	44.10	21.30	21.30	21.30	21.30	21.30
Inc. Work. Cap. Inv. (W) (%)	N/A	19.90	11.10	7.62	10.76	8.95	8.86
Cash Inc. Tax Rate (Tc) (%)	N/A	15.29	39.58	39.58	39.58	39.58	39.58
Discount Rates							
Average Cost of Capital (%)	15.30						
Long-Term Cost of Capital	15.30						
Internal Rate of Return (%)	32.05						
Memo: Avg. Cost of Capital and IRR based on forecast data							
Data IRR uses Pre-Start. Resid. Value as investment ($433.673 million)							

Reconciliation for Sample Company—Year 1: Most Likely Scenario ($ in millions)

	Earnings	Adjustments	Cash Flows
Sales	$2,414.0		
Less: Incr. in Accts Receivable		20.0	
Cash Receipts			$2,394.0
Cost of Goods Sold	1,834.7		
Less: Incr. in Accounts Payable		25.0	
Plus: Total Incr. in Inventories		18.2	
Cash COGS			1,827.8
Gross Profit	$ 579.4		
Total SG&A Expense	303.8		
Plus: Incr. in Cash		5.7	
Less: Incr. in Income Tax Payable		5.3	
Cash SG &A Expense			304.3
Increm. Working Cap. Invest.		$13.6	
Other Operating Income	0.9		0.9
Depreciation Expense	61.0		
Plus: Depreciation Expense: Funds		61.0	
Depreciation in Other Items			0.0
Fixed Capital Investment		98.9	98.9
Operating Profit	$ 215.4		
Interest Income	20.5		
Interest Expense	13.0		
Other Nonoperating Income	43.1		
Earnings Before Taxes	$ 266.1		
Provision for Income Taxes	92.9		
Less: Incr. in Deferred Inc. Taxes		13.8	
Cash Income Taxes			85.3
Proceeds (af. tax) Asset Sale			18.3
Cash Flow from Operations			97.0
Net Income	$ 173.2		

Cash Flows and Shareholder Value for Sample Company: Most Likely Scenario
(Average Cost of Capital [%] = 15.3%) ($ in millions)

Year	Cash Flow	Pres. Value Cash Flow	Cum. PV Cash Flows	Pres. Value Residual Value	Cum PV CF+ PV Residual Value	Increase in Value
1	$55.5	$48.2	$48.2	$490.1	$538.3	$104.6
2	97.0	72.9	121.1	550.8	671.8	133.5
3	102.7	67.0	188.1	472.4	660.5	(11.3)
4	117.1	66.3	254.4	454.4	708.8	48.3
5	124.2	60.9	315.3	437.5	752.8	44.0
						319.1

Marketable Securities	70.9
Corporate Value	$ 823.7
Less: Mkt. Val of Debt	63.0
Less: Unfunded Pension Liabs.	16.7
Shareholder Value (PV)	$ 744.0
Shareholder Value per Share (PV)	$ 56.36
Current Stock Price	$ 49.50
Prem/Disc. Over/Under Mkt. (%)	13.86

Profit Margins for Sample Company Most Likely Scenario

Year	Operating Profit Margin	Threshold Margin	Threshold Spread	Incremental Profit Margin	Incremental Threshold Margin	Incremental Threshold Spread
1	7.439%	6.325%	1.115%	19.035%	6.774%	12.261%
2	8.924%	7.278%	1.646%	27.486%	5.270%	22.216%
3	8.326%	8.695%	(0.369)	(1.638)	4.881%	(6.519)
4	8.712%	8.118%	0.594%	15.139%	4.639%	10.500%
5	9.123%	8.472%	0.650%	15.971%	4.482%	11.490%

Valuation Summary for Sample Company: Most Likely Scenario Five-Year Forecast
($ in millions)

Cumulative PV Cash Flows	$ 315.3
Present Value of Res. Value	437.5
Marketable Securities	70.9
Corporate Value	$ 823.7

Less: Mkt. Val. of Debt	63.0
Less: Unfunded Pension Liabs.	16.7
Shareholder Value (PV)	$ 744.0
Less: Pre-Strat. Shar. Value	424.9
Value Contrib. by Strategy	$ 319.1
Shareholder Value per Share (PV)	$ 56.36
Current Stock Price	$ 49.50
Prem/Disc Over/Under Mkt. (%)	13.86
Value ROI (%)	180.62
Value ROS (%)	55.79

Relative Impact of Key Variables on Shareholder Value for Sample Company + Most Likely Scenario ($ in millions)

A 1% Increase In:	Increases Shareholder Value by:	% Increase
Sales Growth Rate (G)	$0.4	0.054
Operating Profit Margin (P)	8.7	1.163
Increm. Fixed Capital Investment (F)	(1.2)	(0.164)
Increm. Working Capital Investment (W)	(0.5)	(0.074)
Cash Income Tax Rate (Tc)	(2.8)	(0.377)
Residual Value Income Tax Rate (Tr)	(4.0)	(0.543)
Cost of Capital (K)	(4.2)	(0.560)

The approach, shown in **Exhibit 4.3**, yields a histogram that shows the probability distribution. (A histogram is a graph that shows frequencies as bars, indicating what proportion of cases fall into two or more categories.) (For more on the use of statistics in finance, see Appendix E. For use of Monte Carlo simulation in stock investments, see Appendix J.)

The Monte Carlo approach is not foolproof. Consider the 2008–2009 experience with derivative securities based on anticipated mortgage payments from subprime borrowers. When creating models based on cash flows from these anticipated payments, some analysts used a broad range of variables, including some not in financial statements, and some of the variables turned out to be false. This was the great lesson of the mortgage market meltdown.

Exhibit 4.3 Monte Carlo Cash Flow

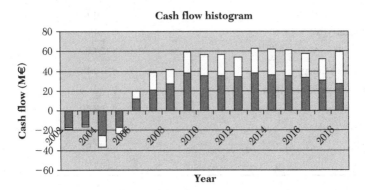

Cash flow histogram

Source: Adapted with permission from Portfolio Management of Strategic Investments in Metal Products Industry, by Juha Martikainen, Helsinki University of Technology Department of Engineering Physics and MathematicsPre. http://www.sal.hut.fi/Publications/pdf-files/tmar02 .pdf. (Thanks also to Professor James M. Grayson of Hull College of Business Administration at August State University for his materials on this topic.)

IASB Open Question

Would a direct method of presenting operating cash flows provide information that is decision-useful?

We acknowledge that a direct method of presenting operating cash flows leads to a clear presentation with respect to information about payment and receipt of cash as compared with an indirect method. Therefore, as it enables the users of financial statements to understand the operating cash flow more easily, we believe such method provides users with decision usefulness. However, since it is expected that preparation of cash flow statements based on a direct method would be very costly due to systems development and other circumstances, in practice, entities would often be forced to use a simplified method in preparing their cash flow statements based on a direct method. In order to address such cases, we believe that the final standard should include an example that illustrates the use of a simplified method in the preparation of cash flow statements based on a direct method.

—Kiyoshi Ichimura, executive board member, Accounting Standards, Japanese Institute of Certified Public Accountants (in a letter to the FASB dated April 14, 2009)

Using Cash Flow to Calculate Amortized Cost

Now that the standard setters have discovered cash flow, it has become a part of other accounting standards, such as recording the value of assets. The value of an asset can change over time. A change for the worse is called "impairment."

Under ASC 360 (FAS 144), a company may give a "probability-weighted cash flow estimate" of impairment for some financial assets.[23] This is not the case globally, however. IAS 39 recognizes impairment of financial assets using an incurred loss model. An incurred loss model assumes that all loans will be repaid until evidence to the contrary (known as a "loss" or "trigger event") is identified. Only at that point is the impaired loan (or portfolio of loans) written down to a lower value. But the IASB is proposing an expected loss model based on *expected cash flows*. Under that model, "expected losses are recognized throughout the life of a loan or other financial asset measured at amortized cost, not just after a loss event has been identified."[24]

IFRS Impact on Cash Flow

In the switch to global accounting (reconciling GAAP to IFRS), slated for 2014, of highest concern is the possible discontinuation of the first-in/first-out (FIFO) choice for inventory accounting, used by about one-third of public companies. Under the FIFO accounting method, when a company records a sale out of inventory, the price used for the sale is the price paid for the oldest item (the first one that came in), as if reaching to the back of a warehouse full of identical items. In contrast, under the LIFO (last-in/first-out) method, sales are booked based on the price of the most recently purchased items. Companies that want to lower their reported net income (in order to reduce taxes) tend to use LIFO, whereas other companies (about a third of them) use FIFO. The FIFO approach occurs typically in companies that have low profit margins and that need to boost reported net income. The change to IFRS could mean the elimination of FIFO, which will lower reported net earnings and cash flow for companies that have been using this approach.[25]

This change will not affect anything "real" in a company; it is merely an accounting convention. It will affect only *reported* cash flow under the *indirect* method, assuming either the inflation or the deflation of prices. But value-minded investors should be aware that if companies switch to IFRS and suddenly show lower cash flow, their value is not really affected. The lower cash flow is a merely a change in accounting approach.

Questions

I am always troubled by *"undistributed earnings from equity affiliates"* when paired with *"other cash payments"* as a kind of plug figure. This may be perfectly legitimate, but it can raise questions. My favorite memory of being right was as a director of the Banque Bruxelles Lambert which owned 30 percent of Drexel Burnham. When I saw the "undistributed" and "other" language, I questioned Drexel's financial statements and was ultimately vindicated when hundreds of millions of dollars, reported as earnings and presumably cash flow, were cruelly contrasted with the reality of zero dividends and ultimate bankruptcy in the historic downfall of the firm and its star, Michael Milken.

——Robert A. G. Monks

Cash Flow Patterns in Industries

Cash flow patterns vary from one industry to another. A good source of information about industry trends is the Georgia Institute of Technology (Georgia Tech), which has published a series of reports on "Cash Flow Trends and Their Fundamental Drivers."[26] The studies' primary focus is on free cash margin, or free cash flow measured as a percentage of revenue. Other trends tracked in the study are median operating cash margin; median operating cushion; median gross margin; median sales, general, and administrative (SG&A) expenses, median receivable days, and median free cash margin.

A July 2009 study by Georgia Tech showed that in 2009, despite overall declines in earnings and stock prices, cash flow did not decline very greatly. Although company revenues were down, so were their expenses—in particular, capital expenditures and working capital requirements. As a percentage of revenue, free cash flow declined to 4.12 percent, down from a peak of 5.14 percent in June 2004, with other highs of 4.93 percent reached in December 2007 and 4.44 percent in September 2008. "With free cash margin at 4.12 percent, corporate America is generating 4.12¢ of free cash flow for every dollar of revenue generated."[27] But a sequel study in July 2009 showed that reporting differences among banks make comparisons difficult.[28]

Chemicals and Other Materials

Chemicals and other industries in the materials sector suffered in the recession that began in 2007. This broad sector, which includes chemicals, construction materials, containers and packaging, metals and mining, and paper and forest products, ended the year 2008 with a median free cash margin of 2.03 percent, the lowest for the time period considered (2000–2008), compared with 4.22 percent for the 12 months ended December 2007. One reason was a rise in median capital expenditures as a percentage of revenue, which rose from 5.10 percent for the 12 months ended December 2007 to 5.73 percent for the 12 months ended December 2008.

Energy

This sector includes energy equipment and services, as well as oil, gas, and consumable fuels. For the 12 months ended December 2008, free cash margin improved slightly to 0.54 percent from the 0.06 percent recorded for the twelve months ended December 2007. That 0.06 percent level was the lowest point reached for the entire review period of March 2000 to December 2008, a period during which free cash margin for the industry had at times reached levels above 3 percent. Operating cash margin, which increased from 25.82 percent in December 2007 to 29.98 percent in December 2008, was the driver of the increase in free cash margin. Capital expenditures as a percentage of revenue experienced no appreciable change during the reporting period.

Financials

The Georgia Tech series does not cover financial firms, whose cash flow analysis has a different application because of the definition and measurement of debt and reinvestment. But investors can value banks using DCF, with certain adjustments.[29]

The analysis of the cash flows of banks became more meaningful under GAAP with. Statement 104, *Statement of Cash Flows—Net Reporting of Certain Cash Receipts and Cash Payments and Classification of Cash Flows from Hedging Transactions*, says that a cash flow statement from a bank, savings institution, or credit union can include net cash receipts and cash payments for (1) deposits placed with other financial institutions and withdrawals of deposits, (2) time deposits accepted and repayments of deposits, and (3) loans made to customers and principal collections of loans.

This statement also permits cash flows resulting from futures contracts, forward contracts, option contracts, or swap contracts that are accounted for as hedges of identifiable transactions or events to be classified in the same category as the cash flows from the items being hedged, provided that accounting policy is disclosed.

Lens Check

Like assets and earnings, cash flow is best seen through various lenses:

➤ *Time: Short term versus long term.* By definition, discounted cash flow has time built into it. The investor discounts from a future point back to the present. The farther out the time period goes, the more difficult the discount rate is to estimate. Even the most sophisticated investors say that beyond seven years, it is almost impossible to estimate a discount rate with any certainty.[30]

➤ *Place: Market versus nonmarket.* In analyzing cash flow, it is important to ask (as we did for earnings) will the cash-generating conditions for the company persist?

➤ *Slope: Level versus skewed playing field.* Cash flow statements are considered to be less susceptible to fraud than income statements, but with the indirect method, some discretion is required, and where there is discretion, there are gray areas. Certainly when it comes to the future, there are many ways to slant the truth.

➤ *Volition: Willing versus unwilling buyer or seller.* Discounted cash flow takes on different meanings depending on the buyer or seller motivation. If the buyer is more eager than the seller, its negotiators are much more willing to accept a high present value based on optimistic projections. The opposite applies when the seller is more eager than the buyer.

➤ *Quality: Level of certainty of return (high, medium, or low) based on investing standards.* Investors' individual goals for future returns shape what kind of current cash flow they want to see. As explained in the earnings chapter, a fund with a short-term horizon doesn't care for a company with currently thin cash flow because it is making capital investments for the future. Conversely, a pension fund with a 10-year horizon for returns *is* interested in such a company, absent other problems.

➤ *Purpose: Private versus public.* A private-sector investor is more likely to pay close attention to cash flow than will a public-sector investor, which may have a greater variety of cash sources, due to its relatively large size and power.

Conclusion

Cash flow analysis has achieved a solid place in the kit of tools for investment analysis. Endorsed and taught by the great valuation experts, it is worthy of attention. This kind of analysis is complex. The investor must know how long it will hold its investment, what its cost of capital will be (what percentage return it must achieve at a minimum), and, most important, what the company's future economic and financial performance—hence cash flow—will be. This kind of analysis is more complex than the analysis of a company's assets or earnings. It moves us into a very dynamic realm—the perfect segue into the next chapter, on valuation methods based in stock prices.

Appendix 4.1: AT&T Example[31]

By making certain simplifying assumptions investors can convert the operating section of the cash flow statement from the indirect to the direct method format. When done properly, the total cash from operating activities does not change. That is, the form of the statement does not alter the substance (the end result). This is best accomplished by using the working capital adjustments the firm has given in its indirect method cash flow statement. Note also that when recast into the direct method, items such as depreciation expense and gains or losses never appear. Since the calculation does not begin with net income, there is no need to adjust these noncash or nonoperating items out of the operating section.

Although the total cash flow will not change, the cash flows for each recast line are merely estimates. Actual categories of direct cash flows may differ. Furthermore, the changes working capital items reported on the balance sheet may differ from the change reported on the cash flow statement. This can occur for several reasons, including acquisitions, dispositions, non-wholly-owned subsidiaries, or exchange rate effects.

AT&T presented its operating cash flows (reproduced below) in indirect method *format*:

AT&T Inc.
Consolidated Statements of Cash Flows
Dollars in millions, increase (decrease) in cash and cash equivalents

	2006	2005	2004
Operating Activities			
Net income	$ 7,356	$ 4,786	$ 5,887
Adjustments to reconcile net income to net cash provided by operating activities:			
Depreciation and amortization	9,907	7,643	7,564
Undistributed earnings from investments in equity affiliates	(1,946)	(451)	(542)
Provision for uncollectible accounts	586	744	761
Amortization of investment tax credits	(28)	(21)	(32)
Deferred income tax (benefit) expense	(87)	(658)	646
Net gain on sales of investments	(10)	(135)	(939)
Income from discontinued operations, net of tax	-	-	(908)
Retirement benefit funding	-	-	(2,232)
Changes in operating assets and liabilities:			
Accounts receivable	519	(94)	282
Other current assets	30	34	(102)
Accounts payable and accured liabilities	(2,213)	74	408
Stock-based compensation tax benefit	(18)	(3)	(5)
Other-net	1,519	1,055	162
Total adjustments	$ 8,259	$ 8,188	$ 5,063
Net Cash Provided by Operating Activities	$15,615	$12,974	$10,950

The direct method presentation attempts to mirror the income statement, but on a cash basis rather than an accrual basis. Therefore, it would not start with net income, but rather from cash collected from customers. This can be estimated as sales plus the change in accounts receivable.

The second line on a direct method cash flow statement is cash paid to suppliers. This can be estimated by taking cost of goods sold from the income statement and subtracting the changes in two working capital accounts from the indirect method presentation of cash flows: inventory and accounts payable.

Other cash operating expenses can be estimated in a similar manner. In AT&T's case, this means adjusting selling, general and administrative expense by subtracting the changes in other working capital accounts as follows: $15{,}511 - 30 - (18) - 1519 = 13{,}980$ in 2006. This measure is an imprecise estimate, as it is lumping several categories together. If the company had separately disclosed, for example, wages payable, this could be used to offset SG&A while changes in rent payable could offset rent expense. Wherever the "plug" is used to fill any gaps that did not have an appropriate offset between the income and cash flow statements, the investor should be aware of the imprecision involved in the estimate.

To finish producing the direct method cash flow statement, we need to account for any cash flows related to income statement "other income and expense" items. Recall that accounting standards require separate disclosure of cash paid for interest and for taxes. AT&T provides this disclosure in Note 13 to its 10K, partially reproduced below:

Statements of Cash Flows	2006	2005	2004
Cash paid during the year for:			
Interest	$1,666	$1,395	$1,043
Income taxes, net of refunds	2,777	2,038	506

The other income and expense items are interest received, equity in net income of affiliates, and other income. Since interest received and payments from affiliates are inflows, we put them at the top of our direct method presentation. The equity in net income from affiliates was not all received as a cash inflow, so only the net amount (less the cash flow statement adjustment) is recorded. The information available was sufficient to create a report that came close to the cash from operations reported indirectly, but a plug was still needed to make the statements "foot," or agree with each other.

Given this information, it is now possible to recast the indirect method presentation of cash flow from operations into a direct method presentation as follows (italicized data represent significant assumption effects that cannot be verified from the financial statements):

	2006	2005	2004
Cash collected from customers	$63,574	$43,670	$41,015
Cash collected from affiliates	97	158	331
Cash received as interest	16	14	922
Equals total cash receipts	$63,687	$43,842	$42,268
less			
Cash paid to suppliers	29,562	18,935	16,953
Cash operating expenses	13,962	9,855	9,847
Cash paid for interest	1,666	1,395	1,043
Cash paid into retirement accounts	-	-	2,232
Cash paid for taxes	2,777	2,038	506
Other cash payments (receipts)	105	(1,355)	737
Cash from operating activities	$15,615	$12,974	$10,950

For more information:

Cash Flow Statement
For the month ended January 31, 2002

Operating Activities	
Net Income	$ 7,000
Plus Depreciation Expense	1,000
Less Gain on Sale of Stock	(500)
Less Increase in Accounts Rec.	(10,000)
Less Increase in Inventory	(5,000)
Plus Increase in Interest Pay.	20,000
Plus Increase in Interest Pay.	500
Cash flow from operating activities	$ 13,000
Investing Activites	
Purchase of equipment	$ (60,000)
Purchase of securities	(3,000)
Sale of securities	3,500
Cash flow from investing activities	$ (59,500)
Financing Activities	
Issuance of stock	$200,000
Increase in notes payable	50,000
Repurchase of treasury stock	(100)
Cash flow from financing activities	$249,900
Total cash flow	$203,400
Beginning cash	0
Ending cash	$203,400

This indirect format links the cash from operating activities to the accrual accounting income statement results, clarifying the distinction between the two. The income statement reflects the operations of the firm, measured on the accrual basis, rather than on a cash basis. Most of the items in an income statement are related to operating activities as defined by the cash flow statement rules. Therefore, it is possible to reconcile the net income from the income statement to the cash from operating activities. This is accomplished by removing the effects of items that appear on the income statement but do not affect cash such as depreciation and amortization expense, items where the timing between accrual and cash is different (e.g., changes in accounts receivable, accounts payable, prepaids) as well as a few items that appear on the income statement but are not categorized as operating activities for cash flow purposes (e.g., gains or losses from sale of PP&E—remember, cash flows from sale of PP&E are included in the investing activities section).

Companies can choose to do one of the following:

➤ Report the cash flow statement under the direct method, with an indirect reconciliation provided as supplementary information.
➤ Report the cash flow statement under the indirect method.

Understandably, most firms opt to create only one format, the indirect method, and present it on the face of the cash flow statement. Only rarely does a firm provide the direct method format.

Cash Flow Statement—The Direct Method (for the Month Ended January 31, 2008)

Operating Activities

Cash collected from customers	$ XXXXX
Cash paid for rent	($XXXXX)
Cash paid to employees	($ XXX)
Cash paid for utilities	($ XXXX)

Cash flow from operating activities XXXX (may be positive or negative)

Cash Flow Statement
For the month ended January 31, 2002

Operating Activities	
Cash collected from customers	$ 20,000
Cash paid for rent	(2,000)
Cash paid to employees	(3,000)
Cash paid for utilities	(2,000)
Cash flow from operating activities	$ 13,000
Investing Activities	
Purchase of equipment	$ (60,000)
Purchase of securities	(3,000)
Sale of securities	3,500
Cash flow from investing activities	$ (59,500)
Financing Activities	
Issuance of stock	$200,000
Increase in notes payable	50,000
Repurchase of treasury stock	(100)
Cash flow from financing activities	$249,900
Total cash flow	$203,400
Beginning cash	0
Ending cash	$203,400

In the direct method format, each line of the operating activities section represents a sum of all checks or deposits in a particular category. For example, the operating activities section would include such items as cash received from customers; cash paid to suppliers; cash paid for interest; cash paid for wages; cash paid for research and development; cash paid for selling, general, and administrative costs; and any other relevant summary lines.

The investing activities section would include such items as cash paid for acquiring capital assets and cash received from disposals of the same classes of assets. Also included in this section would be the cash paid to invest in the stock of another firm, as well as the proceeds from the subsequent sale of the stock.

The financing activities section would include cash received from stockholders' investing in the firm and any cash returned to stockholders, whether in the form of stock repurchases or dividends paid. The liability component of financing activities would include cash received from debt holders who have loaned money to the firm during the period and any principal payments made by the firm back to those debt holders.

Both U.S. GAAP and IAS encourage companies to present operating cash flows using the direct-method format, but another format, the indirect method, is also available. The direct format would provide the summarized detail from the cash account, as described above, corresponding to deposits made and checks written. The items in this intuitive format are straightforward and easy for the analyst to understand. In fact, under both IAS and U.S. GAAP, the financing and investing activities sections are presented in just this manner.

Appendix 4.2: ASC 230 Summary

This Statement (ASC 230, formerly SFAS 95, as Amended in SFAS 104) establishes standards for cash flow reporting. It . . . requires a statement of cash flows as part of a full set of financial statements for all business enterprises in place of a statement of changes in financial position.

This Statement requires that a statement of cash flows classify cash receipts and payments according to whether they stem from operating, investing, or financing activities and provides definitions of each category.

This Statement encourages enterprises to report cash flows from operating activities directly by showing major classes of operating cash receipts and payments (the direct method).

Enterprises that choose not to show operating cash receipts and payments are required to report the same amount of net cash flow from operating activities indirectly by adjusting net income to reconcile it to net cash flow from operating activities (the indirect or reconciliation method) by removing the effects of (a) all deferrals of past operating cash receipts and payments and all accruals of expected future operating cash receipts and payments and (b) all items that are included in net income that do not affect operating cash receipts and payments. If the direct method is used, a reconciliation of net income and net cash flow from operating activities is required to be provided in a separate schedule.

This Statement requires that a statement of cash flows report the reporting currency equivalent of foreign currency cash flows, using the current exchange rate at the time of the cash flows. The effect of exchange rate changes on cash held in foreign currencies is reported as a separate item in the reconciliation of beginning and ending balances of cash and cash equivalents.

This Statement also requires that information about investing and financing activities not resulting in cash receipts or payments in the period be provided separately.

Appendix 4.3: Summary of IAS 7

Objective of IAS 7

The objective of IAS 7 is to require the presentation of information about the historical changes in cash and cash equivalents of an enterprise by means of a statement of cash flows, which classifies cash flows during the period according to operating, investing, and financing activities.

Fundamental Principle in IAS 7

All enterprises that prepare financial statements in conformity with IFRSs are required to present a statement of cash flows. [IAS 7.1]

The statement of cash flows analyses changes in cash and cash equivalents during a period. Cash and cash equivalents comprise cash on hand and demand deposits, together with short-term, highly liquid investments that are readily convertible to a known amount of cash, and that are subject to an insignificant risk of changes in value. Guidance notes indicate that an investment normally meets the definition of a cash equivalent when it has a maturity of three months or less from the date of acquisition. Equity investments are normally excluded, unless they are in substance a cash equivalent (e.g. preferred shares acquired within three months of their specified redemption date). Bank overdrafts which are repayable on demand and which form an integral part of an enterprise's cash management are also included as a component of cash and cash equivalents. [IAS 7.7–8]

Presentation of the Statement of Cash Flows

Cash flows must be analyzed between operating, investing and financing activities. [IAS 7.10]

Key principles specified by IAS 7 for the preparation of a statement of cash flows are as follows:

➤ **Operating activities** are the main revenue-producing activities of the enterprise that are not investing or financing activities, so operating cash flows include cash received from customers and cash paid to suppliers and employees. [IAS 7.14]

➤ **Investing activities** are the acquisition and disposal of long-term assets and other investments that are not considered to be cash equivalents. [IAS 7.6]

➤ **Financing activities** are activities that alter the equity capital and borrowing structure of the enterprise. [IAS 7.6]

➤ Interest and dividends received and paid may be classified as operating, investing, or financing cash flows, provided that they are classified consistently from period to period. [IAS 7.31]

➤ Cash flows arising from taxes on income are normally classified as operating, unless they can be specifically identified with financing or investing activities. [IAS 7.35]

➤ For operating cash flows, the direct method of presentation is encouraged, but the indirect method is acceptable. [IAS 7.18]

The **direct method** shows each major class of gross cash receipts and gross cash payments. The operating cash flows section of the statement of cash flows under the direct method would appear something like this:

Cash receipts from customers	xx,xxx
Cash paid to suppliers	xx,xxx
Cash paid to employees	xx,xxx
Cash paid for other operating expenses	xx,xxx
Interest paid	xx,xxx
Income taxes paid	xx,xxx
Net cash from operating activities	**xx,xxx**

The **indirect method** adjusts accrual basis net profit or loss for the effects of non-cash transactions. The operating cash flows section of the statement of cash flows under the indirect method would appear something like this:

Profit before interest and income taxes		xx,xxx
Add back depreciation		xx,xxx
Add back amortization of goodwill		xx,xxx
Increase in receivables		xx,xxx
Decrease in inventories		xx,xxx
Increase in trade payables		xx,xxx
Interest expense	xx,xxx	
Less Interest accrued but not yet paid	xx,xxx	
Interest paid		xx,xxx
Income taxes paid		xx,xxx
Net cash from operating activities		**xx,xxx**

➤ The exchange rate used for translation of transactions denominated in a foreign currency and the cash flows of a foreign subsidiary should be the rate in effect at the date of the cash flows. [IAS 7.25]

➤ Cash flows of foreign subsidiaries should be translated at the exchange rates prevailing when the cash flows took place. [IAS 7.26]

➤ As regards the cash flows of associates and joint ventures, where the equity method is used, the statement of cash flows should report only cash flows between the investor and the investee; where proportionate consolidation is used, the cash flow statement should include the venturer's share of the cash flows of the investee. [IAS 7.37–38]

➤ Aggregate cash flows relating to acquisitions and disposals of subsidiaries and other business units should be presented separately and classified as investing activities, with specified additional disclosures. The aggregate cash paid or received as consideration should be reported net of cash and cash equivalents acquired or disposed of. [IAS 7.39]

➤ Cash flows from investing and financing activities should be reported gross by major class of cash receipts and major class of cash payments except for the following cases, which may be reported on a net basis: [IAS 7.22–24].

  ➤ Cash receipts and payments on behalf of customers (for example, receipt and repayment of demand deposits by banks, and receipts collected on behalf of and paid over to the owner of a property)

  ➤ Cash receipts and payments for items in which the turnover is quick, the amounts are large, and the maturities are short, generally less than three months (for example, charges and collections from credit card customers, and purchase and sale of investments)

  ➤ Cash receipts and payments relating to fixed maturity deposits

  ➤ Cash advances and loans made to customers and repayments thereof

➤ Investing and financing transactions which do not require the use of cash should be excluded from the statement of cash flows, but they should be separately disclosed elsewhere in the financial statements. [IAS 7.43]

➤ The components of cash and cash equivalents should be disclosed, and a reconciliation presented to amounts reported in the statement of financial position. [IAS 7.45]

➤ The amount of cash and cash equivalents held by the enterprise that is not available for use by the group should be disclosed, together with a commentary by management. [IAS 7.48]

You will find sample IFRS statements of cash flows in our *Model IFRS Financial Statements*.

Notes

1. Jan Barton, Bow Hanson, and Grace Pownall, "Which Performance Measures Do Investors Value the Most—and Why?" op. cit., Chapter 1, note 66.

2. Karl Marx, *Das Kapital: A Critique of Political Economy* (Washington, DC: Regnery Publishing, 2000), chapter 3, Money, The Circulation of Commodities, pp. 72 ff. Originally published in German as *Das Kapital*.

3. As noted in Appendix B, double-entry accounting, the foundation for the balance sheet, was first described in Fr. Luca Pacioli's *Summa de arithmetica, geometria, proportioni et proportionalita* [Everything about Arithmetic, Geometry, Proportions, and Proportionalith] (Venice, 1494).

4. "Historically, the 'earnings power view'. . . came about because of investor needs in the late nineteenth century to understand a company's current and future ability to generate a return" (Joel Jameson, "How FASB and the IASB Should Apply Hicksian Theory to Calculate Income," in *Research in Accounting Regulation*, vol. 18, edited by Gary J. Previts, Thomas R. Robeson, and Nandini Chandler (Amsterdam: Elsevier, 2006).)

5. "In the 1940s," according to the Association of Chartered Accountants in the United States (ACAU), "the accounting profession increasingly used the funds statement to measure the actual flow of monies, rather than simply the sum of working capital changes between balance sheet dates. The funds statement increasingly became a staple for the financial statement and, in 1971, the American Institute of Certified Public Accountants began requiring its inclusion in stockholders' annual reports." (Association of Chartered Accountants in the United States, acaus.org.)

6. Interview with Rocky Lee, partner, DLA Piper Beijing, China, July 30, 2009. See also Zhe Lu, A. Liebman, and Zhao Yang Dong, "Power Generation Investment Opportunities Evaluation: A Comparison Between Net Present Value and Real Options Approach," *Power Engineering Society General Meeting, 2006, IEEE* (2006). Zhe Lu et al. note that "the traditional net present value (NPV) criteria has the ability to capture the present value of the project's future cash flow, but it fails to assess the value brought by market uncertainty and management flexibility. By contrast with NPV, the real options approach (ROA) method has the advantage to combining the uncertainty and flexibility in evaluation process."

7. According to the ACAU (note 3), the rise of the cash flow statement coincided with a rise in institutional investors.

8. International Accounting Standards Board, Chapter 1, "The Objective of Financial Reporting May 2008," in *An Improved Conceptual Framework for Financial Reporting*, http://www.iasb.org/NR/rdonlyres/464C50

D6-00FD-4BE7-A6FF-1BEAD353CD97/0/conceptual_framework_
exposure_draft.pdf.

9. Barry J. Epstein and Eva K. Jermakowicz, *Interpretation and Application of
    International Financial Reporting Standards* (Hoboken, N.J.: John Wiley &
    Sons, 2007), 91–97.

10. The analyst has alternatives, according to one classic financial article: "A
    controversial issue is the question of whether the expected values of net
    cash flows should be discounted with a 'risk-adjusted' rate or whether such
    flows should first be adjusted for risk and then be discounted at a 'risk free'
    rate" (Lutz Haegert and R. M. Edelson, "An Analysis of the Kuhn-Tucker
    Conditions of Stochastic Programming with Reference to the Estimation
    of Discount Rates and Risk Premia," *Journal of Business Finance* 1, no. 3
    (September 1974): 319–455).

11. Stanley Foster Reed, Alexandra Reed Lajoux, and H. Peter Nesvold, *The
    Art of M&A: A Merger/ Acquisition/Buyout Guide*, 4th ed. (New York:
    McGraw-Hill, 2007).

12. See, for example, Co Analysis, from Georgia Tech professor Charles Mul-
    ford (http://cwmulford.com/CoAnalysis.htm). The Financial Statement
    Analysis Model consists of several Microsoft Excel worksheets designed
    to do a complete financial statement and cash flow analysis of a company.
    Three years of balance sheet and income statement data are necessary to
    make the model run.

13. Securities and Exchange Commission Releases Nos. 33-8350 (www.sec
    .gov/rules/interp/33-8350.htm) and 34-48960 (http://www.law.uc.edu/CCL/
    regS-K/SK303.html).

14. Ibid.

15. "Canadian Performance Reporting Board, "MD&A Disclosures in Vola-
    tile and Uncertain Times," *CPR Alert: Canadian Performance Reporting*,
    February 2009, http://www.cica.ca/research-and-guidance/mda-and-
    business-reporting/cpr-alert-issues/item13072.pdf. *Note*: The Canadian
    Performance Reporting Board has not adopted, endorsed, approved, or
    otherwise acted on this bulletin. Contributions to this *CPR Alert* from
    Deloitte's Peter Chant, FCA are greatly appreciated."

16. InvestSign is a service that helps companies to formulate project, analyze
    with finance and risk analysis, run Monte Carlo simulations, perform sensi-
    tivity analyses, export financial reports such as investment costs, operational
    costs, financial means, financial sheets and other reports, solve optimiza-
    tion problems, and create decision support.

17. The source for this cluster of formulas is InvestSign, http://www.investsign-
    home.com/Publications_Evaluation_methods.htm.

18. InvestSign (see note 14).

19. A. J. Merrett and Allen Sykes, *The Finance and Analysis of Capital Projects* (New York: John Wiley & Sons, Inc., 1963). See the review at http://www .actuaries.org.uk/__data/assets/pdf_file/0020/25517/0221-0229.pdf.

20. *Journal of International Accounting*, Vol. 91 (1965), pp. 221-229. http://www.actuaries.org.uk/__data/assets/pdf_file/0020/25517/0221-0229.pdf.

21. Alfred Rappaport and Michael Mouboussin, *Expectations Investing* (New York: McGraw-Hill, 2001).

22. This is an updated version of a chart that appears in Stanley Foster Reed, Alexandra Reed Lajoux, and H. Peter Nesvold, *The Art of M&A: A Merger/Acquisition/Buyout Guide*, 4th ed. (New York: McGraw-Hill, 2007).

23. For a good explanation of FAS 144, see http://www.cbe.uidaho.edu/ Acct592/CourseMaterials/FASB%20Update/FASB%20144%20Impairme nt%20of%20Assets.doc.

24. "November 2009: IASB proposes to amend IAS 39 on impairment," http:// www.iasplus.com/agenda/ias39impairment.htm and http://www.iasplus .com/standard/ias39.htm. See also http://www.aicpa.org/caq/download/ CAQ_Alert_2009_97.pdf. The IASM and the FASB are working together on fair value issues and will publish a joint standard by September 2010 (http://www.iasplus.com/agenda/fairvalue.htm).

25. For a discussion of the end of FIFO accounting and other global accounting issues, see http://ifrs.com/updates/aicpa/joa_news_oct.html.

26. "Cash Flow Trends and Their Fundamental Drivers: A Continuing Look, Comprehensive Industry Review (Qtr 4 2008)," © 2009 by the College of Management, Georgia Institute of Technology, Atlanta, GA 30332-0520, http://mgt.gatech.edu/fac_research/centers_initiatives/finlab/finlab_files/ ga_tech_cf_q1_summary_09.pdf.

27. Dr. Charles W. Mulford and Dr. Eugene E. Komiskey, *Cash Flow Reporting by Financial Companies: A Look at Commercial Banks*, July 2009 (College of Management, Georgia Institute of Technology, Atlanta, GA). http://mgt .gatech.edu/fac_research/centers_initiatives/finlab/reports.html.

28. "We surveyed the cash flow reporting practices for a sample of fifteen of the largest, independent and publicly-traded U.S. commercial banks. We adjusted their reported operating cash flows for classification differences noted in the treatment of federal funds transactions, for non-cash transfers of loans and investments between categories that impact operating cash flow, and for the effects of acquisitions on operating cash flow. In the adjustment process we found notable changes to operating cash flow. In particular, we saw declines in adjusted operating cash flow for Bank of America, JP Morgan and Wells Fargo, and increases in adjusted operating cash flow for Citigroup, Fifth Third Bancorp, KeyCorp, PNC Financial

and SunTrust Banks." http://mgt.gatech.edu/fac_research/centers_initiatives/finlab/reports.html

29. Dennis Schoen, "The Relevance of Discounted Cash Flow (DCF) and Economic Value Added (EVA) for the Valuation of Banks," dissertation, Northumbria Business School, http://www.diplomarbeiten24.de/vorschau/27621.html.

30. The Quantitative Finance group on Linkedin.com had an extended discussion on this topic after June 2009, when Chris Cloke Brown, managing partner of Brave Partners, posted the question, "How do you price long-term equity volatility?" This would seem to be a recurrent question that life insurers and pension funds wrestle with, especially when there are sharp drops in the markets. The question is, how much does the price of an equity today matter when it is held to meet a liability in twenty years' time? The next chapter deals with this question.

31. This appendix was created by valuation expert Thomas Robinson. His *Financial Education* web site is at http://financial-education.com.

CHAPTER 5

Valuation Based on Securities Prices

Financial markets should not be treated as a physics laboratory but as a form of history.

—George Soros, "Anatomy of a Crisis" April 9, 2010
(at King's College, Cambridge)

TO ESTIMATE THE VALUE of a company's securities, investors can study its assets, earnings, and cash flow—the subjects of our opening chapters. But another indicator of securities' value—a deceptively simpler one—is their current *price*: the dollars and cents that other investors are willing to pay for them right now on the open market. This chapter is for prospective investors who already know about a company's financial statements but who want to glean information from current stock prices as well.

It may seem obvious at best—and tautological at worst—to say that a security's current price tells you something significant about its value. But in fact what does price, by itself, really tell you? It indicates only what other investors are willing to pay during the time of the price: it sets a temporary floor for buying today. A security's price shows the market's expectations about the company right now. The real question for investors is, what will the price be in the future when it's time to sell? Thus price-based analysis anticipates price change from the moment of purchase to the moment of sale, whether one day or 30 years hence. This analysis varies according to the investor's theory of stock market values.

This chapter compares different stock market value theories and explains their relevance to different kinds of investors.

Overview of Securities Prices

Public markets are the generally accepted mode for valuing securities, but the prices they set may miss the mark when it comes to true value. Lord John Maynard Keynes famously characterized the process of valuing publicly traded securities as a beauty contest. He noted that investors are highly intelligent people trying to guess what the average person thinks.[1] And in 1993, Peter Drucker wrote to the senior author of this book:

> And one of the basic problems is that management has no way to judge by what criteria outside shareholders value and appraise performance—the stock market is surely the least reliable judge or, at best, only one judge and one that is subject to so many other influences that it is practically impossible to disentangle what, of the stock market appraisal, reflects the company's performance and what reflects caprice, affects the whims of securities analysts, short-term fashions and the general level of the economy and of the market rather than the performance of a company itself.[2]

Drucker's wisdom notwithstanding, the world needs marketplace values even though they are demonstrably flawed. Economists have gone so far as to base value theories on the premise that all information is known by the market—the "efficient market" thesis. Though this view may be a convenient myth for those who wish to use stock price as a short cut to the hard work of valuation, it is demonstrably untrue. One need look no further than 10 percent, $1 trillion drop in equity values on May 6, 2010, to understand that the market can be an overly emotional creature. True, the drop was only temporary, and due largely to technical glitches. Still, there were enough panicked sellers to show the mad side of markets. The great success that many investors have in purchasing and selling securities is the best evidence of "inefficiency."

Bad values are better than none. They make up a universally agreed-on frame of reference that investors and others can use to make comparisons between companies, between industries, and between countries. A valuation reference point can also help companies determine compensation for executives, account for collateral in transactions, and fulfill ratios required by statute. So investors who understand the thinking behind valuation methods can do a better job of analyzing compensation, collateral, and statutory ratios.

In this century, the marketplace has weakened its connection to corporate information and instead has become itself the object of a massive statistical orientation for so-called "quant" analysis, classification, security design, and trading. Quant has become the largest industry in the world and provides the largest paychecks.

Sophisticated mathematical thinkers would persist and explain that numbers are not the precise measure of reality commonly assumed but rather, in their turn, also approximate expressions. This is the central premise of this chapter: that valuation based on security prices is a matter of estimation, requiring as many tools of knowledge and thought as possible. This book is only a bare beginning in offering these tools, and it will present them one at a time.

The "Fix"

Everyone knows the market is an amalgam of utterly different energies, ranging from the delusions of fools to profit maximizing formulas of geniuses—sometimes emanating from the same individual in a single day! No sane investor believes that these energies can be identified, quantified, and ranked in any definitive way. But investors have come to rely on the innocence of these energies. The July 10 Goldman Sachs settlement, in which the company neither admitted nor denied charges of fraud, introduced the element of premeditation and front-running into the market—a flaw that could bring down the system if not addressed. As in the case of juries, all manner of ignorance can be tolerated, but not a fix.

Robert A. G. Monks

Definition of Stock Price

Even assuming that a reported price paid for a security is a proxy for value, the question is which quoted price to use. There are several possibilities.

Should investors use the current closing price or the average price over the past year, month, week, or day? In the mergers and acquisitions area, analysts often use a 14-day or 20-day figure, that is, the average of the closing prices of the security over the past 14 or 20 trading days. For initial public offerings (IPOs) and secondary markets, shorter time periods are used. (See Bob Ferris's comments about IPOs in Chapter 8.)

Furthermore, few people consider the other factors that affect the price of a company's securities. Are takeover rumors inflating the price? Are overhanging blocks depressing the price? What is the trading supply? Has an investment banker—or, worse, a deal principal—been front-running on the stock? These things not only can happen, they do.[3]

In this chapter, unless otherwise defined, *price* is the most recent day's *closing price* in an ordinary *noncontrolling* transaction. The focus is on *closing price* to distinguish it from other prices. For example, instead of closing price, some valuation methods consider a day's price to be at the midpoint between the opening and closing prices because closing prices are subject to some manipulation.[4] Also, the focus is on ordinary *noncontrolling* transactions because Chapter 8 presents a discussion of *controlling* transactions (mergers or acquisitions). The two types of transactions are substantially different (see **Exhibit 5.1**):

➤ In a *noncontrolling* transaction, investors value stock while assuming that the current board and management will stay the same. Future changes in the decision makers will be gradual, coming

EXHIBIT 5.1 Controlling versus Noncontrolling Transactions

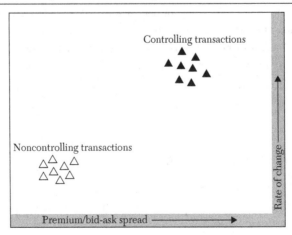

from a combination of board rotation, management succession, or shareholder involvement (proxy voting on governance matters). Investors buy and sell in an open market. The bid-ask spread (the difference between what the buyer will pay and what seller will sell for) is narrow, reflecting ordinary supply and demand.

➤ In a *controlling* transaction, investors value stock while assuming that there will be a new board and management. Future changes may be rapid—coming from postmerger management. Investors buy and sell via a tender offer with a premium price. The bid-ask spread is wide; buyers set a premium price to provoke selling. Sellers evaluate that premium and decide whether to sell or hold.[5]

Seven Basic Points of Departure to Determining the Value of a Security

So, for the purposes of this chapter, what information can we glean from a closing stock price in a noncontrolling transaction? The answer depends on the type of investor.

Investors can make buy, sell, and hold decisions in a variety of ways based on how they think the stock market behaves:

➤ If investors think the stock market responds to the financial state of companies (the subject of Chapters 2 through 4), they buy stocks that are undervalued, using *fundamental analysis*.

➤ If they think the market follows patterns (generally going up and down), they look at securities to buy at the bottom of a pattern, using *technical analysis*.

➤ If they believe that stock prices move randomly toward equilibrium in an efficient market, they *diversify*.

➤ If they believe that the market is somewhat efficient but has enough noise to merit analysis, they engage in *expectations analysis*.

➤ If they believe that it is possible to create a formula based on any or all of the preceding assumptions, they engage in *algorithmic trading*.

➤ If they think that some events—aka *Black Swans*—cannot be anticipated and can cause large losses it is important to avoid, they strive to anticipate and avoid major risk.

➤ If they think the market can have equilibrium but has feedback loops that can cause major self-delusional mistakes, they bet against the crowd judiciously, to avoid the bad effects of *reflexivity*.

We'll look at each of these seven approaches to valuation based on stock price, and then, after a brief discussion of the equity premium, conclude with our usual "lens" on value.

Approach 1: Ratios or Formulas That Include Stock Prices

Fundamental analysts look at stock price in relation to financial reports, and they buy stocks that have a low stock price in relation to reported financials (e.g., a low price-to-earnings or conversely a high earnings per share). If you want to know what the stock price tells you, factoring in fundamentals—or value—is always a good idea. The most famous investor known for this approach is Warren Buffett, but he's not the only practitioner. A whole class of mutual funds advertise themselves as "value funds"—funds that buy stock with a low ratio of stock price to key accounting variables, such as the price-to-earnings (P/E) ratio.

To maintain a fundamentalist view of stock performance, an investor must have reasonable confidence in three key propositions:

1. Financial statements reflect current financial performance.
2. Past financial performance can help predict future financial performance.
3. Stock prices respond to reported financial performance.

These assumptions are true enough to be useful, but each requires a caveat:

1. Regarding the first proposition, as seen in previous chapters, financial statements do not (and are not intended to) mirror financial performance exactly. Interpretation is required.
2. As for the second proposition, history's lesson is that past performance provides clues, but no guarantees. Even if financial statements could mirror performance exactly, the past is not the same as the future.
3. Finally, as for the third proposition, stock prices do not always respond in the same way to reports of financial performance.

Research suggests, for example, that if a firm's financial reporting is more *transparent* than that of its peers (i.e., it discloses more information with higher accuracy), investors will pay more for the stock. And investors will pay an especially high premium for transparency in markets with low investor protections.[6] In a similar vein, high earnings announcements have their highest impact in early-stage IPOs; they have an increasingly lessened impact on stock prices the longer a company is operating, and the more additional information it generates about its performance.[7]

On a macroeconomic scale, Tobin's Q ratio (comparing market value of equities to net worth) could be considered a way of valuing equity based on fundamentals. For the market as a whole, as well as for individual companies, the Federal Reserve provides the data in its annual and quarterly Flow of Funds Reports. Over time (from 1900 through mid-2010), the average Q ratio is 0.70. During periods of exuberance it has been above that point, while during periods of pessimism it has fallen below it. As of mid-2010, the Q ratio stood at 0.68 percent.[8]

Another approach is called the relative Graham value (RGV), named after Benjamin Graham, coauthor of the classic *Security Analysis*. The value V in RGV can be determined as follows:

$$V = \left(EPS \times \frac{8.5 + 2g \times 4.4}{Y} \right)$$

where

V	=	intrinsic value
EPS	=	the company's last 12-month earnings per share
8.5	=	the constant represents the appropriate P/E ratio for a no-growth company as proposed by Graham
g	=	the company's long-term (five years) earnings growth estimate
4.4	=	the average yield of high-grade corporate bonds in 1962, when this model was introduced
Y	=	the current yield on AAA corporate bonds

To apply this approach to a buy-or-sell decision, determine each company's RGV by dividing the stock's intrinsic value V^* by its current price P:

$$RGV = \frac{V^*}{P}$$

An RGV less than 1 indicates an overvalued stock and should not be bought, whereas an RGV greater than 1 indicates an undervalued stock and should be bought.

Because of the measures it uses, difficulties may be encountered.

Approach 2: Technical Analysis of Stock Price Movements

So-called technical analysis, also known as "charting," tries to predict the movement of stock prices based on past movements. The analyst looks at price changes and attempts to detect recurrent patterns, such as waves.

The application of advanced mathematics to this approach has given it the nickname "technical," but the fundamental notion underlying such analysis is the opposite of technical; it is mass psychology—even hysteria. At times, it seems more like reading tea leaves—a common dig at charting. So despite some solid evidence that technical approaches can help as stock movement predictors,[9] the academic community has tended to favor analysis based on company financial performance (fundamentals) rather than market movements.

The general consensus is that technical approaches work but that they must always be tempered by common sense. Charting approaches cannot always be converted into an algorithm that works automatically. Some human intervention is needed. During the recent bear market, six of eight technical methods tested failed to anticipate movements and so lost money, according to one study for Bloomberg.[10] When asked to explain the seeming failures of their models, the chartists typically explain that their approaches have to be combined with others.

Here are some of the more common charting approaches, labeled geometrically and organized alphabetically.[11]

Angles

One basic approach to charting involves angles (see **Exhibit 5.2**). The best-known approach was developed by William D. Gann.[12] Calculating a *Gann angle* is equivalent to finding the derivative of a line on a chart. Each geometrical angle (or line) divides time and price into proportionate parts. Gann proposed a series of angles: 1×1, 1×2, 1×3, 1×4, and so forth. The 1×1, or the 45°, angle represents one unit of price for one unit of time. Gann drew a perfect square and then drew a diagonal line

Exhibit 5.2 Gann Angles

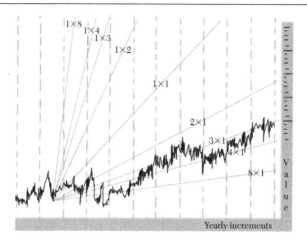

from one corner of the square to the other to show a 1×1 angle, which moves up one point per day. A 2×1 moves up two points per day. The emphasis is on change. Angles—by definition—go either up or down.

Bands

Bands are horizontal trendlines running across a graph of stock price movements. One well-known band is the Bollinger band, a technical trading tool created by John Bollinger, president of Bollinger Capital Management, in the early 1980s (see **Exhibit 5.3**).

Bollinger bands define highs and lows for stock price movements. The bands manifest themselves as a trio of curves. The middle band, which delineates a moving average, serves as the base for the upper band and the lower band. The distance between the upper or lower band and the middle band is determined by volatility, based on the standard deviation of the data used for the average. The inventor of the band suggests default parameters of 20 periods and two standard deviations, but these may be adjusted to suit an investor's purposes.[13]

Bollinger bands can help an investor see when a security rises too high or falls too low by comparing its price to the average level over the past 20 days. According to the Bollinger system, if the stock gains or drops too much from the average—two standard deviations or more—a turnaround may be at hand.

Band systems should not be automated for purposes of trading, but they can be used to check trades.

Exhibit 5.3 Bollinger Bands

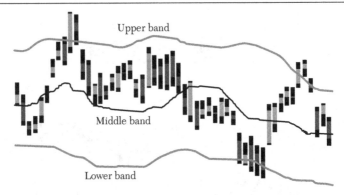

Candlesticks

The candlestick method depicts each day's results as a candlestick—a long vertical line with a wick (closing price) and tail (opening price). If the closing price is higher than the opening price, the candlestick is hollow (white). If the closing price is lower, the candlestick is filled (black). The technique was developed in the eighteenth century by a Japanese rice trader, Munehisa Homma. Today, candlestick gurus include Steve Nison and Greg Morris.[14] (See **Exhibit 5.4.**)

A number of methodologies use candlestick charting. One source, based on the work of Nison and Morris, produces a proprietary score using the following formula:

$$\text{Day Score for individual securities:} \quad \frac{x \times \sqrt{z_1}}{y \times y} \times 1{,}000$$

$$\text{Day Score for individual candle patterns} = \frac{x \times \sqrt{z_2}}{y \times y} \times 1{,}000$$

where

n = 1st, 2nd, 3rd, 4th, 5th

x = n day median gain for the given security and candle pattern

y = standard deviation of all n day median gains

z_1 = count of the candle pattern found for the given security over the entire date range of the database

z_2 = count of the candle pattern found over the entire date range of the database[15]

Exhibit 5.4 Nison Candlesticks

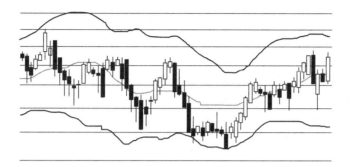

A high score represents a high reward-to-risk ratio for long positions (buy, then sell). Conversely, a low score motivates a short position (sell, then buy). For example, let us compare a stock with the following first-day percentage gains (+5%, +4%, +7%) to another stock with the following first-day percentage gains (−12%, +10%, +5%). The first stock would have a higher score than the second one.

Channels

Channels, referred to as price channels or commodity channels, help investors determine buy and sell signals based on price breakouts (see **Exhibit 5.5**). The upper price channel is the highest high over a time

Exhibit 5.5 Price Channels

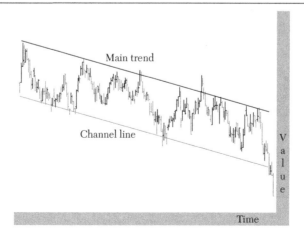

period as defined by the user, and the lower price channel is the lowest low over a time period as defined by the user.[16]

Generally, the user-defined period is 20 days.

➤ *Price channel buy signal*. Buy when the price closes above the upper bands. This is like buying a breakout above resistance; the resistance just happens to be whatever the highest high was of the past 20 trading days.

➤ *Price channel sell signal*. Sell when the price closes below the lower bands. This is like selling a breakout below support, but the support in this case is whatever the lowest low was of the previous 20 trading days.

Directional Movement

The directional movement indicator (DMI), developed by J. Welles Wilder in 1978, is a moving average of range expansion over a given period (see **Exhibit 5.6**). The default period is 14 days. The DMI distinguishes between positive and negative direction. When stock moves upward, is the movement just a blip that will correct, or is it part of a long-term trend up? The DMI attempts to make this determination. The positive directional indicator measures how strongly price moves upward, whereas the negative one does the opposite.

Each DMI is represented by a separate line. The two lines show the respective strength of the optimists and pessimists (buying bulls versus selling bears). The dominant DMI (on top of the chart) is more likely to predict the direction of price. When the lines cross over, the market is changing its directional movement. This movement is called a crossover, and some day traders use it to go long or short.

Exhibit 5.6 Directional Price Movement

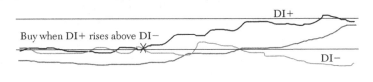

Geometry

Drummond geometry is a respected form of technical analysis (see **Exhibit 5.7**). This approach has a combination of three basic categories of trading techniques:

1. A series of short-term moving averages (P dot)
2. Short-term trendlines (Average of P dots)
3. Multiple time period overlays (multiple averages of P dots)

In the first case, short-term moving averages are calculated from the high, low, and close prices for a given period. So, for example, the investor can take prices for a stock during a three-week period. The average high, the average low, and the average closing price are averaged for week 1, week 2, and week 3. The investor then calculates a point, which is then plotted as a dot and as representative of that week. (The dot is placed within a larger bar that shows the full range of prices from high [H] to low [L] as well as close [C].)

The formula to calculate the first point is:

$$\text{Avg } [H_1, L_1, C_1] + \text{Avg } [H_2, L_2, C_2] + \text{Avg } [H_3, L_3, C_3]\}$$

The second and third points—and subsequent time periods—are calculated in the same way, and an overall average is plotted.

Exhibit 5.7 Drummond Geometry

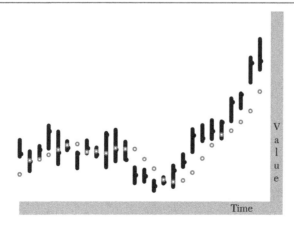

P dots tend to move in straight lines and thus are predictable during a trend. Drummond geometry says to trade with the trend if the market is on one side of the dot, but stay at the dot if the market has closed on both sides of the dot. So, for example, if the trend is $11, $12, $13, you can pay up to $14. But if the trend is $11, $12, $11, you should not offer more than $12.[17]

Investors should look at the averages that are slightly longer term than their own trends. Day traders should look at weekly averages, weekly traders at monthly averages, and monthly traders at yearly averages.

Line Charts

The simplest kind of technical analysis used in valuation is the line chart (see **Exhibit 5.8**). A line chart can show stock price movements from hour to hour during a day or from day to day during a longer time period. One simply plots daily prices over time. These zigzagging charts are so common that they have come to symbolize the stock market.

By superimposing line charts from different industries, one can see general market trends. And it is possible to see performance over time of multiple stocks or sector, relative to the stock's own performance or relative to the performance of other stocks.[18]

Moving Averages Convergence/Divergence

Another technical approach is based on moving averages convergence/divergence (MACD). This approach, developed by Gerald Appel, is

Exhibit 5.8 Line Chart

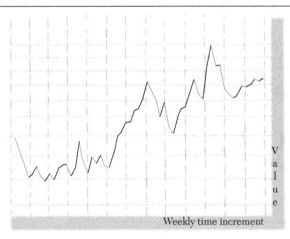

Exhibit 5.9 Appel's MACD

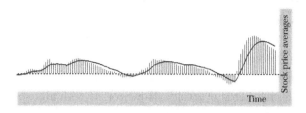

based on a moving average crossover system (see **Exhibit 5.9**).[19] It gives the investor buy and sell signals based on patterns in a histogram (called a "histogram" because vertical bars are used to show the difference between the two lines on the chart) showing faster versus slower exponential moving averages. A buy signal occurs when the faster line crosses above the slower one and both lines are below zero. A sell signal takes place when the faster line crosses below the slower one from above the zero line. Weekly signals take precedence over daily signals. An MACD histogram plots the difference between the two lines and gives even earlier warnings of trend changes.

One of the most popular moving averages is called a "golden cross." This is a short-term average moving faster than a long-term average. Crosses are defined in different ways.[20]

Parabolic Systems

This stop loss system prompts a sell if an investment does not continue to generate returns. The system is based on the shape of a parabola, from analytic geometry. These systems are required by any kind of quantitative trading.

Percentage Range

This type of chart, created by Larry Williams, calculates the difference between a security's closing price and its highest price, and then it compares the result with its average over fourteen days. Larry Williams defines the following trading rules for his %R:

➤ *Buy* when %R reaches 100 percent, five trading days have passed since 100 percent was last reached, and after which the %R again falls below 85–95 percent.

➤ *Sell* when %R reaches 0 percent, five trading days have passed since 0 percent was last reached, and after which the %R again rises to about 15/5%.

Trader Jim Wyckoff advises to sell when %R reaches 20 percent or lower (the market is overbought) and buy when it reaches 80 percent or higher (the market is oversold). However, as with all overbought or oversold indicators, wait for the indicator price to change direction before initiating any trade.

Relative Strength Indicator

A relative strength indicator (RSI) compares the magnitude of recent gains to recent losses, in order to determine whether an asset is overbought or oversold. The formula for calculating it is

$$RSI = 100 - \frac{100}{1 + RS}$$

with *RS* being the average of *x* days' up closes ÷ average of *x* days' down closes.

The RSI chart shows ranges from 1 to 100. An asset is deemed to be overbought when the RSI reaches 70 or above. Conversely, if the RSI is 30 or lower, it may be oversold and may be undervalued.[21]

Stochastics

Stochastics examines what happens in unpredictable systems (those that involve an element of chance), such as changes in share prices. When stochastics is applied to the stock market, it predicts a security's movement based on how close its price is to the highest or lowest levels.[22]

Waves

Technical analysis becomes more difficult for very long-term periods, but approaches do exist. The Elliott wave principle, like other technical approaches, identifies patterns in market prices. (See **Exhibit 5.10.**)

Exhibit 5.10 Elliott Wave

In this case, the patterns are likened to waves of two types: impulsive and corrective:

➤ An *impulsive wave* is made up of five subwaves. It moves in the *same* direction as the trend of the next larger size.

➤ A *corrective wave* is made up of three subwaves. It moves against the trend of the next larger size.

These basic patterns build to form five- and three-wave structures of increasingly larger degree.[23]

Another kind of wave theory, developed by John Ehlers, is called a mesa sine wave (see **Exhibit 5.11**). It uses two sine plots to show whether the market is in a *trend mode* (with current direction likely to continue for near future) or in a *cycle mode* (with current trends about to change).[24]

Exhibit 5.11 Ehler's Sine Wave

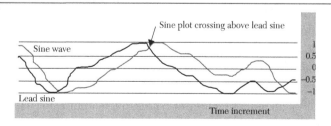

This chart contains two plots: one line depicting the sine of the selected angle over time and the other the sine of the angle advanced by 45, the lead sine. The crossings of the sine and lead sine provides a precise and advanced picture of cycle mode turning points:

➤ *Trend mode.* The plots start to "wander." In a trend mode, the sine and lead sine plots typically move into a sideways pattern around the zero point, running distant and parallel from each other.

➤ *Cycling mode.* The two plots look like a sine wave.

Approach 3: Analysis of Values According to Efficient Market–Random Walk Hypothesis

It would make analysis simple if all stock market theories could be classified as either fundamental (setting a value based on the condition of the companies) or technical (setting a value based in the movement of markets). Better yet, it is tempting to combine the two approaches for stronger analysis. But as every experienced investor knows, another theory, called the efficient (or perfect) market or random walk hypothesis, refutes both fundamentalism and technical analysis entirely.

This theory states that stock market prices already reflect fundamentals as accurately as possible. Movements simply reflect the market recalibrating itself (perfectly), based on new information that reaches participants randomly. In other words, the stock price is smarter than you can possibly be. You can't beat the market. To approximate the market, you must make a random selection of stocks (which, by definition, will be diverse.)

The random walk theory, named after a seminal book by Burton G. Malkiel, *A Random Walk Down Wall Street*,[25] basically says that the market is entirely unpredictable because it is random. However, research since Malkiel's publication indicates that stock prices do not move randomly, a finding that supports technical analysis (which sees predictable patterns) and refutes the efficient market hypothesis (which asserts randomness).[26]

The investor who adheres to this theory is not interested in valuation, whether fundamental or technical. Rather, such an investor has a highly diverse portfolio and tends to invest in index funds.

About Equity Indexes

An *index fund* has been defined as "a mutual fund or exchange-traded fund (ETF) with clearly defined rules of ownership, that are held constant regardless of market conditions."[27] Such a fund attempts to approximate the market (or a market sector), on the assumption that the market will rise and investors can go with it.

Ironically, none other than Benjamin Graham, a pioneer of fundamentals investing, anticipated the index fund. Writing his memoirs late in life, he opined:

> I have little confidence even in the ability of analysts, let alone untrained investors, to select common stocks that will give better than average results. Consequently, I feel that the standard portfolio should be to duplicate, more or less, the DJIA.[28]

How ironic: the very man who wrote a bible on value investing—a true believer in market beating—said that it can't be done. But these are his words. And he wrote them at the very time that the first real index fund was being constructed—in 1971, by bankers from Wells Fargo for the old Samsonite Corporation's pension fund. And only a few years later, indexing became widely available through mutual funds, thanks to pioneer Jack Bogle of Vanguard.[29]

Many major pension funds are significantly indexed—for example, about half for the California Public Employees Retirement System. This mode of investment is particularly attractive for public funds (funds for public sector retirees) because of restrictions on investment.

In the retail world, the percentage is lower but growing. In 2008, index funds accounted for 13 percent of equity mutual funds' total global net assets of $3.7 trillion, up from 3.3 percent in 1994, according to the Investment Company Institute.[30] The use of index funds is growing.[31]

Although index funds are contrasted with so-called actively managed funds, index funds are not entirely passive; they are rebalanced from time to time as the rules of ownership change.[32] Fees for such funds tend to be about half of the fees for active funds (e.g., 0.74 percent versus 1.46 percent),[33] but the high minimum investment needed for some index funds hardly makes them the investor's version of free checking.[34]

One does not need to be a random walk disciple to appreciate the value of indexes. Even for fundamental and/or technical analysts, indexes make sense as a way of tempering or replacing human judgment, which can be flawed (see Appendix K). For this reason, many institutional investors, out of an abundance of caution, invest part of their funds in indexes, such as the Dow Jones Industrial Average or the S&P 500.

Over the past several years, indexes have become more sensitive to investors' varying needs. Now each of the main indexes has several versions. Meanwhile, an entire professional community has grown up around indexes, and there are even awards for good indexes and for research on indexing.[35]

Approach 4: Stock Valuation Based on Expectations

Expectations is a theory developed a decade ago by Alfred Rappaport and Michael J. Mauboussin.[36] Expectations investing says that the investor should start with stock price and then use additional information to adjust the valuation. Information can include signals from managerial actions such as mergers and acquisitions and share buybacks. The investor estimates the impact of such information on share price.

As Rappaport notes, the collective wisdom of the market typically does a better job of forecasting than a single individual. So, instead of forecasting cash flows, the investor should begin with the current price and then determine the expectations for a company's future cash flows that justify the price.[37] Rappaport calls this approach "price-implied cash flow expectations." To earn above-average-market returns, investors must correctly anticipate changes in a company's prospects that are not already reflected in the current price.

The expectations investing theory is an extension and modification of Rappaport's earlier theory of free discounted cash flow (Chapter 4). Both theories fall under the general rubric of so-called shareholder value, a concept defined in various ways. One definition links it to free cash flow.[38] Another associates it with a rise in share price. Unfortunately, many investors and companies focus on short-term rises in share price, a focus that has led to distortions in company values. With a pressure to create short-term gains, companies have sacrificed long-term value. This is not what shareholder value means.[39]

Approach 5: Valuations Implicit in Algorithmic Trading

Algorithmic trading is the analysis, identification, placement, and execution of buy, sell, and hold orders based on trading strategies formulated to meet predefined trading goals.[40] The goals are expressed in algorithms, a kind of formula named after a ninth-century Persian mathematician with the last name al-Khwarizmi.[41] Research suggests that as of the date of publication for this book, approximately half of all trading is done by traders using algorithms.[42]

Of the great number of kinds of algorithms in mathematics (see Appendix E), for investment purposes, the four basic algorithms are volume-weighted average price, time-weighted average price, volume participation, and implementation shortfall (the difference between the decision price and the final execution price).[43] Clearly, none of these is based on fundamentals, the subject of Chapters 2 through 4. Rather, they are based on market prices and thus use some sort of technical analysis.[44]

"Algo trading" makes eminent sense for most market conditions. It is an approach that says that if you have criteria for investing, you should be able to express them in a formula and that, once you have done so, you can automate them to some degree. The goal of algorithmic trading is to take the human factor out of trading as much as possible to avoid the irrational aspects of fear (economic panics) and greed (irrational exuberance).[45] There is one catch, though. Sometimes the market goes through periods in which a feedback loop occurs, magnifying bad information. At those times algorithms can lead to losses. For this reason, a good program needs to have a stop loss mechanism.

There is no good reason for algorithmic trading to focus only on stock price movements. It can have more diverse criteria for trades. Bjorn Schubert predicts that algorithmic trading will become more customized and may even replace traders to some degree (but not entirely). This strongly suggests that algorithms will be keyed to fundamentals, such as the full text of earnings announcements or other financial statements. This prospect is all the more possible now that companies can use computer language to express their financial results; XBRL (extensible business reporting language) can help algo traders customize further.

As Francesco Bertoluzzo and Marco Corazza have noted, when economic agents invest in financial markets, they make decisions under uncertainty. In such a context, they want to cope with financial risk in order to maximize some predetermined measure of profitability. They call the tools used to support these decisions a "financial trading system." To create such a system (or, one might say, algorithm), the investor needs to:

➤ Identify one or more variables (e.g., closing stock price) related to the behavioral changes of one or more quantities of interest (e.g., a trading signal to buy, sell, or hold).
➤ Use the current and the past values of these variables to extract information concerning the future values of the quantities of interest.
➤ Use these predictions/information to implement a trading strategy by which to make elective trades.[46]

Clearly fundamentals may be used for such a purpose as well. Just add a program language (if, then, do, do not, etc.), and you have a trading program.[47]

Approach 6: The Black Swan Approach to Stock Price Valuation

The Black Swan approach to valuation says that, in setting the value of any asset or group of assets, the investor must allow for the possibility of a

---

Mad Scientist Myth

Articles on Wall Street's mad scientist blowing up the lab seem to come out every month in one major publication or another . . . . There is a constant theme in these articles . . . that quants generally, and quantitative risk managers specifically, missed the boat by thinking, despite all evidence to the contrary, that security returns can be modeled by a normal distribution. This is a straw man argument. It is an attack on something that no one believes.

—Richard Bookstaber, in blog of March 10, 2009, http://rick.bookstaber .com/2009/03/fat-tailed-straw-man.html breakdown in the model. In statistical terms, there are risks with tails so fat that they destabilize the system. Nicholas Taleb popularized the Black Swan in a book by that name, as well as several technical articles referencing the concept.[48]

Approach 7: Reflexivity Theory and Stock Values

Reflexivity—a theory developed by global investor George Soros (introduced in Chapter 1)—takes a tack that is very different from the efficient market/random walk theory. Rather than dismissing fundamentals and market movements altogether as irrelevant, reflexivity acknowledges their doomed interrelationship and builds an approach on that assumption. Reflexivity means that an investor's perception of a company's fundamentals (e.g., assets, earnings, and cash flow) affect the value of the company's stock. In turn, the value of the company's stock affects the fundamentals. In other words, company fundamentals and stock prices are in a continual loop: fundamentals influence stock prices and stock prices influence fundamentals. So stock prices not only mirror the value perceptions of investors, but they also influence that perception. Prices have power as well as meaning.

This much of the reflexivity theory is well-known, but there is more to it. In his 1987 book, *The Alchemy of Finance*, Soros raises a number of additional points that have not met with the attention they deserve.

Lack of Equilibrium Despite the Existence of Market

The stock market has all the attributes of a competitive market, notes Soros: a central place of exchange, homogeneous products, relatively low transaction and transportation costs,[49] instant communications, a large number of participants to spread influence, and safeguards against manipulation. In theory, then, prices (adjusting for changes in conditions) should move toward equilibrium, as supply and demand balance out, but in fact the stock market does not move toward equilibrium: instead, it has constant, seemingly unpredictable volatility unrelated to underlying events. The classical economic notions of supply and demand do not work in markets that have thinking participants. *There doesn't seem to be a correlation between changes in stock prices and changes in underlying conditions.*

This observation by Soros, if true, might seem to strike a mortal blow at fundamental analysis and indeed at valuation itself! If there is no correlation between conditions and prices, what is the point of trying to value stocks? The random walk theory would say, precisely, there is no point. The reflexivity theory is quite different. Soros says that "financial markets can affect the so called fundamentals which they are supposed to reflect. When that happens, markets enter into a state of dynamic disequilibrium and behave quite differently from what would be considered normal by the theory of efficient markets." Soros notes that such boom-bust sequences, while rare, are significant because they affect the fundamentals of the economy.

Creating a New Reality

More broadly, Soros points out that when participants think about a situation in which they participate, their thoughts affect the situation. So all our theories about social events are distorted. This includes the efficient market theory and its investment corollary, modern portfolio theory. Reflexivity goes beyond Heisenberg's uncertainty principle because it deals not merely with the impact of observation on what is observed and reported, but with the role of thinking itself in generating observable phenomena.

Soros identified a phenomenon called equity leveraging; that is, companies can use inflated expectations to issue new stock at inflated prices, and the resulting increase in earnings per share can go a long way to validate the inflated expectations. There are also debt ratios. The examples Soros gave years ago could have applied to our current financial situation: "banks relied on so-called debt ratios, which they considered as objective measurements of the ability of [borrowers] to service their debt, and it turned out that these debt ratios were themselves influenced by the lending activity of the banks." Here is the crux of the fallacy, as Soros describes it:

> Any divergence from a theoretical equilibrium has the capacity to validate itself. This self-validating capacity encourages trend-following speculation, and trend-following speculation generates divergences from whatever may be considered the theoretical equilibrium. The circular reasoning is complete.[50]

This reflexive law dooms the market to booms and busts. Ideas are mutually self-reinforcing at first, moving both thinking and reality in a certain direction, but they then become unsustainable and engender a move in the opposite direction.

This pattern would seem to suggest a great opportunity for charting, but Soros emphasizes that reflexivity is intermittent. He acknowledges that some repetitive aspects can be explained and predicted by universally valid laws whose validity can be tested by scientific method and that lend themselves to statistical generalizations. But, contrary to the technical analysts' assumption that patterns are discernible, he says that "each instance may have some unique features and there is a lot more to be gained from understanding the unique features than the repetitive pattern." This is especially true in situations that are far from equilibrium.

Soros distinguishes between normal conditions, in which valuation is possible, and far-from-equilibrium conditions, in which valuation could be futile.

> So we can observe three very different conditions in history: the "normal," in which the participants' views and the actual state of affairs tend to converge; and two far-from-equilibrium conditions, one of apparent changelessness, in which thinking and reality are very far apart and show no tendency to converge, and one of revolutionary change in which the actual situation is so novel and unexpected and changing so rapidly that the participants' views cannot keep up with it.[51]

In a brief passage that has served as an eloquent prologue to the current Wall Street chaos theory, Soros likens the far-from-equilibrium conditions to edge-of-chaos conditions, likening them to the "strange attractors" necessary to create such conditions. (When a system repeats a motion, it is said to be "attracted" to the motion. More on strange attractors is said later in this chapter.)

When Soros wrote these words in 1987, he could hardly have predicted the financial meltdown of 2008, but that crisis, unfolding as we wrote this book, fits the third description well. In 1998 and again in 2008, Soros repeated his warnings: "I have cried wolf three times: first with *The Alchemy of Finance* in 1987, then with *The Crisis of Global*

Capitalism in 1998, and now. Only now did the wolf arrive." It is time to heed them by ending our assumptions that markets move toward equilibrium.

> The fact that the new paradigm does not claim to predict the future explains why it did not make any headway until now, but in the light of recent experience it can no longer be ignored. We must come to terms with the fact that reflexivity introduces an element of uncertainty into financial markets that the previous theory left out of account. That theory was used to establish mathematical models for calculating risk and converting bundles of subprime mortgages into tradable securities, as well as other forms of debt. Uncertainty by definition cannot be quantified. Excessive reliance on those mathematical models did untold harm.[52]

The authors are in agreement with Soros on this point. Therefore, any financial models cited in this book should be seen with extreme skepticism. This gives us the perfect raison d'être for discussing chaos theory.

An Overview of Chaos/Complexity Theory

More than a decade ago, in *The Emperor's Nightingale*, Monks ("smithed" by Lajoux) argued that the corporation is a complex adaptive system. In this book, the authors acknowledge, like many before them, that the stock market itself is a large, complex system. The market fits the definition of such systems because it shows patterns in its growth and change over time; it is neither too chaotic nor too static. Its booms and busts suggest a nonlinear system.[53] The question is, can we call it adaptive? Is it on the edge of chaos—the place where the system begins to organize itself, rather than fall apart?[54] Soros has noted that there seems to be little correlation between fundamentals and stock prices. Rappaport gets around that by urging a study of fundamentals (such as future discounted cash flow) to revise expectations; he does not urge an approach that is based entirely on market price patterns.

Chaos theory does. It notes that there is no direct proportional relationship between the inputs into a market (such as earnings) and the output (the price). The chaos thinkers conclude that markets have to be studied as chaotic, nonlinear systems.

Fractals

A key concept is the *fractals*, which is a shape made of parts similar to the whole in some way. A fractal set is more irregular than those of classical geometry, but it is still a set. A fractal is an object or quantity that exhibits self-similarity on all scales. The object need not exhibit *exactly* the same structure at all scales, but the same type of structures must appear on all scales. A fractal pattern is a recurring pattern in a chaotic environment. A defining characteristic of a fractal pattern in stock price patterns is that the pattern is self-similar as it moves through time; that is, the smaller components of movement have the same basic shape and pattern as the larger components of movement.

According to the chaos theorists, financial markets are fractal. They base this assumption on the similarities of patterns in minute-to-minute, day-to-day, and month-to-month trading. Fractal market analysis seeks to see the order hidden in what seem to be random financial markets, and then it builds on the order of this logic to estimate the probability of future events and thus to price the value of stock.[55]

Strange Attractors

Another key concept is strange attractors. From fractals, we get the shapes of movements. From strange attractors, we get the driving force behind the shapes.

To trace chaotic motion, the investor can make a phase diagram of the motion, showing trajectories and their limits. When a system repeats a motion, it is said to be "attracted" to the motion, and this kind of motion is called an "attractor for the system." Some attractors are simple in shape (a point or a loop), and others are more irregular—or fractals. The latter are called "strange attractors," and they are a hallmark of complex systems, including the stock market.[56]

Professor Andrew Lo of the Sloan School uses the adaptive markets hypothesis to explain many of the anomalies that seem to contradict the efficient market theory. Lo says there is a method, if you will, to market madness. His adaptive markets hypothesis asserts that the degree of market efficiency is related to environmental factors characterizing market ecology, such as the number of competitors in the market, the magnitude of profit opportunities available, and the adaptability of the market participants.[57]

Valuation Requires Markets

Reactivating the capital markets is essential to realistic asset valuation and to enabling banks to divest toxic assets when they judge it appropriate.

———————————

—Lawrence H. Summers, "Responding to an Historic Economic Crisis: The Obama Program," March 13, 2009, http://www.brookings.edu/~/media/Files/events/2009/0313_summers/0313_summers_remarks.pdf

---

Securities Valuation as an Asset on the Balance Sheet

A good litmus test for pricing a security is to find out how the regulators expect companies to price the securities they hold as current assets. This kind of pricing—removed from the freedom and hurly-burly of minute-by-minute stock trading—is formula based.

As mentioned in Chapter 1, during the financial 2007–2009 crisis, the U.S. federal government pledged to take ownership of securities held by troubled financial institutions, under the Troubled Asset Repurchase Program (TARP). As of the end of 2009, the U.S. federal government became a major investor in these securities and is receiving dividends from them.[58]

The Duff & Phelps Valuation Model

A Congressional Oversight Panel asked the securities rating agency Duff & Phelps (D&P) to value preferred stock and warrants under the TARP program, resulting in a report published in February 2009.[59] Duff & Phelps used data from the public debt, equity, and derivatives markets to estimate discount rates, volatility, and default assumptions.

Here is a summary of D&P's conclusions and methodology. (See Appendix D for the full text. For insights on the valuation of derivative securities, see Appendix L.)

The D&P Approach for TARP Preferred Stock

For purposes of its analysis, D&P defined the fair market value of securities as the price at which property would change hands between a willing buyer and a willing seller when neither is acting under compulsion and when both have reasonable knowledge of the relevant facts. As such, the analysis attempted to address the question, "What price would a third party pay for these investments, given their terms, on their respective valuation dates?"

D&P noted (despite the evidence regarding reflexivity) that security prices determined in the financial markets provide the best indications of economic value. But D&P also noted that the financial markets turmoil leading to the TARP created some concern that transaction prices do not always indicate a security's fair value.

To mitigate this concern, D&P used several different valuation approaches, analyzed numerous publicly traded debt and preferred stock securities, and analyzed certain major market transactions the occurred during the relevant time period.

D&P estimated the fair market value of the TARP preferred stocks and the TARP warrants as of the valuation dates for the respective investments. Because the securities are not publicly traded, D&P could not use closing stock prices. Rather, the valuation dates it used were the first trading dates following the announcement of the purchase of the troubled assets by the Treasury. These are the first dates that the financial markets would have incorporated information related to the purchases. To value securities, D&P used data obtained from the public debt, equity, and derivatives markets to estimate certain parameters, such as discount rates, volatility, and default assumptions.

D&P employed three methodologies to value the TARP preferred stocks:[60]

1. *Yield-based DCF approach.* The TARP preferred stocks are perpetual securities that are callable by the issuer. Therefore, the holder of the TARP preferred stock (1) is long a perpetual security and (2) is short (has sold or written) a call option on the perpetual security. In the yield-based DCF approach, D&P valued each of the components (1) and (2) by analyzing the observed yields on other publicly traded preferred and debt securities issued by the Purchase Program Participants. Therefore, this approach allowed

direct comparisons of the TARP preferred stocks with very similar securities.

D&P valued the perpetual component of the TARP preferred stocks by discounting the contractual cash flows (dividends) at a discount rate that reflects the risk of each TARP preferred stock. This discount rate was derived from the option-adjusted yield on the purchase program participants' publicly traded securities. D&P valued the call option (which is a negative value to the holder of the TARP preferred stocks) using additional methodologies described in its report.

2. *Contingent claims analysis.* In contingent claims analysis, a firm's securities can be modeled as derivative securities on its assets. In the simplest case, a firm has one debt instrument outstanding, which is zero coupon debt. Upon maturity, if the asset value exceeds the face value of debt, the residual value belongs to the equity holders. Therefore, the equity of the company can be valued as a call option on the assets of the company. The strike price of the option is the face value of the debt, and the values of the option and debt are equal at maturity.[61]

3. *CDS-based DCF approach.* D&P also used a DCF analysis using as its information base credit default swap (CDS) rates. These rates are akin to bond spreads and provide direct observation of the market's perception of the credit risk of the program participants. The credit default swap market has high liquidity, so its rates are attractive for assessing credit risk. However, because the rates are for bonds issued by the companies, D&P had to modify them in order to apply them to the valuation of the TARP preferred stocks.

D&P analysts applied the standard approach to using CDS rates to value fixed income securities; that is, they used the CDS rates to infer the adjustment to the promised cash flows that incorporates both the probability of default and the risk premium that default requires. They estimated the fair market value of the TARP preferred stocks as the *sum of the present value of the probability adjusted cash flows*.

Revisiting Mark-to-Market

The D&P report is part of a larger movement on the part of regulators and standard setters to get a good feel for how a company can put a value on a security held as an asset. Investors can learn a great deal from what regulators have said about the valuation of securities at market value, or so-called mark-to-market. The mark-to-market issue is an accounting issue. It sets limits on how companies that have invested in securities need to value those securities on their balance sheets. In theory, the principles of mark-to-market accounting should apply to the valuation of a company's securities in general. Currently, the mark-to-market literature is directed at companies that issue stock and to their accountants. But much wisdom can be gleaned for investors as well.

The SEC's Office of the Chief Accountant released some clarifications that may act as guidance to investors. The guidance builds on the work of the International Accounting Standards Board (IASB) Expert Advisory Panel's September 16, 2008, draft document, the work of the Financial Accounting Standard Board) (FASB) Valuation Resource Group.[62] One basis for all this work is the fair value measurement guidance in FASB Statement No. 157, *Fair Value Measurements* (Chapter 2).

The SEC and FASB made four key points, reviewed here from the perspective of investors:

1. Management's internal assumptions (e.g., expected cash flows) can be used to measure the fair value of a security when relevant market evidence does not exist. Statement 157 discusses a range of information and valuation techniques that a reasonable preparer is permitted to use to estimate fair value when relevant market data may be unavailable, including expected cash flows from an asset. The SEC's recent guidance adds a twist to the three levels of value set forth in Statement 157 (Chapter 2). The Commission says that in some cases using unobservable inputs (level 3) might be more appropriate than using observable inputs (level 2); for example, when significant adjustments are required to available observable inputs, an estimate based primarily on unobservable inputs may be appropriate. The determination of fair value often requires significant judgment. In some cases, multiple inputs from different sources may collectively provide the best evidence of fair value. In these cases, expected cash flows are considered alongside other relevant information. The weighting of the inputs in the fair value estimate depends on the extent to which they provide information about the

value of an asset or liability and are relevant in developing a reasonable estimate.

2. Broker quotes may be an input when measuring fair value, but only in some cases. Broker quotes are not necessarily determinative if an active market does not exist for the security. In a liquid market, a broker quote should reflect market information from actual transactions. However, when markets are less active, brokers may rely more on models with inputs based on the information available only to the broker. In weighing a broker quote as an input to fair value, an entity should place less reliance on quotes that do not reflect the result of market transactions. Further, the nature of the quote (e.g., whether the quote is an indicative price or a binding offer) should be considered when weighing the available evidence, says the SEC.

   The SEC also says that results of distressed or disorderly transactions (fire sales) are "not determinative" when measuring fair value. The concept of a fair value measurement assumes an orderly transaction between market participants. An orderly transaction is one that involves market participants who are willing to transact and that allows for adequate exposure to the market. Distressed or forced liquidation sales are not orderly transactions, and thus the fact that a transaction is distressed or forced should be considered when weighing the available evidence.

3. Transactions in an inactive market can affect fair value measurements. A quoted market price in an active market for the identical asset is most representative of fair value. Investors should use that price (just as accountants must). Transactions in inactive markets can be useful as inputs when measuring fair value, but investors should not rely on them. If they are orderly, transactions should be considered in an estimate of value. But if prices in an inactive market do not reflect current prices for the same or similar assets, adjustments may be necessary to arrive at fair value. A significant increase in the spread between the amount sellers are asking and the price that buyers are bidding, or the presence of a relatively small number of bidding parties, is an indicator that should be considered in determining whether a market is inactive.

4. Securities rarely go bad overnight; it takes time for them to rot (i.e., become impaired). In general, the greater the decline in value, the greater the period of time will be until anticipated

recovery; the longer the period that a decline has existed, the greater the level of evidence necessary to reach a conclusion that an other-than-temporary decline has not occurred. Determining whether impairment is other than temporary is a matter that often requires the exercise of reasonable judgment based on the specific facts and circumstances of each investment. This includes an assessment of the nature of the underlying investment (for example, whether the security is debt, equity, or a hybrid), which may have an impact on a holder's ability to assess the probability of recovery.

To assist in making this judgment, the FASB's Staff Accounting Bulletin lists factors that should be considered:

➤ The length of the time and the extent to which the market value has been less than cost.

➤ The financial condition and near-term prospects of the issuer, including any specific events that may influence the operations of the issuer such as changes in technology that impair the earnings potential of the investment or the discontinuation of a segment of the business that may affect the future earnings potential.

➤ Or the intent and ability of the holder to retain its investment in the issuer for a period of time sufficient to allow for any anticipated recovery in market value.

All available information should be considered in estimating the anticipated recovery period.

Can We Bring Back the Equity Premium?

Institutions with very long-term investments especially need to appreciate the market as a system—and hopefully one that will continue to deliver a return on equity that is superior to the return on debt. A comment on an April 2009 IASB project made a very good point about equity: "Equity participations are those financial instruments issued by the entity which participate *without upward limit* in the proceeds of a disposal of the reporting entity or a business within the entity."[63] That lack of an upward limit on proceeds—compared to the fixed limits from debt instruments—give equity special appeal to the investor.

Investors have often assumed that over time equity will provide a superior—if more volatile (risky)—return compared to bonds. Conversely, bonds are considered to be more secure, even if their returns are not as high. As investors look at stock prices for the purpose of valuing companies based on stock price, they see that some of the old equity-versus-debt paradigms are shifting. The equity premium, in a phrase, ain't what it used to be.[64]

A new perspective on the difference between the two instruments could affect corporate valuation based on stock and bond prices. Bradford DeLong and Konstantin Magin of the University of California at Berkley put it this way: *Instead of an equity return premium, perhaps we have a debt return discount puzzle.* They reason that if the equity premium is merely a function of debt returns, it cannot be sustained over time. Yet the equity premium is important to the economy and should be sustained. The recent problems with target date funds (which got burned due to low returns from debt securities) makes continuing confidence in the equity premium all the more important. (See Chapter 8 for more on the target date subject.)

Because companies and investors alike benefit from a high equity premium, it is important to conceive of it as true in its own right.[65] As the authors note, for companies "replacing high priced equity capital with low priced debt capital would seem to be as profitable a strategy for a long lived company as investing in high return equity rather than low return debt is for a long term investor."

Investors can graph out expected returns and expected fluctuations affecting the likely outcomes of their investment. The graph can be

---

Cliché

I have been mulling over that dreadful cliché "risk adjusted." All analysts today conclude with a bromide to the effect that investment returns must be ramified by "risk adjustment." Fiduciary = The Law of the Gadarene Swine: you're acting appropriately if you follow the other pigs over the cliff. Such a large portion of the "market" is comprised of so-called fiduciaries who are essentially paid for "covering their ____ " that there is a factor of comfort—otherwise known as risk adjustment—that may be the underlying dynamic of market value.

—Robert A. G. Monks

based on a random process, so there is uncertainty built into the result, similar to market investments. The investor chooses an investment with a specified return and volatility, and the graph produces a bell curve of possible outcomes. The area of the negative return zone is proportional to the probability of loss.[66]

Reconnecting with the Good Old Capital Asset Pricing Model

Every financial professional is familiar with the dogma of portfolio diversification, as well as the theory underpinning it. This theory may be worth revisiting. After all, a security is a capital asset, and no one has found a single formula to price it better than the Capital Asset Pricing Model (CAPM), developed by William Sharpe, with similar work being done in parallel by other financial economists.

CAPM assumes a relationship between risk and expected return. It is written as follows:

$$\bar{r}_a = \bar{r}_f + \beta_a (\bar{r}_m - r_f)$$

where

r_f = risk-free rate
β_a = beta of the security
$\bar{r}_m$ = expected market return

The basic idea of CAPM (expounded in every article about it) is that investors need to be compensated for the risk they take and for the time they lose while they are waiting for their returns (i.e., the time value of money, implicit in present value calculations). The time value of money is represented by the risk-free (r_f) rate in the formula. It compensates the investors for giving up their money in any investment over a period of time. The other part of the formula represents risk and calculates the amount of compensation the investor requires for taking on additional risk. This is calculated by estimating the volatility of the stock in relation to other stocks (beta) and multiplying by the expected market return, minus the risk-free rate. That is, investors will make 12 percent, but if they had bought Treasury bonds, they could have made 2 percent; so only 10 percent is counted—or $(r_m - r_f)$.[67]

Stock Price Patterns in Industries

Over periods of time, the market accords different P/Es to different industries. However, these P/Es by themselves do not say much about a stock's value—merely the position of the company's industry at a given time with respect to the other fundamentals, including especially prospects for growth in earnings (Chapter 3).

Notably, however, stock price *volatility* does vary predictably by industry and subindustry; so any valuation method based in technical analysis or charting should be adjusted for industry patterns.[68] Most technical analysts are more interested in overall market patterns; so it is rare to find a technical analysis of an individual industry.

Lens Check

Like assets, earnings, and cash flow, securities prices need to be seen through various lenses:

➤ *Time: Short term versus long term.* It is well-known that investors have time horizons for stock. With respect to the discount rate for cash flow, the further out the time period is, the more difficult it is to estimate.

➤ *Place: Market versus nonmarket.* In analyzing securities prices, there is by definition a market. Valuation can differ. However, it is important to ask (as for earnings), will the cash-generating conditions for the company persist?

➤ *Slope: Level playing field or skewed.* Any trading based on non-public information can slant the field for pricing securities. One theory is that the stock market is an incomplete market; that is, the units being traded are more plentiful than the "states" being represented by the units. This theory obviously has implications for valuation, but they are too untested to discuss here.[69]

➤ *Volition: Willing versus unwilling buyer or seller.* Securities prices take on different meanings depending on the buyer or seller motivation. If the buyer wants control, there will be a premium.

➤ *Quality: Level of certainty of return (high, medium, or low) based on investing standards.* An investor's goals for future returns shape the timing and nature of returns.

➤ *Purpose: Private versus public.* In the short term, private and public goals differ, but in the long term they converge. This is why long-term investors such as pension plans can be such a positive force in a nation's economic system.

Conclusion

Share prices reflect what all investors think about a security today. To develop their own views, investors can begin by measuring momentum: Is the price higher, lower, or the same as yesterday? If it has changed, why has it changed?

If 100 investors think Stock A is worth $20, this expectation increases the likelihood that the hundred and first investor will think it is worth $20 as well. But to make a sound investment, that hundred and first investor can exercise independent thought.

The day trader wants to buy low today and sell higher tomorrow, but the longer the time span is, the more uncertain the return. The long-term investor cannot rely on one approach alone. Therefore, the next chapter looks at hybrid approaches to valuation.

Notes

1. John Maynard Keynes, *The General Theory of Employment, Interest, and Money* (London: Macmillan, 1936), p. 156.
2. Letter from Peter Drucker to Robert A. G. Monks, June 17, 1993.
3. It is a well-known fact that stock prices rise on news of a takeover because acquirers pay a premium for control. See Stanley Foster Reed, Alexandra Reed Lajoux, and H. Peter Nesvold. *The Art of M&A: A Merger/Acquisition/Buyout Guide*, 4th ed. (New York: McGraw-Hill, 2006). For a general discussion of rumors (including mention of takeover rumors), see Nicholas DiFonzo. *Rumor Psychology: Social and Organizational Approaches* (New York: American Psychological Association, 2006). At the end of the last merger boom, takeover rumors were adding up to 31 percent to the price of a stock, according columnist John R Dorfman ("Heard on the Street," *Wall Street Journal*, May 28, 1991).
4. P. Hillion and M. Suominen, "The Manipulation of Closing Prices," *Journal of Financial Markets* 7 (2004): 351–375, http://project.hkkk.fi/finfaculty/files/HillionSuominen_The%20manipulation%20of%20closing%20prices.pdf.
5. "On individual equities, there are proportionally more premium sellers than there are on the index side"

(FDAXHunder, "Dispersion: A Guide for the Clueless," July 2004. Version 1.1, http://nuclearphynance.com/User%20Files/2/Dispersion%20-%20A% 20guide%20for%20the%20clueless%201.1.pdf).

6. Mark H. Lang, Karl G. Lins, and Mark H. Maffett, "Transparency, Liquidity, and Valuation: International Evidence," Working Paper Series, last revised June 14, 2009, http://papers.ssrn.com/sol3/papers.cfm?abstract_ id=1323514. This paper says, "Increase in transparency in a low investor protection country [is] associated with a decrease in bid-ask spread from 1.9% to 0.9%." See also Mark H. Lang, "Time-Varying Stock Price Response to Earnings Induced by Uncertainty about the Time-Series Process of Earnings," *Journal of Accounting Research* 29, no. 2 (Autumn, 1991).

7. Victor J. Defeo, "An Empirical Investigation of the Speed of the Market Reaction to Earnings Announcements. *Journal of Accounting Research* 24, no. 2 (Autumn 1986).

8. For an explanation, see "The Q Ratio and Market Valuation," June 11, 2020, http://dshort.com/articles/Q-Ratio-and-market-valuation.html. For the raw numbers, see Federal Reserve, "Z.1: *Flow of Funds Accounts of the United StatesFlows and Outstandings First Quarter 2010*, http://www. federalreserve.gov/releases/z1/Current/z1.pdf, as well as Flow of Funds Accounts of the United States Flows and Outstandings, 2005-2009 http:// www.federalreserve.gov/releases/z1/Current/annuals/a2005-2009.pdf.

9. Andrew W. Lo, Harry Mayamaysky, and Jiang Wang, "Foundations of Technical Analysis: Computational Algorithms, Statistical Inference, and Empirical Implementation," available at Social Science Research Network, http://ssrn.com/abstract=217470. In this article the authors use nonparametric kernel regression to recognize patters for a 31-year period ending in 1996. They tested several technical patterns and found that some provide "incremental information" that can be useful to predicting stock prices.

10. Michale Tsang and Eric Martin. "Stock Charts Fail Forecast Test in Complete S&P Miss," Bloomberg, May 4, 2009 (third update), http://www.bloomberg .com/apps/news?pid=20601087&sid=aM76hi1IDeOo&refer=home.

11. In addition to the techniques listed in this chapter, there are many more: alpha, trend channel (descending, ascending, horizontal), trendline (descending, ascending, horizontal), bar chart, diamond, beta, dormant bottom, broadening formation, double top, climactic top, closing the gap, confirmation/divergence, linear/logarithmic scale, cup and hand, right-angled broadening triangle, and cycle. (http://www.iqchart.com/101/patterns.asp).

12. W. D. Gann. *The Basis of My Forecasting Method* (1935), http://www .esnips.com/doc/ab65d890-a241-491d-a937-dc2425788da5/W.D-Gann-The-Basis-of-My-Forecasting-Method.

13. This description of Bollinger Bands is based on the official web site for the founder, http://www.bollingerbands.com/.

14. See Steven Bigalow, *Profitable Candlestick Trading: Pinpointing Market Opportunities to Maximize Profits* (Hoboken, N.J.: John Wiley& Sons, 2001); Gregory Morris, *Candlestick Charting Explained: Timeless Techniques for Trading Stocks and Futures*, 3rd ed. (New York: McGraw-Hill, 2006); and Steve Nisson. *Japanese Candlestick Charting Techniques: A Contemporary Guide to the Ancient Techniques of the Far East* (Upper Saddle River, N.J.: Prentice Hall: 2001).

15. This formula is based in the writings of Steve Nison, *The Candlestick Course* (Hoboken, New Jersey: John Wiley & Sons, 2003); and Gregory L. Morris, *Candlestick Charting Explained: Timeless Techniques for Trading Stocks and Futures* (New York: McGraw-Hill, 1995), summarized at http://www .hotcandlestick.com/index.html.

16. For more information, see "Price Channels" at the web site Online Trading Technique, http://www.onlinetradingtechnique.com/TA.php?id=Price %20Channels.

17. "Drummond Geometry—Mapping Future Market Activity," *Chartpoint*, http://www.tedtick.com/downloads/chartpoint1.pdf.

18. To create your own free charts, go to Stockcharts.com, Charting Tools, http://stockcharts.com/charts/.

19. Gerald Appel, *Winning Market Systems—83 Ways to Beat the Market* (Greenville, S.C.: Traders Press, 1980); and Gerald Appel and Marvin Appel, *Beating the Market, 3 Months at a Time: A Proven Investing Plan Everyone Can Use* (London: Financial Times Press, 2008).

20. A reliable source defines this as the fifty-day average moving faster than the 200-day average. See Elizabeth Stanton and Jeff Kerns, "S&P 500 'Golden Cross' Signals Stock Gains: Technical Analysis," *Bloomberg*, June 24, 2009. By contrast, an anonymous investor, who calls himself "stock chartist," defines these as "stocks where the price is more than the 90-day moving average and the 90-day moving average is above the 180-day moving average" (http:// stockchartist.blogspot.com/2008/12/where-are-todays-leading-stocks.html).

21. For a good article, see "Relative Strength Index," http://www.investopedia .com/terms/r/rsi.asp.

22. The weak form of the efficient market hypothesis (EMH) states that current market price reflects fully the information from past prices and rules out prediction based on price data alone. No recent test of time series of stock returns rejects this weak form hypothesis. This research offers another test of the weak form of the EMH that leads to different conclusions for some time series. The stochastic complexity of a time series is a measure of the number of bits needed to represent and reproduce the information

in the time series. In an efficient market, compression of the time series is not possible because there are no patterns and the stochastic complexity is high. In this research, Rissanen's context tree algorithm is used to identify recurring patterns in the data and to use them for compression. The weak form of the EMH is tested for 13 international stock indexes and for all the stocks that comprise the Tel-Aviv 25 index (TA25), using sliding windows of 50, 75, and 100 consecutive daily returns. Statistically significant compression is detected in 10 of the international stock index series. In the aggregate, 60 to 84 percent of the TA25 stocks tested demonstrate compressibility beyond randomness. This indicates potential market inefficiency.

23. Ralph N. Elliott, *The Wave Principle* (Detroit, Mich.: Charles J. Collins, Investment Counsel, 1935).

24. John F. Ehlers, *Cybernetic Analysis for Stocks and Futures: Cutting-Edge DSP Technology to Improve Your Trading* (Hoboken, N.J.: John Wiley & Sons, 2004), http://www.forexrealm.com/technical-analysis/technical-indicators/mesa-sine-wave.html.

25. Burton G. Malkiel, *A Random Walk Down Wall Street*, 7th ed. (New York: W.W. Norton, 2000). First published in 1973.

26. Armin Shmilovici, Yael Alon-Brimer, and Shmuel Hauser, "Using a Stochastic Complexity Measure to Check the Efficient Market Hypothesis," *Computational Economics* 22 (October–December 2003): 273–284. According to Shmilovici et al., "The weak form of the Efficient Market Hypothesis (EMH) states that current market price reflects fully the information from past prices and rules out prediction based on price data alone. . . . The stochastic complexity of a time series is a measure of the number of bits needed to represent and reproduce the information in the time series. In an efficient market, compression of the time series is not possible, because there are no patterns and the stochastic complexity is high. . . . The weak form of the EMH is tested for 13 international stock indices . . . Statistically significant compression is detected in ten of the international stock index series . . . This indicates potential market inefficiency."

27. Index Funds, http://www.indexfunds.com/.

28. Benjamin Graham, *Memoirs of the Dean of Wall Street* (New York: McGraw-Hill, 1996). This publication was posthumous; Benjamin Graham died in 1976.

29. John C. Bogle, *Common Sense on Mutual Funds* (Hoboken, N.J.: John Wiley & Sons, 2000).

30. "Burned Investors Give Index Funds Big Boost," Reuters, July 8, 2009, http://news.alibaba.com/article/detail/markets/100132260-1-analysis-burned-investors-give-index-funds.html. See also Eleanor Laise, "More

Index Funds Sought for 401(k)s," *Wall Street Journal*, July 18. 2009, http://online.wsj.com/article/SB124787372758560721.html.

31. Craig Carmin, "Active Managers Get the Cold Shoulder," *Wall Street Journal*, June 22, 2009, http://online.wsj.com/article/SB124561990371635281.html.

32. Jie Kai and Todd Houge, "Index Rebalancing and Long-Term Portfolio Performance," Social Science Research Network, March 2007, http://ssrn.com/abstract=970839.

33. John Morgan, "Industry Opposes Mandatory Index Funds in 401(k) Plans," *Financial Planning Executive*, June 1, 2009, http://www.financial-planning.com/news/industry-opposes-mandatory-index-funds-401k-2662140-1.html.

34. Russel Kinnel, "Silly Season for the Active/Passive Debate," *Morningstar*, http://news.morningstar.com/articlenet/article.aspx?id=298876.

35. The William F. Sharpe Indexing Achievement Awards, http://indexbusiness-association.org/industry-awards/.

36. Alfred Rappaport and Michael J. Mauboussin, *Expectations Investing: Reading Stock Prices for Better Returns* (Boston: Harvard Business School Press, 2001). The authors also have a web site, expectationsinvesting.com.

37. Alfred Rappaport, "The Economics of Short-Term Performance Obsession," *Financial Analysts Journal* 61, no. 3 (2005). See also Rappaport and Mauboussin, note 35.

38. One definition of shareholder value is the value of the company minus the future claims (debts). The value of a company can be calculated as the net present value of all future cash flows plus the value of the nonoperating assets of the company. This definition is based on the legal fact that the shareholders are the last to be paid in the event of insolvency.

39. Justin Fox, "Ignore Your Investors: Shareholder Value Isn't So Dumb. Using Today's Stock Price to Gauge Success Is," *Fortune*, May 18, 2009, http://money.cnn.com/2009/05/15/news/economy/fox_value.fortune/index.htm.

40. Bjorn Schubert, *Evolution of Algorithmic Trading and Challenges of the Future* (Saarbrucken, VDM, 2009).

41. Abu Abdullah Muhammad Musa al-Khwarizmi introduced Arabic numerals (1, 2, 3, as opposed to Roman numerals i, ii, iii), as well as algebraic concepts, into European mathematics.

42. In 2006, algorithmic trading represented 33 percent of all equities trading and at current growth rates could reach 53 percent by 2010 (B. Bailey and S. Lee, in "Bulge Bracket Firms and Algorithmic Trading: The Bigger Get Bigger," *Aite Group Report*, November 2006, cited in Schubert, http://www.aitegroup.com/reports/200611081.php.

43. For a good discussion of volume-weighted average price, see Robert Kissel and Morton Glantz, *Optimal Trading Strategies: Quantitative Approaches for Managing Market Impact and Trading Risk* (New York: Amacom, 2003). Their formula is min $\varsigma(x)$ s.t. $R(x)$ R^* This formula calculates the minimum cost [ς] of a trade [x] while ensuring that the risk of the trade [$R(x)$] will be within an acceptable level of risk [R^*] for an investor.

44. For a good look at the inner working of a trading algorithm, see the Patent of Donato Petrino for an "Algorithmic Trading System, a Method for Computer-Based Algorithm Trading and a Computer Program Product," http://www.faqs.org/patents/app/20090119224.

45. Linkedin.com's Quantitative Finance Group has an excellent discussion at the question, "Does anyone have any insight on the growing popularity of algorithmic execution systems and how they affect market behavior?"

46. Francesco Bertoluzzo and Marco Corazza, "Recurrent Reinforcement Learning-Based Trading Systems." Bertoluzzo is with the department of statistics, University of Padua Via Cesare Battisti, Padua, Italy, fbertoluzzo@stat.unipd.it. Corazza is with the department of applied mathematics, University Ca' Foscari of Venice Dorsoduro, Venice, Italy, corazza@unive.it.

47. If your program is in English, key words would include: START, BEGIN, END, STOP, DO, WHILE, DO WHILE, FOR, UNTIL, DO UNTIL, REPEAT, END WHILE, END UNTIL, END REPEAT, IF, IF THEN, ELSE, IF ELSE, END IF, THEN, ELSE THEN, ELSE IF, SO, CASE, EQUAL, NOT, TRUE, FALSE, AND, OR, GET, WRITE, PUT, UPDATE, CLOSE, OPEN, CREATE, DELETE, EXIT, FILE, and READ. Structured English is based on certain principles, such as all logic should be expressed in operational, conditional, and repetition blocks:

    ➤ Operation statements are written as English phrases executed from the top down.

    ➤ Conditional blocks are indicated by keywords such as IF, THEN, and ELSE.

    ➤ Repetition blocks are indicated by keywords such as DO, WHILE, and UNTIL.

    For a classic article on this subject, see P. R. Bagley, "Principles and Problems of a Universal Computer-Oriented Language," *The Computer Journal* 4 (1962): 305–312. Consider also "fuzzy logic" (incorporating unknown uncertainties). This has been used by the OK-Score rating system to pick stocks from the Dutch AEX index. From 2003 to mid-2010 (as we go to press), the index achieved 3 percent return; the OK-Score portfolio's return was 128 percent.

48. Nassim Nicholas Taleb, *The Black Swan: The Impact of the Highly Improbable* (New York: Random House, 2007). Taleb calls the book

a "literary-philosophical essay." His more technical work—including thoughts on what to do about the Black Swan—appear in separate academic papers. See, for example, "Black Swans and the Domains of Statistics," *The American Statistician* 61, no. 3 (August 2007); and "Errors, Robustness, and the Fourth Quadrant," Social Science Research Network (February 14, 2009), http://ssrn.com/abstract=1343042.

49. In paraphrasing Soros's point about transaction cost, the authors added the modifier "relatively" because they do not agree that costs associated with the issuance and exchange of equity securities are in fact low. See shareholdercoalition.com for a discussion of problems with the proxy voting process that has led to high costs for issuers.

50. George Soros, *The Alchemy of Finance* (New York: Wiley, 1987).

51. Ibid.

52. Ibid.

53. For an interesting paper about a bubble as nonlinear, see Ehsan Ahmed, "Emerging Markets and Stock Market Bubbles: Nonlinear Speculation?" (December 2008), http://cob.jmu.edu/rosserjb/EMERGING%20MARKET%20AND%20STOCK%20MARKET%20BUBBLES%201.doc.

54. Les Oxley and Donald A. R. George, "Economics on the Edge of Chaos: Some Pitfalls of Linearizing Complex Systems," *Environmental Modeling and Software* 22, no. 5 (May 2007): 580–589, http://www.sciencedirect.com/science?_ob=ArticleURL&_udi=B6VHC-4JHMFSH-2&_user=10&_rdoc1&_fmt=&_orig=search&_sort=d&_docanchor=&view=c&_searchStrId=961459731&_rerunOrigin=google&_acct=C000050221&_version=1&_urlVersion=0&_userid=10&md5=16d7f2e67721834708cae1dc5f11a109.

55. See, for example, the writings of David Nichols, past editor of the *21st Century Market Report*, "Fractal Market Analysis," Fractal Market Report, http://www.fractalmarketreport.com/fmr-analysis.php.

56. Feng-tao Liu, "Criterion and Measurement of Complexity of Stock Market: From Chaos, Fractal to Complexity Degree," in *International Conference on Wireless Communications, Networking and Mobile Computing, WiCom 2007* (September 21–25, 2007): 4093–4096 (Digital Object Identifier 10.1109/WICOM.2007.1011).

57. Andrew W. Lo, "Reconciling Efficient Markets with Behavioral Finance: The Adaptive Markets Hypothesis," *Journal of Investment Consulting*, 7 (2005): 21–44. See also Nicholas T. Chan, Blake LeBaron, Andrew W. Lo, and Tomaso Poggio, "Agent-Based Models of Financial Markets: A Comparison with Experimental Markets," MIT Sloan Working Paper No. 4195-01.

58. Section 105(a) Troubled Assets Relief Program Report to Congress for the Period June 1, 2009, to June 30, 2009, http://www.financialstability.gov/docs/105CongressionalReports/105aReport_07102009.pdf.

59. Valuation Report, Congressional Oversight Panel, February 4, 2009, http://cop.senate.gov/documents/cop-020609-report-dpvaluation.pdf.

60. For the valuation of the TARP warrants, D&P used an options pricing approach implemented with a Monte Carlo simulation, which accommodates time-varying interest rates and volatilities, and incorporated adjustments to account for the issuer's ability to cancel one-half the warrants through a qualifying equity offering (defined further in the full report).

61. The authors have rephrased this formula according to their interpretation of its meaning. The original text says "maturity" instead of "value at maturity."

62. SEC Office of the Chief Accountant and FASB Staff Clarifications on Fair Value Accounting, Release 2008-234, http://www.sec.gov/news/press/2008/2008-234.htm; and Section 105(a) Troubled Assets Relief Program Report to Congress for the Period June 1, 2009 to June 30, 2009, http://www.financialstability.gov/docs/105CongressionalReports/105a Report_07102009.pdf. As of December 30, 2009, the Treasury has invested more than $200 billion in 793 financial institutions, and received more than half of those funds back in capital repayments. Finally, more than $4 billion in warrant proceeds have been repurchased by financial institutions or sold by the Treasury (http://www.financialstability.gov/docs/transaction-reports/1-4-10%20Transactions%20Report%20as%20of%2012-30-09.pdf).

63. April 2009—Project Earnings per Share Topic Summary of responses to questions in the ED (Appendix 10B of the IASB document), http://www.iasb.org/NR/rdonlyres/F2B79DFA-9727-4BC2-850F-DFF6624A5F0B/0/EPS0904b10BappBobs.pdf.

64. John Authers, "Is It Back to the Fifties?" FT.com, March 24, 2009, http://www.ft.com/cms/s/680b46b0-18a7-11de-bec8-0000779fd2ac, Authorised=false.html?_i_location=http%3A%2F%2Fwww.ft.com%2Fcms%2Fs%2F0%2F680b46b0-18a7-11de-bec8-0000779fd2ac.html%3Fnclick_check%3D1&_i_referer=&nclick_check=1.

65. J. Bradford DeLong and Konstantin Magin, "The U.S. Equity Return Premium: Past, Present and Future," preliminary draft. DeLong is professor of economics, University of California at Berkeley. Magin is a postdoctoral fellow there.

66. Try *Money Chimp's* Monte Carlo simulation using your own investment criteria at http://www.moneychimp.com/articles/risk/longterm.htm.

67. For more, see David E. Hampton, "Mean-Variance Capital Asset Pricing Model for Long Short Equity Hedge Fund Portfolios," EDHEC Business School, HedgeFundSciences.com, March 14, 2009, confirming classical CAPM. For a review of basics, see this introductory article at http://www.investopedia.com/terms/c/capm.asp.

68. The classic article on this topic is by Edward Altman and Robert A. Schwartz and, "Volatility Behavior of Industrial Stock Price Indices," *Journal of Finance* 28, no. 4 (September 1973): 957–971. Their empirical results showed that the stability of volatility ranking is of high significance by nonparametric statistical tests. See Appendix E for a discussion of parametric versus nonparametric statistics. For a recent application in a specific Asian stock market, see Lan-Jun Lao, "Inter-industry Volatility Patterns in Chinese Stock Market," *Machine Learning and Cybernetics, 2005: Proceedings of 2005 International Conference* 6, nos. 18–21 (August 2005): 3458–3462.

69. J. Geanakoplos, M. Magill, M. Quinzii, and J. Drèze, "Generic Inefficiency of Stock Market Equilibrium When Markets Are Incomplete," Cowles Foundation Paper 751, *Journal of Mathematical Economics*, 19 (1990): 113–151, http://cowles.econ.yale.edu/P/cp/p07b/p0751.pdf.

CHAPTER 6

Hybrid Techniques
for Valuation

The purpose of science is not to analyze or describe but to make useful models of the world. A model is useful if it allows us to get use out of it.

—Edward de Bono

VALUATION HAS MANY FACETS, as explained in preceding chapters. Valuing a company requires appreciation for what the company owns (assets minus liabilities), for how the company can generate future funds (via earnings and cash flow), and for how the capital marketplace perceives this wealth-creating potential (stock price). Careful analysis of any *one* of these aspects of value can improve an investor's sense of a company's worth and hence the possible price ranges for buy, sell, and hold decisions. But valuation need not stop there. These elements can be even more powerful as valuation tools *in combination*. But how? It starts with the effort to obtain a useful model for valuation.

Building vs. Buying a Model

As in many business decisions, an investor can build or buy a formula for valuation, that is, either create a formula for valuing a company or adopt one already in use.

Many investors choose the build route. These do-it-yourself, innovative investors express their valuation idea as a formula and then create software, using open source technology or combining or adapting proprietary technology. The software operationalizes the formula into a proprietary and confidential model.[1] At the simplest level, this can consist of putting a formula into a spreadsheet, but programming extends far beyond this tool.[2] We hope the information contained in this book (combined with other more specialized guides) can help investors build new models or improve the ones they have.

The other option is to buy, or at least to adopt, a preexisting formula and model—an approach used by 15 percent of companies.[3] A number of time-tested ones are available for general use, most of them developed in the 1970s during a period of financial innovation and popularized in the 1980s in an active market for corporate control (aka "merger boom"). We call these programs "hybrid" because they combine a variety of elements; they do not operate strictly in the domain of assets, or earnings, or cash flow, or stock price. We call them "approaches" because they are more than a ratio; they are not just one number compared to another (such as price-to-earnings, Wall Street's most popular metric).

This chapter presents 14 of these existing hybrid approaches to valuation, focusing on the ones that have received some level of attention (based on Web hits) in writings about valuation by investors, managers, regulators, and academics.

A few of these approaches are associated with developers and/or trademarks or patents, but most are in the public domain, having been developed through common practice and, in some cases, being "obvious" and therefore nonprotectable.[5] Interestingly, whatever their origin, most of these models tend to use the same six key elements as part of their formulas:

1. Some kind of earnings
2. Some kind of cash flow
3. Some kind of market value
4. Some kind of invested capital
5. Cost of capital
6. Some measure for return on capital

Other elements appearing in models include cash on hand, debt, book value of equity,[6] and market value.

Exhibit 6.1 Google Hits for Various Valuation Approaches (June 28, 2010)

Search Term	Number of Hits
Return on Capital Employed	1,530,000
Shareholder Value Added	1,430,000
Discounted Free Cash Flow[4]	869,000
Enterprise Value	590,000
Return on Net Assets	538,000
Cash Value Added	450,000
Cash Flow Return on Investment	223,000
Economic Value Added	219,000
Total Shareholder Return	180,000
Cash Flow Return on Equity	156,000
Market Value Added	42,700
Economic Margin Framework	29,600
Economic Value Management	15,600
Cash Return on Gross Investment	1,690

Note: Hits are only a very rough proxy for popularity. The number of hits changes daily and sometimes varies wildly, depending on whether the search engine is counting duplicates. Also, popularity is not necessarily correlated to effectiveness. We put all search terms in quotes, e.g., "economic value added."

Disclaimer: Some phrases may be used outside the realm of corporate valuation. For example, "enterprise value" clearly can be used in a nontechnical sense. Also, hits include a good deal of duplication and chaff. Nonetheless, even if we allow for a very high standard deviation of error across the board, the list proves that many of these approaches have achieved some measure of acceptance or at least recognition.

A Word about Building a Model Within a Model

We are aware that we are offering valuation advice "one company at a time" for investors who have multiple investments. When a stock is part of a portfolio, the individual stock risk-return can be defined as an additional risk-return to the portfolio. The analyst can then compute the covariance of the risk and the return of the stock versus the portfolio. This can be a time-consuming process, which is why many investors use indexes and/or algorithms rather than conducting analysis.

Clearly, any model used to value individual stocks needs to be correlated to a larger model for portfolio management.[7] The skills used in building one valuation model can transfer to the building of the other.

The analyst who can value a complex portfolio can apply those same skills to value a complex company.

One of the world's most successful investors, Warren Buffett, has never laid out a valuation methodology, much less a formula. Rather, he speaks through his actions. Buffett followers report that he favors a relatively small selection of carefully selected, well analyzed stocks; that he eschews exclusive reliance on any single ratio (such as P/E); and that he anticipates (and discounts) future cash flow. Predicting future cash flow is, of course, the ultimate mystery (see Chapter 7). This chapter is concerned with developing a workable valuation formula that factors in the future.

Words of Caution

The list of 14 commonly used approaches to corporate valuation in this chapter come great caution for several reasons:

➤ First, *the list is not comprehensive*. There are, in fact, countless models. A simple visit to Professor Aswath Damodaran's Web page for valuation models[8] makes it abundantly clear that there are scores of them.

➤ Second, *no sane person would buy a security based on these valuation techniques alone*; the techniques provide a reality check on a decision arrived at otherwise.

➤ Third, investors need not take solutions off the shelf; it is better to *build one's own*. Indeed, many companies do. (This discussion contains occasional examples of companies using these approaches to judge corporate performance. Note, however, that companies change their approaches over time, as needed, and sometimes abandon off-the-shelf models to create their own.)[9]

Fourteen Approaches

However we believe this list of 14 valuation approaches can be very useful to investors or to anyone who wants to analyze the value of a corporation. There are a couple of reasons:

➤ If a technique is widely used, then knowing it (and running its numbers) can help an investor predict how others will value a stock—the Keynes beauty contest. Also, these formulas provide content for the algorithms that quantitative traders use.

➤ A corporation's use of a particular model influences its strategic choices, its compensation programs, and its message to the world. So the model becomes a self-fulfilling prophecy. The kind of wealth generated by a corporation focused on one model is different from the kind of wealth created by a corporation using another model.

To be sure, everything gets translated into cash; so all the models are after the same goal. Nonetheless, the reason for and the timing of the cash varies according to the model used. And this really does matter. Unless cash is connected to something that is not merely cash—something pertaining to value (a product or service that meets a need in society)—then the cash flow will cease. The more elements models include beyond cash, the more likely they are to predict sustainable value.

Here is a simplified list of the approaches, along with the general valuation terms—e.g., "earnings"—for the elements they add, subtract, divide, and/or multiply (See the following section for the specific terms used by each approach—e.g., "operating surplus" in the cash-value-added approach.):

1. Cash Flow Return on Equity™ (uses cash flow, equity)
2. Cash Flow Return on Investment® (uses assets, cash flow, invested capital)
3. Cash return on gross investment (uses cash flow, invested capital)
4. Cash value added (uses cash flow, invested capital)
5. Discounted free cash flow (uses cash flow, invested capital)
6. Economic Margin Framework
7. Economic Value Added™ (uses earnings, invested capital)
8. Economic value management (earnings, invested capital)
9. Enterprise value (uses liabilities, equity [preferred stock], market cap, cash equivalents)
10. Market Value Added® (uses invested capital, market value)
11. Return on capital employed (uses earnings, assets, liabilities)
12. Return on net assets (uses earnings, assets, invested capital)
13. Shareholder value added (uses liabilities, cash flows)
14. Total shareholder return (uses stock price appreciation plus dividends paid)

Chapter 7 presents a fifteenth model that is based in qualitative factors. These multiple approaches are analogous to the groups of chemicals seen the periodic tables of chemistry. As equity valuation practices improves, some day it should be possible to arrange valuation approaches in a "periodic table for valuation" based on shared elements.

The following sections provide more details on these common approaches to corporate valuation.

Cash Flow Return on Equity™

Cash Flow Return on Equity (CFROE) measures how well a company is doing with its shareholders' capital. It was created for use by financial services firms, but it is also in use at some other types of service firms, such as media.[10] The approach is similar to cash flow return on investment (CFROI), which some use to value industrial firms.

The basic formula is

$$CFROI = \frac{Cash\ flow\ from\ operations}{Shareholders'\ equity}$$

The cash flow measured is for a particular period. If it is for a future period, it will be discounted to present value and is hence a discounted cash flow (DCF) measure. Credit Suisse First Boston, which owns a valuation company called CSFB Holt, released a valuation model based on CFROE in 2005 with great fanfare. As of mid-2010, this measure still appears to be less popular than its older sibling, CFROI.

Cash Flow Return on Investment®

Cash Flow Return on Investment (CFROI®) was developed by Bart Madden at Holt Value Associates (now part of Credit Suisse First Boston). It is used for industrial firms, such as aerospace companies.[11] Madden calls this metric "a proxy for the firm's economic return." He explains that it is "an inflation-adjusted (real) ROI metric constructed from annual financial statements to approximate the average real ROIs being achieved on the firm's portfolio of on-going projects."[12]

This metric has two main variables: cash flow and investment. The figures used are gross figures, and one is divided into the other. Hence, very simply,

$$CFROI = \frac{Gross\ cash\ flow}{Gross\ investment}$$

➤ *Gross cash flow* is current dollar annual cash flow. These are the inflation-adjusted gross cash flows available to all capital owners in the company.

➤ *Gross investment* is defined as net asset value plus cumulated depreciation on assets plus current dollar adjustment. Another way of expressing this is:

Current dollar gross investment = Inflation − Adjusted
total assets − Nondebt liabilities and intangibles[13]

➤ This is the inflation-adjusted gross investment made by the capital owners.

The approach then converts this ratio into an internal rate of return (IRR) by recognizing the finite economic life of depreciating assets and the residual value of nondepreciating assets. The CFROI of the investment must exceed a hurdle rate, which is the total cost of capital for the corporation. This is calculated as the cost of debt financing and the equity investors' expected return on equity investments. An investor can adjust the formula to account for depreciation.[14] In the end, the CFROI® result approximates the economic return produced by the firm's projects.

The standard CFROI calculation is a five-year projection. Over time, cash flow return on investment drops, depending on the stage of growth, from a high innovation stage with high CFROI to "fading," "mature," and "failing" phases when the CFROI is progressively lower. The CFROI analyst includes "fade" in the valuation for the company. The rate of the fade is based on where the company is in its life cycle, as well as past performance and future prospects.

Right Number, Wrong Deal

The CFROI approach assumes that over a five-year period returns will gradually decline (or "fade") toward the market norm because of competitive pressures. The rate of decline is determined in part by the volatility of the company's historic CFROI levels.

(*Continued*)

(Continued)

Valuation journalist Randy Myers once asked, "What Snapped at Quaker?" Myers noted that when analysts used CFROI on Snapple in 1994, they found a very high CFROI and a very high asset growth rate—25.5 percent and 35 percent, respectively. The analyst (Sam Eddins of Holt) calculated a value for Snapple's stock as if its CFROI would fade at an average rate and calculated Snapple's asset growth rate at a slightly above-average rate. That left it with a CFROI of 17 percent and an asset growth rate of 21 percent five years out. Discounting those values back to 1994, it suggested a price for Snapple of $19.55 per share—well above the $14 per share Quaker actually paid in 1994 and far above the $2.80 per share that Quaker sold Snapple for in 1997. At the time, Myers and others claimed that Quaker overpaid for Snapple. The CFROI measure appeared to be overly optimistic.

But this example shows how complex valuation is. As it turns out, the Snapple property really did have value. The problem was that its operations did not integrate well with the Quaker operations. Today, after changing hands a number of times, Snapple is part of Dr Pepper Snapple Group, a collection of beverages that, between June 25, 2009, and June 25, 2010, traded in a range of $28.69 to $38.93—well above the original CFROI number, even accounting for inflation.

—Robert A. G. Monks and Alexandra R. Lajoux

According to Credit Suisse First Boston, the CFROI approach corrects many common distortions found in traditional accounting measures of performance, such as inflation, depreciation method, asset mix, asset life, deferred taxes, pension accounting, research and development, off-balance-sheet items, inventory accounting, asset holding gains or losses, acquisition accounting, investments, and revaluations. Thus, true economic wealth creation or destruction can easily be assessed to determine a company's warranted value.

Cash Return on Gross Investment

Cash return on gross investment (CRGI) involves both earnings and invested capital. The formula is

$$CRGI = \frac{EBITDA - Tax}{Gross\ invested\ capital}$$

(EBITDA is earnings before interest, taxes, depreciation, and amortization.)

This is a good metric for companies in the industrial sector because the key number includes interest, depreciation, and amortization, which can distort earnings.[15] At the same time, these factors can correct earnings; so this ratio should never be used as a central metric of corporate value.

Cash Value Added

The cash value added (CVA) approach is calculated as follows:

CVA = Operating cash flow − Operating cash flow demand

where

Operating cash flow[16] = Operating surplus + Change in working capital − Nonstrategic investments
Operating surplus = Sales − Costs
Operating cash flow demand = Operating cash flow needed to meet the capital costs of the company's strategic investments – The opportunity cost of capital (expressed as a cash amount; not as a percentage)

As one expert put it,[17] CVA represents the cash flow needed to meet the investors' financial requirements of the company's strategic investments. Interestingly, despite its name, this is not considered a discounted cash flow method; rather, it is considered to be a residual method.

The CVA metric seems appropriate for a consumer products company because so much of the consumer products business depends on the efficient movement of products. Also, consumer products companies—and industrials in general—have a wide variety of significant stakeholders. The CVA metric can be presented to show what cash value each group of stakeholders receives, enhancing a company's corporate responsibility profile.[18]

Discounted Cash Flow (DCF)

Discounted cash flow is as simple as it sounds. Take the cash flow expected in the future, and calculate its present value, using a discount rate based on the cost of capital for the firm. Depending on the perspective of who's expecting the money, the cash can come from dividends (dividend discount model), from operating cash flow (present value of operating cash flows), or from free cash flow (present value of free cash flows to equity). In the case of earnings-based cash flow, DCF is calculated by taking projected annual earnings over some future period, getting its present value according to a discount rate, which is the weighted cost of raising capital by issuing debt or equity.

One kind of DCF involves free cash flow, that is, cash flow net of taxes. Another term for this is net operating profits after taxes (NOPAT). For any period of time (past, present or future), the calculation is

$$\text{Free cash flow} = \text{NOPAT} - \text{Change in capital employed}$$

where
Change in capital employed = Percentage by which capital employed (Capital employed = Equity + Long-term debt) changes for the period

The DCF methodology is helpful to companies that may not have strong current revenues but project strong revenues, such as pharmaceuticals companies.[19]

The discounted cash flow model typically proceeds in two periods: a known forecast period and some terminal value. For each year in the known forecast period, there is an individual forecast of free cash flow. By contrast, all of the years in the posthorizon period are represented through one continuing value formula, being the steady-state value of the firm's producing assets at the horizon. Continuing value is typically derived by applying the so-called Gordon formula to a simple extrapolation of free cash flow at the end of the explicit forecast period.[20]

Continuing value at the end of the DCF attempts to project value well into the future. It gives a two-stage formula in which the first part is a known period of investment, and the second part is after the known period. Breaking returns into two parts enables two things. First, because the first part of the formula is short term, the analyst can include detailed assumptions that would be difficult to forecast far into the future. Second, by adding the second tier, it extends the usefulness of the formula.

The formula for DCF can also be used to produce a simple metric called continuing value. DCF is the present value of future economic profit (EP); so the calculation is as follows:

$$\text{Continuing value} = \frac{\text{Economic profit}_{T+1}}{\text{WACC}}$$

$$+ \frac{\text{NOPLAT}_{T+1} \times \dfrac{g}{\text{RIOC}} \times \text{ROIC} \times \text{ROIC} \times \text{WACC}}{\text{WACC} \times (WACC - g)}$$

where

Economic profit $_{T+1}$ = Normalized economic profit in the first year after the forecast period (that is, EP = Net operating profit after tax [NOPAT] less a capital charge)

NOPAT = invested capital cost of capital

g = expected growth rate of return in NOPLAT in perpetuity

ROIC = expected rate of return on net new investment

WACC = weighted average cost of capital

WACC is exactly what it says: the cost of capital. If the capital is in the form of debt, it is the interest rate charged times whatever time period and compounding may apply. If the capital is in the form of equity, it is the expected return. The weighted average part pertains to a portfolio. WACC is the expected return on a portfolio of all a firm's securities. The weights are determined by the distributions of the securities (equity and/or debt).

DCF is often combined with other approaches (see, for example, the CFROI metrics above). By itself, DCF may not be robust enough to value a complex company. However, it is very appropriate to value a company unit.[21]

Economic Margin Framework

Economic Margin Framework, a proprietary model of the Applied Finance Group, is calculated as:

(Operating cash flow – Capital charge)/Invested capital

Its creators believe that it combines the best of CFROI and EVA, because it calculates an economic value (like EVA), while at the same time incorporating a fade rate (like CFROI).[22]

Economic Value Added™

Economic Value Added™, developed by Joel Stern and trademarked by Stern Stewart & Co., enables investors or lenders to determine the value they will receive for the funds they loan or invest. EVA estimates the amount that future earnings will differ from the required minimum rate of return (against comparable risk) for providers of capital. The formula is

$$EVA = (r-c) \times K = NOPAT - c \times K$$

where

r	=	return on invested capital = NOPAT/K
NOPAT	=	net operating profit after tax
c	=	weighted average cost of capital (WACC)
K	=	capital employed

This model, like cash value added, is considered a residual model, rather than a discounted cash flow model. It's also called an "economic measurement" to distinguish it from market-based measures. The vendor of this approach, Stern Stuart, offers more than 150 ways to customize it, although users reportedly make only a few adjustments.

Because this is one of the more widely accepted approaches and because of the ability to customize it, this metric is particularly suitable for a large, diversified company.[23]

Economic Value Management (EVM)

Economic value management, developed by Eleanor Bloxham, is a valuation approach created for managers, rather than investors; so it is in a class by itself. Nonetheless, it is worthy of inclusion because it shows the narrowness of some of the other concepts. EVM is broader than shareholder value because it examines economic value management from the perspective of all the potential constituents of an organization and their roles.

Many people have written about stakeholders, but Bloxham makes a significant contribution by analyzing them by role: she sees a central role for internal and external suppliers. Internal suppliers are board, management, and employees. Externally, on the one side, we have providers of capital (equity and debt) and on the other we have consumers (customers). Other important stakeholders are citizens and regulators who represent them, as well as observers (critics, the media). Bloxham sees value as a function of all these relationships. Although this approach does not easily lend itself to simple formulas and models, it can be very useful for running company or, in the case of investors, for evaluating how well a company is run.

In some applications, the theory of EVM emphasizes economic profit, which says the value of a company is the amount of capital investment plus a premium equal to the present value of the value created in each year going forward. The main formula for this is:

$$\text{Economic profit} = \text{Invested capital} \times (\text{Return on invested capital} - \text{WACC})\,[24]$$

For an example of the use of economic profit as part of economic value management, see Appendix 6.1. In that example:

$$\text{EP} = \text{Net operating profit after tax (NOPAT)} - \text{Capital charge}$$

where
$$\text{NOPAT} = \text{Invested capital} \times \text{Cost of capital}[25]$$

Enterprise Value

The enterprise value formula is a financial rather than a strategic concept, and its value is close to liquidation value. Therefore, company managements don't often use it. This measure seems to be more common in academic and investor circles.[26] This metric assumes that the worth of a company is the sum of all outstanding obligations (stocks, bonds, and debts) minus the cash the company has on hand. The formula is as follows:

$$\text{Enterprise value} = \text{Market capitalization} + \text{Preferred stock} + \text{Debt} - \text{Cash equivalents}$$

where

Market capitalization = Shares of stock outstanding × Current stock price

Preferred stock = Value of preferred stock (as found on the balance sheet)

Debt = Long-term debt + Short-term debt (all debt from the balance sheet)

This is considered a residual value measure, rather than a cash flow measure.

Market Value Added

Market value added (MVA) is the difference between the equity market value of a company (total shares outstanding multiplied by current stock price) and the sum of the adjusted book value of debt and equity capital invested in the company. The simplest formula is

$$\text{MVA} = \text{Market value} - \text{Invested capital}^{27}$$

or, expressed more mathematically,

$$\text{MVA} = V - K$$

where

MVA = market value added

V = the market value of the firm, both equity and debt

K = the capital invested in the firm

Total market value is the sum of the *market* values of debt and equity, while total capital supplied is the sum of the *book* values of debt and equity. Some analysts use the book value of debt as a proxy for the market value of debt.[28] However, when they do this, the formula becomes simply market value of equity minus book value of equity (because the debt cancels out).

MVA is equivalent to the present value of all future expected EVAs. Positive MVA means the value that management's actions have contributed to the company are higher than the value of that capital markets have contributed. (See Chapter 7 for more thoughts on management genius.)

The drawback of this approach is that it cannot be used for a company unit. Also, it does not take dividends into account. [29]

Return on Capital Employed (RCE)

Return on capital employed is calculated as follows:

$$RCE = \frac{Earnings\ before\ interest\ and\ taxes}{Capital\ employed} \times 100\%$$

where
  EBIT = earnings before interest and taxes
  Capital employed = Total assets − Current liabilities

Based on one example, a positive return is in the order of 18 percent.[30]

Return on Net Assets (RONA)

This measure's formula is

Profit after tax/(Fixed assets + Working capital)

Enthusiasts of this approach point out that it is simpler than some measures (such as CFROI).[31]

Shareholder Value Added

The shareholder value added (SVA) approach, developed by valuation expert Alfred Rappaport (see also Chapter 4), attempts to measure what a company is worth to shareholders. SVA estimates the total net value of a company and divides this figure by the value of shares. This metric has gained wide acceptance and is used by a number of blue-chip multi-national companies.[32]

The value-added part says a company adds value for its shareholders only when equity returns exceed equity costs. Once the amount of value has been calculated, targets for improvement can be set, and shareholder value can be used as a measure for managing performance. (The management of shareholder value requires more complete information than traditional measures.)

A company's shareholder value can be calculated as follows:

Shareholder value = Total business value − Debt

The value given to shareholders is found by subtracting the market value of any debts owed to the company from the total value of the company:

$$\text{Total business value} = \text{Present value of future cash flows} + \text{Residual value of future cash flows}$$

In his writing, Al Rappapport identifies seven drivers of cash flow: operating profit margin; the ratio of operating profit to net sales; income tax rate; working capital investment; fixed capital investment; cost of capital; and value growth duration.

If total business value is greater than 1, then the company is worth more than the invested capital and value is being created.

Total Shareholder Return

Total shareholder return (TSR), also called total business return in a more generic sense, is a simple valuation measure that can be used as a check point for an investment. It is a forward-looking internal rate of return.

$$\text{Total business return} = \begin{array}{l} \text{Terminal value for end of period} \\ - \ \text{Gross cash investments at beginning of period} \\ + \ \text{Gross cash flows between periods} \end{array}$$

TSR, or holding period return (HPR), as it is sometimes called, is the return a shareholder earns over a specified period of time. It is derived using the following formula:

$$TSR = \frac{SP_1 - SP_0 + D}{SP_0} \times 100\%$$

where
SP_1 = share price at end of period
SP_0 = share price at beginning of period
D = dividends paid during the period

Using Metrics to Measure Management

Metrics open two windows for investors.[33] First, investors can use them to decide whether to buy, sell, or hold, and within what price range. Second, they can find out what metric managers are using and form an opinion of how good the managers are as stewards of value.

➤ In his classic article entitled "Measure for Measure," financial journalist Randy Myers noted that if a company wants to promote balance sheet efficiency, control working capital, increase asset turnover, and improve receivables, managers can use RONA, DCF, or EVA, all of which link profits to the balance sheet. However, if assets are depreciating, then either CFROI or return on gross investment ROGI, a simplified CFROI, is best because it is sensitive to depreciation. In the CFROI model, the cash on cash ratio is converted to an internal rate of return by recognizing the finite life of capital, classifying a portion of the original investment as depreciating and a portion as nondepreciating.[34]

➤ Growth-oriented companies tend to avoid return measures such as ROE, return on capital employed (ROCE), RONA, ROGI, and CFROI. These companies should choose from EVA, CVA, net present value, or TBR (mentioned above) because they don't insist on efficiency.

➤ Obviously any company without hard assets would find it challenging to use value-based performance metrics that include assets.

A Basic Distinction: Residual Income vs. Discounted Cash Flow

The approaches discussed so far may be grouped into two types of metric: one based on return (what investors get compared to what they give) and those based on flow (what investors get compared to what they could get elsewhere). Return metrics include anything with the word "return" or "added" in the title, such as cash value added, Economic Value Added (EVA)®, and enterprise value added. Interestingly, all yield the same values as discounted cash flow models.[35]

Residual Income Value

When used to value stocks, the residual income model separates value as the sum of two components: the current book value of equity plus the present value of expected future residual income. The expected future residual income is

$$\text{The sum from time } t = 1 \text{ to } \infty \left(\frac{\text{RI}}{\left[1 + r \right]_t} \right)$$

This model can be used to value the firm based on this formula or to value a share (by using a per-share measure). The blog operated by William Trent, CFA, makes an interesting point about residual value: "Unlike models that discount dividends or free cash flow, in which a significant portion of the estimated value is the terminal value, a residual income model tends to be front-end loaded by the reliance on book value. This can be an advantage since forecasting errors tend to magnify over time."[36]

Residual income springs from the economic concept of residual value. In classic accounting, residual value is either the value something can be sold for at the end of its useful life or the value of an asset or property one if leasing at the time the lease expires It also means, philosophically, cash flows arising after the normal planning period. It has been estimated that as much as two-thirds of the value of a business can be attributed to cash flows arising after the normal planning period (usually 5 to 10 years). Viewed another way, only one-third of the value of a business results from cash flows arising during the normal planning period.

Out-of-the-Box, or Generic, Valuation Models

As already shown, a number of percentages and ratios have risen to the level of an approach to value. An analyst can easily turn the simpler ones into spreadsheets. The proprietary models are more complex and require engaging a vendor. If investors or others don't feel a need to understand the logic of a model, out-of-the-box software enables them to put in numbers and get a result. However, even if investors know the variables, this approach still seems like a black box. Investors should want to know the formula or algorithm that drives the factors.[37]

To Do It Yourself, You Must Take Steps

Investors are constantly valuing aspects of securities, and so they rarely see their process as a series of steps. Yet there are indeed paths to valuation, paths that may vary (even though all roads lead to Rome). For example, Matt Richey, a popular financial blogger, lists these as his steps:

1. Calculate operating free cash flow.
2. Calculate expected growth.
3. Factor in dilution from options.

4. Set a discount rate.[38]
5. Calculate terminal value.[39]
6. Calculate cash per share.[40]
7. Run assumptions through a DCF.
8. Set a range of fair value estimates.
9. Link the DCF value back to the price-to-free-cash-flow (P/FCF) multiple.[41]

This seems to be a good series of steps and constitutes a very useful approach to consider, if the only information you have is from financial statements and ticker tapes. See Chapter 9 for the author's series of steps.

Reconciling the Balance Sheet and Income Statement

Many hybrid approaches combine elements from the balance sheet (assets, liability, equity) and/or income statement (sales, expenses, earnings), in combination with some reference to cash flow and/or market value. This catholicity is key to their effectiveness. But digging deeper, the analyst may want to break down the silos of value represented by these domains. Doing so requires a fundamental change to accounting.

For example, consider a proposal from Joel Jameson, an independent economist based in Los Altos, California. In a July 2008 comment letter to the SEC,[42] Jameson presents a hybrid of two basic views of income: one based on assets and liabilities, and the other based on revenues and expenses. He derives operating income via a present value calculation and then posts it in a double-entry bookkeeping framework based on credits and debits. In this way, Jameson attempts to bridge the balance sheet and the income statement. His resulting formula integrates a fair-value market-based balance sheet with an equally fair-value market-based income statement. The formula employs stochastic calculus via an ex-ante equation (that is, before the period being measured), to estimate instantaneous asset-and-liability incomes. All nonequity postings pass through the income statement.

In this financial reporting model, all income streams, coupled with operating income, yield a measure Jameson calls "permanent income." They don't include windfalls, which always present noise to the value-minded analyst; windfalls are presented in a separate statement.

The Jameson formula calculates asset-and-liability windfalls based on "instantaneous" incomes and market-value changes. Permanent income plus windfalls yield fair-value economic income on a clean surplus income statement. The only data needed, claims Jameson, are the data already collected for fair value accounting. The overall result, he states, provides both a meaningful earnings (income) number and an asset-and-liability stewardship metric.[43]

Ex Ante Equation

The ex ante equation is as follows:

$$\text{Ex ante income} \ = \ \frac{r \times \text{Capital value}}{1 + r}$$

where
  r = expected appreciation or discount rate

In this equation, capital value is not defined, other than to say (later in the paper) that it means "end of period account balances." (In classical economics, "capital value" is a leasing term. The capital value of a rentable item or property is equal to the discounted value of its future rents.) Jameson continues: r times capital value yields mathematically expected ex post income, which is discounted to the present to yield ex ante income.

Windfall Equation

Jameson's windfall equation is defined as:

$$\text{Windfall} = \text{Ex post income} - \text{Ex ante income}$$

If a capital value performs as suggested by the r value, then the windfall value is zero.

Jameson's ex ante equation is equally applicable to assets and liabilities, where end-of period account balances are used as the capital value parameter. In practice, r should either be the same r used in the present value calculation, be equal to the risk-free interest rate for publicly traded assets and liabilities (because of the no-arbitrage theorem[44]), or be based on existing asset depreciation schedules, in which case it is negative. For appreciating assets, ex ante income is positive; for depreciating assets and for liabilities, ex ante income is negative.

The ex ante equation yields a mathematically expected instantaneous income, scaled to span the upcoming period, says Jameson. Implicitly, it is assumed that the capital value parameter follows a stochastic process. The capital value stochastic process has a mean appreciation rate (r), which is used to calculate ex ante income. Assuming unbiased capital and r values, the yielded ex-ante income is also unbiased, that is, on average correct.

The yielded income of the ex ante equation is based only on the capital value, not any history of that value. Whether the capital value has been increasing or decreasing prior to the application of the ex ante equation is not considered and does not impact the calculation of ex ante income. The advantage with the ex ante equation's not considering any history is that it yields a true indication of ex ante value, defined as the mathematically expected value that can be perpetually and constantly consumed, beginning at the time of measurement, on a periodic basis.

Will Jameson's idea ever be accepted as a new approach to accounting, either in GAAP or in the global accounting framework with which it is now being integrated? Change is slow, deliberate, and collective in these domains, so we cannot be sure. Nonetheless, this model may find some utility in the realm of valuation. Whereas by definition accounting must follow generally (and now *globally*) accepted practices—as approved by authorities (the Financial Accounting Standards Board and the International Accounting Standards Board)—valuation is another matter. When it comes to willing buyers placing valuations on corporations in a free market, there may be guidelines and precedents, but there is still a great deal of flexibility.

Reconciling the Income Statement to the Statement of Cash Flows

As the Jameson formula reveals, one of the challenges in valuation is the use of financial statements with no clear correlation. Jameson reconciles the income statement with the balance sheet, but what about the cash flow statement? An SEC committee focused on this challenge and came up with an approach that aligns these two major financial statements, the income statement and the cash flow statement. See **Exhibit 6.2,**

Exhibit 6.2 Reconciliation of the Statements of Income and Cash Flows

	A	B	C	D	E	F	
			Noncash Items Affecting Income				
	Cash Flow Statement	**Cash Flows Not Affecting Income**	**Accruals and Systematic Allocations**	**Recurring Valuation Changes**	**Other Valuation Changes**	**Income Statement A + B + C + D + E**	
Operating							
Cash received from sales	$2,700,000		$ 75,000			$2,775,000	Sales
	0		$ 9,000		($15,000)	($ 9,000)	Depreciation expense
	0				($15,000)	($ 15,000)	Impairment expense
				$7,500		($ 7,500)	Forward contract adj.
Investing							
Capital expenditures	($ 500,000)	$500,000				0	
Sale of available-for-sale securities	$ 5,000	$ 4,900		$ 350		$ 450	Realized gain on sale
Financing							
Interest paid	($ 125,000)	($100,000)				($ 225,000)	Interest expense

Source: SEC Advisory Committee on Improvements to Financial Reporting, Substantive Complexity Subcommittee Update, http://sec.gov/rules/other/2008/acifr-scsupdate-050208.pdf.

which shows that the amounts recorded on the income statement are totals from cash flows, accruals, allocations, and valuation changes.

One of the challenges in valuation is the use of various financial statements with no clear correlation. An SEC committee focused on this challenge and came up with an approach that aligns two major financial statements, the income statement and the cash flow statement.

A New Balance Sheet Metric

The preceding reconciling approaches, although untested, are logical. At the same time, they both remain firmly within the realm of currently accepted accounting principles; they reconcile concurrent paradigms. To break out of the box of conventional accounting, the most urgent tasks ahead—as indicated in Chapter 1 and discussed in greater detail in Chapter 7—may be to include the value of nonbooked intangible assets (and debts) as part of the valuation formula. The approaches discussed in this chapter try to do this indirectly (by including market value or by using value-sensitive present value and/or discount rates). However, a more direct approach to the problem is possible.

Here are the calculations that one analyst uses to convert reported accounting data into a meaningful foundation for public value of a well-known company:

1. Calculate average pretax earnings for the past three years. Let's say $3.694 billion.[45]
2. Go to the balance sheet and get the average year-end tangible assets for the same three years: $12.953 billion.
3. Divide earnings by assets to get the return on assets: 29 percent. (A nice business, pills!)
4. For the same three years, find the industry's average return on assets.
5. Calculate the excess return, comparing the company and its peers. For this company, the excess is $2.41 billion. (That's how much more Merck earns from its assets than the average company in its industry does.)
6. Pay taxes. For this company, the average tax rate is 31 percent: $1.66 billion.
7. Calculate the net present value of the premium: $11.1 billion.

And there it is: the calculated intangible value (CIV) of Merck's intangible assets—the ones that don't appear on its balance sheet.

On the liabilities side are undisclosed liabilities in the form of externalities. Although the corporation has the power to place costs elsewhere, it doesn't truly have the right to do so, and, over time, displaced costs have a way of coming home to roost, whether through regulation or market forces. Because the value of a corporation is intimately connected to its future, and because its future is clearly affected by assets and liabilities that extend beyond normal accounting standards, the analyst must take a broader look.

Use of Hybrid Valuation Approaches in a Key Industry: Energy

In addition to these valuation approaches used across industries, there are some hybrid approaches within specific industries.

Energy

Here are six widely used hybrid valuation techniques in the oil and gas energy sector, especially applicable to the exploration and production (E&P) subindustry, according to JPMorgan Chase:[46]

1. *Price/cash flow (P/CF)*. Divide stock price by discretionary cash flow (cash flow from operations before changes in working capital). In times of low commodity prices, multiples expand, and in times of strong commodity prices, multiples contract. This metric, while easily calculated, can be misleading in cases of above-average or below-average financial leverage.

2. *Enterprise value/EBITDAX* (earnings before interest, taxes, depreciation, amortization, and exploration expense [X]). This is a better metric than P/CF because it adjusts for financial leverage (i.e., a highly leveraged company may look cheap on a P/CF basis but more average or even rich on an EV/EBITDAX basis). Earnings are less of a concern for E&P investors. In times of low commodity prices, multiples expand, and in times of strong commodity prices, multiples contract. The E&P sector has traded at 5.0 times EBITDAX on average during the past five years, with a high of 7.2 and a low of 3.2.

3. *Enterprise value/FCF (free cash flow).* This multiple captures important differences in maintenance capex (expenditures required to keep production flat)/finding efficiency among the companies. Thus it should be a better indicator of sustainable growth potential. Free cash flow, as the authors define it, is unleveraged cash flow (i.e., discretionary cash flow less cash taxes and interest expense) minus maintenance capex. The underlying concept with EV/FCF is to assess what an investor is paying for the sustainability of a given asset base's growth profile, which is a direct function of its free cash flow.

4. *Enterprise value/normalized EBITDAX.* This is the same calculation as EV/EBITDAX. However, the EBITDAX is based on a theoretical normalized value that is estimated assuming midcycle commodity prices, defined as the level of oil and gas pricing that would enable the sector on average to earn its cost of capital in a given year. Unlike EV/EBITDAX, this multiple contracts in times of low commodity prices and expands in times of strong commodity prices. The E&P sector has traded at 5.0 times the normalized EBITDAX on average during the past five years, with a high of 7.9 and a low of 3.6.

5. *Enterprise value/normalized asset value*: A discounted cash flow analysis that assumes midcycle commodity prices, defined as the level of oil and gas pricing that would enable the sector on average to earn its cost of capital over the course of a year. The DCF analysis mimics the Securities and Exchange Commission's mandated present value calculation (estimated pretax future net income discounted at 10 percent, commonly known as "PV 10"), which is required to be disclosed in the reserve section of companies' 10-Ks. The SEC calculation requires the assumption of whatever the prevailing commodity prices were at the end of a reporting period. This leads to significant volatility in the PV 10 calculation from one year to another, simply because of fluctuating commodity prices. Unlike the SEC approach, this calculation assumes that the normalized or midcycle price prevailed in every given year. Stocks can trade at discounts or premiums to their normalized asset values, depending on the commodity price cycle. The E&P sector has traded at 93 percent of normalized asset value on average during the past five years, with a high of 135 percent and a low of 65 percent.

6. *Enterprise value/reserves.* This is a simple valuation tool that requires no estimates or assumptions. In general, this metric should not be used as a primary valuation multiple, because reserves vary, but it can be a useful benchmark. For example, acquirers often use it in the valuation of property acquisitions, when little is known about the specific potential of the acquired reserves to generate cash flow. Companies also sometimes prefer to repurchase stock if the shares are trading below the EV/reserve multiples of potential corporate or property acquisitions. In general, the longer the reserve life of a company or property, the lower the EV/reserve multiple, all other things being equal. This is because reserves with a longer reserve life (reserves/production ratio, or R/P ratio) take longer to produce and are therefore worth less on a time-value-of-money basis. The proportion of proved undeveloped reserves (PUDs) in the reserve base also affects this multiple. In general, according to JPMorgan analysts, the greater the proportion of proven undeveloped reserves, the lower the EV/reserve multiple, all other things being equal. Reserves that are less abundant also trade at a discount, all other things being equal.

Spark Spread

In addition, there are special considerations for the valuation of power plants, which may have fuel supply contracts (usually gas) and firm power sales agreements that lock in a gross margin from power generation.[47] The purchaser of the power plant is purchasing what is called a positive contracted "spark spread," defined as the electricity revenue less the cost of gas to produce that revenue. Given a positive spark spread, valuation analysts can proceed as follows:

➤ Project gross margins and operating margins for the generating assets for the duration of the applicable contracts, making reasonable assumptions thereafter.
➤ Apply a terminal multiple to the last year of the period projected.
➤ Examine the applicable contracts to determine how firm they are under all circumstances.
➤ Examine regulatory context (regulated entities are more financially stable and less likely to default, especially when the contracts at issue are regulated).

➤ Review the creditworthiness of contract counterparties to identify the weakest ones, using credit agency ratings and spreads where appropriate.

➤ Discount cash flows using a worst-case discount rate that keys off the weakest link.

Concluding Caveat and a Fifteenth Model

This chapter summarized some of the most respected off-the-shelf formulas for corporate valuation. These approaches are all valid, but analysts should not take them as magic bullets—as single, elegant solutions to the corporate valuation problem. There is no such thing. Valuation is hard work, and investors must look beyond the next corner, as well as over their shoulder.

In closing, here are wise words from economist Paul Krugman, in an essay that appeared over Labor Day weekend after one of the most economically challenging years in the history of finance:

> It will be a long time, if ever, before the new, more realistic approaches to finance and macroeconomics offer the same kind of clarity, completeness, and sheer beauty that characterizes the full neoclassical approach. . . . The vision that emerges may not be all that clear; it certainly won't be neat; but we can hope that it will have the virtue of being at least partly right.[48]

The same message applies to valuing an individual corporation. By all means use an elegant formula and mode, but remember to make adjustments. The result may not look as beautiful, but it will be truer to life.

So, in addition to the 14 commonly referenced models, another one goes well beyond them. It is based in market value drivers, a model developed by senior author Monks:[49]

➤ *Genius*. Respect for the gifts of the individual.

➤ *Liberty*. A product of culture, history, and economy—a tradition of respect for power outside government, societal support for wealth based on performance, and a viable trading system.

➤ *Law*. An effective legal system to protect rights of minority shareholders and other stakeholders.

➤ *Markets.* A mechanism for the purchase and sale of securities based in perceived value.

➤ *Governance.* Accountability to owners based on disclosure and compliance with legal and ethical standards.

➤ *Values.* Social and economic values in harmony with public well-being.

Many of these elements are difficult to quantify and do not lend themselves to formulaic expression. Nonetheless, they are indispensable to the valuation process. The following chapter explores these elements in greater detail.

Appendix 6.1: National Standard Company: Description of Bonus Plan Based on EVA[50]

1. What Is Economic Value Management?

Economic value management (EVM) is an integrated approach to managing a business, with the primary goal of maximizing its economic value by maximizing its generation of economic profit (EP). This integrated approach includes:

➤ *Measuring economic profit.* EP is not the same as net income as defined by generally accepted accounting principles (GAAP). It is a better measure of value creation than traditional accounting measures of financial performance because it incorporates the full cost of capital; i.e., the cost of both debt and equity.

➤ *Strategic assessment and planning.* EVM begins with an assessment of business strategies and financial performance from a value perspective. It focuses on the development of new strategies and plans intended to maximize economic profit.

➤ *Changing management processes.* Financial reporting, cost, and capital reporting, and other systems need to be aligned to support management's abilities to make decisions that create value.

EP is a measure of net operating profit after-tax that takes into account all economic costs. The principal cost that is not considered in calculating GAAP net income is the cost of equity. The "cost" of equity is a reasonable return to shareholders given the risks of their investment:

EP = Net operating profit after tax (NOPAT) less a capital charge or

$$NOPAT-(Invested\ capital \times Cost\ of\ capital)\ [51]$$

The focus of plan (described the next section) participants should be to increase EP. Increasing EP can be accomplished in the following ways:

➤ Increasing NOPAT without increasing capital.
➤ Decreasing capital without decreasing NOPAT.
➤ Increasing NOPAT at a greater rate than capital increases.

EP can also be increased by investing in new products or markets that provide the incremental return on capital in excess of the cost of capital. Finally, business units and activities that will never earn enough NOPAT to cover the cost of capital employed should be divested or outsourced.

2. Introduction to the Plan

This bonus plan (the "plan") is part of the company's strategy to approach business operations from an EVM perspective.

The primary performance measure of EVM is EP. Shareholder value is created when EP is positive or when the trend in EP is positive. The plan rewards participants for creating this shareholder value by linking bonus awards with the actual EP generated by the company.

In each year of the plan, a target level of EP will be established based on the prior year EP result and an Expected Improvement in EP. The expected improvement (EI) factor will be set at the beginning of the plan and will be in effect for the life of the plan, which is three years initially.

Target bonus amounts will be directly linked with target EP performance. Actual bonus accruals by participants will vary up or down with actual EP results relative to target EP performance.

3. Plan Objectives and Core Concepts

The objectives of the plan are to:

➤ Link the interests of management and shareholders.
➤ Encourage participants to invest in projects and activities that exceed the cost of capital.

➤ Allow participants to share in the increase in the value of the company.
➤ Reward participants for achieving, or beating, EP targets that meet investor expectations.

The core concepts/key features of the plan are:

➤ *Sustained performance over time.* The EP goals are in effect for a multiyear period and tied to a bonus bank concept which accrues individual awards below threshold or above the annual payout maximum for the life of the plan. This feature ensures that participants are motivated to sustain superior performance over time. Each participant's account balance in the bank may increase or decrease depending on EP results in each year of the plan.
➤ *Improvement goal derived from shareholder expectations.* The Expected Improvement in EP is based on shareholder expectations and the Company's strategic plan. Once the Expected Improvement goal is established at the beginning of the plan, it is added to the year-end EP result of the prior year to obtain the goal for the current year.
➤ *Unlimited upside.* There is no limit, or cap, to the amount of bonus participants may earn in the plan.

Notes

1. For a useful paper on using proprietary versus open source software, see Romain Saha, "The New Rules of Engagement: Bridging the Gap Between 'Open' and 'Commercial' Software," QNX Software Systems, http://photon.qnx.com/download/download/18280/bridging_the_open_commercial_gap_paper.pdf/download/download/18280/bridging_the_open_commercial_gap_paper.pdf.
2. This can be done with a worksheet change event. For example, a formula would kick in a code whenever D1 changes (http://forums.techarena.in/software-development/1074829.htm).
   Sample code:
   ```
   Change (By Target Value As Range)
   If Target Address = $D$1 Then
   If Target = "Yes" Then
   Target Offset (0, −1) = Range ("A1") = Range ("B1")
   Else
   ```

Target Offset $(0, -1) =$ "$= A1 + B +$
End If
End If

For more on computer programming, see Chapter 5, note 46, citing **P. R. Bagley,** "Principles and Problems of a Universal Computer-Oriented Language," *The Computer Journal* 4 (1962): 305–312.

3. Source: *2010 NACD Public Company Governance Survey.* For an explanation of results and additional resources, see Chapter 2, note 2.

4. Total is number of hits for both "discounted free cash flow" and "discounted cash flow."

5. The United States Patent Office does not commonly grant patents to computer software programs, rejecting many claims as being too obvious. The following is from the U.S. Patent and Trademark Office: "Obviousness is covered by 35 U.S.C 103. Under this statute, a patent may not be obtained if the differences between the subject matter sought to be patented and the prior art are such that the subject matter as a whole would have been obvious at the time the invention was made to a person having ordinary skill in the art to which said subject matter pertains. In a rejection under this statute, it is necessary to modify a single reference or to combine it with one or more other references. The term 'obvious' applies to this modification/combination. If the modification/combination is obvious, then the rejection is proper.

To determine if a modification/combination is obvious, three basic criteria must be met. First, there must be some suggestion or motivation, either in the references themselves or in the knowledge generally available to one of ordinary skill in the art, to modify the reference or to combine reference teachings. Second, there must be a reasonable expectation of success. Finally, the prior art reference (or references when combined) must teach or suggest all the claim limitations. (See MPEP 2142." http://www.uspto .gov/web/offices/com/iip/transcriptsn_s.htm.)

6. In the case of insurance companies, equity may be termed "statutory surplus." See discussion by Ravi Nagarajan, "Berkshire Hathaway Intrinsic Value—Part III. Insurance Subsidiaries Valuation." He sees the Berkshire Hathaway value as being based on a series of valuations, for each part of the business. For the insurance part of the business, the key metrics are statutory surplus and policy holder float.

7. Thomas S. Y. Ho and Sang Bin Li, *The Oxford Guide to Financial Modeling: Applications for Capital Markets, Corporate Finance, Risk Management, and Financial Institutions* (Oxford: Oxford University Press, 2004).

8. Valuation, http://pages.stern.nyu.edu/~adamodar/New_Home_Page/valuation/val.htm.

9. See, for example, the change announced at the New Zealand–based Transnet Company: "In the year ahead CFROI will be replaced with Shareholder Value Add (SVA). SVA will establish a single Group value concept, by integrating financial and operational KPIs," http://onlinewebstudio .co.za/online_reports/transnet_ar09/over_indicators.html.

10. "The annual bonus plan for the CEO and CFO was comprised of a combination of cash flow return on equity (CFROE), achievement of operating profit targets in the individual business units and meeting personal objectives. CFROE. We believe that CFROE, which focuses on the company's generation of cash flow against the equity capital employed, is an important measure in assessing our financial performance. We make adjustments to the CFROE calculation to focus the calculation on the actual financial performance of Torstar's operations." (Information Circular. Torstar Corporation, March 1, 2009, http://www.torstar.com/pdf/informationcircular.pdf.)

11. For example, Northrop Grumman, 2009 Annual Report, p. 36, http://www .northropgrumman.com/images/annual_report/2009_noc_proxy.pdf.

12. J. Bartley Madden, "Maximizing Shareholder Value and The Greater Good," white paper, 2005.

13. This formula assumes current dollar value of nondepreciating assets, inflation-adjusted treatment of current assets and land asset life, and uses an average depreciation term for all assets

14. Michael J. Maubossin quoted an analysis by CSFB, that, measured by CFROI, the performances of companies tend to converge after five years in terms of their survival rates (Michale J. Maubossin, *More Than You Know: Finding Financial Wisdom in Unconventional Places* (New York: Columbia University Press, 2006)). The CFROI for a firm or a division can then be written as follows:

$$CFROI = \frac{\text{Gross cash flow} - \text{Economic depreciation}}{\text{Gross investment}}$$

This annuity is called the economic depreciation.

$$\text{Economic depreciation} = \frac{\text{Replacement cost in current dollars}\,(K_c)}{[1 + K_c]n - 1} \quad \text{where}$$

n is the expected life of the asset. For one person's (possibly biased) comparison of CFROI to other valuation techniques, see http://www.valueanalytix .com/articles/sva_vs_cfroi.html.

15. CROGI is used as a key metric by the Norwegian fertilizer and fertilizer byproducts company, Yara. http://www.yara.com/doc/Financial%20review %202008.pdf.

16. Operating cash flow is synonymous with Earnings before Depreciation, Interest, and Tax (EBDIT). See Buctaru Dumitru, "Analysis Model of Company Treasury in the European Theory and Practice," http://steconomice .uoradea.ro/anale/volume/2008/v3-finances-banks-accountancy/017.pdf.

17. J. H. M. de Jonge, an analyst based in the Netherlands, at http://www .valuebasedmanagement.net/methods_cva.html.

18. Brown-Forman, "Corporate Responsibility," http://www.brown-forman.com/ responsibility/priorities/economic-contribution.aspx.

19. "Precedent Transactions Analyses to estimate potential acquisition value. Using base case financial forecasts provided by our management, which assume positive I2S clinical trial results as well as the successful commercialization of all other pipeline programs, SG Cowen estimated our company's potential acquisition value, based on precedent acquisitions in our industry. SG Cowen arrived at an acquisition value range of $15.78 to $28.27 per share. . . . Again using management's base case forecasts, and again assuming positive I2S clinical trial results and the successful commercialization of all other pipeline programs, SG Cowen performed a discounted cash flow analysis of our company as an independent entity which yielded a range of standalone value for our company of $21.56 to $36.76 per share." ("Board of Directors Urges TKT Stockholders to Vote 'FOR' Shire Transaction," press release of July 12, 2005, http://www.shire.com/shire/NewsAndMedia/ News/showtktshirepress.jsp?ref=2&tn=3&m1=8&m2=36.)

20. The Gordon formula states that the real return from buying and holding a stock forever and consuming the dividends is equal to the dividend yield plus the real rate of dividend growth. See Kenneth S. Reinker and Edward Tower, "Predicting Equity Returns for 37 Countries: Tweaking the Gordon Formula," July 12, 2002, http://www.econ.duke.edu/Papers/Other/Tower/ Equity_Returns.pdf. See also L. Peter Jennergren, "Continuing Value in Firm Valuation by the Discounted Cash Flow Model," presented at the 32nd meeting of the EURO Working Group on Financial Modelling, London, April 2003.

21. The third quarter 2009 report for US Concrete states, for example, "The estimated fair values of the Company's reporting units were based on discounted cash flow models derived from internal earnings forecasts and other market-based valuation techniques" (http://www.faqs.org/sec-filings/091105/ US-CONCRETE-INC_8-K/v164900_ex99-1.htm).

22. Daniel J. Obrycki and Rafael Resendes, "Economic Margin: The Link Between EVA and CFROI," in *Value-Based Metrics: Foundations and Practice*, Ed. by Frank L. Fabozzi and James L. Grant (New Hope, PA: FJF, 2000).

23. For a description of why and how Allianz uses EVA, see https://www.allianz .com/en/investor_relations/share/value_based_management/page1.html.

24. An alternative formula is Net Operating profit – Adjusted taxes.
25. See Appendix 6.1 for further explanation.
26. See, for example, the discussion of enterprise value in Joshua Rosenbaum and Joshua Pearl, *Investment Banking: Valuation, Leveraged Buyouts, and Mergers and Acquisitions* (Hoboken, N.J.: John Wiley & Sons, 2008).
27. A more expanded formula is:

$$MVA = V - K_0 = \sum_{t=1}^{\infty} \frac{EVA_t}{(1 + c)^t}$$

28. "The purpose of the analysis is to assess the addition to shareholders' wealth; determining the market value of most corporate debt issues is difficult because they are not actively traded; debt market values are usually relatively close to book values; and the market value of an organization's debt is more closely tied to interest rate movements than to managerial actions that influence shareholder wealth. Essentially, the assumption is made that the market value of debt equals its book value." (Louis C. Gapensky, "Using MVA and EVA to Measure Financial Performance," *Healthcare Financial Management* (March 1996), http://findarticles.com/p/articles/mi_m3257/is_n3_v50/ai_18193961/. Monks and Lajoux comment that it is important to calculate the *market* value of debt in the MVA formula; otherwise the two debt values cancel each other out and the formula is less robust as a valuation measure.
29. 12 "Manage: The Executive Fast Track," http://www.12manage.com/methods_mva.html.
30. Toromount, http://www.toromont.com/company.asp.
31. Northrop Grumman, http://www.northropgrumman.com/images/annual_report/2009_noc_proxy.pdf.
32. John Deere, http://www.deere.com/en_US/compinfo/speeches/2009/090225_lane.html.
33. In insightful commentary well over a decade ago, Randy Myers noted: "The universe of value-based performance metrics is rapidly expanding. " And he asked, "How can CFOs determine which metric is best for their companies?" (Randy Myers, "Measure for Measure," *CFO Magazine*, November 1997.)
34. "Ironbridge Process: The CFROI Framework," http://www.ironbridgellc.net/process/cfroi.asp.
35. "In this paper we show that the three residual income models for equity valuation always yield the same value as the discounted cash flow valuation models. We use three *residual income measures*: *Economic Profit, Economic Value Added (EVA) and Cash Value Added.* . . . Specifically, we first show that the present value of the Economic Profit discounted at the required

return to equity plus the equity book value equals the value of equity. The value of equity is the present value of the Equity Cash Flow discounted at the required return to equity. Then, we show that the present value of the EVA discounted at the WACC plus the Enterprise Book Value (equity plus debt) is the Enterprise Market Value. The Enterprise Market Value is the present value of the Free Cash Flow discounted at the WACC. Then, we show that the present value of the Cash Value Added discounted at the WACC plus the Enterprise Book Value (equity plus debt) is the Enterprise Market Value. The Enterprise Market Value is the present value of the Free Cash Flow discounted at the WACC." (Pablo Fernández, "Three Residual Income Valuation Methods and Discounted Cash Flow Valuation," IESE Research Paper D-487, http://www.iese.edu/research/pdfs/DI-0487-E.pdf.)

36. The blog was founded by Thomas Robinson, who is now with the CFA Institute (cfainstitute.org) and no longer blogs. Trent's blog is http://financial-education.com/2007/10/30/the-residual-income-valuation-model/.

37. See, for example, Business Valuation Model for Microsoft Excel, http://www.spreadsheetstore.com/p-1-business-valuation-model-for-excel.aspx.

38. His default was 11 percent, based on 100 years of stock returns as of 2002.

39. Richey: Price-to-free-cash-flow (P/FCF) multiple to the year T FCF estimate, discounted that figure back to present value. A growth rate of 3 percent and a discount rate of 11 percent, would give a P/FCF of 12.5.

40. Divide earning power, plus any excess cash, by shares outstanding.

41. Matt Richey, http://www.fool.com/news/foth/2002/foth020917.htm.

42. Joel Jameson, "The Third Way: A Financial Reporting Synthesis," July 3, 2008, http://www.sec.gov/comments/265-24/26524-98.pdf.

43. For a related patent, see USPTO Patent Application 20070088637, in the section on financial accounting methods and systems to account for assets and liabilities.

44. The no-arbitrage theorem means that there are no free lunches. Here is a good technical explanation of it: "Recall that, loosely speaking, an arbitrage opportunity is a way of getting something for nothing. The arbitrage assumption is defined thanks to the existence of a strategy leading to a non negative and non zero payoff. Under a technical condition, the assumption no-arbitrage implies the existence of an interest rate and a particular probability measure which make the sum of the investments' expected value non-positive if there are short-selling constraints and equal to zero otherwise." (Laurence Carassus and Elyes Jouini, "A Discrete Stochastic Model for Investment with an Application to the Transaction Costs Case," *Journal of Financial Mathematics* 33 (2000): 57–80.)

45. This example is based on the annual report of Merck cited in Robert A. G. Monks, *The Emperor's Nightingale: How the Emerging Dynamics*

of Corporate Complexity Will Restore Integrity to Economic Life in the New Millennium (London: Capstone, Oxford: 1998); *Nightingale* was also released by Basic Books with the subtitle *Restoring the Integrity of the Corporation in the Age of Shareholder Activism.*" The full text of this book is available at ragm.com.

46. North American Equity Research, November 18, 2005, Shannon Nome.

47. The discussion of valuing the spark spread in energy assets is based on Part II of an article by John Barry, managing director, Prospect Street Ventures, entitled "Valuation of Energy Assets," *Energy Pulse*, http://www .energypulse.net/centers/article/article_display.cfm?a_id=716.

48. Paul Krugman, "How Did Economists Get It So Wrong?" *New York Times*, September 2, 2009, p. 8.

49. See the ragm.com home page, at "What Drives Corporate Value?"

50. Excerpted from SEC Info, National Standard Co., 10-Q for 12/31/97, EX-10, http://www.secinfo.com/drTA7.71e.d.htm.

51. "It should be noted that calculating capital for the purposes of this plan requires balance sheet adjustments, including adjustments to inventory (LIFO reserve), interest expense for operating leases, and RD&E."

Market Value Drivers of Public Corporations

Genius, Liberty, Law, Markets, Governance, and Values

Everything that can be counted does not necessarily count; everything that counts cannot necessarily be counted.
—Attributed to Albert Einstein, from a sign posted at his desk at the Institute for Advanced Study, Princeton, New Jersey

LET'S RECAP. Chapter 1 summarized, with caveats, existing valuation techniques. Chapter 2 identified the main kinds of *assets* found on a balance sheet and urged analysts to consider values that lie beyond. Then, turning to *earnings*, Chapter 3 advised analysts to select operating earnings rather than total earnings, to eliminate windfalls. Chapter 4 focused on *cash flow*, with an emphasis on the importance of understanding the accrual method (which is subject to manipulation) and the recommendation to select reasonable revenue projections and discount rates when forecasting. Chapter 5 dealt with *stock price*, listing price points (single day opening, average, or closing, and their multiday versions), and summarized the sobering findings of behavioral finance—human foibles and the madness of crowds. Then, Chapter 6 discussed *hybrid valuation approaches*, specifically a number of well-known approaches that combine aspects of these four main sources of valuation information.

This penultimate chapter transcends *all* of these elements and presents the theoretical work of the senior author. Using a "rocket" analogy, the authors offer valuation guidance based on six factors: genius, liberty, law, markets, governance, and values.

If all this sounds high flown, the authors apologize. Having the combined experience of being professionally involved in corporate governance for a hundred years, they are keenly aware that a false promise from an equity issuer is only "so many feet of blue sky."[1] On the other hand, a company's reach should exceed its grasp, and value lies in the margin between what is and what can be. The purpose of this chapter, therefore, is to explore this other less quantitative domain, namely management quality and factors relating to the company and the economy.

The Nonmarketability Discount

Let's return to a subject introduced in Chapter 2: the premium paid for marketability and, conversely, the discount offered for nonmarketability. As explained in that chapter, tax court valuation rulings focus on nonmarket discounts, with the IRS trying to give a relatively shallow nonmarket discount (or conversely a higher marketability premium) in order to collect more taxes. Taxpayers have used expert witnesses to establish steeper discounts and have generally prevailed, with discounts ranging from 30 to 50 percent (and conversely, premiums in that same range).[2]

The classic valuation case of *Mandelbaum v. Commissioner*, which established a healthy 30 percent discount for lack of marketability, listed factors to consider when valuing any company. The key to this case lay in some nontraditional factors. To be sure, *Mandelbaum* cited accounting results reported on financial statements, including the balance sheet, income statement, and cash flow statement. The case also mentioned the cost of a similar corporation's stock, or the firm's own stock, if applicable. But significantly, it also mentioned management quality, as well as factors relating to the company, its history, its industry, and the economy.[3] In public companies, as discussed in Chapter 2, these latter elements make an even greater contribution to value.

Six Key Elements

We propose a general theory of corporate value rooted in the following six elements:

➤ *Genius*. Respect for the gifts of the individual.

➤ *Liberty*. A product of culture, history, and economy—a tradition of respect for power outside government, societal support for wealth based on performance, and a viable trading system.

➤ *Law*. An effective legal system to protect rights of owners against appropriation by government and, conversely, right of government to protect society from overarching powers of corporations and their owners.

➤ *Markets*. A mechanism for the purchase and sale of securities based in perceived value.

➤ *Governance*. Accountability to owners based on disclosure and compliance with legal and ethical standards.

➤ *Values*. Social and economic values in harmony with public well-being.

The investment world is ready for such a big-picture approach to valuation. Consider the work of the International Corporate Governance Network (ICGN) Nonfinancial Business Reporting Committee. The nonfinancial areas under review include not only corporate governance, which is a central focus of the ICGN's mission, but also intellectual capital, human capital, the environment, customer goodwill, reputation, human rights, anticorruption practices, suppliers, and community relations.[4] The ground is therefore laid for a very inclusive look at corporate valuation.

This list is valid, but its specificity may be more suited to a proxy voting card than to a book on valuation. The authors take a more ontological view. Here are the six basic elements we see.

Element 1: Genius

Corporate equity securities can have more value than alternative investments if the people issuing the securities possess, individually and collectively, genius—from the Latin *gignere*, to beget or produce. Though the notion of a genius spirit existed in the Age of Faith, it was not until the Age of Commerce (aka the Renaissance) that genius was attributed to individual human beings. The very existence of a thriving global market brought forth this larger-than-life quality in humanity. Add to this the well-known value of a person's networks (through which any other person may be reached in six steps or fewer, the urban legend says), and the value-generating value of a human being becomes even more obvious.[5]

Robert K. Steel, undersecretary for domestic finance, U.S. Department of Treasury, put it well, in a speech before the Council on Competitiveness: "Markets serve as a bridge, connecting suppliers of capital with users of capital. They connect those who have resources to invest with those who could use this capital to turn new ideas into businesses, generating jobs and contributing to the economy." He goes on to describe the role of the Treasury Department. "We seek to ensure that the policies in place for managing our bridge are effective in protecting investors and consumers, while at the same time enhancing the *entrepreneurial spirit and innovation* that has made America great." Undersecretary Steel's words underscore the importance of *genius* as a driver of enterprise value.[6]

The existence of commercial genius resolves a basic paradox of equity: if this is such a bargain, why sell it? Esteemed valuation authors Richard A. Brealey, Stewart C. Myers, and Franklin Allen, writing during the financial crisis, note:

> Since corporate managers know more about their company than outside investors, investors are likely to infer from corporate decisions to issue equity that the firm is overvalued (otherwise, why not issue debt instead?):[7]

Following this same logic, one might say that investors can infer that *any* equity outstanding is overvalued; otherwise, managers would buy it back! Add to that the cost of transfer (the John Coase theory of economics), and we have ourselves a very poor deal in equity for sure. So is it true that *all* equity, by its *very existence*, is fundamentally overvalued? The answer is no, for two reasons:

➤ One reason is obvious: liquidity issues. Like people, corporations have times when they need money. So they can sell highly valuable shares of stock for a price less than their worth just for the cash. It is one of the oldest stories in the human family.[8]

➤ A second and perhaps more compelling reason is that knowledge goes only so far. Corporate managers *know* more about their company than investors, but they don't necessarily *understand* their company better than investors. Why not? Because managers themselves drive the value, and they cannot be objective about themselves. *Investors alone have the objectivity needed to confirm and support management genius.*

So what exactly is management genius, and how does it translate into value for securities? In their classic book on *Security Analysis*, published just five years after the crash of 1929, Benjamin Graham and David Dodd stated that:

In selecting stocks, great emphasis is laid on the question whether the company enjoys efficient management. This must imply that many companies are poorly directed. Should not this mean also that the stockholders of any company should be open-minded on the question whether its management is efficient or the reverse?[9]

Elaborating, Graham and Dodd assert that the interests of management may not be the same as shareholders—a point made earlier by their contemporaries Adolf Berle and Gardiner Means in the 1932 classic on the *Modern Corporation and Private Property*.[10]

Consider decisions about business expansion, compensation, dividends, disclosure, and spinoffs, sales, and liquidations, say Graham and Dodd. Managers and directors, absent ethical or legal constraints, can enlarge the business in order to pay themselves high amounts. They can also cut dividends and withhold information while trading on it. Also, under some circumstances, they can keep the business going even when spinning it off, selling it, or liquidating it would serve the shareholders' purposes better.

Graham and Dodd's insights on pay give pause. A trend toward megacorporations has coincided with a trend toward megapay. Although the multiple of CEO pay to lowest worker pay is down from its historic high of 525 in 2000, it is still high, at 319 a decade later.[11] Without the huge scale of the companies these CEOs head, these multiples would be impossible.

But this issue is complex. To really sabotage shareholders' interests, managers would pay themselves entirely in cash, depleting the shareholders' coffers. In fact, today, most senior executive (especially CEO) pay is awarded in equity. Although this has the downside of dilution, it also has the upside of aligning manager pay and shareholder pay. This is true of director pay as well. One study showed that of every governance reform ever generated, only one shows a consistent link to higher corporate performance, and that is paying directors in stock.[12]

Investors who wish to assess the value of management can logically start with the concept of genius, including executive leadership, strategic originality, value of technology, and human capital. A key indicator is how CEOs and senior managers are selected and compensated. To maximize value by leveraging genius, companies need:

> *Bench strength.* This requires ongoing succession planning based on the development of talent from within (rather than offering a generous package to recruit a "star"). Such planning should be part of an overall human capital system that recruits, develops, rewards, and retains the best.[13]

> *Benchmarks.* Reasonable compensation must be based on measurable performance goals, based on long-term share value, and have no ability to adjust upward if a goal is not reached.[14]

Investors have gained an increased ability to impact compensation. Since 2003, at companies listed on the New York Stock Exchange or Nasdaq, shareholders have had the right to approve any new compensation plan that includes equity.[15] Under the Wall Street Reform and Consumer Protection Act of 2010, this right was broadened to include all senior executive pay at all public companies in the United States, through a so-called say-on-pay provision. To help shareholders assess pay, proxy advisory and research firms have developed products for compensation analysis.

Globally, the ICGN has been active on this issue, issuing and periodically updating Executive Remuneration Guidelines on how companies should be structuring pay for the long term, disclosing policies and seeking shareholder support.[16]

The good news is that investors have a better window into the pay structure. Over the past two decades, the Securities and Exchange Commission (SEC) has been increasing compensation disclosure requirements. Landmarks have included a compensation table and the Compensation Disclosure and Analysis Statement (CD&A). The CD&A in particular is a gold mine for investors seeking clues about company value. It must "focus on the material principles underlying the company's executive compensation policies and decisions, and the most important factors relevant to analysis of those policies and decisions."[17] Performance indicators often combine traditional financial indicators (such as operating earnings) as well as value-building accomplishments such as increased market share or strategic accomplishments (selling or buying business units).[18]

Troika

Given a chance to name the attributes that contribute to their success, the troika of strong customer relationships (65%), employees who understand the business (51%), and quality products/services (51%) led the way.

Source: Forbes, US Middle Market Outlook 2009.

Assuming that a company has the right people paid the right amount in the right way, *how exactly do those people create value?* What moves them from genius to gold? Investors don't need to reinvent the wheel to answer this question. Two theoretical economists have done the work for us. Roland Burgman and Göran Roos have theorized that the origin of corporate value lies in the deployment of corporate assets and that this is particularly true of intellectual capital assets.[19] For example, a firm that has "control of a group of competent people" can have those people:

➤ *Work for hire for others*. The firm can transform the human resource into a monetary resource by leasing their time.
➤ *Craft a prototype*. The transformation of a human resource into a physical resource.
➤ *Generate a new customer*. The transformation of a human resource into a relational resource.

➤ *Design a new process.* The transformation of a human resource into an organizational resource.

➤ *Train another person.* The transformation of a human resource into another human resource.

Investors evaluating a company need to ask, which of these things are happening, and for what value? Unfortunately, most intellectual capital goes uncaptured in the valuation process. As one scholar notes, trying to fit existing popular frameworks to gather intellectual capital measurements inside organizations has little relevance to understanding the value-creation process. Intellectual capital measurement has relied heavily on "accountingization."[20]

But some investment analysts are making it very clear that management, interpreted broadly, adds value. The value adders are not merely stellar CEOs, but entire management teams and employee cultures. This was the kind of element that made one analyst state that Dupont shares were being undervalued as the well managed company headed into a bad economy in early 2009.[21]

Sensitivity of Financial Performance to Operating Style

One aspect of management genius is found in operating style, which can affect its financial performance. Here is a summary of research,[22] highlighting seven key operating elements that human capital expert Price Pritchett has identified as central to any enterprise: decision-making process, power and authority, communication practices, work and spending habits, performance management metrics, organization structure, and corporate culture.

Decision-Making Process

Corporate culture consists of the set of values and decisions that determine how individuals perform their activities within the organization and that define which behaviors are considered appropriate.[23] The best-selling book, *In Search of Excellence*, looked at the most frequent characteristics of successful firms and found that sharing basic values is a condition for performance improvement because it implies less coordination effort.[24]

The more directly an organization can make decisions, the more efficiently it will create economic value. This is consistent with the theory of transaction cost economics, based in John Coase's theory of economics.[25] Formal control requires rules for behavior, codified procedures, and organizational routines; informal control is based on shared norms and values. Informal control is less expensive and more effective.[26]

Power and Authority

Cooperative culture entails more delegation, better controls, and improved coordination.[27] According to one study, drawing on previous studies of culture, there are three kinds of cultures: orientation toward results (result-oriented culture), power development (power-oriented culture), and the human aspect (human-oriented culture). For each of these three sets of corporate culture estimates, Carretta and colleagues conducted extensive research in the banking industry and found evidence to support the theory that a cooperative culture can help boost economic performance. The study, which measured shareholder value as the ratio of economic value added and invested capital, found a negative link between a power-oriented corporate culture and/or results-oriented culture, but a positive link to a human-oriented culture.[28]

Communication Practices

When employees use a term drawn from the vocabulary of their organization, "what they are really doing is making reference to an individual cognitive representation transformed into organizational behaviors shared by and common to the organization to which they belong."[29] According to one study in the banking industry, an "open leadership style" that includes "broad communication flows" is associated with a human-oriented culture, which in turn is associated with higher profits and higher share price performance.[30]

Work and Spending Habits

Efficient work habits can lead to higher stock returns.[31]

As for spending habits, corporate expenditures are constrained by budgets that show greater or lesser degrees of financial discipline and a higher or lower tolerance of financial risk. Companies in the bottom 10 percent of research and development spending as a percentage of sales underperform competitors on gross margins, gross profit, operating profit, and total shareholder returns.[32] Research also shows that profitability can lead to the infusion of more capital.[33]

Firm culture and leadership (including the allocation of resources—spending) can predict firm performance.[34] Corporate culture can increase the effectiveness of the allocation of a firm's resources (and thus its financial performance) due to a few key elements that affect individual efforts toward common goals. (Banking examples are used.)[35]

Performance Management Metrics

When setting performance goals for managers, companies should look beyond the traditional ones, which are not always predictive of firm performance.[36]

Organization Structure

As stated earlier, the human-oriented culture created more shareholder value than power- or results-oriented cultures. Also, the presence of small groups (tribes or clans) and a considerable involvement of individuals in the performance of different tasks could be at the root of superior results, compared with bureaucratic and power-based organizations.[37] Power-orientation reduces the propensity to share and cooperate.[38]

Corporate Culture

Corporate culture predicts firm performance, allowing organizations to adapt to the environment's constantly changing conditions.[39] Organizational factors explain about twice as much variance in profit rates as economic factors, concluding in their study that the intangible attributes of firms are crucial for their performance.[40]

Corporate culture can be a source of competitive advantage if the environment is characterized by high competition.[41] Employee satisfaction and customer loyalty positively influence bank financial performance (using data from the branches of a large U.S. regional bank).[42] Firm culture is related to firm performance via human and social capital and differences in performance.[43]

And so that returns to the original question: Does a company's managerial genius affect its financial performance? The evidence is that the answer is yes.

Element 2: Liberty

Liberty is a product of culture, history, and economy—a tradition of respect for power outside government, societal support for wealth based on performance, and a viable trading system. "Liberty" is such a politically powerful word that some have risked death for it.[44]

From an economic standpoint, liberty (or freedom) has the following hallmarks, according to the Cato think tank, in its annual report on Economic Freedom of the World.[45]

The report defines four cornerstones of economic freedom:

1. Personal choice (rather than collective choice)
2. Voluntary exchange coordinated by markets rather than allocation via the political process
3. Freedom to enter and compete in markets
4. Protection of persons and their property from aggression by others.

Year after year, this annual report offers evidence that high levels of economic freedom are strongly correlated to increased prosperity and human well-being.[46] The 2009 report covers 141 sovereign nations. In recognition of the economic crisis and resultant increase in regulation, the 2009 report expresses concern that governments may try to restrict economic freedom, but it offers research showing that "economic freedom remains on the rise." The average economic freedom score rose from 5.55 (out of 10) in 1980 to 6.70 in the most recent year for which data are available. Of the 103 nations with chain-linked scores going back to 1980, 92 saw an improved score and 11 saw a decrease. In the 2009 Cato index, Hong Kong retains the highest rating for economic freedom, 8.97 out of 10, followed by Singapore, New Zealand, Switzerland, Chile, the United States, Ireland, Canada, Australia, and the United Kingdom.

In 2009, Hong Kong and Singapore, as in the past, took the top two positions. The other nations in the top 10 were New Zealand, Switzerland, Chile, United States, Ireland, Canada, Australia, and the United Kingdom. The rankings of other major countries include Germany (27th), Japan (30th), Korea (32nd), France (33rd), Spain (39th), Italy (61st), Mexico (68th), China (82nd), Russia (83rd), India (86th), and Brazil (111th). The 10 lowest-rated countries were Niger, Chad, Democratic Republic of Congo, Guinea-Bissau, Central African Republic, Republic of Congo, Venezuela, Angola, Myanmar, and, again in last place, Zimbabwe.

High-income industrial economies generally rank quite high for legal structure and security of property rights, access to sound money, and freedom to trade internationally. For some Western European countries, however, ratings were lower for the size of government and regulation of credit, labor, and business, pushing these countries further down on the list (e.g., Italy, at 61st place). In assessing the stock of global companies, these lessons are surely worth noting.

Along the same lines, the Heritage Foundation has created a country-by-country index for Economic Freedom of the World. The 2010 *Index of Economic Freedom* covers 183 countries around the world, ranking 179 of them with an economic freedom score based on 10 measures of economic openness, regulatory efficiency, the rule of law, and competitiveness. The basic principles of economic freedom emphasized in this *Index* are individual empowerment, equitable treatment, and the promotion of competition. [47]

Element 3: Law

Law means an effective legal system to protect rights of owners against appropriation by government and, conversely, the right of government to protect society from overarching powers of corporations and their owners.

Law addresses the relationship of public to private power. It must be above both political and economic power. Law must restrain governments from expropriating private wealth. Conversely, law must restrain the private sector from inappropriate lobbying that interferes with the workings of a free, yet just, economy (for example, by obtaining protectionist or lax legislation).[48]

Research has shown that investors are more willing to finance firms when their rights are protected because better protection provides a greater chance that company profits will be returned as interest or dividends, as opposed to being expropriated by those who control the company.[49] Investors must have absolute confidence that the fair economic return from their investments will be enforced by the prevailing jurisdiction.

The Governance Principles of the Organization for Economic Cooperation and Development (OECD) explicitly depend on a legal framework.

OECD Principles

I. Ensuring the basis for an effective corporate governance framework
The corporate governance framework should promote transparent and efficient markets, be consistent with the rule of law and clearly articulate the division of responsibilities among different supervisory, regulatory and enforcement authorities.

II. The rights of shareholders and key ownership functions
The corporate governance framework should protect and facilitate the exercise of shareholders' rights.

III. The equitable treatment of shareholders
The corporate governance framework should ensure the equitable treatment of all shareholders, including minority and foreign shareholders. All shareholders should have the opportunity to obtain effective redress for violation of their rights.

IV. The role of stakeholders in corporate governance
The corporate governance framework should recognize the rights of stakeholders established by law or through mutual agreements and encourage active co-operation between corporations and stakeholders in creating wealth, jobs, and the sustainability of financially sound enterprises.

V. Disclosure and transparency
The corporate governance framework should ensure that timely and accurate disclosure is made on all material matters regarding the corporation, including the financial situation, performance, ownership, and governance of the company.

VI. The responsibilities of the board
The corporate governance framework should ensure the strategic guidance of the company, the effective monitoring of management by the board, and the board's accountability to the company and the shareholders.

Source: Organization for Economic Cooperation and Development, published 1999; revised 2004, http://www.oecd.org/dataoecd/41/32/33647763.pdf.

UN Work in Legal Frameworks: The Freshfields Study

The long arm of the law also reaches into fund management. Some investors hesitate to factor in nontraditional metrics for fear that they may be sued for not maximizing returns. In fact, the opposite may be true. Two studies—let's call them Fiduciary I and Fiduciary II—make this point.

Fiduciary I

Fiduciary I was published in 2005, when the United Nation's Enviromental Program, through its Asset Management Working Group,[50] sponsored a Finance Initiative report titled "A Legal Framework for the Integration of Environmental, Social, and Governance Issues into Institutional Investment." Pro bono legal work came from Freshfields Bruckhaus Deringer.[51]

Freshfields studied the state of law in Australia, Canada, Europe, Japan, and the United States. Its findings show that fiduciary responsibility is not legally limited to the maximization of short-term financial returns. In all the jurisdictions examined in the Freshfields report, investment fiduciaries have some discretion, but the scope of the discretion varies:

➤ In many pension funds, the discretion is wide. Very few express limits are typically placed on how the fund may be managed.
➤ In specialized mutual funds, the discretion is narrower. The beneficiary specifies the asset profile and the investment decision maker can only implement that profile through day-to-day stock selection and other management tasks.

Some funds, notes the study, are subject to considerable control from regulators. Certain legal rules define investment decision makers' ability to integrate environmental, social, and governance considerations into their decision making. The pertinent restrictions come from specific laws (for example, about the types of assets that are permitted for certain types of investment) and from general duties that must be fulfilled (such as ensuring that investments are adequately diversified or that fiduciaries select fund managers with care). In the common law jurisdictions (the United States, the United Kingdom, Australia, and Canada), the rules are articulated not only by statute and code (as elsewhere) but also by decisions of the courts. In the common law jurisdictions some "rules" are more flexible, being open to reinterpretation over time or when applied to new facts.[52] This can be a double-edged sword for investors.[53]

In any event, no matter what kind of legal system applies, it is up to decision makers to figure out how they can integrate nonfinancial considerations into their decisions and still meet their legal obligations in the particular circumstances.

Fiduciary II

In 2009, Freshfields produced a sequel: Fiduciary Responsibility: Legal and Practical Aspects of Integrating Environmental, Social and Governance Issue into Institutional Investment. This report examines the legal aspects of incorporating nonfinancial elements into investment and recommends that they become a routine part of the investment process. Specifically, the report recommends that asset managers who are signatories to the Principles for Responsible Investment be proactive in raising social investing with their clients.

Government Involvement

Government's tendency to intervene in the affairs of industries and companies has a major effect on value, creating premiums and discounts that would not have existed in a marketplace based on supply and demand and supported by a rule of law.

For example, in recent years when various large institutions encountered financial distress, government stepped in and changed the rules of the game.

> ➤ In the case of General Motors and Chrysler, government in effect altered the agreed-upon priorities of creditors in support of public/political objectives. This created a kind of premium in value owing to the worth of a guarantee for which no premium payment had been paid.
> ➤ Another example of effects from government involvement can be seen in the differing fates of the rescued Bear Stearns and AIG shareholders versus the abandoned Lehman Brothers shareholders.

There's a nickname for government help for GM, Chrysler, AIG, Bear Stearns, and other large institutions that benefited from government involvement: "too big to fail."[54] Taxpayers and politicians alike rail against this approach, yet it persists. Unless and until the "too big to fail" approach is replaced with market-based approaches, valuation will be distorted through government involvement. Investors need to increase valuations to reflect the safety net that public policy has placed underneath corporate mismanagement. Conversely, they need to decrease valuations to recognize when that net will be taken away.[55]

Element 4: Markets

Markets enable exchanges of goods, services, money, and promises. Securities markets, for example, enable the purchase and sale of securities based on perceived value.

Are securities markets efficient? In Chapter 5, that question was answered yes and no. Markets are efficient enough to provide useful information to investors, but not efficient enough to relieve investors from their obligation to analyze value. Ideally, given time and funds, investors consider a variety of metrics, including assets, earnings, cash flow, stock price, along with the broader elements described in this chapter. The greatest economic minds have offered metaphors to describe global markets—from the invisible hand of Adam Smith[56] to the mammoth coordinator of Charles Lindblom.[57] So-called black swan or fat-tail events will always be around to throw markets into chaos.[58] But markets can nonetheless maintain an open and orderly structure; otherwise, there could be no transactions.

The orderliness of markets requires both government and private-sector cooperation. Governments around the world have been active in regulating markets, with each set of regulators facing a unique set of issues.[59] But government alone cannot ensure orderly securities markets. Issuers and traders must help.

In 2009, the International Corporate Governance Network (ICGN) released its *Global Corporate Governance Principles, Revised,* including this one: "Corporations should disclose relevant and material information concerning the corporation on a timely basis, in particular meeting market guidelines where they exist, so as to allow investors to make informed decisions about the acquisition, ownership obligations and rights, and sale of shares."[60]

More recently, the ICGN applied this same principle to troubled markets. The group has called on countries around the world to take "steps to secure fair and transparent markets in which large speculative positions cannot be built up in obscurity."[61] This would reduce the need for excessive regulation, says the group. In its *Statement of Principles on Institutional Shareholder Responsibilities* (2007), ICGN highlights the responsibilities of investors both in their external role as owners of equity and their internal governance responsibilities to their beneficiaries.[62]

Many stock and bond issuers also want to do their part to keep markets working. For example, in 2008, nine European and global trade associations representing issuers published *Ten Industry Initiatives to Increase Transparency in the European Securitisation Markets.* Here are the 10 (using American spelling):

1. Increase transparency in the reporting of securitization exposures.
2. Organize comprehensive, frequent and relevant statistical data.
3. Develop issuer disclosure code of conduct/principles.
4. Develop transparency and disclosure principles.
5. Widen access to transaction information.
6. Develop industry data portals.
7. Develop issuer/manager directories.
8. Improve standardization and digitization of reporting templates and granularity of information.
9. Standardize definitions.
10. Develop investor credit assessment and valuation principles.[63]

But investors and issuers cannot do it all. Some market reforms only regulators can bring about. The work of the Securities and Exchange Commission is globally known. Less well-known are reforms underway for other markets. The conversion of many European currencies to a single currency created a "natural experiment" that, in turn, sparked ongoing reforms in that market.[64]

Each specific stock market can benefit from similar scrutiny. Investors, issuers, and regulators need to work together to keep their markets worthy of the name.

Marketplace as Commons

The marketplace is a Commons. The ancient need for all who use the Commons is to contribute to its upkeep and avoid its abuse. We are passing through a period of time in which the cost of the "bailout" of the Commons exceeds $3 trillion. . . . It now appears clear that many of the transactions accepted by banks had no commercial purpose beyond the generation of fees. These transactions created huge losses. Should the taxpayers be responsible entirely for these losses, or should the banks (and their principal officers) who collected fees for their origination and trading share in the loss?

_____

Robert A. G. Monks, in a letter to Lloyd C. Blankfein, chairman and CEO, Goldman Sachs, April 14, 2010.

Element 5: Governance

Another key element in the construction of corporate value is governance, a broad term with many possible definitions. We define it as accountability to owners based on disclosure and on compliance with legal and ethical standards.

A number of international or national organizations have issued governance guidance, including:

➤ Organization for Economic Cooperation and Development (cited above)
➤ International Corporate Governance Network, *ICGN Global Corporate Governance Principles—2009* [65]
➤ National Association of Corporate Directors, *Key Agreed Principles to Strengthen Corporate Governance for U.S. Publicly Held Companies* (2008)[66]

The corporate governance structure of a company can impact its value. This is why over the past century shareholders have been increasingly active in setting forth proxy resolutions about governance. (This activism itself adds value—a point explored in Chapter 9.)

The governance-value connection has given rise to governance rating methodologies, which compare corporations based on a variety of governance practices. Definitions of exactly what constitutes governance vary. The dominant system may be one that traces its origins to Institutional Shareholder Services (ISS). (ISS was cofounded by Robert Monks.) The current ISS system, replacing the Corporate Governance Quotient or CGQ, is called Governance Risk Indicators™, or GRId. It gives a color code as high, medium, or low risk based on 70 variables in four areas: audit, board, compensation/remuneration, and shareholder rights.[67] But GRId is not the only system. There are many more, including, for example, Governance Metrics International and The Corporate Library (also cofounded by Monks). The major securities rating agencies (Fitch, Moody's, and Standard & Poors) include governance among the factors they rate.

The Corporate Library has identified the following red flags for governance traits associated with poor financial performance:

➤ Promanagement bias in board and committee makeup (e.g., lack of independence in composition of the board and key committees)
➤ Runaway agency costs (e.g., CEO compensation that is poorly aligned with shareholder interests)
➤ Management and/or board entrenchment (e.g., overly powerful takeover defenses)
➤ Poor board oversight of accounting (e.g., failure to prevent a finding of weak internal controls under Sarbanes-Oxley 404)
➤ Subordinated minority shareholder interests (e.g., dominant or controlling shareholder concerns)[68]

Negative Proof

There is little evidence that "good corporate governance," as currently defined, adds value:[69]

➤ We can prove conclusively that weak corporate governance puts shareholder value at risk, and will, over time, in most cases result in actual value loss. We can prove this with regard total shareholder returns, and also with regards losses as defined through successful securities litigation. We can *infer* from this that good corporate governance is essential to achieving and maintaining maximum

value. But this is still not the same thing as proving that good
corporate governance adds value.

➤ The main flaw in this premise is that there cannot possibly be one
single model of good corporate governance that can be applied
equally well to all public corporations; both ownership and corporate maturity must be taken into consideration, and a flexible spectrum of good corporate governance models supported. The typical
good corporate governance model embraced by the proxy advisory firms and most other observers (including the authors of the
Corporate Governance by Robert A. G. Monks and Nell Minow)
is most appropriately applied to relatively mature, widely held
corporations, but has far less relevance to controlled companies,
founder firms, most family firms, and many recent IPOs. The most
conclusive studies have sidestepped the full impact of this problem
by focusing on just one aspect of governance at a time, such as
takeover defenses or compensation. The main point is that good
governance is not additive but essential.

Some recent studies have suggested that commercial governance
ratings cannot be used to predict financial performance. One study
team, led by Robert Daines of Stanford University, tested to see whether
ratings by three of the services—Governance Metrics International,
and the Corporate Library—could predict five events:

1. Accounting restatements and class action lawsuits
2. Accounting operating performance
3. Tobin's Q
4. Excess stock returns
5. Alpha

Daines and colleagues found that predictive ability was low, although
they did find that the Corporate Library's governance scores predicted
a company's future operating performance and future earnings'
multiples.[70]

Sanjai Baghat of the University of Colorado took it one step further
and critiqued to test the correlation of corporate governance to corporate performance using a variety of multifactor indexes, both academic
and commercial. Baghat wanted to know which, if any of them, were the

best predictors of positive performance (measured by return on assets). But he and his team found only weak correlations using multifactor indexes and concluded that the use of such indexes raises econometric problems (such as distortions caused by subjectivity in weighting). They concluded that one governance practice with a strong correlation to stock price is director ownership of stock.[71] See Appendix 7.1 for a summary of the governance elements they studied before arriving at this conclusion.

But these problems do not prove that investors can safely ignore governance. Recent studies point to some meaningful correlations.

Stock Exchange Study

The Australian Treasury did a study of financial performance of firms on the Australian Stock Exchange that did not comply with the 10 principles and 28 best practices recommended by that exchange. The study showed a high correlation between compliance and return on assets.[72]

Pension Fund Investment Results

The CalPERS Focus List Program, the earliest such program by any pension fund, has produced excess returns on CalPERS assets in the order of about 3 percent per year.[73] Every year, the program identifies companies whose domestic internal equity portfolio show both poor economic performance and poor corporate governance. CalPERS focuses on reforming the companies' governance practices with an emphasis on accountability, transparency, independence, and discipline, in an attempt to improve shareowner wealth.

Some of the governance rating organizations have published studies showing that positive ratings on their systems correlate to positive financial performance. For example, Governance Metrics International, which institutional investors regard highly,[74] has identified six studies that show the correlation of positive GMIR to positive stock performance.[75]

Conversely, there is evidence that poor corporate governance hurts performance.[76]

And there is evidence that special-purpose funds that invest based on governance do better than comparable funds (see Chapter 8). Overall, however, the problem may be too complex to solve.

In any event, investors are heeding governance. As Robert Ferris of RF|Binder told us:

> Institutional investors are much more attuned to corporate governance measures/policies undertaken by issuers. Of course, setting standards of accountability is not a recent phenomenon. What's changed is that managements and boards, post Enron and SOX, have really taken this to heart in terms of implementation and enforcement. More important, foreign issuers and regulators have modeled corporate governance platforms on the U.S. system (in part, of course, because unlike most securities regulations, SOX compliance is applicable to foreign issuers whose securities trade in the U.S.).[77]

Disclosure

To value the securities of a corporation, investors need to see not only what the company discloses but also how it discloses the information. One of the Catch-22s of disclosure is that the more companies that are required to disclose, the more diluted the impact of each disclosure becomes (because it get buried in an avalanche of disclosure). Also, the time that it takes for companies to prepare the information becomes a tax on productivity.

The solution is to communicate key points simply and honestly. The Berkshire-Hathaway 2008 annual report is a great example of this solution. The company lost money that year, and said so.

To the Shareholders of Berkshire Hathaway Inc.:

Our decrease in net worth during 2008 was $11.5 billion, which reduced the per-share book value of both our Class A and Class B stock by 9.6%. Over the last 44 years (that is, since present management took over) book value has grown from $19 to $70,530, a rate of 20.3% compounded annually.

> The table on the preceding page, recording both the 44-year performance of Berkshire's book value and the S&P 500 index, shows that 2008 was the worst year for each. The period was devastating as well for corporate and municipal bonds, real estate and commodities. By yearend, investors of all stripes were bloodied and confused, much as if they were small birds that had strayed into a badminton game.
>
> As the year progressed, a series of life-threatening problems within many of the world's great financial institutions was unveiled. This led to a dysfunctional credit market that in important respects soon turned non-functional. The watchword throughout the country became the creed I saw on restaurant walls when I was young: "In God we trust; all others pay cash."
>
> ———————
> —Opening paragraphs of the 2008 annual report of Berkshire Hathaway

Once companies start down the road to candor, accounting models can change. Consider the proposal by Al Rappaport for a new kind of corporate performance statement. The new statement would separate cash flows from accruals and classify accruals by their levels of uncertainty, from low to high. Accruals not relevant to realized cash flows would be eliminated. The statement would spell out all assumptions and risk levels. This would enable managers and investors to make better predictions of future cash flows.[78] Rappaport says the new statement would go far in helping analysts and investors estimate future cash flows. He wants the equity market to forsake its obsession with short-term earnings as the metric to measure value and stick with long-term cash flows instead. Better disclosure is at the center of enabling the market to make better calculations of future cash flow. This new corporate performance statement would be the source of that better disclosure.

XBRL

XBRL can help disclosure as well. As mentioned in Chapters 1 and 2 and explained in Appendix O, XBRL is way of tagging electronic records so that they can be totaled, compared, grouped, and otherwise treated as data. Certainly this is a great tool for investors. We would agree with the American Institute of Certified Public Accountants (AICPA) that "the use of XBRL will provide major benefits in the preparation, analysis, and communication of business information through cost savings, greater efficiency, and improved reliability to all those involved in supplying or using financial data."[79] Furthermore, XBRL can be used for the reporting of social values, our final and perhaps most important element.

Element 6: Values

Values are the social and economic values in harmony with public well-being. These values are often referred to as corporate social responsibility (CSR). Some evidence shows that companies demonstrating CSR values do better than those that do not. In the words of attorney and ethicist Ben Heineman Jr., investors seek "high performance with high integrity."[80] In his overview on "Valuing Values" (see Appendix N), Stephen Jordan offers support for this general proposition.

Equation

Integrity *is* the business.

—Ben W. Heineman Jr., in a conversation with R.A.G. Monks

Many public companies today recognize the link between socially conscious values and long-term share values. Such "good companies" are admirably profiled in *Philanthrocapitalism*, by Matthew Bishop and Michael Green.[81]

Some companies are publishing manifestos in their annual reports or other documents, so that shareholders can see the connection. For example, the annual report of Iino Kaiun Kaisha states:

> It is a matter of course that an enterprise is established to make a profit. Therefore, we also have to improve our middle and long term performances in order to raise the enterprise value; however,

we must not raise the enterprise value without losing social benefits. We must demonstrate a positive contribution to our society. We must always keep in mind that we are operating not only for the company, but also for mankind.[82]

Work of the Enhanced Business Reporting Initiative

In January 2003, the American Institute of Certified Public Accountants established a Special Committee on Enhanced Business Reporting. Based on earlier work at the AICPA led by Edmond L. Jenkins,[83] the consortium aimed to improve the quality and transparency of information used for decision making.

After two years, the committee launched a consortium of investors, creditors, regulators, management, and other stakeholders to the Enhanced Business Reporting Consortium. The Consortium is currently working to develop an internationally recognized framework of voluntary, international guidelines for business reporting. The framework will provide structure for the presentation of nonfinancial components of business reports, including key performance indicators. The group hopes to facilitate the integration of financial and nonfinancial components industry by industry. The framework assumes full use of XBRL, which can help to provide useful taxonomies for the nonfinancial components of the reporting package, including the narrative portions of the 10K and proxy statements. The Consortium will work with industry representatives to develop generally accepted components developed on an industry basis:

➤ Definitions, measurements, and voluntary disclosure guidelines for industry-specific, process-oriented value drivers, and key performance indicators

➤ Voluntary disclosure guidelines for information about opportunities, risks, strategies and plans, and about the quality, sustainability, and variability of cash flows and earnings

The Framework can be viewed in Appendix 7.2.

Work of the Aspen Institute

The Aspen Institute has spearheaded a number of private sector initiatives to encourage long-term investing. In June 2007, Aspen released

Long-Term Value Creation: Guiding Principles for Corporations and Investors, which to date has received endorsement from 26 groups, corporations, firms, and individuals prominent in governance.[84] In late 2009, Aspen published a sequel intended for a more macroeconomic approach, *Overcoming Short-Termism: A Call for a More Responsible Approach to Investment and Business Management*. In this publication, a group of 28 individuals sounded the same themes in a "call for a more responsibility approach to investment and business management."[85] This 2009 Aspen publication recommends the following:

➤ *Market incentives.* More patient capital.
➤ *Fiduciary duty.* Better alignment of interests between financial intermediaries and their investors.
➤ *Transparency.* Strengthening of investor disclosures.

Work of the Caux Roundtable

No discussion of values in business would be complete without reference to the Principles of the Caux Round Table, as follows:

➤ Respect stakeholders beyond shareholders.
➤ Contribute to economic, social, and environmental development.
➤ Respect the letter and spirit of the law.
➤ Respect rules and conventions.
➤ Support responsible globalization.
➤ Respect the environment.
➤ Avoid illicit activities.

This short list is a good litmus test for any investors who want to make sure that their money is placed in a company that is worthy of long-term investment. The Caux Principles for Business appear in greater detail in Appendix 7.3, along with some more recently proposed guidelines for the owners of corporate wealth.

GE Profile

When a company gives back to society, this can increase their value to shareholders. Consider the example of General Electric Company (GE). The analytical service Morningstar makes a significant point about the company: "Like its industry peers, General Electric Company is a large-cap issue. However, it differs in that it has an *extreme value bias*." By "value bias," Morningstar means that investors attribute a value to the stock above and beyond the numbers. It is reasonable to assume that the enormous investment GE has made in citizenship has made a positive impact on its stock value. GE has affirmed its commitment to the following areas:

➤ *Compliance and governance.* "Our strong culture of integrity strengthens compliance and governance at GE and is the cornerstone of our reputation."

➤ *Environment, health, and safety.* "Operational excellence shapes the tools and measurements that help keep employees safe while reducing our impact on the environment."

GE tracks a great deal of data on this topic. For example, here are some highlights from its 2008 Performance Highlights:

➤ Injury and illness rate: ↓ 12 percent.
➤ Lost time rate: ↓ 17 percent.
➤ Air exceedances: ↓ 53 percent.
➤ Wastewater exceedances: ↓ 8 percent.
➤ Spills and releases: ↓ 29 percent.
➤ Greenhouse Gas: ↓ 1 percent.
➤ Water use: Flat.
➤ 29 new VPP/Global Star sites in 14 countries.
➤ 650 external environmental health and safety excellence recognitions from governments and customers.

Notably, GE put in a strong performance in 2008, according to Morningstar analysts:[86]

➤ *Public policy.* "It is our priority to work with governments and political leaders to build relationships that serve the pursuits of both business and society."

➤ *Suppliers.* "GE expects our suppliers to treat their workers fairly, provide a safe and healthy work environment and act responsibly toward the environment."

➤ *Customers.* "Our approach to customers entails working closely to define a joint roadmap toward addressing and solving their unique challenges."

➤ *Employees.* "The GE commitment to nurture employee relations has helped to create healthy workplaces that are both challenging and stimulating."

➤ *Products and services.* "GE makes strategic investments in our products and technologies based on social, demographic and environmental needs."

➤ *Human rights.* "We are guided and strengthened by our human rights principles, which advance our business relationships in all countries in which we operate."

➤ *Communities and philanthropy.* "GE acts as a good citizen by making sure that our contribution to our world extends far beyond the bottom line."

These could be seen as rhetoric, but GE backs them up with metrics. See **Exhibit 7.1**.

Investing in Citizenship

General Electric stock performs well, in part, because it has invested in citizenship. The citizenship dimension is not fully reflected in the financial reports; so GE produces a separate *GE Citizenship Report* signed by CEO Jeffrey R. Immelt, General Counsel and Senior Vice President Brackett B. Denniston III, and Vice President for Corporate Citizenship Robert L. Corcoran. At-a-glance metrics in this report include such highlights as:[87]

➤ Injury and illness rates

➤ GE Safety and Excellence Programs (number of sites) versus injuries and illnesses (incidence per one hundred employees)

➤ Air and wastewater exceedances

➤ GE U.S. toxic release inventory (Tri) on-site data 2002–2006

➤ Water in use (billions of gallons)

➤ Waste generation

➤ GE greenhouse gas emissions

Exhibit 7.1 Performance Metrics: Environmental, Health, and Safety Data

	2004	2005	2006	2007	2008
Injury & Illness Rates[a]					
Recordable rate	1.62	1.64	1.52	1.39	1.23
Lost-time rate[b]	.42	.45	.46	.42	.35
GE Safety Excellence Programs (number of sites) vs. Injuries & Illnesses (incidence per 100 employees)					
Total VPP/Star sites	134	157	183	210	238
GE recordable injury and illness rate	1.62	1.64	1.52	1.39	1.23
Air & Wastewater Exceedences					
Air	25	14	21	30	14
Wastewater	98	98	101	74	68
GE U.S. Toxic Release Inventory (Tri) On-Site Data 2002–2006[c]					
TRI on-site releases (in millions of pounds)	5.00	4.92	3.09[d]	0.42[e]	—
Water Use (in billion gallons)[f]					
Total	—	—	12.29	—	12.32
Noncontact cooling waters (NCCW)	—	—	5.88	—	6.6
Waste Generation					
Hazardous waste (metric tons)	—	—	39,807	—	43,215
Nonhazardous waste (metric tons)	—	—	209,509	—	204,740
GE Greenhouse Gas Emissions[f,g]					
GE operational GHG emission (million metric tons of CO_2 equivalent emissions)	7.50	—	—	—	6.49

(Continued)

Exhibit 7.1 (Continued)

GE operational GHG intensity (metric tons per $ million revenue)	60.58	—	—	—	35.58
GE operational energy intensity (MMBtu per $ million revenue)	496.69	—	—	—	312.75
GE operational energy use (million MMBtu)	61.50	—	—	—	57.08
Additional Metrics					
Global paid penalties (in $ thousands)	351	323	365	236	96
Training Units Completed (millions of units)					
U.S.	1.10	1.42	1.45	1.42	1.78
Non-U.S.	.45	.59	.62	.62	.68
Agency Inspections					
U.S.	694	753	861	740	776
Non-U.S.	767	736	640	474	485
Spills & releases	36	65	66	98	70

Source: General Electric, © 2010 General Electric Company, http://www.ge.com/citizenship/performance_metrics/ehs.jsp.

[a] Rates are based on 100 employees working 200,000 hours annually.

[b] Lost-time rate uses the OSHA calculation for days away from work cases (transfer or restricted cases are excluded).

[c] This data will always lag by a year since U.S. TRI data for the prior year are not submitted until July 1 as a matter of law.

[d] Does not include the former GE Advanced Materials business as it was divested in December 2006.

[e] On-site TRI Releases not including GE Plastics, which was divested in August 2007.

[f] For data associated with reductions in greenhouse gas emissions and water usage, please visit www.ge.com/citizenship/ehs.

[g] For GHG-related metrics, each year GE adjusts its 2004 baseline inventory to account for divestments and acquisitions. 2005, 2006 and 2007 fuel and electricity use and other GHG emission data were not collected for new acquisitions. As a result, adjusted results for 2005, 2006, and 2007 are not available.

➤ Additional metrics:
   ➤ Global paid penalties
   ➤ Training units completed
   ➤ Agency inspections
   ➤ Spill and releases

All this is not a signal to "buy GE." The point is merely that institutional investors who want to take a long position in a corporate stock should seek and receive some assurance that the company managers are conscious of social values because such consciousness tends to strengthen long-term financial performance.

Shareholder Resolutions

One sign of CSR's connection to long-term financial value is the existence of shareholder resolutions seeking to minimize negative environmental or social impacts from operations. Nearly half (45 percent) of all shareholder resolutions are related to CSR. Resolutions targeted at climate change receive particularly strong support. These resolutions draw a connection between environmental risk and risk to shareholder value.[88]

Criteria

Some institutional investor "investment criteria" include various levels of compliance with SOX and governance best practices, so to the extent that this governs "investment or not," effective compliance has an impact on liquidity, and therefore on valuation. Furthermore, non-compliance or faulty compliance is indeed a detractor to investor confidence, and could have a negative impact on valuation, in real terms.

—Robert Ferris, executive managing director, RF|Binder, New York City

---

Given the perceived connection between CSR and shareholder value, the oldest and largest proxy advisory firm, RiskMetrics Group (acquirer of the pioneering Institutional Shareholder Services), not surprisingly, has studied performance by companies deemed "notable" for their sustainability reports—or "communications on progress," comparing it to peer companies. To be considered notable, a communication on progress must have:

➤ A strong statement of continued support for the Global Compact
➤ A clear and detailed description of practical actions taken in implementing Global Compact principles and/or UN goals
➤ A measurement of outcomes
➤ Reporting on progress

RiskMetrics found that from March 2007 to March 2009, the notable companies outperformed the MSCI World Index by 7.3 percent (see **Exhibit 7.2**).[89] Despite the sharp market drop in October 2008, the notables outperformed the market by 6 percent, suggesting possible market valuation benefits associated with progressive disclosure on ESG issues. As of March 31, 2009, the notables achieved 10 percent higher

Exhibit 7.2 UN Global Compact Notables' Return versus MSCI World Index (performance as of March 31, 2009)

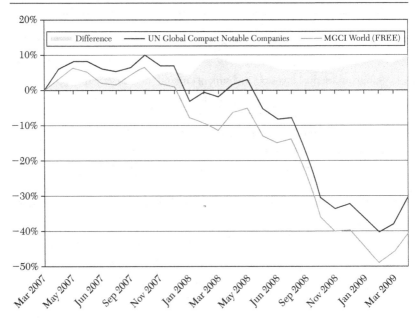

Source: RiskMetrics Group.

returns than the MSCI World Index, with notables down 30 percent for the period compared to a 40 percent decline for the MSCI World Index.

On July 21, 2009, the Social Investment Forum (SIF) wrote to the SEC recommending mandatory environmental, social, and governance (ESG) reporting and using XBRL to facilitate that change.[90] One step in that direction would be to tag the content of management's discussion and analysis (MD&A). In the United Kingdom, UK Sustainable Investment and Finance (UKSIF) has been publishing a series of annual reports as part of the UKSIF Sustainable Pensions Project. Recent surveys show a universal interest in environmental, social, and governance issues among large UK pension funds, as well as growing interest in corporate social responsibility.[91]

➤ Four-fifths of UK funds surveyed now have a responsible investment (RI) policy, compared with only two-thirds in 2007.
➤ Almost all the trustees of larger funds now believe (in 2009) that ESG factors can have a material impact on the fund's investments in the long term, increasing from three-quarters in 2007. Overall, trustees of three-quarters of participating funds agree, up from two-thirds.
➤ A third of funds give "great" significance to alignment with the plan sponsor's CSR/sustainability policy, up from a fifth.

For an example of special-purpose investment funds that focus on the environment, see Chapter 8.[92]

To the Point

Unlike many market strategists at investment banks, who cloak their recommendations in buzzwords and hedge them until they are meaningless, Buffett is to the point and says what he means. His emphasis on corporate governance puts most institutional investors to shame.

———
—Aswath Damodaran, blogging on May 2, 2009, http://aswathdamodaran .blogspot.com/feeds/posts/default.

Long-Term Investing

It's a cliché to say that investors must look to the long term. The World Economic Forum in Davos, Switzerland,[93] is doing something about it. The group has created a Global Agenda Council on Long-Term Investing, chaired by the senior author of this book.[94] Issues before the Council include:

➤ *Alignment of interest* between institutional investors and fund managers.
➤ *Risk management* to capture the complexity of market and product interrelationships.
➤ *Time frames*—adopting a long-term perspective in a short-term world.
➤ *Mitigating risk* through public/private partnership.
➤ *Mitigating protectionism* aimed at sovereign wealth funds.[95]
➤ *Climate and sustainability*—transitioning into a low-carbon economy.

Carbon: A Crucial Environmental Issue

On this last point, investors have been particularly active in environmental issues, including climate change and carbon emissions.

Green Eyeshades

Today, the imperative is for a market system that promotes sustainability and, essential to the success of that, are reliable flows of relevant and accurate information. This is the domain of the accounting profession. The CDSB's [Climate Disclosure Standards Board's] reporting framework, of which we and other accountancy bodies as well as chartered accountants from business and the firms have played a vital role, is a great example of how the profession has and can continue to play its part.

—Michael Izza, chief executive of the Institute of Chartered Accountants in England and Wales

To develop a true understanding of corporate value, value-minded investors can therefore integrate environmental factors into the analysis process. For example, they can consider the carbon and other environmental impact costs the company is incurring—both those that the company discloses and those that the company externalizes. Over the long term, those external costs may become internalized, and valuation must take account of the cost shift. See Appendix 7.4 for a profile of Trucost, a service that calculates and tracks such costs.

Another place where the environmental movement meets the investor movement is at the Climate Disclosure Standards Board (CDSB), founded in January 2007 at the Annual Meeting of the World Economic Forum.[96] The CDSB has launched a Carbon Disclosure Project (CDP), which holds the largest corporate climate change database in the world. The purpose of the project is to help companies implement the corporate accounting and reporting standard developed by the Greenhouse Gas Protocol Initiative.[97]

BP

The BP explosion and oil spill of April 2010 offered tragic proof of the link between environmental and economic goals. Within two months of the spill, BP had already spent more than $2 billion cleaning up the spill, with more costs expected. As a June 25, 2010, press release notes:

> To date, almost 74,000 claims have been filed and more than 39,000 payments have been made, totalling almost $126 million. The cost of the response to date amounts to approximately $2.35 billion, including the cost of the spill response, containment, relief well drilling, grants to the Gulf states, claims paid, and federal costs. On June 16, BP announced an agreed package of measures, including the creation of a $20 billion fund to satisfy certain obligations arising from the oil and gas spill. It is too early to quantify other potential costs and liabilities associated with the incident.[98]

Cost estimates for recovery in the region over the next 25 years range from $80 billion to $100 billion.[99] Many of these costs will be borne by national and state taxpayers and BP's insurers. Nonetheless, it is clear that the company itself has paid and will continue to pay for its environmental errors—perhaps all the more dearly due to its status as a multinational.[100] On April 20, the day of the oil spill, BP's stock was trading at $60 with a market capitalization of cost to $200 billion as of the end of the first quarter. By the end of June, BP stock was trading at below $30, and the company's market cap was under $100 billion.

Clearly, investors need to consider environmental issues when making buy/sell/hold decisions. Moreover, they need to keep such issues in mind when they hold stocks. Given the decline in stock price suffered in catastrophes, it would be unwise to pay at high levels for any company known to be underspending on environmental safety.

Default

For a long time, I have been persuaded of the unique superiority of BP's corporate governance structure involving a separate Secretariat reporting to an independent chairman. The cruel irony arises in the apparent dichotomy between governance and management. BP continues to fail to consolidate the acquisitions made by Lord John Brown of American oil companies in the sense of imposing a company wide standard of quality and care. There continues to be a nagging default setting to preferring the least expensive alternative, irrespective of risk. This might have been understandable in a world of $10 oil; it is a serious indictment in today's world.

——————

—Robert A. G. Monks, June 25, 2010.

RAGM served as an expert witness in the civil litigation arising out of the March 2005 Texas City explosion in which BP was a defendant.

A Note on Valuation for Divestment

With respect to portfolio management, the art of valuation for investment can also be seen as valuation for *divestment*. Once again, the investor community is not monolithic. For example, some investment funds may choose (for social and/or economic reasons) to divest shares of companies with bad social records, whereas some investors in those funds may disagree with this choice. But suing the funds for the divestment may be difficult as long as the reasons are disclosed. This is the case with the Sudan Accountability and Divestment Act of 2008[101] and might also be the case in future social divestment scenarios.

Golden Rule

[T]he use of positive screening for environmental, social, and ethical factors is entering mainstream investment analysis particularly where such screening may potentially yield superior financial performance by targeting companies that adopt socially responsible practices and thereby avoid future liabilities and losses. [A Mercer] study revealed that 70 percent of fund managers believe the integration of environmental, social, and ethical factors into investment analysis will become a mainstream part of investment management within three to 10 years.

—A Legal Framework for the Integration of Environmental, Social, and Governance Issues Into Institutional Investment (United Nations, 2009).

Conclusion

A corporation of value is founded on individual *genius* and shows respect for it. But to turn genius into value, five other elements are required, starting with *liberty*: a corporation of value must have a relatively unfettered ability to create and to recreate for the good; overregulation kills investment value. Another essential principle is *law*, based in fairness. There must be fairness as well as good orderly direction to support it. A corporation of value is founded on concepts of fair treatment for all investors. An analogy can be traced to the courts of equity in England, the ancestors of Chancery business courts today. The existence of a *market* for goods is also obviously a driver of value; without it, value has no real meaning. Also, a corporation of value has a system of accountability in step with the aspirational *governance* standards of its time. Finally, a corporation takes responsibility for its actions in society, operating in harmony with the public well-being and so possessing what we call *values*.

The early chapters described financial metrics and provided a "lens" for using them (flagging the importance of time, place, slope, volition, and utility). This book has also addressed the subject of stock price volatility. In this chapter is a summary of the nonfinancial elements that drive market value. By paying attention to *all* these elements, institutions can invest successfully for the long term.

The next chapter will show how these principles apply throughout the corporate and investment life cycles.

Appendix 7.1: Rating Governance

Governance is important, but what is it? The following passages are excerpted from Sanjai Bhagat and coauthors, in their landmark article, "The Promise and Peril of Corporate Governance Indices."[102]

I. Gompers, Ishii & Metrick (GIM) Governance or "G" Index

Groupings of the governance provisions in the index:

1. *Delay*. Four provisions for delaying hostile takeover bidders (the presence of blank check preferred stock, a classified board, restrictions on shareholders' ability to call special meetings, and restrictions on shareholders' ability to act by written consent).

2. *Voting*. Six provisions involving shareholder voting rights (supermajority voting for business combinations, dual class stock, limits on shareholders' ability to amend certificate of incorporation, limits on ability to amend bylaws, absence of cumulative voting or confidential voting).

3. *Protection*. Six provisions protecting directors and officers from legal liability or compensating them for termination (limited liability provisions, indemnification provisions in charters or bylaws, indemnification contracts, golden parachutes, severance contracts not conditioned on control changes, and compensation plans with changes in control provisions).

4. *Other.* Six other takeover defenses (the presence of antigreenmail charter provisions, fair price provisions, other constituent provisions, poison pills, silver parachutes, and pension parachutes).

5. *State.* Incorporation in a state with one of six state takeover laws (antigreenmail, business combination freeze, control share acquisition, fair price, other constituencies and redemption rights statutes).

Because of overlap between some of the tracked firm-level provisions and state takeover laws, the 28 tracked provisions are collapsed into 24 unique provisions. Note that the groupings can be questioned for lack of internal coherence. For example, blank check preferred is classified in the *delay* category but it is used in the creation of poison pills, which are placed in the *other* category.

II. Bebchuk, Cohen & Ferrell (BCF) Entrenchment or "E" Index

Subset of provisions in the G index used (GIM's grouping in parentheses):

1. Classified boards (Delay).
2. Limitations to shareholders' ability to amend the bylaws (Voting).
3. Supermajority voting for business combinations (Voting).
4. Supermajority requirements for charter amendments (Voting).
5. Poison pills (Other).
6. Golden parachutes (Protection).
7. Brown and Caylor Gov-Score.

III. Examples of RiskMetrics Standards[103]

1. *Audit.* audit committee consists solely of independent outside directors; auditors ratified by shareholders at most recent annual meeting; consulting fees paid to auditors less than audit fees paid; company has formal policy on auditor rotation

2. *Board of directors.* These factors include the following: managers respond to shareholder proposals within 12 months of meeting; CEO serves on no more than two other public corporation boards; all directors attended at least 75 percent of board meetings or had valid excuse for nonattendance; size of board between 6 and 15;

no former CEO is a director; no CEO related-party transactions listed in proxy; board has more than 50 percent independent outside directors; compensation committee comprised solely of independent outside directors; CEO and Chairman positions are separated or lead director is specified; shareholders vote on directors selected to fill vacancies; *annual director elections*; shareholder approval to change board size; nominating committee comprised solely of independent outside directors; governance committee meets at least once a year; *cumulative voting rights*; board guidelines in proxy statement; policy requiring outside directors to serve on no more than five additional boards.

3. *Executive and director compensation.* No interlocking directors on compensation committee; nonemployees do not participate in pension plans; no option repricing in past three years; shareholder approval of stock incentive plans; directors receive all or part of fees in stock; no corporate loans to executives to exercise options; average options granted in past three years as percentage of basic shares outstanding no more than 3 percent (option burn rate); prohibition on option repricing; expenses stock options

4. *Shareholder rights.* No staggered boards, only shareholder-approved poison pills, no authority to issue blank check preferred stock.

IV. Proprietary Governance Indices

a. The Corporate Library Board Effectiveness Rating

The Corporate Library (TCL), an investor research firm established by Nell Minow, an investor activist, and that produces research reports and commentary on corporate governance, has developed a proprietary measure of the quality of firms' governance, called the "Board Effectiveness" rating, which is a letter grade from A to F, representing a weighted average of an assessment of the effectiveness of seven governance components and an eighth personal assessment of the TCL analyst of the company's governance quality.

Components in the rating:

1. *Board Composition.* Described as the only component not based primarily on board actions and decision making, and related to an analysis of the historical governance patterns of firms that experienced

governance failures, it consists of screens on director tenure, age, and independence, the number of active or former CEOs on the board, and whether a past CEO is chairman, and director over-commitment (sitting on more than four other boards)

2. *CEO Compensation.* Depends on the balance of fixed and variable pay, how much variable pay is in the form of stock, with numerical red flags, such as base salary over $1 million, excessive options and high perquisite payments, and disclosure practices.

3. *Shareholder Responsiveness.* History of board's response to successful shareholder proposals (those receiving a majority of the votes).

4. *Litigation & Regulatory Problems.* Based on the incidence of litigation and assessed fines, includes an evaluation of the amount of disclosure of current or potential liability exposure, and the existence of repeated regulatory infractions or fines.

5. *Takeover Defenses.* Detailed information provided on defenses, with better ratings assigned for unidentified "more shareholder friendly" defenses.

6. *Accounting.* Screen compares current quarter reports against prior four quarters for indicators of potential earnings management or other accounting concerns.

7. *Strategic Decisionmaking.* Focuses on board approval of mergers and acquisitions (with lower ratings assigned to approvals of mergers resulting in significant loss of shareholder value).

8. *Analyst Adjustment.* Analyst may adjust the board rating up or down for reasons that fall outside the regular scoring system.

The first two components, board composition and CEO composition, comprise half of the overall rating, with equal weights applied to the other five governance components. The analyst adjustment is described as "determined on an individual basis."

TCL also reports a Best Practices Compliance score or benchmark, developed from other organizations' guidelines, that ranges from 0 to 100. It considers the effectiveness rating, and not the compliance score, as the preferable metric of a company's governance quality. TCL's Best Practices Compliance Score is based on the following factors: whether the firm has a classified board, majority outside directors, independent chairman or lead director, audit committee of only independent directors, formal governance policy, and the number of directors who are over 70 years old, serve on more than four other boards, and/or have more than 15 years of service.

b. GovernanceMetrics International (GMI) Market and Industry Indices

GovernanceMetrics International is an international governance rating organization, founded by individuals experienced in the investor relations and advising industry, that markets research and analyses principally to institutional investors. It provides advisory services to a variety of nonprofit organizations, such as stock exchanges, as well as to investors, but it does not provide proxy voting advisory services. Its "overall rating" governance score, which ranges from 1 to 10 and is derived from a statistical algorithm assigning numerical values to individual metrics falling within six general governance areas, is computed as a comparative score based on the governance practices and policies of other firms in the rated company's home state or region (the "home market" rating) or all firms in GMI's universe (the "global" rating).

Governance Areas ("Research Categories")

1. Board Accountability
2. Financial Disclosure and Internal Controls
3. Shareholder Rights
4. Executive Compensation
5. Market for Control and Ownership Base
6. Corporate Behavior and Corporate Social Responsibility Issues
7. Institutional Shareholder Services (ISS) Corporate Governance Quotient

RiskMetrics (as acquirer of ISS) is the market leader in the provision of proxy advisory and corporate governance services to institutional investors. It also provides governance and proxy consulting services to issuers (an activity currently under scrutiny for possible conflict of interest).[104] It has been in the advisory business for over two decades, during which it acquired competitors and expanded its services (acquiring most recently the proxy research firm, IRRC, in 2005, before it was itself acquired in 2006 [by RiskMetrics]). ISS rates companies according to a "Corporate Governance Quotient," which is derived from 63 governance factors (also referred to as governance criteria) that are grouped into four key governance areas, combining eight governance categories on which companies are evaluated. The weights assigned to the individual components are a function of their correlations with performance measures. The ratings are calculated as percentages indicating where a firm stands in relation to other firms in its industry or market. (For example, a value of 97.5 means that the company outperformed 97.5 percent of firms in its industry or stock market index, according to ISS' statistical algorithm combining governance factors.)

Governance Areas and Weights

1. Board of directors—40 percent
2. Compensation—30 percent
3. Takeover defenses—20 percent
4. Audit—10 percent

The eight most important governance variables that enter into the rating, in order of their weighting, are: audit committee with all independent outside directors; average options granted in past three years as percentage of basic shares outstanding no more than 2 percent or less or within one standard deviation of industry mean (option burn rate); all audit committee members are financial experts; board controlled by supermajority (over 90 percent) of independent outside directors; board has only one nonindependent director; directors subject to stock ownership requirements; board controlled by supermajority (between 75 and 90 percent) of independent outsiders; incorporation in state with no takeover statutes.

c. Sixteen Measures

The 16 performance measures ISS used to test its governance rating factors, which are divided into four categories of performance, are as follow:

1. *Risk*. Two measures: Volatility; Altman's Z score (probability of bankruptcy).
2. *Market*. Two measures: Total Shareholder Return; Tobin's Q.

3. *Valuation*. Three ratio measures: Price to Book; Price to Cash Flow; Price to Earnings.
4. *Profitability*. Nine measures: Dividend; Return on Invested Capital; Return on Equity; Return on Investment; Cash Flow Return in Investment; Net Profit Margin; EBITDA Margin; Sales Growth; Free Cash Flow to Sales.

The factors that ISS uses change over time, reflecting changing trends in corporate governance. For example, it no longer includes a factor for whether firms expense options, because that accounting treatment is now required and no longer voluntary. In addition, it now includes a factor for whether the company has majority vote director elections, a governance issue that first appeared on activist institutional investors agenda in any serious form in 2005, and a factor for whether the company has backdated options, an accounting issue—some would call it a scandal—that first came to light in 2006.

d. Egan-Jones Proxy Services Corporate Governance Ratings

Egan-Jones Proxy Services provides assistance in proxy voting, offering research, recommendations and voting services (such as automated vote execution, recordkeeping and vote disclosure reporting). Although its affiliated business has provided credit rating analysis for many years, it began to offer proxy recommendations commercially in 2003 (in conjunction with the increased emphasis on corporate governance and particularly the new SEC regulations regarding disclosure of mutual funds' voting). In addition to offering general voting evaluating the impact on "shareholder value," it provides voting guidelines tailored to certain labor union funds' needs that ensure that "the rights and interests of labor are respected." Egan-Jones provides an "overall" rating and specific ratings on the following five factors:

1. Voting process
2. Board independence
3. Board skills
4. Financial performance
5. Disclosure/controls

How, if at all, it combines the five factors into an overall rating is not publicly disclosed. All six ratings are in the form of letter grades (with pluses and minuses).

e. Glass Lewis & Company

Glass Lewis & Company, which provides research and advisory services to institutional investors, was established in 2003 by Lynn Turner, chief accountant of the Securities and Exchange Commission during Arthur Levitt's chairmanship. It markets a governance ranking, termed the "Board Accountability Index," that is derived from BCF's research, and which it considers a "governance-enhanced" S&P 500 index. It uses a "modified market-cap weighting algorithm" that adjusts an S&P 500 index company's weight by the presence or absence of five of the six components of BCF's entrenchment index. The component that Glass Lewis excludes is the supermajority requirement for charter amendments.

Appendix 7.2: Enhanced Business Reporting Framework[105]

EBRC Framework Version 2.1

A. Business Landscape

A. 1. Business Landscape—Summary	A summary of the key issues in the items below. This can be provided in lieu of a discussion of each category or can be omitted if each category is discussed specifically.
A. 2. Economic	Management's perspective on the macroeconomic environment in the countries and regions in which the company has operations including key factors such as GDP growth, interest rates, inflation rates, currency exchange rates.
A. 3. Industry Analysis	Discussion of competitive environment in the industries in which the company operates including strategies, strengths and weaknesses of major competitors; customer preferences and trends; supplier capabilities, dynamics of supply and demand, and management's view of the industry's prospects.
A. 4. Technological Trends	Discussion of the key technologies and their trends which affect the company and all the members of its supply chain including competing technologies, intellectual property issues, and pace of technological innovation.

(Continued)

(Continued)

A. 5. Political	Analysis of the major political issues in the countries where the company has operations including such things as potential shifts in power between "pro-business" and "anti-business" parties, trade policies and relevant pending legislation.
A. 6. Legal	Discussion of legal cases and decisions, new regulations and regulatory actions that can affect the ways in which the company operates, including the way in which it delivers its products and services and which products and services it will be able to deliver in the future.
A. 7. Environmental	Discussion of key environmental issues and concerns that are related to the company's operations, the stakeholder groups actively involved in these issues and concerns, and what these groups are trying to accomplish and through what means.
A. 8. Social	Management's analysis of key demographic and lifestyle trends, social attitudes and norms, consumer preferences and media influences.

B. Strategy

B. 1. Corporate Strategy—Summary	A summary of the key issues in the items below. This can be provided in lieu of a discussion of each category or can be omitted if each category is discussed specifically.
B. 2. Vision and Mission	Management's description of its long-term vision for the company and the mission it sees the company has having with respect to all of the stakeholders it defines as relevant.
B. 3. Strengths	Management's perspective on the company's absolute and relative strengths in the context of its Business Landscape.
B. 4. Weaknesses	Management's perspective on the company's absolute and relative weaknesses in the context of its Business Landscape.
B. 5. Opportunities	Management's perspective on the opportunities facing the company in the context of its Business Landscape.
B. 6. Threats	Management's perspective on the threats facing the company in the context of its Business Landscape.
B. 7. Goals and Objectives	Statement of financial and nonfinancial goals and the objectives that must be accomplished to achieve them.
B. 8. Corporate Strategy	Description of the company's overall corporate strategy, which sets the context for specific business unit strategies.
B. 9. Business Unit Strategies	Description of the strategies for the company's major business units.
B. 10. Business Portfolio	Discussion of the relationships between the different business unit strategies such as vertical and horizontal integration, common customers, and shared distribution channels.

C. Resources and Processes

C. 1. Resources and Processes— Summary	A summary of the key issues in the items below. This can be provided in lieu of a discussion of each category or can be omitted if each category is discussed specifically.	
C. 2. Resource Form	C. 2. a. Monetary capital	Tangible monetary capital is reported on the balance sheet but monetary capital also has intangible aspects, identified by management, which affect the ability of a company to fund its operations and investments such as borrowing capacity/access to capital, quality of earnings, the character and reputation of the company's major debt and equity investors and the stability of the shareholder base.
	C. 2. b. Physical capital	Tangible physical capital is reported on the balance sheet but physical capital also has intangible aspects, identified by management, which affect its value, such as a plant location, plant adaptability, raw material accessibility and reliance on strategic resources.
	C. 2. c. Relationship (Social) capital	Management's identification of relationships with other organizations and third parties that it regards as important; these can be both tangible (e.g., contracts, license agreements, joint venture agreements, and alliances) and intangible (e.g., long-term relationships with no contractual basis and personal relationships).
	C. 2. d. Organizational (Structural) capital	Management's identification of organizational resources not reported on the balance sheet and that are independent of its employees; these can be both tangible (e.g., patents, trademarks, copyrights, formulas and data bases) and intangible (e.g., employed but undocumented methodologies and processes).
	C. 2. e. Human capital	Management's identification of any attributes of its workforce (both employees and contractors) that it regards as important; these can be both tangible (e.g., employment contracts) and intangible (e.g., education, skills and abilities, experiences, attitudes, and accomplishments).

(Continued)

(Continued)

C. 3. Key Processes	C. 3. a. Develop Vision and Strategy	Description of the processes (possibly including benchmarking comparisons) by which the company develops its vision and strategy at the corporate and business unit levels, how it determines the appropriate overall business portfolio and the capital allocation process.
	C. 3. b. Manage Internal Resources	Description of the processes (possibly including benchmarking comparisons) used for managing internal resources like financial, human capital, information technology, property and knowledge.
	C. 3. c. Manage Products and Services	Description of the processes (possibly including benchmarking comparisons) used for managing the design and development, marketing and delivery of products and services.
	C. 3. d. Manage External Relationships	Description of the processes (possibly including benchmarking comparisons) used for managing external relationships with suppliers, customers, government and regulatory agencies, and NGOs.
	C. 3. e. Manage Governance and Risks	Description of the processes (possibly including benchmarking comparisons) used for ensuring that the interests of shareholders and other stakeholders are properly represented and for managing risk on both a category and enterprise-wide basis.

D. Performance

D. 1. Performance—Summary	A summary of the key issues in the items below. This can be provided in lieu of a discussion of each category or can be omitted if each category is discussed specifically. For each category, the company can provide segment information as appropriate.
D. 2. GAAP-based	Discussion of outcomes on key GAAP-based measures such as revenues, earnings, and gross margins.
D. 3. GAAP-derived	Discussion of outcomes on performance measures (including definitions) relevant to all industries which are based on but not defined by GAAP, such as return on invested capital and revenue growth.

D. 4. Industry-based	Discussion of outcomes on key performance indicators (including definitions) which are commonly used in an industry, including both financial (e.g., sales per square foot in retail) and nonfinancial (manufacturing yield rates in semiconductors) metrics.
D. 5. Company-specific	Discussion of outcomes on key performance indicators (including definitions) which are specific to a company's strategy, including both financial (e.g., percentage of revenues from products introduced in the last three years) and nonfinancial (e.g., employee turnover) metrics.
D. 6. Capital market-based	Discussion of outcomes on performance measures (including definitions) which are based on the company's performance in the capital markets such as total return to shareholders, debt ratings, and weighted average cost of capital.

Appendix 7.3: The Caux Round Table Principles

Principles for Business[106]

The CRT Principles

The Caux Round Table's approach to responsible business consists of seven core principles as detailed below. The principles recognize that while laws and market forces are necessary, they are insufficient guides for responsible business conduct.

The principles are rooted in three ethical foundations for responsible business and for a fair and functioning society more generally, namely: responsible stewardship; living and working for mutual advantage; and the respect and protection of human dignity.

The principles also have a risk management foundation—because good ethics is good risk management. And they balance the interests of business with the aspirations of society to ensure sustainable and mutual prosperity for all.

The CRT Principles for Responsible Business are supported by more detailed Stakeholder Management Guidelines covering each key dimension of business success: customers, employees, shareholders, suppliers, competitors, and communities. These Stakeholder Management Guidelines are as follows.

Principle 1—Respect Stakeholders Beyond Shareholders

➤ A responsible business acknowledges its duty to contribute value to society through the wealth and employment it creates and the products and services it provides to consumers.

➤ A responsible business maintains its economic health and viability not just for shareholders, but also for other stakeholders.

➤ A responsible business respects the interests of, and acts with honesty and fairness toward, its customers, employees, suppliers, competitors, and the broader community.

Principle 2—Contribute to Economic, Social and Environmental Development

➤ A responsible business recognizes that business cannot sustainably prosper in societies that are failing or lacking in economic development.

➤ A responsible business therefore contributes to the economic, social and environmental development of the communities in which it operates, in order to sustain its essential operating' capital—financial, social, environmental, and all forms of goodwill.

➤ A responsible business enhances society through effective and prudent use of resources, free and fair competition, and innovation in technology and business practices.

Principle 3—Respect the Letter and the Spirit of the Law

➤ A responsible business recognizes that some business behaviors, although legal, can nevertheless have adverse consequences for stakeholders.

➤ A responsible business therefore adheres to the spirit and intent behind the law, as well as the letter of the law, which requires conduct that goes beyond minimum legal obligations.

➤ A responsible business always operates with candor, truthfulness, and transparency, and keeps its promises.

Principle 4—Respect Rules and Conventions

➤ A responsible business respects the local cultures and traditions in the communities in which it operates, consistent with fundamental principles of fairness and equality.

➤ A responsible business, everywhere it operates, respects all applicable national and international laws, regulations and conventions, while trading fairly and competitively.

Principle 5—Support Responsible Globalization
➤ A responsible business, as a participant in the global marketplace, supports open and fair multilateral trade.
➤ A responsible business supports reform of domestic rules and regulations where they unreasonably hinder global commerce.

Principle 6—Respect the Environment
➤ A responsible business protects and, where possible, improves the environment, and avoids wasteful use of resources.
➤ A responsible business ensures that its operations comply with best environmental management practices consistent with meeting the needs of today without compromising the needs of future generations.

Principle 7—Avoid Illicit Activities
➤ A responsible business does not participate in, or condone, corrupt practices, bribery, money laundering, or other illicit activities.
➤ A responsible business does not participate in or facilitate transactions linked to or supporting terrorist activities, drug trafficking, or any other illicit activity.
➤ A responsible business actively supports the reduction and prevention of all such illegal and illicit activities.

The Caux Round Table Proposed *Principles for the Ownership of Wealth*[107]

Fundamental Principle: The Ownership of Wealth Entails Stewardship

The ends of holding wealth encompass more than meeting self-centered desires for dominion and indulgence. There is a fiduciary aspect to the ownership of capital. Wealth is to be consciously devoted to meeting the needs of society, of others, and the challenges of the future. Wealth should be of benefit to society.

General Principles

1. *Wealth should be used to enhance other forms of capital: finance, physical, human, reputational, and social.* First, wealth should be used to sustain and improve the institutions that permit the creation of wealth. Accumulated over time, wealth can influence the future. Wise use of wealth avoids immediate consumption and invests in the creation of better outcomes for future generations. When wealth is invested in the creation of additional finance capital, it should invest in those businesses and productive enterprises that adhere to the Caux Round Table Principles for Business. In particular, the current wealth of advanced industrial countries (some US$79 trillion) should be increasingly directed towards the creation of conditions for sustained economic growth in poor, developing and emerging market nations. Wealth should be used to enhance all forms of capital formation in nations that adhere to the Caux Round Table Principles for Governments.

2. *The desires of owners for self-satisfaction should be balanced against society's need for robust accumulation of new capital in all forms.* Philanthropy is incumbent upon those who possess wealth. The social function of wealth is to finance a greater good. Those who are to inherit wealth should be expected to assume the fiduciary responsibilities of stewardship that accompany the possession of wealth.

3. *Wealth must support the creation of social capital.* Social capital—the reality of the social compact incubating successful wealth creation and permitting the actualization of human dignity—is created over time by governments and civil society. From the rule of law to physical infrastructures, from the quality of a society's moral integrity and transparency of its decision making to the depth and vitality of its culture, social capital demands investment of time, money, imagination and leadership. Wealth should pay its fair share in taxes to support public programs enhancing social capital and should invest in the private creation of social capital through philanthropy.

4. *Wealth should be invested in institutions enhancing human capital.* Education and culture can be funded from public budgets on a consumption basis, but wealth should shoulder the principal

responsibility in a society of providing permanent endowments for institutions of education and culture.

5. *Private wealth should supplement public expenditures for the social safety net.* Private charity and philanthropy should respond to the health and human services needs of the less fortunate.

6. *No one is morally entitled to the use and enjoyment of wealth procured by fraud, corruption, theft, or other abuse of power.* Those who control such wealth should make restitution of such wealth to public bodies or civil society. Use of private property rights to shelter such wealth is ethically suspect.

Appendix 7.4: Trucost[108]

The efficient-market hypothesis (EMH) asserts that financial markets are "informationally efficient. That is to say that prices on traded assets, such as stocks and bonds, already reflect all known information. In its strongest form it suggests share prices reflect all information, and no one can earn excess returns. Support of the EMH comes from studies showing that the return of market averages exceeds the return of actively managed mutual funds.

However, there are many examples where markets do not behave consistently with the efficient-market hypothesis, especially in its strongest form. EMH requires a stock's price to reflect the best possible estimate of that performance that can be made with publicly available information:

➤ It is a fact that complete and comparable data on companies' environmental performance (resources used and quantities of emissions) are not widely known and so cannot be factored into asset prices.

➤ It is also a fact that, until relatively recently, many environmental impacts have not resulted in a cost to the company that creates them. That cost remains external to the company.

This briefing looks at the implications of such external costs being paid by companies. It shows how investors can use environmental and carbon footprint data to understand and measure risk in individual companies and portfolios and how to adopt investment strategies that address environmental risk and potentially improve financial returns.

Understanding External Cost

In economics, external cost refers to an element of an economic transaction, consumption or production that is not moderated by price. As this cost is often borne by society it is sometimes referred to as "social" cost. An example of an external cost would be the cost borne by health services due to particulate emissions. The World Health Organization estimates that 300,000 premature deaths are caused by particulate emissions in Europe alone. These emissions typically arise as a result of the combustion of fuel. Thus, a company with a car fleet may be responsible for a cost borne by the health service, but does not pay for this cost, hence the cost is "externalized."

Markets are unable to act efficiently when the price signal does not accurately reflect the real cost of the transaction. Governments are increasingly studying such costs with the aim of internalizing them so that the private costs more accurately reflect the social costs. *Forward-looking, long-term investing anticipates these future costs.*

In terms of emissions, such as carbon dioxide, the internalization of external costs is known as the "polluter pays" principle. The EU Emissions Trading Scheme (ETS) introduced in Europe in 2005 is an example of the principle, being applied (with the caveat of the allocation of carbon credits process). The cap and trade scheme results in a cost for CO_2 emissions. The current price for Phase 2 of the ETS (2008–12) is €28 and at present, the ETS covers 46 percent of carbon dioxide emissions. This mechanism prices an environmental impact directly for specific companies and for all companies through increased electricity prices. Financial analysts can now look at the cost of carbon allowances and the increased costs of energy and put these into their models to see the effects on a company's fair value.

The ETS regulates just CO_2, and just 46 percent of European emissions. Nonetheless, ETS impacts on company margins can be significant even now. Furthermore, the questions that investors need to consider long-term are

> ➤ What would be the impact on companies should the scheme regulate other green house gasses and other sectors?
> ➤ What will be the impact on companies as other environmental external costs become regulated?

➤ What impacts will occur directly and what as a result of company's supply chains (connections to vendors) or demand chains (products in use)?

➤ How will the impact of rising fuel and energy costs play out in company returns?

Using Environmental and Carbon Footprint Data to Understand and Measure Risk in Individual Companies and Portfolios

Investors increasingly understand the need to measure the environmental risks in equity investments. Asset valuations are set to take greater account of environmental issues such as climate change, greenhouse gas emissions, waste disposal, landfill, pollution of land or water, and resource use.

These environmental issues may stem from beyond the normal financial reporting boundaries. Monitoring supply chain performance, increasingly regarded as good business practice, may alert an organization to significant environmental issues that arise outside its normal reporting boundaries.

In relation to carbon, the impact for companies through regulation is apparent. A European Commission Green Paper stated that "a swift transition to a low carbon economy is the central pillar of the EU's integrated climate change and energy policy."[109] Most EU countries are not on track to meet their share of the EU's emission reduction target under the UN Kyoto Protocol. Carbon taxes are planned and sectors under the expanded EU Emissions Trading Scheme will have to make deeper cuts between 2012 and 2020.

America and Australia look set to have some form of carbon pricing by 2012 and a global scheme appears increasingly likely. Where carbon pricing has led other greenhouse gases will follow and investors need to be aware of the potential impacts of environmental factors on company valuations.

As an environmental research organization, Trucost enables investors to understand not only carbon but all environmental impacts in quantitative and financial terms. As regulation imposes environmental costs on companies—that is, makes the polluter pay—the risks can be identified and managed.

Trucost has developed a cost-effective tool to measure the carbon and environmental footprints of companies using its unique, comprehensive database of the resource use and emissions of over 4,000 listed companies.

Recent analysis by a number of blue chip asset managers who use Trucost data suggests that taking the environment into account in the investment process positions portfolios well in respect to rising environmental costs, and what is more, has led to better financial returns.

Previously, environmental factors have not been widely integrated into investment analysis and decision making due to the lack of standardized and comprehensive data on companies' comparable environmental performance. Since 2000, Trucost has built a database of the environmental impacts and disclosures, particularly in the area of climate change where it holds the world's largest repository of greenhouse gas disclosures. This unique knowledge enables investors to understand the environmental impacts of business activities in quantity and financial terms:

> *Risk audit*. Calculating a footprint allows a fund manager or asset owner to assess the potential environmental risk to the value of investments. Footprints provide a tangible tool to measure and monitor environmental performance of equity holdings.
> *Tool for investment managers*. A footprint report will identify the largest contributors to environmental risk both at an individual stock level and as a result of sector allocation decisions. Footprints enable fund managers to understand potential risk areas in a portfolio in order to prepare for environmental regulation. Asset managers can then consider incorporating environmental factors into their investment decisions and consider strategies such as carbon optimising investments.

Investment Strategies That Address Environmental Risk

Trucost maintains the world's largest comprehensive database of standardized environmental disclosures. Uniquely, this means that Trucost can perform very sophisticated back-testing of different investment strategies. Trucost data can be used to create a range of environmentally conscious investment options aimed at investors across a range of risk-reward characteristics. This could include the "greening" of an existing alpha or beta strategy (the data can be used to lighten the environmental impact of a portfolio while preserving the alpha or beta generated) through to specific carbon intensity plays in sectors such as utilities or aviation.

Below are three example analyses of how environmental issues could affect company valuations:

➤ Analysis by Trucost shows that electricity prices could rise by almost 50 percent in some countries if utilities pass on carbon costs. This analysis explains how global carbon emissions trading or tariffs would financially affect producers in different sectors and countries. In particular, the research examines how indirect carbon costs could cut the profits of Alcoa, BHP Billiton, and Rio Tinto by up to 30 percent.

➤ Trucost looked at the carbon risk exposure of vehicle manufacturers in Europe. The EU Environment Council met recently to debate draft legislation to set performance standards for passenger car carbon dioxide emissions. Currently manufacturers are not disclosing appropriate data for investors to assess exposure to carbon regulatory risk either through their own operations or via EU legislation to target passenger car CO_2 emissions. To help fill the gap, Trucost analyzed seven EU carmakers, and found that some would be better placed than others under the proposed carbon constraints.

➤ Trucost analyzed 500 of the largest companies in the United States finds that financial risk from carbon costs varies greatly. The study, commissioned by the Investor Responsibility Research Center Institute (IRRCi), examines the global greenhouse gas emissions, carbon intensity and exposure to carbon costs of companies in the S&P 500 Index.[110]

To enable investors to consider a company's environmental impacts both upstream (supply chain) and downstream (products in use), Trucost has developed a Hybrid Life Cycle Analysis (LCA) approach, which combines the detail of process LCA with the complete supply chain coverage of input output modeling. This enables the environmental analysis of a company to include for example GHG emissions from the input of capital goods and intermediate services in production processes, and those of the company's own operations as well as use phase emissions.

Examples of Improved Financial Returns

The rest of the briefing looks at two specific funds that have been created to take advantage of environmental data in their investment strategies and a discussion regarding the technique and benefits of carbon optimization.

GLG Partners is one of the largest European alternative investment managers with circa $25 billion AUM (i.e., assets under management).

In April 2007 GLG launched the GLG Environment fund (see **Exhibit 7.3**). The Fund is not an environmental exclusive fund (with negative screening, i.e., avoiding whole sectors like oil and gas or utilities) or an alternative energy fund—often characterized by volatile performance. Trading carbon credits were the impetus behind the funds creation. GLG saw that there were big differences in environmental liabilities between companies among the same sectors.

At the moment, carbon trading applies to a few sectors only, yet all sectors are exposed if not directly than through increased input costs through their supply chains. Therefore, GLG felt the need to assess the environmental liabilities and exposure of each company in which they are invested.

GLG's quantitative work highlighted that applying a "green" filter to current investments could actually add value and generate extra returns.

Exhibit 7.3 GLG Clean European Equity Strategy: Proven Green Alpha Creation

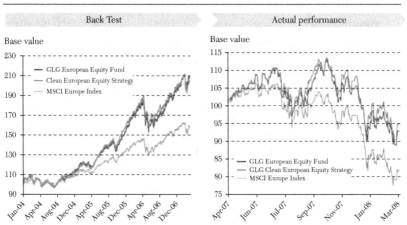

Source : GLG Partners, March 2008.

GLG Partners has a long-only fund filtering the greenest companies from its $1.5 billion European Equity strategy. The fund uses Trucost data to find the companies in each sector with a lighter environmental footprint. A three-year back-test showed 1.19 percent annualized out performance over their European Equity Fund. The environmental fund would have produced annualized returns of 27.62 percent after fees, in the past three years, against the 26.44 percent annualized rise from the European Equity fund. The fund has now been running for one year and the performance demonstrate, in GLG's words, "proven green alpha creation."

UBS

The financial firm UBS points out that some "green" investments have either used a negative screening process (e.g., excluding high carbon sectors like Oil & Gas) or have focused on solution providers (e.g., Alternative Energy).[111] Their view is that negative screening can, other things being equal, results in unbalanced portfolios in which the risk-reward ratio may be sub-optimal against the Benchmark Indices. They argue that to be fully invested in equities in volatile markets it makes more sense to rebalance portfolios towards carbon-efficient companies within sectors, across the full range of sectors.

UBS has created an index that rewards carbon efficiency across the economy by systematic carbon reduction, but preserving financial efficiency relative to the Benchmark. Through this mechanism, investors are able to receive index returns on a lower carbon footprint portfolio. The portfolio is well positioned should carbon prices rise (see the forecast in **Exhibit 7.4**), in essence providing a free call option on carbon price rises.

The UBS ECO Index is a carbon-optimized index based on DJ Stoxx 600 (see **Exhibit 7.5**). The UBS Index matches the sector weightings of the benchmark but overweighs the carbon efficient and underweighs the carbon-inefficient companies within the sectors. The tracking error is approximately 0.46 percent and has a lower carbon footprint by about 30 to 35 percent volume.

Carbon Optimization

The above UBS Eco Index provides a carbon optimized tracker fund.

Exhibit 7.4 UBS EU ETS CO2 Price Forecast

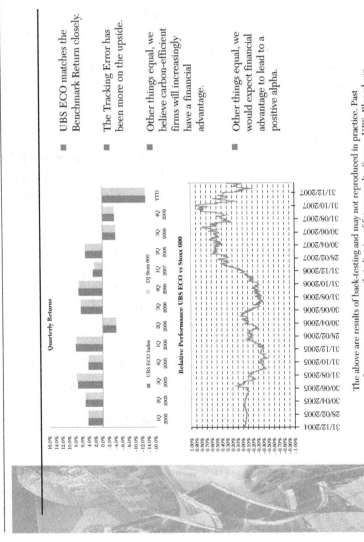

- UBS ECO matches the Benchmark Return closely.

- The Tracking Error has been more on the upside.

- Other things equal, we believe carbon-efficient firms will increasingly have a financial advantage.

- Other things equal, we would expect financial advantage to lead to a positive alpha.

The above are results of back-testing and may not reproduced in practice. Past performance is not necessarily indicative of future results; Source: UBS, Bloomberg

Source: UBS estimates.

350

Exhibit 7.5 Quarterly Returns: UBS ECO Index vs. Stoxx 600

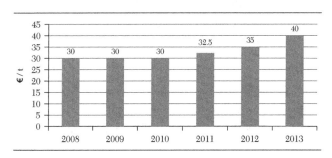

■ EU ETS CO2 Price per February 2007 is around 20 EUR/t

Source: UBS estimates.

To demonstrate that it is possible to reduce the carbon burden associated with any investment strategy, Trucost applied the carbon optimization technique to the holdings of an existing Growth fund. Although this type of fund may not be specifically required to invest in high-intensity sectors, for the purposes of maintaining a similar risk profile, sector weightings for the case study were maintained.

The fund was underexposed to both the basic resource and Oil & Gas sectors. In terms of its carbon footprint, it had slightly better stock selection in these sectors compared to its benchmark. On the other hand, it was overweight in the utilities sector with more carbon-intensive stocks that its benchmark. The effect overall was that the particular fund had a higher carbon risk profile than the index. By cross-referencing holdings data against Trucost's Environmental database, the fund was reweighted to reduce carbon exposure while maintaining sector weightings and keeping the stock universe constant.

This strategy resulted in a 21 percent reduction in the carbon footprint. The financial returns for the fund following optimization increased by 0.1 percent compared to the nonoptimized portfolio over the period analyzed.

In an era of rising energy costs the benefits of carbon optimization need not rely on the internalization of external CO_2 costs. The carbon intensity of a company—that is the ratio of its carbon use (directly and through its supply chain) to that of its turnover is a very close proxy for its exposure to margin risk through rising energy costs. High intensity, without the benefit of relatively inelastic demand, should be a red flag for both companies and their investors.

Conclusion

Climate change presents a new category of risk and opportunity for individuals, companies and investors alike. When Sir Nicholas Stern released his report "Economics of Climate Change" in October 2006, he identified climate change as the "biggest market failure the world has ever seen." Increased recognition that investments contain carbon and other environmental risk has driven demand for investment analysis that specifically addresses this issue.

Companies are more and more aware that they may face higher costs as they are increasingly forced to bear the environmental costs of their own operations and those in their supply chain. Trucost helps companies and investors to identify and manage this risk.

Notes

1. *Hall v. Geiger Jones Co.*, 242 U.S. 539 (1917), citing unnamed precedent, http://supreme.justia.com/us/242/539/case.html.
2. In chronological order, the cases (and *discount* verdicts) are as follows: *Gallo v. Commissioner*, 50 TCM (CCH) 470 TCM (RIA) 85363 July 22, 1985 (36 percent); *Howard v. Shay*, 100 F 3d 1934 (9th Circ.) November 22, 1996 (50 percent); *Mandelbaum v. Commissioner*, 69 TCM (CCH) 2852, TCM (RIA), 195, 255, June 12, 1995) (30 percent); and *Davis v. Commissioner*, 110 TC 530 (June 30, 1998) (32 percent). For a discussion of these cases, see Shannon P. Pratt, *The Market Approach to Valuing a Business*, 2nd ed. (Hoboken, N.J.: John Wiley & Sons, 2005).

   Just prior to 2003, tax court cases implied acceptance of discounts ranging from 7.5 percent up to 25 percent with an average marketability discount of 17.5 percent and a median of 20 percent. These tax court cases are based on situations that were strongly contested by the IRS and thus on the low end of the spectrum. (Source: *Federal Tax Valuation Digest*, Thomson [2009].) Expert witnesses in valuation cases often cite federal tax court cases. For example, Exhibit F in the "Valuation of Valrico Bancorp, Inc. in Amendment to Tender-Offer Statement—Going-Private Transaction," Schedule 13E-3, includes a summary of valuation cases accumulated by the 2003/2004 *Federal Tax Valuation Digest*. The range of discounts for the lack of marketability ranges from 0 to 45 percent with an average and median discount of 25.4 and 25.0 percent, respectively, for the 42 cases identified.

3. *Mandelbaum v. Commissioner*, 69 TCM (CCH) 2852, TCM (RIA), I95, 255, June 12, 1995. The six other factors were:
   ➤ Dividend history and capacity
   ➤ Restrictions on transfer
   ➤ Holding period
   ➤ Policy for redeeming stock
   ➤ Costs of listing the stock
   ➤ Segree of control transferred with the subject block
   All of these are related to stock price. For more details, see Chapter 5.

4. International Corporate Governance Network (ICGN), *ICGN Statement and Guidance on Nonfinancial Business Reporting* (London: ICGN, 2008), http://www.icgn.org/files/icgn_main/pdfs/best_practice/buss_reporting/icgn_statement_&_guidance_on_non-financial_business_reporting.pdf; or http://ec.europa.eu/enterprise/newsroom/cf/document.cfm?action=display&doc_id=5312&userservice_id=1.

5. For a primer on degrees of separation, see David Easley and John Kleinberg, Chapter 20, "The Small-World Phenomenon," *Networks, Crowds, and Markets: Reasoning About a Highly Connected World* (Cambridge: Cambridge University Press, 2010), 629–662, http://www.cs.cornell.edu/home/kleinber/networks-book/networks-book-ch20.pdf.

6. Robert K. Steel, Under Secretary for Domestic Finance, "Remarks before the Council on Competitiveness 'Strengthening our Capital Markets Competitiveness,'" U.S. Department of the Treasury, http://www.ustreas.gov/press/releases/hp409.htm.

7. Richard A. Brealey, Stewart C. Myers, and Franklin Allen, "On Real Options," *Journal of Applied Corporate Finance* 20, no. 4 (Fall 2008): 49–57.

8. Every family with any commercial engagement has its story of the cash-strapped ancestor who sold something (or passed up on buying something) that subsequently grew geometrically in value. Perhaps the most poignant image comes from the Native American's sale of Manhattan Island to Dutch colonists in exchange for what in retrospect was a paltry amount. Here is a partial transcript of that transaction.

Recep.7 November 1626 High and Mighty Lords, Yesterday the ship the Arms of Amsterdam arrived here. It sailed from New Netherland out of the River Mauritius on the 23d of September. They report that our people are in good spirit and live in peace. The women also have borne some children there. They have purchased the Island Manhattes from the Indians for the value of 60 guilders. It is 11.000 morgens in size [about 22,000 acres]. . . . Herewith, High and Mighty Lords, be commended to the mercy of the Almighty, Your High and Mightinesses' obedient P. Schagen

"The Purchase of Manhattan," *Memory of the Netherlands - Background: Atlantic World*, http://www.kb.nl/coop/geheugen/extra/tentoonstellingen/atlanticworldEN/tentoon5.html.)

9. Benjamin Graham and David Dodd, *Security Analysis* (New York: McGraw-Hill, 1934).

10. Adolf Berle and Gardiner Means, *The Modern Corporation and Private Property* (New York: Modern Classics, 1932).

11 "Trends in Executive Pay," Institute for Policy Studies with data through December 2008. 2009 data was not available as of June 27, 2010. For latest data see http://www.aflcio.org/corporatewatch/paywatch/pay/

12. Sanjai Baghat, Brian Bolton, and Roberto Romano, "The Promise and Perils of Corporate Governance Indices," *Columbia Law Review* 108, no. 8 (2008).

13. For a financially oriented (return-on-investment) view of human resource management, see Brian S. Friedman, James A. Hatch, and David M. Walker, *Delivering on the Promise: How to Attract, Manage, and Retain Human Capital* (New York: Free Press, 1998).

14. See the report for Colfax Corporation for the quarter ending July 3, 2009: "The Committee shall retain the discretion to adjust any Awards downward, either on a formula or discretionary basis, or any combination as the Committee determines. Annual Incentive Awards may not be adjusted upward from the level of performance achieved," Colfax Corporation, Form 10-Q, for the quarter ended July 3, 2009. quhttp://shareholder.api.edgar-online.com/efx_dll/edgarpro.dll?FetchFilingRTF1?sessionid=frMFWInOmFoWnoi&ID=6726507&PageBreakStyleID=2.

15. SEC Release 34-48108 (June 30, 2003).

16. International Corporate Governance Network, ICGN Remuneration Guidelines. http://www.icgn.org/files/icgn_main/pdfs/best_practice/exec_remun/2006_executive_remuneration.pdf.

17. Securities and Exchange Commission, Executive Compensation and Related Person Disclosure Agency, http://www.sec.gov/rules/final/2006/33-8732a.pdf.

18. The Colfax Corporation (note 9) has a list of key performance indicators that include both financial and *strategic* benchmarks (emphasis added). Here is the list: earnings (net, operating, pre-tax; EBIT, EBITDA); earnings per share; *sales or revenue growth, whether in general, by type of product or service, or by type of customer*; gross or operating margins; return measures, including return on assets, capital, investment, equity, sales or revenue; cash flow; productivity rations; expense targets; *market share*; financial ratios as provided in credit agreements of the Company and its subsidiaries; working capital targets; *completion of acquisitions/divestitures of business or companies*; any combination of any of the foregoing business criteria. This list of key performance indicators for management has the virtue of being quantitative/measurable. The next frontier will be to enrich such a list with more qualitative factors (or hard data that points to such factors)." (http://shareholder.api.edgar-online.com/efx_dll/edgarpro.dll?Fe tchFilingRTF1?sessionid=frMFWInOmFoWnoi&ID=6726507&PageBr eakStyleID=2.)

19. Dr. Roland Burgman and Prof. Göran Roos, "The New Economy: A New Para- digm for Managing Shareholder Value," unpublished paper, http://www.intcap .com/downloads/ICS_Article_2004_The%20New%20Economy%20-%20 a%20New%20Paradigm%20for%20Managing%20for%20Shareholder%20 Value.pdf.

20. John C. Dumay, "Intellectual Capital Measurement: A Critical Approach," *Journal of Intellectual Capital* 10, no. 2 (2009).

21. Jefferies & Co. analyst Laurence Alexander said Wall Street is not yet pricing in DuPont's potential to rally before the economy improves, and its ability to transform its product line, http://www.emailwire.com/release/20900- Technical-Trade-Alerts-on-Diversified-Chemical-Stocks-ASH-DD-SHW- APD-DOW-ROH.html.

22. This section of the chapter is based on a model developed by Price Pritchett. The research was directed by Jim Jeffries, founder, M&A Partners, Dallas, Texas. The authors wish to acknowledge guidance of an unpub- lished article by Alessandro Carretta, Vincenzo Farina, Franco Fiordelisi, and Paola Schwizer, in "Corporate Culture and Shareholder Value in the Banking Industry," 2006, http://mpra.ub.uni-muenchen.de/8304. The study of corporate culture, in terms of power orientation, result orientation, and human resource in this paper is drawn from the *Harvard IV Psychosocial Dic- tionary* (Zuell, Weber, and Mohler 1989) and the *Lasswell Value Dictionary* (Lasswell and Namenwirth 1969). The different intensities of these catego- ries, expressed in terms of "orientations," characterize the concepts and allow a comparison of the corporate culture against various benchmark contexts.

23. See E. H. Schein, *Organizational Culture and Leadership* (San Francisco: Jossey-Bass, 1985).

24. See T. Peters and R. Waterman, *In Search of Excellence* (New York: Harper & Row, 1982).

25. A general theory of negotiating cost was developed by Oliver Eaton Williamson, Edgar F. Kaiser Professor Emeritus University of California, Berkeley. See Oliver E. Williamson, "Transaction Cost Economics and Business Administration," *Scandinavian Journal of Management* 21, no. 1 (March 2005): 19–40; and G. M. Hodgson, "Corporate Culture and the Nature of the Firm," in *Transaction Cost Economics and Beyond*, edited by John Groenewegen (Boston: Kluwer Academic Press, 1996).

26. See J. Van Maanen, "The Smile Factory," in P. J. Frost, L. F. Moore, M. R. Louis, C. C. Lundberg, and J. Martin, eds., *Reframing Organizational Culture* (London: Sage, 1991).

27. See E. J. Van den Steen, "Culture Clash: The Costs and Benefits of Homogeneity," working paper, 2004.

28. Here is a director quote from the Carretta et al. study (see note 21): "It turns out that there is a statistically significant (at the 10% confidence level) negative link between a power-oriented corporate culture and the shareholder value created over a given time period. Namely, if a bank was to increase the power-orientation of their corporate culture by 10% (e.g. by 20% to 30%), the ratio between EVA and invested capital would decline by 1.49% in the following year. We have found that the estimated regression coefficient for the human-oriented corporate culture is positive and statistically significant (at the 5% confidence level) showing that banks with a human-oriented capital have an advantage in creating EVA: namely, if a bank was to succeed in increasing the human-orientation of its corporate culture by 10% (e.g. by 10% to 20%), the ratio between EVA and invested capital would rise by 2.44%. . . . [T]he estimated regression coefficient for the result-oriented corporate culture is slightly negative and non-statistically significant (even at the 10% confidence level). This result lives up to our expectation that bank with a result-oriented culture have no advantage in creating shareholder value, as it shows that when a bank requests its workforce to attain considerable results in the short run, it is bound to assume higher risk and the overall result is a shareholder value destruction."

29. See P. Di Maggio, "Culture and Cognition," *Annual Review of Sociology* 23, no. 1 (1997): 263–288, described in Carretta et al. (see note 21).

30 "Does banking culture affect shareholder value?" asks Carretta et al. (see note 21). "The answer is affirmative although selectively. Banking strategies are paying greater attention to the use of culture as a potential for

leading change and enhancing innovation. In order to promote strategic change and match short term with long-term goals, organization restructuring involves hard and soft value drivers. A flexible and eclectic culture, built on such values as human resources' motivation and satisfaction, broad communication flows and information sharing, which is pervasive through an open leadership style, is likely to support integration needs following growth processes and diversification strategies and to create a competitive advantage."

31. See, for example, E. Beccallie, B. Caus, and C. Girardone, "Efficiency and Stock Performance in European Banking," *Journal of Business, Accounting and Finance* 33 (2006): 218–235. (See also the discussion of corporate energy.)

32. Booz Allen Hamilton, *Global 1000: Money Isn't Everything* (2004).

33. G. C. Biddle and G. Zhang, "When Capital Follows Profitability: Nonlinear Residual Income Dynamics," *Review of Accounting Studies* 6 (2001): 229–265.

34. C. Wilderom and P. T. Van Den Berg, "Firm Culture and Leadership as Firm Performance Predictors: A Resource Based Perspective," working paper n. 2000-03.

35. See A Carretta, ed., *Il governo del cambiamento culturale in banca: Modelli di analisi, strumenti operativi, valori individuali* [The management of cultural change in a bank: Analytical models, implementation, and individual values] (Rome: *Bancaria Editrice*, 2001 and "M&A and Post Merger Integration in the Banking Industry: The Missing Link of Corporate Culture, MPRA Paper 8300, University Library of Munich, Germany. Working Paper 8300, posted 2007. Page updated June 27, 2010.

36. See M. E. Barth and W. H. Beaver, "The Relevance of the Value Relevance Literature for Financial Accounting Standard Setting: Another View," *Journal of Accounting and Economics* 31 (2001): 3–75; P. Fernandez, "EVA, Economic Profit and Cash Value Added Do Not Measure Shareholder Value Creation," University of Navarra, IESE, Research Paper no. 453, 2002.

37. See A. L. Wilkin and W. G. Ouchi, "Efficient Cultures: Exploring the Relationship Between Culture and Organizational Performance," *Administrative Science Quarterly* 28 (1983): 468–481.

38. R. Harrison, "Understanding Your Organization's Character," *Harvard Business Review* 50, no. 3 (1972): 119–128.

39. G. G. Gordon and N. Di Tomaso, "Predicting Corporate Performance from Organizational Culture," *Journal of Management Studies* 29 (1992): 783–798.

40. G. S. Hansen, and B. Wernerfelt, "Determinants of Firm Performance: The Relative Importance of Economic and Organizational Factors," *Strategic Management Journal* 10 (1989): 193–206.

41. R. S. Burt, S. M. Hgabbay, G. Holt, and R. Moran, "Contingent Organization as a Network Theory: The Culture Performance Contingency Function," *Acta Sociologica* 37 (1994): 346–370.

42. G. W. Lovemean, "Employee Satisfaction, Customer Loyalty, and Financial Performance: An Empirical Examination of the Service Profit Chain in Retail Banking," *Journal of Service Research* 1 (1998): 18–31.

43. J. M. Pennings and A. Van Witteloostujin, "Human Capital, Social Capital and Firm Dissolution," *Academy of Management Journal* 41 (1998): 425–440.

44. Patrick Henry's words before the Virginia Convention in March 1775: "Give me liberty, or give me death," inspiring a vote to go to a war that became known as the American Revolution. During that same war, General John Stark of New Hampshire penned the motto, "Live free or die."

45. James Gwartney and Robert Lawson, et al., *Economic Freedom of the World: 2009 Annual Report* (Washington, D.C.: Cato Institute, 2009), http://www.cato.org/pubs/efw/index.html.

46. The first *Economic Freedom of the World Report*, published in 1996, was the result of a decade of research by a team that included several Nobel laureates and over 60 other leading scholars in a broad range of fields, from economics to political science, from law to philosophy. This is the thirteenth edition of the report. The EFW index is calculated back to 1970 as the availability of data allows; see the Country Data Tables at http://www.freetheworld.com, for information from past years. Because some data for earlier years may have been updated or corrected, researchers are always encouraged to use the data from the most recent annual report to assure the best quality.

47. *2010 Index of Economic Freedom* (Washington, D.C. The Heritage Foundation, 2010). http://heritage.org/index/PDF/2010/Index2010_Executive-Highlights.pdf.

48. "The ultimate commercial accomplishment is to achieve regulation under law that is purported to be comprehensive and preempting and is administered by an agency that is in fact captive to the industry." Robert A. G. Monks and Nell Minow, *Power and Accountability* (New York: Harper Collins, 1992).

49. Rafael La Porta, Florencio Lopez-de-Silanesb, Andrei Shleifer, and Robert Vishny, "Investor Protection and Corporate Governance," Harvard University Working Paper Series No. rwp01-017, http://ksgnotes1.harvard.edu/Research/wpaper.nsf/rwp/RWP01-017/$File/rwp01_017_lopezdesilanes.pdf.

50. The Asset Management Working Group was composed of investors, both pension funds and asset managers.

51. UNEP Finance Initiative, "A Legal Framework for the Integration of Environmental, Social and Governance Issues into Institutional Investment," http://www.unepfi.org/fileadmin/documents/freshfields_legal_resp_20051123.pdf.

52. "The rules applicable in the civil law jurisdictions, by contrast, are more rigid as they are and are not generally interpreted by reference to decided cases but rather by reference to the principles and purposes behind their enactment" (UNEP Finance Initiative, see note 49).

53. "The common law system gives courts the authority to develop rules of law based on accretion of case by case decisions. Such a system has decided strengths in the creation of responsive doctrines of private law governing the legal dealings of private actors with each other. On the one hand, the authority of public law, particularly laws establishing the structure and function of various participants in the political process, derives entirely from the democratic composition of the law-giving body. Widely representative legislative bodies can act to restructure American politics and can be held accountable for their actions in political elections. On the one hand, when courts act to change the political playing field, they are in no way accountable for the havoc that their decisions may wreak." Robert A. G. Monks and Peter L. Murray, "Chief Justice Roberts: Judicial Activist for Corporate Power," August 2009.

54. This phrase became engrained in the English language thanks to a popular book by *New York Times* journalist Andrew Ross Sorkin, *Too Big to Fail*: **The Inside Story of How Wall Street and Washington Fought to Save the Financial System—and Themselves** (New York: Viking Adult, 2009).

55. The rating agencies recognize that "the removal of implicit federal support would probably lower the creditworthiness of some banks. Source Dawn Kopecki and Michale J. Moore, "S&P Says It May Take Months to Assess Bank Downgrades After Financial Bill." Bloomberg May 26, 2010.

56. Adam Smith is widely regarded as the world's first modern economist. But he did not write *ex nihilo*. For precedents, read *Economic Thought before Adam Smith: An Austrian Perspective on the History of Economic Thought*, vol. 1 (Cheltenham, U.K.: Edward Elgar, 1995) by the late Murray N. Rothbard, formerly S. J. Hall Distinguished Professor of Economics, University of Nevada, Las Vegas.

57. Charles E. Lindblom, *The Market System: What It Is, How It Works, and What to Make of It* (New Haven: Yale University Press 2001), http://dannyreviews.com/h/Market_System.html.

58. Ian Bremmer and Preston Keat, *The Fat Tail: The Power of Political Knowledge in an Uncertain World* (Oxford: Oxford University Press, 2010).

59. In Europe, there are "challenges for financial reforms in an increasingly integrated market," notes Jean-Claude Trichet, president of the European Central Bank, in his review of *Handbook of European Financial Markets and Institutions*, edited by Xavier Freixas, Philipp Hartmann, and Colin Mayer (Oxford: Oxford University Press, 2008). In India, challenges stem from fragmentation. One study showed that the Indian stock market could benefit from:

➤ Single authority;
➤ Demutualization;
➤ Prescribing capital adequacy norms;
➤ Stricter registration of brokers;
➤ Margin requirements.

(Amitabh Anand, director, Corporate Affairs, NSB, Bangalore, India, in an email October 1, 2009.)

60. [International Corporate Governance Network, *ICGN Global Corporate Governance Principles: Revised (2009)* http://www.ecgi.org/codes/documents/icgn_global_corporate_governance_principles_revised_2009.pdf

61. International Corporate Governance Network, "ICGN Statement on the Global Financial Crisis,"http://www.icgn.org/ press/press-releases/articles/-/page/222/.

62. International Corporate Governance Network, http://www.icgn.org/organisation/. For example, the ICGN's Securities Lending Code of Best Practice (2007) clarifies the responsibilities of all parties engaged in stock lending, http://www.icgn.org/organisation/documents/slc/SL_Best_Practice_rev_060707.pdf.

63. *Ten Industry Initiatives to Increase Transparency in the European Securitisation Markets* http://www.afme.eu/document.aspx?id=2852.

64. Edmond Cannon and Giam Petro Cipriani. "Euro-Illusion: A Natural Experiment." *Journal of Money, Credit, and Banking*, August 1, 2006.

65. *ICGN Global Corporate Governance Principles—2009*http://www.icgn.org/files/icgn_main/pdfs/best_practice/global_principles/short_version_icgn_global_corporate_governance_principles-_revised_2009.pdf.

66. See National Association of Corporate Directors, *Key Agreed Principles to Strengthen Corporate Governance for U.S. Publicly Held Companies* (2008)https://secure.nacdonline.org/StaticContent/StaticPages/DM/NACDKeyAgreedPrinciples.pdf.

67. See FAQ Transition Plan for Institutional Investors—RiskMetrics Governance Risk Indicators, http://www.riskmetrics.com/sites/default/files/FAQ-GRId-institutional.pdf.

68. Ric Marshall, "Investing in Corporate Governance: Realizing Alpha by Mitigating Risk," white paper, The Corporate Library, October 2009. This

paper includes an annotated bibliography of 15 recent studies variously finding or disputing a connection between a corporation's governance and its financial performance.

69. This paragraph and the following were contributed by Ric Marshall, Chief Analyst, The Corporate Library, Portland, Maine.

70. Robert Daines, Ian Gowe, and David Larcker, "Rating the Ratings: How Good Are Commercial Governance Ratings?" http://shareholdercoalition.com/ StanfordProxyRatingsStudyJune2008.pdf. But note: "The metrics they used to find this relationship are common in the academic world (e.g., Tobin's Q) but almost never used by investors, banks, or insurance companies" (Eric Jackson, "Does Corporate Governance Impact Performance?" http://seekingalpha. com/article/151050-does-corporate-governance-impact-performance).

71. "Corporate law provides the board of directors with the authority to make, or at least ratify, all important firm decisions, including decisions about investment policy, management compensation policy, and board governance itself. The board's pivotal role suggests focusing on its attributes in order to identify a single governance variable that might serve as an alternative to an index. It is theoretically possible, and intuitively plausible, that an independent board, or board members with stock ownership, will have adequate incentives to provide effective oversight of important corporate decisions and monitoring of management action implementing those decisions. Accordingly, board independence or outside board members' stock ownership are excellent candidates for a single characteristic that could best an index as a proxy for overall good governance" (Sanjai Baghat, et al., see note 10). For economic models in which outside directors have incentives to build reputations as expert monitors, see Eugene Fama, "Agency Problems and the Theory of the Firm," *Journal of Political Economics* 88 (1980): 288–307; and Eugene Fama and Michael Jensen, "Separation of Ownership and Control," *Journal of Law and Economics* 26 (June 1983): 301–325. For the legal literature has long held this view of independent directors, see Melvin A. Eisenberg, *The Structure of the Corporation* (Frederick, Md.: Beard, 1976); and of the incentives provided by directors' stock ownership, see Charles M. Elson, "The Duty of Care, Compensation and Stock Ownership," *University of Cincinnati Law Review* 63, no. 2 (1995): 649–711. For an economic model that suggests that equity compensation for outside directors will increase board monitoring, see Benjamin E. Hermalin and Michael S. Weisbach, "Endogenously Chosen Boards of Directors and Their Monitoring of the CEO," *American Economic Review* 88 (1998): 96–111. Evaluating the quality of a firm's governance from a single board characteristic rather than a multifactor index might be justified on econometric grounds as well.

72. Treasury Working Paper 02-2009. March 2009, http://www.treasury.gov .au/documents/1495/PDF/TWP_2009-02.pdf.

73. "The average targeted company produced excess returns of 15.4% above their respective benchmark return on a cumulative basis, or 3% per year on an annualized basis."Andrew Junkin, CFA, CIMA, managing director, and Thomas Toth, CFA, vice president, Wilshire Associates, "The 'CalPERS Effect' on Targeted Company Shares Prices," July 31, 2009. This Wilshire Associates study examined the performance of 139 companies targeted by CalPERS Focus List from the beginning of 1987 through the fall of 2007.

74. "GMI Named Top Corporate Governance Research Firm: Firm Seeks to Promote 'Investment Grade' Governance," http://www.gmiratings .com/Release_GMI_Top_CG_Firm_6_22_09.pdf.

75. Governance Metrics International, "GMI Governance and Performance Studies," http://www.gmiratings.com/(5s02rdfrqtocf555cwiyhnvx)/Performance.aspx.

76. "Poor Corporate Governance Hurts Performance," re the hypothetical Governance Alpha Fund, created by The Corporate Library, http://srimonitor .blogspot.com/2009/07/poor-corporate-governance-hurts.html.

77. Robert Ferris, in correspondence with Alexandra Lajoux, May 27, 2009.

78. William F. Mahoney, "Creating the Corporate Performance Statement," ValuationIssues.com, summarizing *Financial Analyst's Journal*, May–June 2005.

79. American Institute of Certified Public Accountants, "XBRL," http://www .aicpa.org/Professional+Resources/Accounting+and+Auditing/BRAAS/ XBRL.html. See also http://www.xbrl.org/Home/.

80. Ben W. Heineman Jr., *High Performance with High Integrity* (Boston: Harvard Business School Press, 2008).

81. Matthew Bishop and Michale Green, *Philanthrocapitalism: How the Rich Can Save the World* (London: Bloomsbury, 2008).

82. See, for example, Iino Kaiun Kaisha, "Corporate Profile," http://www.iino .co.jp/kaiun/english/company/philosophy.html.

83. Edmond Jenkins, as chair of the ACIPA Special Committee on Financial Reporting, issued a report in 1994 titled "Improving Business Reporting— A Customer Focus." Many of the concepts in the current enhanced business reporting movement are founded in this landmark work.

84. *Aspen Principles for Long-Term Value Creation: Guiding Principles for Corporations and Investors* (New York: Aspen Institute, June 2007), http:// www.aspeninstitute.org/sites/default/files/content/docs/pubs/Aspen_ Principles_with_signers_April_09.pdf.

85. *Overcoming Short-Termism: A Call for a More Responsible Approach to Investment and Business Management* (New York: Aspen Institute, 2009).

86. Morningstar's article on GE's performance in 2008 can be found at this link: http://news.morningstar.com/articlenet/article.aspx?id=83572&.

87. For the full report, see *Resetting Responsiblities* http://www.ge.com/files_citizenship/pdf/reports/ge_2008_citizenship_report.pdf. The sequel for 2009 had not been published by press time in June 2009, but GE maintains current metrics on its website at http://www.ge.com/company/citizenship/index.html.

88. Robert A. G. Monks, Anthony Miller, and Jacqueline Cook, "Shareholder Activism on Environmental Issues: A Study of Proposals at Large US Corporations (2000–2003), United Nations Natural Resources Forum, http://www3.interscience.wiley.com/journal/118771647/abstract?CRETRY=1&SRETRY=0. The general points made in this paper remain true as of late 2009.

89. The MSCI World Index is one of several created by MSCI Barra. See, for example, http://www.mscibarra.com/products/indices/index.jsp. See also "Notable Performers Outperform Key Stock Index," http://www.unglobalcompact.org/NewsAndEvents/news_archives/2009_06_18.html.

90. See the letter at http://raasconsulting.com/Documents/ESG_Letter_to_SEC%2021Jul09.pdf. See also http://raasconsulting.com/ Documents/ESG%20SEC%20Letter%20Aug%2005%2009-1.pdf.

91. UKSIF Sustainable Pensions Project, "Responsible Business: Sustainable Pension—How the Pension Funds of the UK's Corporate Responsibility Leaders Are Approaching Responsible Investment," 2009. This project is supported by Hermes Fund Managers, KBC Asset Management, and the members of the Sustainable Pensions Advisory Board, including representatives of several professional services firms involved with employee benefits (Hewitt, Mercer, and Watons WorldWide).

92. Interview with Mark Mills, director, Generation Investment Management LLP, http://www.generationim.com/; and interview with Steven Brown, Governance for Owners, http://www.governanceforowners.com/news/49.

93. For a four-decade history of the Forum, see http://www.weforum.org/en/index.htm.

94. Through its Global Agenda Councils (GACs), the Forum has created a network of leading experts from different regions, industries, and organizations to cover the most important issues of the world's agenda. There are seventy GACs as of late 2009. All of its members meet once a year in Dubai for a summit on the Global Agenda. For each of these GACs, the Forum has identified and convened 15 to 25 of the world's leading experts. These experts do not necessarily need to be involved in other activities of the Forum. Each GAC covers one specific topic and are often linked to particular industries. There is no predefined content when a GAC is being created; the Forum provides a platform and sets the framework, and the members of the GACs themselves define the agenda.

95. See Chapter 8 for a discussion of sovereign wealth funds.

96. CDSB operates through a board representing the World Economic Forum (chair and convenor) and the following additional members: Carbon Disclosure Project; Ceres, The Climate Group, The Climate Registry, International Emissions Trading Association, and the World Resources Institute. CDSB's proposed framework is available for download at cdsb-global.org.

97. Greenhouse Gas Protocol Initiative, ghgprotocol.org.

98. "Update on Gult of Mexico Oil Spill," BP Press Release dated June 25, 2010. http://www.bp.com/genericarticle.do?categoryId=2012968& contentId=7063132gul.

99. Albert Hunt, "BP Spill Cleanup Alone Won't End Gulf's Suffering," *BusinessWeek*. June 27, 2010, 11:16 AM EDT http://www.businessweek. com/news/2010-06-27/bp-spill-cleanup-alone-won-t-end-gulf-s-suffering-albert-hunt.html

100. Globilization is often discussed in glowing terms but companies operating outside their own domiciles face special risks. For example, U.S. law has criminalized many business practices that might be considered civil matters in other jurisdictions. In the absence of genuine global law, multinational enterprises run the risk of local vagaries.

101. Summary from the SEC: "The Securities and Exchange Commission is adopting amendments to its forms under the Securities Exchange Act of 1934 and the Investment Company Act of 1940 that will require disclosure by a registered investment company that divests, in accordance with the Sudan Accountability and Divestment Act of 2007, from securities of issuers that the investment company determines, using credible information that is available to the public, conduct or have direct investments in certain business operations in Sudan. The Sudan Accountability and Divestment Act limits civil, criminal, and administrative actions that may be brought against a registered investment company that divests itself from such securities, provided that the investment company makes disclosures in accordance with regulations prescribed by the Commission. Effective Date April 30. 2008."

102. Sanjai Baghat, et al., see note 66.

103. This title and list is updated to be current as of June 2010. according to RiskMetrics, http://www.riskmetrics.com/sites/default/files/FAQ-GRId-institutional.pdf.

104. A report from the General Accountability Office exonerated all the proxy advisory services from this charge in 2007, http://www.gao.gov/new.items/ d07765.pdf. However, as of late 2009, the issue is being raised again by both the SEC and trade groups with an interest in the issue of proxy

voting. See, for example, http://www.gao.gov/new.items/d07765.pdf and http://www.shareholdercoalition.com/proxyadvisory.html.

105. American Institute of Certified Public Accountants, Enhanced Business Reporting Initiative, ebr360.org.

106. Reprinted with permission, The Caux Round Table.

107. This appendix was created by Stephen B. Young, global executive director, The Caux Round Table.

108. The following essay is provided by Trucost.com and reprinted with permission. Trucost is owned by a group of investors, including Robert A. G. Monks. We have updated the content and Americanized the spelling and punctuation. For a report on recent Trucost analysis jointly with *Newsweek*, see http://www.newsweek.com/id/215522.

109. EuroEnviron, "Environmental Themes," http://www.euroenviron.net/climate.htm.

110. Carbon Risks and Opportunities in the S&P 500, June 2, 2009. TruCost enables investors to rebalance investment holdings to favor companies that are more carbon efficient (and less prone to regulatory repercussions) than their sector peers. TruCost data and analysis can offer support in demonstrating solid environmental credentials to stakeholders and United Nations Principals for Responsible Investment (UNPRI), http://www.trucost.com/newsweek/links.php.

111. UBS," ubs.com.

CHAPTER 8

Situational Valuation
Equity Values throughout the Corporate Life Cycle

CORPORATE VALUATION IS situational, known more for its exceptions than its rules. This stands to reason. Corporations, like the people who create them, have a life, and where there is life, there is change.

This chapter provides guidance aimed at equity investors willing to hold on to their investments during times of change in the life cycle of a corporation. For the benefit of these longer-term investors (particularly funds that focus on equity), we identify valuation issues that can arise during an entire life cycle of a corporation.[1]

The most important aspect of this chapter is not so much the bits and pieces of its content. Like all content in any book today, the material here is already well-known in bits and pieces to many in the business world. With the World Wide Web at hand, the facts are only a keyword search and a second away. Rather, the message of the following pages is the *relativity of value*.

Previous chapters explained the fundamentals of assets, earnings, cash flow, and stock price; identified common methodologies that put these together; and shared the authors' view of the seven main drivers of corporate value. This chapter shows that all these elements are merely like parts of a kaleidoscope. Like the "lens" used for viewing fundamentals, the corporation's particular situation makes all these value indicators fall into place.

Scenarios

For example, consider the company that is under pressure to put itself up for sale by the government of the country that permits it to stay in business. This is happening now in the United States. (Yes, states grant corporate charters, but federal fiat can quickly halt a going concern. Just ask the former partners of Arthur Andersen.) For this dramatic reason, this final chapter starts with the emerging topic of public sector ownership.

The chapter then moves on to the more ordinary events in corporate life under private ownership: corporate formation, initial public offerings (IPOs), secondary offerings, stock splits, dividends, buybacks, pension funding, mergers, spin-offs and divestitures, shareholder-led governance changes, bankruptcy, and emergence from bankruptcy. Whether buying, holding, or selling, investors can profit from understanding the valuation issues that each of these events may entail.

Valuation of Shares Under Public Policy Pressure: A Story *in Medias Res*

The story of public sector valuation has barely begun; so its impact on valuation remains to be seen. The following two short stories speak volumes.

When it became clear that AIG was going to be bankrupt absent government intervention, the U.S. government stepped in. On the evening of September 16, 2008, the Federal Reserve Bank of New York loaned AIG $85 billion at LIBOR plus 8.5 percent, plus a commitment fee on the loan principal and a fee on the undrawn portion of the loan. The U.S. government was entitled to 79.9 percent equity ownership of the company through preferred stock. The remaining 20.1 percent could trade freely on the market.

The U.S. Department of the Treasury (U.S. Treasury) purchased, through the Troubled Asset Relief Program (TARP), $40 billion of newly issued AIG perpetual preferred shares; AIG used the proceeds to pay down a portion of the government loan.[2] The term sheet for the transaction states that warrants exercised to purchase these preferred shares were valued at $2.50 per share, representing the par value of the stock on the date of investment.[3] Under Delaware corporate law, this was the minimum price at which AIG's board could sell the stock. But some analysts believe that the government in effect paid a much lower price.[4] In any event, the price the government paid was far lower than the price the market delivered on the 20.1 percent that was trading freely.[5]

Jamie Dimon could have taken a similar approach to the share price JPMorgan paid for Bear Stearns under federal pressure, but he took pity on the shareholders (including the managers who owned shares) and elevated the price to $10.[6]

In both cases, the prices were a steal—literally—and all for public policy reasons. These transactions were akin to appropriation conditions that can be antithetical to economic freedom and prosperity.

Today, a concern with employment makes it important for public policy reasons to keep some entities going for the sake of employees and vendors, even if at owners' expense. This concern is the exact opposite of that in the 1980s era of restructuring, when companies pared jobs to boost returns to shareholders. The theme of public value led by policy makers (rather than private value led by owners) is discussed further later in this chapter.

Now, for a more time-tested perspective on value, we return to the private sector.

Valuation of Shares at Par (or No Par)

Every corporation has a par value. At its origin, prior to being publicly traded, equity has little if any value separate from the company that issues it. The company has value as a whole, but not in small parts. This fact is well symbolized by the low amounts set for par value. Traditionally, therefore, corporations set only a nominal value for each share, called par value, which has little or no correlation to market value. Par value is low in order to limit the liability of shareholders and the exposure of creditors. Indeed, the trend now is to declare that the stock has no par value.

The investor who buys a company with only par (or no par) value stock is well advised to ignore that written par value and to value the company's other value indicators: assets, earnings, cash flow, and general drivers of value—but not stock price. The main concern for any investor at this stage is with the control over operations and with the protection of the rights of minority shareholders.

Valuation of Shares in IPOs and Secondary Offerings

The new issues valuation expert can benefit from knowing the formulas behind pricing trends for initial public offerings and secondary offerings. What could be a better laboratory for securities valuation than setting an offering price for stock? The stock may be in a newly public company (an IPO) or in an existing public company (a secondary public offering), and valuation techniques will vary accordingly. Ultimately, though, the pricing of all new securities conform to the same general laws.

IPOs are a relatively rare event and prone to volatility in frequency and returns, making generalizations about IPO values difficult. As of the end of June 2010, there have been 114 IPOs during the most recent 12 months. Returns varied from −48.5 to +128.0. And in the first six months of 2010, when there were 67 IPOs, the spread was similar.[7]

Research has shown a positive correlation between high returns and many different elements, including the following:

➤ Longer involuntary wait periods before going to market[8]
➤ Intentional underpricing intending to increase demand[9]
➤ Presence of independent directors on the board of the issuing company[10]
➤ Ownership by insiders[11]

Experienced Wall Street advisor Robert Ferris calls the new issue valuation process the "same old story in IPO financings." According to Ferris, the bankers (still highly selective) reel potential issuers in with best-case valuation scenarios, then soft-pedal through the due diligence and registration period, inevitably coming in at the low end of the pricing band. (Explanations for this practice include conflicts of interest by managers who own the stock and profit by selling after a rise in stock value.[12])

The Wall Streeters expect that the market euphoria created by the syndicate "buzz" will support and/or enhance the offering price and cover the underwriting discount for at least a short period (of weeks) after the deal goes effective. After that, the issuer essentially faces the cold, cruel world on its own. Few if any bankers continue to support the stock in the aftermarket. In fact, empirically there has been less and less support from sell-side research, which undoubtedly will soon be extinct.

One study found that the best predictors of future prices in under-priced IPOs were multiples and discounted cash flow. The multiples were earnings per share and enterprise value or latest 12 months of revenue.[13]

Follow-on and secondary offering pricing, of course, is principally tied to current market performance (typically five-day average pricing). This approach can get complex in the many cases of lock-ups, which have a planned chronology of stock issuance to the aftermarket (from insiders and venture capitalists), usually 180 days out and sometimes in more than one tranche.

IPO value determination, therefore, depends a lot on the issuer's marketing strategy. The so-called go-to-market strategy of brand building, promotional activities, and budget commitments can have a real influence too. So IPO pricing is not always a matter of financial strength, creditworthiness, and current or potential financial performance—but that's the story with stock in any case.

Valuation of Shares upon the Declaration of a Dividend or a Stock Split

A number of academic studies show that stock prices go up after the announcement of a stock dividend or stock split, but the effect is not lasting unless accompanied by other news. The actual value of a firm does not change at the declaration of a dividend, according to the famed second Modigliani-Miller theorem, which has never been challenged. The theory states that, for a given investment policy, the value of a firm is independent of its dividend policy. A dividend increase, for instance, certainly increases shareholders' incomes, but it is neutralized by a corresponding reduction in share value. (For more on Miller and Modigliani, see Appendix F.)

As for stock splits, the price goes up. The combined value of the two or more shares that each shareholder receives in exchange for one is greater than the value the shareholder had with one share. Over time, though, the price goes back down as the market corrects.[14]

Valuation of Shares in Buybacks

In buybacks, the current market price determines the valuation of shares. Unlike a management buyout, where a group is taking a unit private by paying the parent company a lump sum including a premium, in a buyback the company is buying shares on the open market.

Buybacks can send a signal either of confidence or of weakness, depending on context, notes Al Rappaport.[15] Also, different kinds of buybacks have varying effects. An open market purchase operates differently from a Dutch auction or a fixed-price tender offer. Other relevant factors include involvement by insiders, the size of the program, and, of course, the premium paid. The buyback has an impact on earnings per share depending on a variety of factors, including the price-to-earnings multiple. And most obviously, a buyback increases the debt-to-equity ratio because the number of shares outstanding decreases following the buyback.

Valuation of Shares in Companies with Underfunded Defined Benefit Pension Plans

A very common situation in the evolution of a major publicly held corporation is the creation and maintenance of a pension fund. If the fund has defined contributions, its value can be largely determined by forces beyond the company's control; so the company is off the hook for the value of the fund.

Defined benefit plans, however, are a whole different story. The company is accountable to deliver a specific (defined) dollar amount of benefits. The financial performance of a defined corporate pension fund can, in turn, affect the performance of the corporation that sponsors the fund. So a corporate pension fund can be a fund within a fund. When the corporation owning the fund suffers pension fund losses, this in turn affects the value of the corporate shares being held by other funds.

Institutional investors that buy equities already know how to assess performance using risk-adjusted measures; this approach is well established among professionals.[16] When speaking to the managements of companies that take major positions, investors can insist on the use of these same measures to track the performance of corporate pension funds.

Accounting also matters. How corporations apply accounting standards affects balance sheet numbers, in turn, affecting stock price and corporate performance. Under both U.S. and international accounting standards, companies are required to recognize a liability in their balance sheets that is at least equal to the unfunded benefit obligation.[17] In the United Kingdom, auditors have been urging companies to reconsider how they calculate their pension liabilities.[18] They want companies to lower the discount rate they use. The lower the discount rate, the higher the present value of future liabilities will be; conversely, the higher the discount rate, the lower the present value of future liabilities.[19]

Another issue that can affect the value of corporate-sponsored pension funds is the balance of equity and debt securities within the fund. The 2007–2009 crisis in equity markets cast doubt on the proposition that equity returns are higher than fixed-income returns over the long term. Nonetheless, it is still good to ask how valuation can help us compare stock and bonds.

With respect to valuation for portfolio investment, bond valuation is every bit as challenging. The poor performance of bonds in so-called target-date funds has made this point. In 2007, the Department of Labor (DOL) issued a rule to protect 401(k) money in target funds that lose money. This rule caused a rise in target fund investments. In June 2009, the DOL and the Securities and Exchange Commission (SEC) held hearings on target-date funds. An important message from the hearings was that when an institutional investor chooses an investment, it is more important to study the quality of the investment than the label that goes onto the investment. The hearings also emphasized the continuing value of equity investments in a portfolio, including one held by a retirement fund.[20]

The Example of Endowments

Finally, pension funds can learn from the example of endowments. Some endowment funds overvalue nonmarketable assets in their portfolios to mask weak equity values. Harvard Management Corporation, for example, began a recent fiscal year with 17 percent of its assets invested in commodities, a portion of which was in timber or farmland. Do you know anyone who wants to buy New Zealand timber property or a farm in western Iowa? Should there be the same merciless mark-to-market imperative on valuing endowment properties, as there is in the financial sector with publicly traded banks and others that hold securities?

Arguably, one could leave the valuation of New Zealand timber at an aspirational future level—that is, in accordance with a harvesting replanting inflation assumption—but only as long as the balance of assets are sufficient to meet the liquidity requirements. There is no abstract reason why one should have to punish the illiquid holdings when the trustees are under no imperative to convert the assets into cash. Indeed, the applicable legal standard, the Uniform Prudent Investor Act, for trusts, no longer has any restrictions on what is and is not an appropriate vehicle for investment.[21]

Ultimately the critical informing concept is time:

> *Value now.* On occasion, the instantaneous pricing capability of mutual funds—when value must be determined right now—is necessary.

> *Value at a specific future date.* On other occasions, value can be determined at predictable times in the future. As a result, there has developed a rather poorly but graphically named investment discipline: liability management. Literally, this phrase could refer to a defined benefit plan that can with actuarial precision define exactly when it will have to pay out, how much, and to whom.

> *Value over time.* Finally, value need not be associated with any corresponding liability requiring liquidity at a particular time, as is the case, typically, with university endowments or sovereign wealth funds.

The only unique characteristic of value now is that it is real. It is not a bewildering complex of algorithms; it is cash in hand. Although this concept has distinct utility and integrity, as a guide to investing in either the second or third category, it is expensive (why pay a premium for liquidity that you don't need?) and needlessly limiting.

How, then, do investors deal with the problem that an asset's value for a particular time period is not real, or otherwise risky? There are several ways of dealing with this. The simplest is disclosure—so that no one is misled. The second is legal compliance procedures, that is, avoidance of negligence. The third is some kind of self-imposed ratio, such as a percentage of portfolio permitted to be invested in assets not susceptible of real marketplace confirmation.

The need for such solutions finds support in a May 2010 study that identified problems in the so-called endowment model of investing. In *Educational Endowment and the Financial Crisis*, the Center for Social Philanthropy and the Teullus Institute argue that investment risk-tracking has jeopardized the security of endowment income, and that "far from being the innocent victims of the financial crisis, endowments helped enable it" through their investment style—for example, by investing (often through external investment managers) in "opaque, illiquid, and overcrowded asset classes such as commodities, hedge funds, and private equity." The study calls on funds to choose their own investments, to invest in assets with more liquidity and lower volatility, and to become more active as owners in promoting practices that lead to long-term value. "By integrating sustainability factors into investment decisions and becoming more active owners of their assets, endowments can begin to seize the opportunities of long-term responsible stewardship."[22]

Valuation of Shares Tendered, Exchanged, or Retained in Mergers or Acquisitions

A merger creates a number of special valuation scenarios. Certainly mergers are of interest to investors because they are a fairly common phenomenon with some 30,000 transactions announced every year. The related valuation work is highly circumstantial and requires answering multiple questions. In the case of a merger:

> ➤ *Owners of shares in a corporate buyer buying another company* should weigh everything in this book, plus the following considerations:
>> ➤ *Strategy*. Does this transaction make sense strategically for the buyer? Valid strategies might include supplementing a current line of business to grow market share, complementing a current line of business to offset cyclical sales, and so forth.[23]
>> ➤ *Pricing*. Is the premium offered for the stock so high that it will harm the future economic value of the acquirer? (If so, get out of the stock because it will decline in value later.)
>> ➤ *Structuring*. Is the transaction structured in the most value-enhancing way?[24]
>> ➤ *Financing*. How is the deal funded—equity or cash? (Research suggests that cash-funded deals do better.[25])
>> ➤ *Industry valuation quirks*. What are the quirks of the industry that could affect value, and does the acquirer show signs of knowing them?[26]
>> ➤ *Due diligence*. Investors want assurance that the buyer has completed a diligent study of the main sources of risk for postmerger value, namely a study of risks in management, operations, internal

financial controls, external financial reporting, legal exposure of the company to be acquired, and legal risks of the transaction itself. Is the target company practically insolvent but hiding it? If so, there could be litigation of a fraudulent transfer.[27]

➤ *Deal integration.* Will the corporations integrate fully, partially, or not at all, and what is the plan to capture value from any "synergies"? Two plus two can equal five, but managers need to know what they are doing.

➤ *Owners of shares in a target company in a friendly merger* have a choice to hold on to shares in order to trade them in for shares of a the newly combined company or getting out early by selling the shares before the transaction takes place. And *the owner of shares in a target company in a hostile acquisition* have a choice to sell to the first hostile bidder or to hold on to shares in the hopes that the company will remain independent or sell into a future bid. In both cases, whether friendly or hostile, the considerations to weigh include the many already covered in this book, plus these:

➤ How likely is it that the merger will take place? What are the chances of a cancellation?

➤ If the merger does take place, when will that be?

➤ What will happen to the price of the stock while the deal is pending?

➤ How credible are the claims of the managements of the combining companies that they will increase postmerger value? (What does the postmerger stock price history of similar combinations in this industry show about postmerger performance of similar transactions?[28])

➤ Owners of shares in a company that is letting an investor and/or management group take a unit of a public company private (leveraged buyout) need to consider their actions from several points of view. According to one experienced source, most experienced LBO buyers try to determine how much they must pay for a company and then analyze whether the deal will work on that basis. In so doing, they look at a number of standard ratios that focus principally on the relationship of the gross unleveraged price to operating cash flow, operating income, or unleveraged book value. The ratios really perform only a support function to the more practical concerns of actually getting the deal in the first place. A special issue involves conflicts of interest. The people approving the transaction should not be affiliated with the group that will buy the unit.[29]

➤ *For investors who own a company forced to merge by the govern-ment*, it's best to get out while the getting is good. As the events of 2008–2009 showed, the government—loath to be accused of wast-ing taxpayer money—tends to undervalue the equity shares. At the same time, it can force a sale because it has greater power than the private sector. Due process aside, it can rule by fiat.

The buyer of shares in a special-purpose acquisition company—a buyout fund that has gone public to capitalize itself for future acquisitions—needs to assess the merger market as a whole. Share values in such a company are likely to go up if conditions are favorable for deals (e.g., low interest rates and low price-to-earnings multiples), but will languish otherwise. More generally, beware of any publicly traded special-purpose fund. It has permanent capital, unlike a private equity fund, which has temporary capital. The three- to seven-year time frame that a private equity fund has to deliver returns or close provides a dis-cipline. The shares in such companies, like any conglomerate, must be heavily discounted to offset the problem of lack of cohesion or synergy among differing units. The more moving parts there are, the higher the transfer costs will be when doing business. This was the major dis-covery of economist John Coase, whose theory of transfer cost helps to explained why all conglomerates, large or small, trade at a permanent discount. For an investor who must buy, sell, or hold the shares involved in the transaction, the main focus is whether any premium price paid per share is attractive or unattractive in relation to the investor's alter-native investments. In any transaction focused on control, such as a tender offer, the price paid is rarely the trading price of the security because an acquirer will pay a premium for control. So the value of a company is its market capitalization (price per share times shares outstanding), plus an additional amount.

The value-price gap closes at the moment the price is paid because value and price are equal. The per-share value of the target company to the best potential buyer is the same as the price just paid per share. After the transaction, the price per share of the company drops and can become lower than what a willing buyer would pay, and the company could be in play again. The only thing preventing an incessant parade of changes of control is the transaction cost of change of control. You can only flip a house every so often.

Premiums can make sense in a certain narrow range. Purely mathematically (that is, theoretically), a premium can be a negative of more than 100 percent, in which case the seller would be paying another company more than the price of the stock to take it over (much as the frustrated owner of an untunable, low-grade piano might pay a junk dealer to haul the instrument away). It can also be a positive of well over 100 percent (1.5, 2, 3 times or more than the selling price of a stock). Yet premiums are never negative, and when they are positive, they're generally in the low to middle two-digit range.

A premium that is more than 50 percent means either of the following:

➤ The selling company management may have failed to realize the company's value (in which cases, there would have been corrective shareholder action much earlier).

➤ The buying company may be overpaying (in which case, share price will decline, harming shareholders who survive the transaction).

Furthermore, a closer look at transaction pricing from a comparative price setting reveals a greater world of complexity than simply comparative premiums. Thus the astute investor has to learn to think like an investment banker when assessing an M&A transaction for its pricing. In their excellent book *Investment Banking: Valuation, Leveraged Buyouts, and Mergers & Acquisitions*, Joshua Rosenbaum and Joshua Pearl devote Chapter 1 to comparable pricing, and they give these steps:[30]

1. Select the universe of comparable companies.
2. Locate the necessary financial information.
3. Spread key statistics, ratios, and trading multiples (which may include industry-specific rules of thumb).
4. Benchmark the comparable companies.
5. Determine valuation.

As to step 1, comparative market valuation requires not only knowledge of the past selling price of those companies, but also good statistical techniques to ensure the proper selection of benchmarks for comparison.

Investors need to look beyond global industry classification (GIC) codes and company size to consider other factors of comparability. With the wealth of information available for public companies (step 2) this is possible.

But there is a risk in customizing comparisons too much. An investor may think JS Software Company is a peer to Microsoft, but this view may be inflated.[31] Just because two companies are in the same industry does not make them comparable.

Keep it simple. As always, a mathematical approach can help clear away the clutter.

Direct Comparison Math

Expressing the direct comparison approach in mathematical terms yields further insight into how it works and the assumptions on which it depends. Define the value indicator to be V and the observable variable to be x. The critical assumption on which the direct comparison approach depends is that the ratio of V to x for the appraisal target equals (at least approximately) the ratio of V to x for the comparable firms as shown in equation (1).

$$V(\text{target})/x(\text{target}) = V(\text{comparables})/x(\text{comparables}) \qquad (4.1)$$

If equation (4.1) holds, the appraisal procedure is trivial. Solving (1) for the one unknown variable, the value indicator for the appraisal target, gives.

$$V(\text{target}) = x(\text{target}) \times V(\text{comparables})/x(\text{comparables}) \qquad (4.2)$$

Equation (4.2) works for any observable variable x, as long as the ratio of V to x is constant across firms as shown in equation (4.1). . . . A critical step in applying the direct comparison approach is choosing observable variables, x, that have a consistent relation to value, V. In general, the best way to do this is to find x variables that economic theory indicates will be causally related to value.

—Aswath Damodaran, New York University [emphasis added][32]

Having selected a comparative transaction, the two sale prices have to be compared to something else intrinsic to each deal, as described in step 3. This price analysis is rarely if ever a simple sale price number (Peer Company B sold for a merger sale price of N, therefore our Company A should also sell for N). Rather, it is usually analyzed as a premium paid with one or more key ratios, not merely the premium paid over stock price. As Rosenbaum and Pearl chronicle, investment bankers use a great variety of ratios to analyze price. In addition to the usual accounting-based and share-price-based multiples, others are sensitive to industry, such as broadcast cash flow (BCF) for media companies, earnings before interest, taxes, depreciation, and exploration expenses, or EBITDAX (earnings before interest, taxes, depreciation, amortization, and exploration expenses) for oil and gas companies.

Legal Basis for Comparable Pricing

As Aswath Damodaran has noted, courts of law have recognized the idea that valid value indicators can be derived by making direct comparisons. In two landmark decisions, *Central Trust* and *Bader*, the court ruled that the value of a target company could be estimated by capitalizing the company's dividends and earnings.[33]

When deciding whether to buy into a deal, it is good to anticipate how courts may see the transaction with respect to viability and price.

Landmark M&A Valuation and Cancellation Cases

Smith v. VanGorkom (1985). No protection is available for directors who make uninformed judgment on M&A valuation.

Revlon Inc. v. McAndrews & Forbes Holding (1986). Directors have affirmative duty to seek best price when selling the company (once the company is in play).

Time Inc. v. Paramount Communications (1990). It is OK to turn down a higher price if the decision is based on valid strategic plan for greater value.

> *Omnicare v. NCS Healthcare* (2003). An exclusive merger agreement must include a "fiduciary out" (escape clause), at least when the agreement gives target shareholders no other escape.
>
> *Henkel Corp. v. Innovative Brands Holdings* LLC (2008). If an agreement has a "material adverse conditions" clause allowing deal cancellation, the clause must be invoked within a reasonable amount of time, unless otherwise set by agreement.

Strategic Reasons for M&A

Investors considering buying, selling, or holding stocks involved in a merger need to make sure the merger makes sense and can increase share value. In a free market (absent a merger forced by a government), an acquirer may want to gain control of another entity for 10 basic reasons, according to the late J. Fred Weston, merger expert. Nine reasons are good and one is bad. If you are an investor of a company acquiring another, make sure that the motive for the transaction is not number ten. Investors should listen for key messages (and, if they hear number ten, run the other way):

1. *Strategic planning.* Accomplish strategic goals more quickly, successfully: "We want to expand into X field so we can get there first and take the lead."
2. *Operating synergy.* Achieve economies of scale and/or better pricing by buying a customer, supplier, or competitor: "We want to reduce cost of marketing by convincing a competitor to join us."
3. *Market power.* Increase market share: "We want to take them out."
4. *Differential efficiency.* Realize a return on investment by making a firm more efficient: "We want to put our system in."
5. *Inefficient management.* Realize a return by buying a firm with inefficient managers and replacing them: "We want to replace the CEO with our own."
6. *Financial synergy.* Lower the cost of capital by smoothing cash flow and increasing debt capacity: "We want to buy a cash cow."
7. *Undervaluation.* Take advantage of a price that is low in comparison to past stock prices and/or estimated future prices, or in relation to

the cost the buyer would incur if it built the company from scratch (buy versus build): "We want to buy low."

8. *Agency problems.* Assert control in an underperforming company with dispersed ownership: "We want to wake up a management that has been ignoring owners."

9. *Tax efficiency.* Obtain a more favorable tax status: "We want to buy a not operating loss (NOL)."

10. *Managerialism.* Increase the size of a company and therefore increase the power and pay of managers: "We want to be king." (To be avoided!)[34]

Analyzing Organic vs. Merger Growth

Long-term investors with major stakes in an acquisitive company may want to see a what-if scenario without acquisitions. In one instance, when one major nonprofit purchased a for-profit subsidiary, it wanted a report that segregated its organic growth from its acquired growth. Using statistical analysis software, managers added a single variable that segregated the two, rather than separating them by group number. As a press release states, "People could easily look at business growth with and without [the acquisition] in there. All I had to do was add a couple of lines of code . . . and there it was."[35]

Valuation of Shares in Spin-Offs and Divestitures

Spin-offs and divestitures are the opposite of mergers. Instead of taking two companies and creating one, one company creates two. Spin-offs raise values when they have what is called "information asymmetry" compared to their industry and peers. This is a typical problem in conglomerates where not enough is known from unit to unit. Information problems decrease significantly after the spin-off. Gains around spin-offs are positively related to the degree of information asymmetry.[36]

Spin-offs can be complex. In October 2008, for example, Procter & Gamble (P&G) spun off The Folgers Coffee Company to its shareholders and had the entity merge with J. M. Smucker. The transaction gave P&G shareholders majority control of Smucker, and Smucker then owned

Folgers. P&G shareholders didn't have to pay taxes. In a phrase only Wall Street lawyers could love, this was called a "reverse Morris Trust transaction." P&G first spun off Folgers to its shareholders, and the coffee company then simultaneously merged with Smucker. To qualify for tax-free treatment, P&G shareholders had to end up with majority control of Smucker, but Smucker still owns Folgers. As of late 2010, all companies involved were doing fairly well.[37]

A divesting firm likes to say that their company or one of its units is undervalued and that splitting the firm into its component businesses will make it easier for the market to value the components accurately.

Cost-Benefit of Diversification

When firms are undervalued due to unobservability of divisional cash flows, they may resort to divestiture to raise capital while overvalued firms will use external equity. Diversification thus might result in costly future divestiture. Firms trade off this expected cost of diversification against the benefit of higher levels of cheaper internal capital in deciding the scope of the firm.[38]

—Vikram Nanda and M. P. Narayanan

Valuation of Shares Impacted by Shareholder-Led Governance Changes

Shareholder activism is another event in the life of a corporation that can affect value (Chapter 7). For example, consider the hypothetical mutual fund called the Governance Alpha Fund (GAF), which excluded companies identified as having poor corporate governance practices, based on a definition from The Corporate Library.[39] It significantly outperformed its benchmark, according to a study conducted by Northfield Information Services for The Corporate Library.[40]

Furthermore, shareholders who believe that governance has a positive impact on value may use their share ownership to affect changes in company value.

These two factors, governance attributes and shareholder activism, can become a double helix for value growth. As Colin Melvin of the successful Hermes Fund has stated:

> Hermes' corporate governance work is based on the belief that both ensuring compliance with certain governance standards and active ownership based on a larger set of standards "in itself" will improve the performance of investee companies.[41]

Shareholders can take a progression of steps to effect change. For one thing, investors can sell their shares—a move called the "Wall Street walk." But there are other ways, as one experienced investor has noted: periodic review of company performance, positive communications with management, challenging discussions with management, forming an informal shareholder group for joint action, having a first meeting with legal counsel, holding an initial shareholder meeting, proposing a dissident slate, having more meetings with retaining counsel, holding more shareholder meetings, having shareholders' counsel meet with counsel for the board, negotiating, and, as a last resort, a lawsuit.

The Many Faces of Shareholder Activism

Shareholder activism is the way in which shareholders exercise their ownership rights to influence a company's behavior. Activist investors, dissatisfied with certain aspects of a company's management, seek to cause a change within the company by resorting to various forms of activism, ranging from selling off shares to acquisition of controlling interest in the company. In between these extreme steps [are] other actions like issuing private or public communications to the management and the board of directors demanding change in the company decisions, submitting shareholder resolutions, and filing legal cases. . . . Shareholder activism may have both positive and negative effects on companies.

—Robert A. G. Monks, *Shareholder Activism: An Emerging Paradigm*, edited by Madtha Cyril Marcel (Hyderabad: ICFAI, 2007).

The goal of all these steps is to buy low (when the company's value is suffering due to some condition shareholders want to change) and to sell high after the value goes up at some point following shareholder activism.

The following topics are generally considered to be appropriate focus areas for board-shareholder communications (if not outright resolutions[42]), according to a Blue Ribbon Commission representing investors, managers, and directors:

➤ CEO evaluation and succession
➤ Executive compensation
➤ Board nomination and election
➤ Governance issues[43]
➤ Strategic direction
➤ Social issues that impact share value[44]

Enlightened managers and directors welcome shareholder input in these matters. Interestingly, this short list of matters appropriate for shareholder engagement closely parallels the list of value drivers discussed in the previous chapter, even though the two lists were developed entirely independently from each other.

Valuation of Shares in Companies in the Zone of Insolvency or Filing for Bankruptcy

Like mergers, bankruptcies are a fairly common event in the life cycle of companies. According to the American Bankruptcy Institute, business filings in 2008 totaled 43,546. This was up from 28,322 the previous year—and was the largest annual number of bankruptcy filings since 1997.[45]

Many of the institutions that had the greatest challenges during the 2007–2009 financial crisis had embraced illiquid assets. They had bought shares they could not sell. Their difficulties engendered a newfound appreciation for liquidity. Investors henceforth will be much more sensitive to the issue of illiquid assets in the corporations that sell them stock.[46]

Shareholders must remain vigilant to the risk of bankruptcy because this event is almost always devastating to shareholder value. Not only is the company suffering financially—usually with the double whammy of low cash flow and low stock price—but also payments to shareholder returns go to end of the food line, after employees and creditors.

So, during bankruptcy, the key for shareholders is not valuation. By then it is too late. They are powerless to receive any meaningful return. As the Fool in Shakespeare's *King Lear* says, "Nothing comes of nothing." The time to do something about value is before a filing for bankruptcy, when the firm is still solvent. Then the question is, can investors rely on the company to pull out of its troubles before a filing and, if so, what will the shares be worth?

With regard to the latter, the investor must look for different red flags. One is any merger or acquisition. If due diligence has been lax, the acquired company may turn out to be insolvent after the fact, dragging the acquirer down. This is hardly a rare event; indeed, the legal profession (through the American Bar Association) has developed a model law called the Uniform Fraudulent Transfer Act to address this type of scenario. (U.S. law has some 40 "uniform" laws to deal with recurrent business problems.)

The quality of earnings is obviously a key issue. One way to verify earnings quality, notes a source at Morningstar, is to look at other valuation measures such as the price-to-cash-flow ratio, which should not be dramatically higher than the stock's forward price-to-earnings ratio.[47]

To value a firm that is or may be trouble, one can also:

➤ Normalize the earnings for a troubled firm using historical or industry averages.
➤ Estimate the likelihood that a troubled firm will not survive, based on bond ratings as well as bond prices.
➤ Use a free cash flow model that allows the valuation of negative-earnings firms as going concerns.

(For spreadsheets that enable these operations, see the ones created and posted by Aswath Damodaran.)[48]

Investors who want to be active analysts and participants in corporate value are well advised to heed the lessons of a company that was teetering on the edge of bankruptcy. In *Chartwell Litigation Trust v. Addus Healthcare, Inc. (In re Med Diversified, Inc.)*, the question was, what was the company' value? The court had to assess the value of 100 percent of the shares of a company (Addus Healthcare, Inc., a privately held health-care firm) and of a related option payment. Establishing its value required more than one valuation approach. In that case, the wisdom of Judge Stan Bernstein of the Eastern District of New York is instructive.[49] Judge Bernstein barred a self-styled expert (Dr. Shannon Pratt, well-known for his expertise in private company valuation) from testifying in the fraudulent transfer case, based on lack of rigor. The court challenged the defense's expert witness, noting among other facts that he relied too heavily on a single source of expertise—the same source cited by plaintiffs.

Second, the court found that the expert's use of valuation methodologies was too narrow. He used financial multiples, considered comparables but did not show rigor in selecting peer companies, and failed to use a DCF method to check his work—a good lesson for analysts of any type of company, not only private firms in the throes on insolvency.[50]

Valuation of Shares in Companies Emerging from Bankruptcy

Companies that emerge from Chapter 11 bankruptcy are subject to Financial Accounting Standards Board's Accounting Standards, in particular ASC 805, *Business Combinations*, and 852, *Reorganizations* (incorporating multiple earlier standards).[51] Under ASC 852, emerging entities adopt so-called fresh start accounting, which calls for them to apply fair value concepts to determine their reorganization value and start a new basis for financial reporting. Just before confirmation of the company's reorganization plan:

➤ The company must be "balance sheet insolvent"—that is, the reorganized value of its assets must be lower than the sum of its postpetition liabilities and allowed claims.
➤ The holders of the voting shares receive less than 50 percent of the voting shares of the emerging entity.

Under fresh start accounting, the emerging entity allocates its reorganization value to its assets based on their estimated fair value. Essentially, reorganization value is the price a willing buyer would pay for the new entity.

Conclusion

Investors can learn much from news items such as the events identified in this chapter, News affects stock price value—sometimes well after the headlines fade away.[52] Investors seeking superior returns from investments in corporate equity can benefit from monitoring all major life cycle events of a company. Further, they can influence those events through their actions.

Notes

1. We apologize in advance for repeating the phrase "valuation of shares" with almost every heading, but we found it necessary to maintain focus on the point of each subsection.
2. AIG 2008 Annual Report, http://www.asiaing.com/aig-2008-annual-report .html.
3. U.S. Treasury, "TARP AIG SSFI Investment, Senior Preferred Stock and Warrant, Summary of Senior Preferred Terms," http://www.treasury.gov/ press/releases/reports/111008aigtermsheet.pdf.
4. "Formally, Treasury paid a mere $500,000 for the convertible preferred, earlier this month. That is far less than the $30 billion it would take to pay a minimum of $2.50 per share for 12 billion common shares. The deal papers suggest that the parties are assuming that the New York Fed's earlier loans, with a current balance of about $50 billion, somehow count as part of the consideration AIG received for issuing the convertible preferred. Maybe a court could be so persuaded. But it is not free from doubt." (Lawrence Cunningham, "AIG's Unsupervised Capital Structure Conflicts," http://www.concurringopinions .com/archives/2009/03/aigs_unsupervis_1.html.)
5. "Traders Seek Fortune in AIG, a Stock Once Left for Dead," *Wall Street Journal*, September 23, 2009, http://online.wsj.com/article/ SB125366502247832417.html.
6. JP Morgan Chase, "JPMorgan Chase and Bear Stearns Announce Amended Agreement," March 24, 2008, http://jpmorgan.com/cm/cs?pagename=JPM_ redesign/JPM_Content_C/Generic_Detail_Page_Template&cid=115933910 4093&c=JPM_Content_C.
7. "IPOs Priced in the Last 12 Months," http://www.renaissancecapital .com/ IPOHome/Pricings/Year.aspx.
8. "After a long dormant period, companies that would already be public in better times will be coming to market further along the development curve, but at valuations that are far more palatable to investors." Steve

Schaeffer, "IPO Class of 2010," *Forbes*, September 1, 2009, http://www
.forbes.com/2009/09/01/ipo-market-rebound-markets-equities-public-
offerings.html.

9. Michael Adams, Barry Thornton, and Russ Baker, "Asymmetric Price Adjustment: Are Prices for IPOs Too Sticky?" *Journal of Business and Economic
   Research* 7, no. 5 (May 2009): pp. 55–61.http://www.cluteinstitute-online-
   journals.com/PDFs/1674.pdf.

10. Shawn D. Howton, Shelly W. Howton, and Gerard T. Olson, "Board
    Ownership and IPO Returns," *Journal of Economics and Finance*, 25(1)
    (March 2001), http://www.springerlink.com/content/bn3044124824683j/.

11. Howton, see note 10.

12. See Rajesh Aggarwal, Laurie Krigman, and Kent Womack, "Strategic IPO
    Underpricing, Information Momentum, and Lockup Expiration Selling,"
    Journal of Financial Economics 66 (2002): 105–137.

13. Daniella Gelman, "Examining IPO Valuation Methods—Market Compara-
    bles and Discounted Cash Flow," a student paper citing Marc Deloof, Wouter
    De Maeseneire, and Koen Inghelbrecht, Koen, "The Valuation of IPOs by
    Investment Banks and the Stock Market: Empirical Evidence," EFMA 2002
    London Meetings, EFA 2002 Berlin Meetings discussion paper.

14. Aigbe Akhigbe, Jeff Madura, and Stephen P. Zera, "Long-Term Valuation
    Effects of Stock Splits," *Journal of Economics and Finance* 19, no. 3 (Fall
    1995): 119–134.

15. Al Rappaport and Michael J. Mauboussin's *Expectations Investing* (New York:
    McGraw-Hill, 2001) informed this section of our chapter. We list this book
    in the back of our own as one of our top selections on corporate valuation.

16. Eight approaches are common: (1) the standard deviation of returns, (2) the
    Sharpe ratio, (3) value at risk, (4) the Jensen Index. From industry practice,
    the approaches are: (5) the Sortino ratio, (6) the Treynor ratio, (7) the Modi-
    gliani or M-Square Measure, and (8) the Morningstar Rating. See Katharina
    Schwaiger, Cormac Lucas, and Gautam Mitra, "Measuring Pension Fund
    Performance Using Risk-Adjusted Measurements," OptiRisk Systems White
    Paper Series, January 2009, http://www.optirisk-systems.com/papers/opt008
    .pdf. For more on the Sharpe ratio, see William Sharpe, "The Sharpe
    Ratio," *Journal of Portfolio Management* (Fall 1994), http://www.stanford
    .edu/~wfsharpe/art/sr/sr.htm.

17. For details, see Towers Perrin, "Comparison of IAS 19 with FAS
    87/88/106/132(R)/158: Summary of Provisions Affecting Accounting for
    Postretirement Benefits," http://www.towersperrin.com/tp/getwebcached
    oc?webc=USA/2008/200807/IAS19_FAS87_comparison_808.pdf.

18. See Normal Cohen and Jennifer Hughes, "Call for Change in Pension
    Deficit Reporting." *Financial Times*, December 31, 2008.

19. "Discounting the value of pension accounting," February 18, 2009, http://pwc.blogs.com/ifrs/2009/02/discounting-the-value-of-pension-accounting.html.

20. Allison Bell, "Target Funds Draw Ire," *National Underwriter*, June 18, 2009. See also Mariana Lemann, "Funds Resist Regulation of Target Date Pensions," *Financial Times*, July 5, 2006, http://www.ft.com/cms/s/0/40d18954-6827-11de-848a-00144feabdc0.html.

21. As of 1994, "All categoric restrictions on types of investments have been abrogated; the trustee can invest in anything that plays an appropriate role in achieving the risk-return objectives of the trust and that meets the other requirements of prudent investing" (Uniform Prudent Investors Act, National Conference on Uniform State Laws, http://www.law.upenn.edu/bll/archives/ulc/fnact99/1990s/upia94.htm).

22 *Educational Endowment and the Financial Crisis: Social Costs and System Risk in the Shadow Banking System—A Study of Six New England Schools* (Boston, MA: The Center for Social Philanthropy and the Tellus Institute, May 2010.

23. Corporate strategy is worthy of a massive book unto itself, and investors would be well-advised to understand it, especially when it comes to analyzing the value of equities to be purchased or relinquished in a merger. To develop and monitor a strategy requires a vast amount of knowledge, including risk assessment, economic, environmental, and market trends, internal financial information, industry comparisons, market demographics, and competitive information. For more on strategy, see Chapter 4. A good example of an articulated merger and acquisition (M&A) strategy is the one articulated by Dupont Ellen Kullman. Like her predecessor Charles Holliday, she sees acquisitions as an extension of strategy. Dupon sees four megatrends: the increasing demand for food, the need to protect people and the environment, the desire to lessen dependence on fossil fuels, and the growth of emerging markets. Accordingly, Kullman says the company is considering potential acquisitions in the areas of agriculture, safety and protection, alternative energy, electronic materials, and biosciences (Andrew Eder, "Taking Charge of Dupont in Trying Times," *DelawareOnline*, http://www.sparkweekly.com/apps/pbcs.dll/article?Date=20091206&Category=BUSINESS&ArtNo=912060382&SectionCat=&Template=printart).

24. See Alexandra R. Lajoux and H. Peter Nesvold, *The Art of M&A Structuring: Techniques for Mitigating Financial, Tax, and Legal Risk* (New York: McGraw-Hill, 2004).

25. To test this, see the case study that produces a pro forma earnings-per-share estimate for acquisitions funded by debt and then by equity ("Mergers and Acquisitions Modeling," December 1–4, 2009, a course taught by

Nick Antill, with Kenneth Lee, coauthor of *Company Valuation Under IFRS: Interpreting and Forecasting Accounts Using International Financial Reporting Standards* (Hampshire, U.K.: Harriman House, 2005), http://www.euromoneytraining.com/pdf/Mergers%20and%20Acquistion%20Modelling/M&A%20Modelling%20-%20EIF2824-WEB.pdf).

26. "For example, to name just one example out of an infinite variety, if a management team is considering buying or selling shares in an electric company that is buying a plant, the acquirer must understand that where a generating plant benefits from firm contracts creating a positive spark spread, the buyer of the plant is locking in a positive arbitrage between gas prices and electricity prices for the duration of the contracts" ("Valuation of Energy Assets, Part II," http://www.energypulse.net/centers/article/article_display.cfm?a_id=716). Investors need to have the confidence that the directors and officers of the company have assembled a management team with this kind of knowledge. Although the selection of management is not considered a topic suitable for shareholder resolutions, it is considered appropriate for shareholder communications.

27. For a comprehensive discussion, see Alexandra R. Lajoux and Charles M. Elson, *The Art of M&A Due Diligence*, 2nd ed. (New York: McGraw-Hill, 2010).

28. For a discussion of postmerger value, see Alexandra Lajoux, *The Art of M&A Integration,* 2nd ed. (New York: McGraw-Hill, 2006).

29. Stanley Foster Reed, Alexandra Reed Lajoux, and H. Peter Nesvold, *The Art of M&A: A Merger/Acquisition/Buyout Guide* (New York: McGraw-Hill, 2007).

30. *Investment Banking: Valuation, Leveraged Buyouts, and Mergers & Acquisitions* (Hoboken, N.J.: John Wiley & Sons, 2009).

31. Appraiser Randall Schostag said, Companies may be comparable even though in different industries, while many within the same industry are not comparable, depending on capital structure and operating differences" (Randall Schostag, "Portfolio Valuation Using Automation," *Business Valuation*, May–June 2008.) As Aswath Damodaran notes, "Even highly dissimilar companies can be made to appear similar if the data are massaged enough. Thus, the fewer adjustments made to the data, the greater the confidence that generally can be placed in a direct comparison appraisal" (Aswath Damodaran *Investment Valuation: Tools and Techniques for Determining the Value of Any Asset* (Hoboken, N.J.: John Wiley & Sons, 2002)).

32. Aswath Damodaran, see note 31.

33. *Central Trust*, 59-1 USTC par. 9431; 172 F. Supp. 833 (DC Ill.); *Bader,* 62-2 USTC par. 12,092; 304 F 2d 923, cited in Damodaran, see note 31.

34. This classic list is adapted from one that appears in Alexandra R. Lajoux and J. Fred Weston, *The Art of M&A Financing and Refinancing* (New York: McGraw-Hill, 1999).

35. SAS, "A Little Serendipity Goes a Long Way," http://www.sas.com/success/bcbsfla_pmdis.html.

36. Sudha Krishnaswami and Venkat Subramaniam, "Information Symmetry, Valuation, and the Corporate Spin-Off Decision," *Journal of Financial Economics* 53, no. 1 (July 1999): 73–112.

37. "Smucker's Sales Increase with Folgers Purchase," 1/11/2010, http://www.brandchannel.com/home/post/2010/01/11/Smuckers-Sales-Increase-With-Folgers-Purchase.aspx; "JM Smucker Raising Coffee Prices by 9 Percent," 8/3/2010, http://www.marketwatch.com/story/jm-smucker-raises-coffee-prices-by-9-2010-08-03.

38. Vikram Nanda and M. P. Narayanan, "Disentangling Value: Financing Needs, Firm Scope, and Divestitures," *Journal of Financial Intermediation* 8 (1999): 174–204.

39. SRI Monitor, "Poor Corporate Governance Hurts Performance, Study Concludes," http://srimonitor.blogspot.com/2009/07/poor-corporate-governance-hurts.html.

40. The Corporate Library (thecorporatelibrary.com), based in Portland, Maine, is a research company cofounded in 1989 by Robert A. G. Monks and shareholder activist Nell Minow. See Chapter 7 for more details on its corporate governance standards. See also http://srimonitor.blogspot.com/2009/07/poor-corporate-governance-hurts.html.

41. See "Corporate Governance and Performance: A Brief Review and Assessment of the Evidence for a Link Between Corporate Governance and Performance," October 2005; and "Taking the Long-Term View" (undated; accessed June 28, 2010). http://www.eumedion.nl/page/downloads/Corporate_Governance_and_Performance_oct05_1_.pdf and http://www.hermes.co.uk/ic_hff_the_fund.aspx. For more about returns from governance, see *2009 Wilshire Consulting Report on Corporate Pension Funding Levels*. http://www.wilshire.com/BusinessUnits/Consulting/Investment/2009_Corporate_Funding_Report.pdf. Also see Chapter 7 of this book.

42. Most of the items on this list cannot be excluded as ordinary business under Rule 14a-8(i)(8).

43. Board operations, as well as "transparency, disclosure, and general oversight of the company's financial and reputational interests" fall into this category.

44. This list comes from the Report of the NACD Blue Ribbon Commission on Board-Shareholder Communications (Washington, D.C.: NACD, 2008). This report notes that "shareholders care about a host of issues in the social

and environmental domains. In recent times, companies have received shareholder proposals on animal welfare, environmental concerns (including a growing number on global warming), health, human rights, labor standards, political donations, product safety, sexual orientation, and sustainability. Depending on the circumstances, these may or may not be appropriate for direct board-shareholder communication. In any event, directors should be aware of these issues and how they may impact company sustainability and returns to shareholders."

45. "Annual Business and Non-business Filings by Year (1980-2009)," American Bankruptcy Institute," http://www.abiworld.org/AM/AM Template.cfm?Section=Home&TEMPLATE=/CM/ContentDisplay .cfm&CONTENTID=57826.

46. Liquidity of assets has been a major theme at the World Economic Forum in Davos, Switzerland, where Robert A. G. Monks was a keynote speaker in November 2009.

47. Morningstar, "Morningstar's Equity Research," http://news.morningstar .com/articlenet/article.aspx?id=83572&.

48. See the spreadsheets offered by Aswath Damodaran, under the category Troubled Firms, http://pages.stern.nyu.edu/~adamodar/New_Home_Page/ spreadsh.htm.

49. 2005 WL 3077228 (Bankr. E.D.N.Y., 11/14/05). The authors extend thanks to Steve Jubowski, who has analyzed this case in his blog, http://www .bankruptcylitigationblog.com/.

50. *Chartwell Litigation Trust v. Addus Healthcare, Inc. (In re Med Diversified, Inc.), 2005 WL 3077228 (Bankr. E.D.N.Y. 2003)*. The case referenced *Lippe v. Bairnco Corp.*, 288 B.R. 678 (S.D.N.Y. 2003) (citing Shannon P. Pratt et al., *Valuing a Business: The Analysis and Appraisal of Closely Held Companies*, 4th ed.: "Regardless of what valuation approach is used, in order for it to make rational economic sense from a financial point of view, the results should be compatible with what would result if a well-supported discounted economic income analysis were carried out."), *aff'd*, 99 Fed. Appx. 274 (2d Cir. 2004).

51. Fresh start accounting used to be covered under the American Institute of Certified Public Accountants Statement of Position 90-7, *Financial Reporting by Entities in Reorganization Under the Bankruptcy Code*. See Mike A. Antonetti, CPA, CMA, and John A. Grivetti III, CPA, "After The Bankruptcy: Fresh Start Accounting," August 25, 2009, http://www.mondaq.com/article .asp?articleid=83990.

52. Fabio Farnari and Antonio Mele, "Volatility Smiles and the Information Content of News," *Applied Financial Economics*, 11, (2001), 179–186, http:// fmg.lse.ac.uk/~antonio/files/afe01.pdf.

CHAPTER 9

Conclusion

SOCIETY NEEDS PREDICTABLE and consistent measures of wealth in order to conduct commerce. The need is so acute as to allow virtually any measurement that produces a value. The financial crisis of 2007–2009 persisted because of a continuing inability to value securities in a consistent and credible fashion.

Need for Humility in Valuation

This book has presented most, if not all, of the known methods of valuation, along with some of the authors. The need for valuation guidance becomes obvious when one considers the power of the credit rating agencies, renamed as Nationally Recognized Statistical Rating Organizations (NRSROs) under Section 702 of Sarbanes-Oxley.[1] NRSROs are powerful entities with de facto power to determine net capital requirements, the valuation of reserves, prospectus disclosures, and even allowable investment choices.[2] As of late 2010, 10 organizations are designated as NRSROs, including the common defaults of Moody's, Standard & Poors, and Fitch.[3]

Despite numerous attempts at reform—most recently the July 2010 financial reform law—rating agencies remain deeply flawed; yet investors continue to rely on them on the theory that a wrong rating is better than none at all. Reliance on credit ratings becomes even more dangerous in a setting where government intervention can skew values. Consider these words from the bipartisan Congressional Oversight Panel in its June 2010 report, *The AIG Rescue, Its Impact on Markets, and the Government's Exit Strategy*:

> The government's actions in rescuing AIG continue to have a poisonous effect on the marketplace. By providing a complete rescue that called for no shared sacrifice among AIG's creditors, the Federal Reserve and Treasury fundamentally changed the relationship between the government and the country's most sophisticated financial players. Today, AIG enjoys a five-level improvement in its credit rating based solely on its access to government funding on generous terms. Even more significantly, markets have interpreted the government's willingness to rescue AIG as a sign of a broader implicit guarantee of 'too big to fail' firms. That is, the AIG rescue demonstrated that Treasury and the Federal Reserve would commit taxpayers to pay any price and bear any burden to prevent the collapse of America's largest financial institutions, and to assure repayment to the creditors doing business with them.[4]

This quote, which is timely, concludes our book with the immediate concern of flawed values—"poisonous" no less—due to government intervention. This flaw is not limited in time or in place of application; it is an ongoing element of "value" that must be taken into account. One purpose of this book is to provide guidance on valuation methodology so that any individual or institution setting a value on a security can articulate the reason behind the value.

A True Beauty Contest

Language imperfectly defines reality. And, although the use of precise numbers to measure corporate performance—"You can manage what you can measure"—is beguiling, it is conceptually inadequate. The shortcomings of language are particularly evident in the so-called beauty contest definition of value.[6] Lord John Maynard Keynes identified a fatal flaw in these contests when he wrote:

> It is not a case of choosing those which, to the best of one's judgment, are really the prettiest, nor even those that average

opinion genuinely thinks the prettiest. We have reached the third degree where we devote our intelligences to anticipating what average opinion expects the average opinion to be. And there are some, I believe, who practice the fourth, fifth and higher degrees.[7]

The difference between guessing what others will choose as beauty versus true beauty is the difference between a well-designed robot and the young Elizabeth Taylor (or Montgomery Clift, to be fair about it).

No Single Definition for Valuation

The need for valuation exists in many contexts that have irreconcilable frames of reference; that is, the valuation imperative must be addressed in a wide range of often conflicting contexts. As a result, valuations of the same security can vary widely. Although each may be appropriate to its intended purpose, the resulting disparities create confusion and no small degree of skepticism regarding the whole language of valuation.

There is therefore no absolute definition of valuation. Valuation exists to serve particular functions; it has validity at particular times and applies only to the dynamics of a specific situation. In its most common usage—with which this book is concerned—value describes the settlement price at which individuals and institutions decide to sell, hold, or buy a particular publicly traded security.

Publicly traded securities are, by definition, purchased by the general public—including the unsophisticated investor. To protect investors, regulators and exchanges require security issuers to disclose certain types of information. This information is valuable for purposes of comparing the performances of different companies within industries and for illuminating trends over time. It provides a basis for the so-called "value investing" versus the "quant" mode of investment, which purports to identify marketplace anomalies in the available information.

But the required disclosures of public companies, although voluminous, miss the mark. Key information is missing in action. Indeed, the most important informing factors for many sophisticated investors are subjective and not susceptible of being expressed in numerical form.

The inclusion of certain criteria in the valuation process has the effect of increasing their relative importance vis-à-vis excluded items, but only in that particular context. The exclusion of other items, such as the externalized costs of corporate functioning, haunt the process anyway, confounding wealth maximization and the sustainability of a corporate society.

Also, roles matter: are you selling or buying? As the Harvard University endowment fund famously illustrated, no matter how rich you are, if you have to sell to meet claims, you cannot achieve what was previously thought to be a fair value. Warren Buffett's 2008 investments in General Electric Company and Goldman Sachs prove the converse: the value of a security pledged as collateral varies depending on the rights and needs of the lender and on the general condition of the marketplace. If the timing of the valuation is not under the owners' control, they had best make pessimistic assumptions. Regulators' requirements for valuations are essentially based on the need for a fair and thorough process, not an explicit price. One of the founding geniuses of the Securities and Exchange Commission said shortly after passage of the Securities Act of 1933: "The purpose of this act is not to prevent someone from making a fool out of themselves; it is to prevent someone from making a fool out of them."[8]

A Word about Genius

In the previous chapter, genius was listed first among the drivers of securities value—as the most important driver. The reason is that, in some cases, value is the expression of a single human being's creative genius. For example, Edwin Land, holder of more patents that any American other than Thomas Edison, created the empire of Polaroid technology, which flourished as long as he lived. Twice, Stephen Jobs has vitalized Apple. Wise investors—the creator of the Fidelity financial empire Ned Johnson among them—base their buy, hold, and sell decisions on whether the value-driving principals in companies have any "skin in the game." The previous chapter noted a similar concept at work in IPO values: high returns have a positive correlation to insider management ownership. One consequence of this eminently reasonable requirement is that typical executive compensation packages today contain a high percentage of equity (more than half of pay received by many CEOs). If people were angels, this type of scheme would deliver the much-touted "pay for performance." But people are not angels and the definition of company performance is notoriously susceptible to manipulation.

Consider the greats of yesteryear. No CEO in history has had such a mastery of the numbers as ITT's Harold Sidney Geneen, and yet the half-billion dollar write-off of the Rayonier Paper Mill could be charged only after his retirement. Even the "CEO of the Century" was not beyond the temptations of the game: "During the last five years of the Welch era, ended in 2001, GE's reported earnings jumped from 72 cents a share to $1.37, a rise of 65 cents a share, or 90.2%—spectacular for a behemoth like GE. But without a massive under-reserving at its reinsurance unit, the company would have shown a cumulative earnings gain of just four cents, or 5.6%."[9]

Whose valuation is more "real"? Which one should investors accept? CEOs manage their stock in the same way they run their businesses. When their stock is expensive, they use it for acquisitions and raising new capital; when their stock is cheap, they buy it back, sometimes to offset dilution from the exercise of options granted to management. Exxon effected the acquisition of Mobil entirely through the use of Treasury (repurchased) shares, dramatically improving the accounting cost.

Real Impact

Although valuation is usually considered an analytic abstraction, it can have real impact. Consider Norway's Government Pension Fund—Global (formerly Petroleum Fund). The Norwegian Bank of Investment Management (NBIM) formally attempts to ground the value of the securities in the Fund against the value of the oil taken out of the ground that produces the fund's basic source of wealth. As a 2009 research paper stated, "The key characteristics of the Fund that should influence the deviation of its investment policy from a market weight position are its absence of need for liquidity, its very long-term horizon and, at least while cash inflows continue from oil revenue, no explicit liabilities of the fund. . . . [T]he Fund should be able to earn risk premiums from taking exposure to assets that are, for example, somewhat less liquid.[10]

NBIM's mandate is different from virtually all other institutional managers in that there are no counterpart claims against the fund. Thus, it seeks long-term *real* value (real in the sense of not being tied to an index). Knut Kjaer, NBIM's founding CEO, in a speech of November 2, 2006, elegantly summarized the requirements of this approach:

> As foreign investor, Norway earns the return provided by broad investment portfolios in the market. In this part of management there are substantial economies of scale. . . . What is demanding is that active management must also consistently generate added value. This activity is talent based.[11] [For more about this approach, see Appendix S.]

Indeed, talent is a remarkably useful metaphor for the range of skills involved in the various valuation processes described in this book. However, in addition to talent on the part of management, investor talent plays a role.

A Need for Investor Talent

To understand the extent of talent's involvement in the total investment process, it is necessary to review investor classes and the context of their investment. As shown in **Exhibit 9.1**, from McKinsey & Company, besides the miscellaneous group of "others," there are three kinds of investors:

> ➤ *Traders*. The largest group of investors, at 35 percent, trade on technical signals. These investors move in and out of their positions rapidly to earn many small gains. They rarely hold stock for years, much less months; for these, a typical stock holding may be in days or even

Exhibit 9.1 Investor Classes

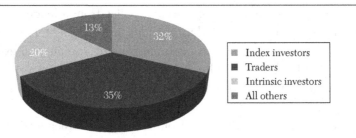

Source: McKinsey on Finance, Number 27 (Spring 2008), http://corporatefinance.mckinsey .com/_downloads/knowledge/mckinsey_on_finance/MoF_Issue_27.pdf.

hours. The problem with this class is that there are transaction costs with every trade; traders must be very good at what they do.

➤ *Indexes.* The next largest segment of equity—a full 32 percent—resides in index funds, which are relatively mechanical in their trades. The only human involvement is in the composition of the index; the investor needs only to choose among various index funds.

➤ *Intrinsic.* This is the least dominant kind of investor, but perhaps the one with the highest level of talent, making the traditional selection of individual stocks, called "intrinsic" or "value investment." Approximately 20 percent of the equity in U.S. markets is held by this type of investors. They study individual stocks and apply criteria such as the ones proposed in this book.

Index investors and traders both use quantitative criteria, often with the help of algorithms. These quant investors' criteria may leave value on the table for intrinsic investors to pocket. McKinsey, speaking of indexes, describes the limitations of the quant investor: "Because their approach offers no real room for qualitative decision criteria, such as the strength of a management team or a strategy, investor relations can't influence them to include a company's shares in an index fund. Similarly, these investors' quantitative criteria, such as buying stocks with low price-to-equity ratios or the shares of companies below a certain size, are based on mathematical models of greater or lesser sophistication, not on insights about fundamental strategy and value creation."

Plainly, the creation of these algorithms is a manifestation of talent. The question is, whether this talent is enough to mine the value intrinsic to securities.

Looking for the Story

According to such acclaimed investors as Warren Buffett and Dean LeBaron, they are apt to be moved by the "story": Who are the leaders, and how do they impress? What is the niche advantage that creates the company's profit flywheel? How wide is the moat that protects this niche from competition or obsolescence? Is the company in a good business? The demonstrable strength of cash flow is the aspect of traditional valuation to which they pay the most attention. Knut Kjaer has recently said that long-term value can only be based on dividends. Buffett has famously said that he would rather have a weak leader in a strong business than a great leader in a weak business. The valuation methodologies described in this book are principally useful as a reality check to provide perspective on decisions arrived at by other means.

On the Social Impact of Corporations and Investors

An unintended consequence of the existing protocols of valuation is that stock purchasers can so easily become enablers of socially destructive conduct because the "social factors" have been traditionally excluded from the accounting reports that are the basis for the investment process. The accounting profession is increasingly pressing to expand holistically the span of factors included in a company review. The European Union is leading efforts to define the regulation of corporations to more closely align their prosperity with that of society as a whole. Investors—most recently, the Public Employees' Retirement System of California (CalPERS)—are including in their investment review process the gamut of elements included in the sobriquet of environmental, social, and governance issues. (The category is now so common that it is referenced as ESG.) But the present practice of accounting tends to encourage "misevaluation" from the perspective of society's interests, giving positive incentive to companies that are successful in placing the costs of their operations onto third parties.

There is increasing evidence that identifiable factors relating to the environmental impact or to the corporate governance of corporations have a measurable impact on their valuation. This development is most important because it compels companies to disclose information far more broadly than before. Corporate governance ratings have their critics[12], but recent analysis by The Corporate Library (TCL) has demonstrated significant marketplace value related to the governance profile of companies. As mentioned in Chapter 7, Robert Daines et alia found that The Corporate Library's governance scores predicted a company's future operating performance and future earnings' multiples—at least according to one economic (Tobin's Q).

From the time of their initial commercial release in July 2003, The Corporate Library's ratings have consistently proven effective in anticipating the most significant corporate losses.

The Corporate Library's corporate governance ratings are intended to focus on governance factors that can be linked to inferior shareholder returns. The Corporate Library currently rates every company in the Russell 3000 universe on a rolling, as-needed basis.[13] Four separate components are identified, for concerns related to the board, compensation, takeover defenses, and SOX 404 compliance. The first two of these, board and compensation, comprise the majority of the overall rating.

In 2010 the Quantitative Services Group (QSG), studied the use of these ratings as investment screens against the stocks that comprise the Russell 1000 index.

QSG's conclusions:

All of these findings indicate that the benefits of considering corporate governance criteria in the investment process can be significant. Corporate governance signals have not historically been leveraged by most traditional portfolio construction models. Consequently, issues related to governance have often been overlooked. Standard financial measures typically look backward and report on current successes. Corporate governance objectives and priorities are forward looking and reveal prospects for future achievement. The results of our detailed efforts to simulate real-world portfolio construction parameters in a governance-driven multifactor environment suggest that the integration of these signals into alpha modeling presents an exciting opportunity, and also one that represents the convergence of a traditional investment approach with that of long-term sustainability.

Good corporate governance and social responsibility tend to be correlated. Comparable work by Trucost suggests that value pivots on companies' environmental profile and their disclosure of efforts to contain them. The hoped for dénouement is that the commercial concept of value will increasingly coincide with society's.

Work in Progress

There can be no conclusion to a work on the valuation of equities. It is a work in progress that must stop because of a publication schedule. The current challenges of BP must suffice. This tale has all the burning questions of value: Is this company well managed? Is it overvalued or undervalued (How do its financial results relate to its stock price?). What are the most important governance and social issues? Are there hidden risks ahead?

In a June 14, 2010, letter to then-BP CEO Tony Hayward, two congressional leaders made a key point:

"Time after time, it appears that BP made decisions that increased the risk of a blowout to save the company time or expense."[14]

Rep. Henry Waxman (D-CA), chairman of the House Energy and Commerce Committee, and Rep. Bart Stupak (D-MI) detail this allegation with many examples, bringing to mind the old proverb penny wise, pound foolish.

Investors know that it takes money to make money. A good investor would never buy a cheap stock merely because it was cheap, nor scorn an expensive stock merely because it was costly. Investors ask, "If I pay X for this now, what will my return be at Y time in the future?" They know that if the value is there, the money will be there. Managers need to ask the same question and take action accordingly, with the help of advanced financial reporting.[15]

Companies need managers who think more like long-term investors and investors who think like more long-term managers. At the end of the investor's 24-hour day, value comes down to this: who wants to buy, hold, or sell, and why? The better the reasons, the more valuable the result.

Notes

1. Sarbanes-Oxley Act of 2002, Pub. L. No. 107-204, § 702(b), 116 Stat. 745 (2002).
2. Securities and Exchange Commission (SEC), "Report on the Role and Function of Credit Rating Agencies in the Operation of the Securities Markets: As Required by Section 702(b) of the Sarbanes-Oxley Act of 2002," January 2003, http://www.sec.gov/news/studies/credratingreport0103.pdf; and "Concept Release: Rating Agencies and the Use of Credit Ratings under the Federal Securities Laws, June 10, 2003," http://www.sec.gov/rules/concept/33-8236.htm. See also Bo Becker and Todd Milbourn, "Reputation and Competition: Evidence from the Credit Rating Industry," working paper (June 2009), http://www.hbs.edu/research/pdf/09-051.pdf.

3. The full list is Moody's Investor Service, Standard & Poor's, Fitch Ratings, A. M. Best Company, Dominion Bond Rating Service, Japan Credit Rating Agency, R&I, Egan-Jones Rating Company, LACE Financial, and RealPoint.

4. The Wall Street Reform and Consumer Protection Act of 2010 included many provisions to enhance "regulation, accountability, and transparency" of nationally recognized statistical rating organizations. Under the law, "Each nationally recognized statistical rating organization shall establish, maintain, enforce, and document an effective internal control structure governing the implementation of and adherence to policies, procedures, and methodologies for determining 15 credit ratings, taking into consideration such 16 factors as the [Securities and Exchange] Commission may prescribe, by 17 rule." The law also included numerous disclosure provisions as well as governance requirements such as having a majority of independent directors on the compensation committee of public companies.
   See the Wall Street Reform and Consumer Protection Act of 2010 http://docs.house.gov/rules/finserv/111_hr4173_finsrvcr.pdf

5. See Congressional Oversight Panel June 2010 report entitled *The AIG Rescue, Its Impact on Markets, and the Government's Exit Strategy.* http://cop.senate.gov/documents/cop-061010-report.pdf. In a proposed rule of Credit Ratings Disclosures (http://www.sec.gov/rules/proposed/2009/33-9070.pdf), dated October 7, 2009, the SEC writes: "We have four principal areas of concern. First, we are concerned that investors may not be provided with sufficient information to understand the scope or meaning of ratings being used to market various securities. . . . Second, we are concerned that investors may not have access to information allowing them to appreciate fully the potential conflicts of interest faced by credit rating agencies and how these conflicts may impact ratings. . . . Third, there has been significant discussion of the possibility that "ratings shopping" may lead to inflated ratings. Finally, even though credit ratings appear to be a key part of investment decisions and are used to market securities, disclosure about ratings is not required in prospectuses currently. As a result, we are concerned that investors may not be receiving even basic information about a potentially key element of their investment decisions."

6. This notion was first introduced in John Maynard Keynes, *General Theory of Employment Interest and Money* (London: Macmillan, 1936), p. 154.

7. Ibid.

8. Attributed to Louis Loss, circa 1934.

9. Jonathan R. Laing, "Jack's Magic," *Barron's*, December 26, 2005.

10. Andrew Ang, William N. Goetzmann, and Stephen M. Schaefer, "Evaluation of Active Management of the Norwegian Government Pension Fund—Global," a study conducted for the fund, published December 14, 2009, http://www.regjeringen.no/upload/FIN/Statens%20pensjonsfond/rapporter/AGS%20Report.pdf.

11. Knut N. Kjaer, "From Oil to Equities, Speech at the Norwegian Polytechnic Society, November 2, 2006. http://www.norges-bank.no/templates/article____51952.aspx.

12. For a general discussion of corporate ratings, see Chapter 7.

13. Rating changes are typically published each Monday, and are available only to subscribers. The ratings employ a letter grade (A, B, C, D, & F) scale, but the investment signal implicit in these ratings can generally be thought of as a binary indicator between those companies where corporate governance practices are believed very likely to have a negative impact on future investment returns (those assigned a D or F rating), and those where The Corporate Library believes corporate governance is less likely to have any measurable investment impact (those assigned an A, B, or C rating). Individual company ratings can be further discriminated by considering the individual component assessments that result in the overall letter grade.

14. Letter to Tony Hayward, chairman, BP, from Rep. Henry Waxman, chairman, House Energy and Commerce Committee (D-CA), and Rep. Bart Stupak (D-MI), chairman, Subcommittee on Oversight and Investigations. http://energycommerce.house.gov/documents/20100614/Hayward.BP.2010.6.14.pdf

15. As we go to press, there are reports of a newly formed International Integrated Reporting Committee that will address not only traditional accounting measures, but also consider management, governance, environmental, and social issues. See Rachel Sanderson, "Initiative to Overhaul Global Financial Reporting," *Financial Times*, August 1, 2010.
Participants in the initiative include Aviva, EDF, HSBC, and Nestlé, as well as the major auditing firms and the accounting standard setters. The *Financial Times* account gives the last word to Ian Powell, PricewaterhouseCoopers chairman: "This is an important step on the journey to create a new corporate reporting model fit for the 21st century."

Equity vs. Debt Securities
A Global Definition

FROM 2007 to mid-2010, a joint task force of the International Accounting Standards Board (IASB) and the Financial Accounting Standards Board (FASB) labored to build the basis for global definition of equity.

During their deliberations on the Financial Instruments with the Characteristics of Equity in April 2007 and for the following year, the task force proposed that "the distinction between equity (risk capital) and liabilities is based exclusively on the ability or inability of capital to absorb losses incurred by the entity, with losses being tentatively understood as accounting losses."[1]

However, at the joint board meeting in October 2007, the IASB used a new definition called the *perpetual approach* (that is, no settlement feature and entitlement to pro-rata share on liquidation of the issuing entity) and the *basic ownership approach* (that is, most subordinated instrument and entitlement to percentage of net assets).

On December 11, 2008, the boards decided that all instruments that *have no contractual settlement requirement* (perpetual instruments) and that entitle the holder to a *share of the issuer's net assets in liquidation* should be classified as equity. The boards also decided that derivatives on an issuer's own equity instruments should be classified as liabilities or assets.

On January 21, 2009, the boards proposed a schema for classification.[2] The following table illustrates the classification results under the approach:

Instrument Classification

Perpetual common or preferred share	Equity
Share redeemable at the option of the issuer (callable)	Equity
Share that is redeemable at the option of the holder (or that is required to be redeemed) only upon the holder's death or retirement	Equity
Share that is redeemable at the option of the holder (or is required to be redeemed) on a specific date or at an event that is certain to occur[3]	Liability
A share that is redeemable at the option of the holder (or is required to be redeemed) upon an event that is not certain to occur[4]	Liability
A share that is redeemable at the option of the holder (or is required to be redeemed) at any time	Liability

Later in 2009, the boards continued to discuss measurement requirements for freestanding equity, liability, and asset instruments and equity hybrid instruments (instruments that are separated into an equity component and a liability or asset component). Professionals who are responsible for recording and analyzing values of freestanding instruments will want to consult this highly technical document.[5]

On March 3, 2010, the boards discussed reclassification of an instrument from debt to equity or from equity to debt and agreed on the following:

1. An instrument should be reclassified if events occur or circumstances change so that the instrument no longer meets the conditions for its existing classification. The reclassification should take place as of the date of the events that changed the classification.
2. An entity should remeasure a reclassified instrument according the requirements for the new classification as if it were a newly issued instrument on the date of the reclassification. An entity should report any difference in measurement on reclassification as an adjustment to a separate equity account and recognize no gain or loss in profit or loss.
3. There is no limit on the number of times an instrument may be reclassified.[6]

In March 2010, the project team began drafting an exposure draft, with plans to produce a global standard by 2011.[7]

Notes

1. Deloitte, "IASB Agenda Project," *IAS Plus*, http://www.iasplus.com/agenda/liabequity.htm.
2. See FASB, "Board Meeting Handout: Financial Instruments with Characteristics of Equity, March 16, 2009, http://www.iasplus.com/usa/fasb/0903fairvalueproposal.pdf.
3. The partnership interest is redeemable upon an event that is certain to occur *other than* the *holder's* retirement or death. For example, a share that is required to be redeemed upon liquidation that will occur on a specific date or a partnership share that is required to be redeemed upon any partner's withdrawal.
4. For example, a change in control, an initial public offering (or failure to make such an offering), or a change in tax legislation.
5. FASB, Financial Instruments with Characteristics of Equity Team, "Minutes of the June 10, 2009, Board Meeting: Financial Instruments with Characteristics of Equity", June 18, 2009, http://www.fasb.org/jsp/FASB/Page/SectionPage&cid=1218220079460 accessed August 13, 2010. See also the overview at Deloitte, "IASB Agenda Project," *IAS Plus*, http://www.iasplus.com/agenda/liabequity.htm.
6. "The staff undertook intensive outreach activities with several large financial institutions to determine how entities measure financial instruments within portfolios in practice. The agenda paper noted two approaches to measurement—the individual instrument approach and the portfolio approach. The staff recommended that a portfolio approach be permitted. In that approach, the unit of account and the unit of valuation might differ. This is the approach currently used in practice for measuring the fair value of financial instruments that are managed within a portfolio." (Deloitte, "Notes from the Special IASB-FASB Joint Meeting, 11 March 2010, *IAS Plus*, http://www.iasplus.com/agenda/1003b.htm. Also of note is the discussion of March 3, 2010.)
7. "Financial Instruments with Characteristics of Equity: Project Milestones." http://www.ifrs.org/Current+Projects/IASB+Projects/Liabilities+and+Equity/Characteristics+of+Equity.htm. Accessed August 13, 2010.

Basic Accounting Concepts for Corporate Valuation

VALUATION-MINDED INVESTORS can benefit from knowing current accounting principles and standards. These two terms are used interchangeably, but they are different. A *principle* is a general concept that can be applied in all situations. A *standard* is a rule that fits a particular situation.

One of the hottest topics in accounting today is principles versus rules. Non-U.S. accounting tends to emphasize principles, whereas U.S. accounting tends to emphasize rules. Although the effort to develop a global standard seems to be headed toward principles, U.S. accounting is still focused on rules. The following materials should make this clear.

Summary of Tentative Global Accounting Decisions on Objectives and Qualitative Characteristics of Accounting

As of mid-2010, the International Accounting Standards Board (IASB) and the U.S. Financial Accounting Standards Board (FASB) were well underway in their plans, launched October 2004, to develop a common conceptual framework, based on and built on both the existing IASB framework (http://www.iasplus.com/standard/framewk.htm) and the FASB Conceptual Framework (http://www.fasb.org/project/cf_phase-a .shtml). Here is the report they issued at their foundational meeting, followed by a current epilogue:[1]

Summary of Tentative Decisions on Objectives

Financial reports should be prepared from the entity's perspective and should aim to provide information to a wide range of users, rather than focus on the information needs of existing common shareholders only. The framework should identify the primary users as present and potential investors and creditors (and their advisors). Later in the project, the boards will consider whether financial reporting also should provide information to meet the information needs of particular types of users, such as different kinds of equity participants.

The objective is to provide information about the entity to the external users who lack the power to prescribe the information they require and therefore must rely on the information provided by an entity's management. The entity's management also will be interested in that information. However, because management has the power to obtain the information it requires, any additional information needs of management are beyond the scope of the framework. Similarly, certain external users (for example, a credit rating agency or a bank lender) generally have the power to prescribe the information they require. Additional information needs, therefore, may be beyond the scope of the framework.

As discussed in the two boards' existing frameworks, the financial statements should provide information to help users assess an entity's liquidity and solvency. However, that objective should be consistent with the overall objective of providing information to a wide range of users. Therefore, the information provided in the financial statements should not be focused on meeting the information needs of particular types of users that primarily use the financial statements to help them assess an entity's liquidity and solvency.

As with the existing frameworks, the boards' converged framework should be concerned with general-purpose financial reports that focus on the common information needs of users. That does not preclude the Boards from concluding, in a standards-level project, that additional information should be provided to meet the information needs of particular types of users.

Summary of Tentative Decisions on Qualitative Characteristics

Relevance is an essential qualitative characteristic. To be relevant, information must be capable of making a difference in the economic decisions of users by helping them evaluate the effect of past and present events on future net cash inflows (predictive value) or confirm or correct previous evaluations (confirmatory value), even if it is not now being used. Being "capable of making a difference," rather than now being used, is a change from the present IASB framework; "confirmatory" rather than "feedback" value is a change from the present FASB framework. Also, the information must be available when the users need it (timeliness).

Accounting information has predictive value if users use it, or could use it, to make predictions. Accounting information is not intended, in itself, as a prediction or as synonymous with statistical predictability or persistence.

Faithful representation of real-world economic phenomena is an essential qualitative characteristic, which includes capturing the substance of those economic phenomena. Faithful representation also includes the quality of completeness. The common conceptual framework will need to discuss thoroughly what faithful representation means and what it does not mean.

Financial information needs to be neutral—free from bias intended to influence a decision or outcome. To that end, the common conceptual framework should not include conservatism or prudence among the desirable qualitative characteristics of accounting information. However, the framework should note the continuing need to be careful in the face of uncertainty.

Financial information needs to be verifiable to provide assurance to users that the information faithfully represents what it purports to represent and that the information is free from material error, complete, and neutral. Descriptions and measures that can be directly verified through consensus among observers are preferable to descriptions or measures that can only be indirectly verified.

Representations are faithful—there is correspondence or agreement between the accounting measures or descriptions in financial reports and the economic phenomena they purport to represent—when the measures and descriptions are verifiable, and the measuring or describing is done in a neutral manner. Therefore, faithful representation requires completeness, not subordinating substance to form, verifiability, and neutrality. Consequently, the common framework should drop the widely misinterpreted term reliability from the qualitative characteristics, replacing it with faithful representation. That replacement is a change from the current IASB and FASB frameworks.

Although empirical research may provide evidence useful in standard-setting decisions, for example, in assessing trade-offs between desirable qualities, the conceptual framework project should not seek to develop empirical measures of faithful representation or its component qualities.

Comparability is an important characteristic of decision-useful financial information and should be included in the converged conceptual framework. Comparability, which enables users to identify similarities in and differences between economic phenomena, should be distinguished from consistency (the consistent use of accounting methods). Concerns about comparability or consistency should not preclude reporting information that is of greater relevance, or that more faithfully represents the economic phenomena it purports to represent. If such concerns arise, disclosures can help to compensate for lessened comparability or consistency.

Understandability also is an essential characteristic of decision-useful financial information and should be included in the converged conceptual framework. Information is made more understandable by aggregating, classifying, characterizing, and presenting it clearly and concisely. Whether reported information is sufficiently understandable depends on who is using it. The information in general-purpose external financial reports should be understandable to financial statement users who have a reasonable knowledge of business and economic activities and accounting and a willingness to study the information with reasonable diligence. Relevant information should not be excluded because it is too complex or difficult for some users to understand.

Materiality relates not only to relevance, but also to faithful representation. Materiality should be included in the converged framework as a screen or filter to determine whether information is sufficiently significant to influence the decisions of users in the context of the entity, rather than as a qualitative characteristic of decision-useful financial information.

Transparency, often cited recently as a desirable characteristic of financial information, seems to be difficult to define. In current usage, it appears to encompass some of the qualitative characteristics already included in the framework. Because it would be redundant, transparency should not be added to the converged framework as a separate, qualitative characteristic of decision-useful financial information.

Other possible characteristics considered, including credibility, high quality and internal consistency, do not describe attributes of decision-useful financial information that are distinct from other qualitative characteristics. Thus, they should not be added as separate qualitative characteristics in the converged framework.

The converged framework should include information about the types of costs that should be considered in deciding what financial information to provide, as well as criteria to help standard setters decide how to take particular types of costs into account. The converged framework should include presumptions not only about the capabilities of financial statement users but also about the capabilities of financial statement preparers and auditors.

The relevant standard here is FRS 18.[2] It says that an entity should judge the appropriateness of accounting policies to its particular circumstances against the objectives of

- ➤ Relevance
- ➤ Reliability
- ➤ Comparability
- ➤ Understandability

FRS Standard 18 also says that an entity should balance its different objectives, as well as balancing the cost of providing information with the likely benefit of such information to users of the entity's financial statements.

The standard notes that an entity's accounting policies should be reviewed regularly to ensure that they remain the most appropriate to its particular circumstances. An entity should implement a new accounting policy if it is judged more appropriate to the entity's particular circumstances than the present accounting policy.

It also requires specific disclosures about the accounting policies followed and changes to those policies, including, in some circumstances, disclosures about the estimation techniques used in applying those policies.

Accounting Principles: U.S. GAAP

U.S. GAAP issued a similar concept a quarter century ago: FASB Statement of Financial Accounting Concept No. 5 (SFAC 5). An item and information about it must meet four fundamental recognition criteria to be recognized (and must be recognized when the criteria are met), subject to a cost-benefit constraint and a materiality threshold.

Those criteria are:

> *Definitions.* The item meets the definition of an element of financial statements.
> *Measurability.* It has a relevant attribute measurable with sufficient reliability.
> *Relevance.* The information about it is capable of making a difference in user decisions.
> *Reliability.* The information is representationally faithful, verifiable, and neutral.[3]

Ironically, despite all the discussion surrounding principles-based accounting rather than rules-based accounting, concept statements like this are considered to be less authoritative than narrow standards.

In June 2009, the FASB issued Statement of FAS No. 168, *Accounting Standards Codification and the Hierarchy of Generally Accepted Accounting Principles,*[4] effective September 15, 2009. The Codification project organized all the FASB standards into one hierarchical system, refreshed through Accounting Standards Updates (ASUs).

The Codification and ASUs do not change GAAP, but they supercede everything else, unless they are grandfathered or issued by the Securities and Exchange Commission. Companies accounting for a transaction must first look to authoritative (codified) standards and only secondly to nonauthoritative standards. Sources of nonauthoritative accounting guidance and literature include, for example, practices that are widely recognized and prevalent either generally or in the industry, FASB concept statements, American Institute of Certified Public Accountants (AICPA) issues papers, International Financial Reporting Standards of the IASB, pronouncements of professional associations or regulatory agencies, Technical Information Service inquiries and replies included in AICPA Technical Practice Aids, and accounting textbooks, handbooks, and articles. The appropriateness of other sources of accounting guidance depends on their relevance to particular circumstances, the specificity of the guidance, the general recognition of the issuer or author as an authority, and the extent of their use in practice, says Statement 168.

Despite this development, companies and their investors can still rely generally on the fundamental concepts of accounting, even if they are not explicitly spelled out in any FASB-codified standard. Such concepts, which underlie the Uniform CPA Examination,[5] are as follows:

➤ *Accounting period.* The income statement should be prepared at *periodic intervals* for purposes such as performance evaluation and determination of taxes. Conventionally, the time span covered is one year.

➤ *Accrual concept.* Expenses incurred for a particular accounting period should be reckoned in the *same period*, regardless of whether these expenses have been paid in cash or not in that year. The same holds true for revenues; that is, revenues earned in a specific accounting period are construed as incomes of the same period, irrespective of their receipts.

➤ *Conservativism concept.* This concept, associated with the reliability factor, says that the accountant should adopt a *worst-case* scenario for reporting. The accountant should anticipate no profits unless they are realized, but at the same time, provide for all probable future losses. Inventory is generally valued at cost or market price, whichever is lower.[6]

➤ *Consistency principle.* This principle requires accountants to apply the *same methods* and procedures from period to period. When they change a method from one period to another, they must explain the change clearly on the financial statements.

➤ *Cost concept*. The assets of the firm are shown at their *acquisition cost*, not at current market value or current worth. (The only exception is for intangibles, per the going concern concept, and for securities, per the fair market value concept.[7]) The rationale for the cost concept is that it provides objective and verifiable basis for accounting records. Market valuation of assets in use, although it is being used increasingly, is difficult to accomplish and is prone to subjectivity and continual change.

➤ *Going concern concept*. This concept implies that the firm will *continue to operate* in the foreseeable future. That is the reason accountants give for recording the value of intangible assets based on the value of goods and services they are likely to produce in future years.[8]

➤ *Matching principle*. This principle requires *matching of expenses or costs incurred to revenues* realized in an accounting period. A related concept is the *double entry concept*. Double entry accounting, the foundation for the balance sheet, was first described in Fr. Luca Pacioli's *Summa de arithmetica, geometria, proportioni et proportionalita* (Venice, 1494). It says that for every change in value of one account in a balance sheet item, there must be an equivalent change in the balancing account. So, for example, if a transaction diminishes an asset, it must increase either a liability or equity (Assets = Liabilities + Equity). This concept is also known as the *principle of balance*.

➤ *Money measurement concept*. Financial reports prepared under GAAP must be expressed in terms of *money*. Any business events and facts that cannot be expressed in cash are excluded, even if they are important. This makes it clear that financial statements do not and cannot provide all the necessary information about a business.[9]

These principles, even if not specifically articulated in any document that has been "codified" as "authoritative," will still hold for accounting. Corporate investors can benefit from understanding them.

Notes

1. Deloitte, "IASB Agenda Project," *IAS Plus*, http://www.iasplus.com/agenda/framework-a.htm.
2. Accounting Standards Board (ASB), "Accounting Policies: FRS 18," December 2000, http://www.frc.org.uk/asb/technical/standards/pub0209.html.
3. http://www.fasb.org/st/status/statpg-con5.shtml.
4. http://www.fasb.org/cs/ContentServer?c=Pronouncement_C&pagename=FASB%2FPronouncement_C%2FSummaryPage&cid=1176156308679.
5. Individuals must pass this exam to be licensed as certified public accountants in any of the 55 U.S. jurisdictions.
6. See FAS No. 157, *Fair Value Measurements*.
7. Ibid.
8. Meanwhile, physical assets are carried at their historic value, with adjustments for deterioration and depreciation. The advent of fair value accounting (see Chapter 2), has begun to erode this physical approach.
9. For an excellent discussion of these fundamental concepts from an online learning course based in India and branded by Macmillan, see http://www.develop.emacmillan.com/iitd/material/DirectFreeAccessHPage/FNFE/ch1_accountingp.html.

Convergence of Global Standards
FASB, IASB, and Their Joint Standards as of June 1, 2010

Current Technical Plan and Project Updates for Joint FASB-IASB Projects in 2010 and 2011

The Financial Accounting Standards Board (FASB) provides the following schedule to help its constituents monitor the progress of and plan for their involvement in the Board's standards-setting activities. The schedule provides a current estimate of the publication dates of due process documents expected to be issued through 2011; that is, Discussion Papers (DPs), Exposure Drafts (Es), and Final Accounting Standards Updates or Final Conceptual Framework chapters (Fs). It also indicates the comment periods that will close in the next six quarters (C) and any roundtable discussions planned during that time period (R). The FASB undertakes its work following established due process procedure's which include extensive consultation with interested parties before reaching conclusions. Therefore, all of the information of this schedule is subject to change depending on input received throughout a project's development.

The Board recognizes that the work plan anticipates the completion of many projects in the 2010 and 2011 time frame. The Board will consider staggering effective dates of those standards to ensure the orderly transition to any new requirements.

Also provided on the schedule are links to staff-prepared summaries of Board decisions that are provided for information purposes only. The decisions are tentative and do not change current accounting. Official positions of the FASB are determined only after extensive due process and deliberations. (See http://www.fasb.org/jsp/FASB/Page/SectionPag e&cid=1218220137074. See also Deloitte, "IASB Agenda Project," *IAS Plus*, http://www.iasplus.com/agenda/framework-a.htm.)

Current Technical Plan and Project Updates

The FASB prepares a project plan to communicate information about its standards-setting activities to stakeholders. The project plan lists all agenda projects and includes:

➤ Estimated publication dates through 2011 (Discussion Papers (DPs), Exposure Drafts (Es), and Final Accounting Standards Updates or Final Conceptual Framework chapters (Fs)

➤ Comment periods expected to close in the next six quarters (indicated by a C)

➤ Roundtable meetings or other public forums planned during the next six months (indicated by an R)

The FASB sets standards following established due process procedures that include extensive consultation. This project plan is subject to change as a result of those consultations or for other reasons.

The project plan anticipates the completion of many projects in the 2010 and 2011 time frame. The Board will consider staggering the effective dates of those standards to ensure an orderly transition to any new requirements.

The project plan includes links to staff prepared project summaries that describe Board decisions and provide other information. The decisions are tentative and do not change current accounting. Official positions of the FASB are determined only after extensive due process and deliberations.

	2010			2011	
Joint FASB/IASB Projects:	**2Q**	**3Q**	**4Q**	**1H**	**2H**
Conceptual Framework Project: *(Updated as of May 26, 2010)*					
Objective and Qualitative Characteristics	F				
Reporting Entity ╱			C	F	
Measurement					
Elements and Recognition					

		2010		2011	
Standards Projects:	**2Q**	**3Q**	**4Q**	**1H**	**2H**
Fair Value Measurement *(Updated April 2, 2010)*	E	R	F		
Consolidation: Policy and Procedures *(Updated April 26, 2010)*	E	R		F	
Accounting for Financial Instruments *(Exposure Draft issued 05/26/10. Updated June 11, 2010)*		C	R	F	
Financial Instruments with Characteristics of Equity *(Updated March 18, 2010)*	E	R		F	
Financial Statement Presentation *(Updated May 6, 2010)*	E	R		F	
Insurance Contracts *(Updated June 1, 2010)*	E	R		F	
Leases *(Updated June 22, 2010)*	E	R		F	
Revenue Recognition *(Updated May 18, 2010)*	E	R		F	
Statement of Comprehensive Income *(Exposure Draft issued 05/26/10. Updated June 1, 2010)*		C		F	
Reporting Discontinued Operations *(Updated February 26, 2010)*	E				
Balance Sheet—Offsetting *(Updated June 21, 2010)*		E		F	
Emissions Trading Schemes *(Updated February 17, 2010)*					
Earnings per Share *(not active)* *(Updated May 7, 2009)*					
Income Taxes *(not active)* *(Updated November 6, 2009)*					
Postretirement Benefit Obligations including Pensions (Phase 2) *(not active)* *(Updated January 21, 2009)*					
Research Projects:					
Financial Instruments: Derecognition *(Updated May 1, 2009)*					

(Continued)

(Continued)

	2010			2011	
FASB PROJECTS:	**2Q**	**3Q**	**4Q**	**1H**	**2H**
Disclosures about Credit Quality and the Allowance for Credit Losses (*Updated June 14, 2010*)	F				
Disclosure of Certain Loss Contingencies (*Updated April 26, 2010*)	E	F			
Going Concern (*Updated April 13, 2010*)	E	F			
Disclosures about an Employer's Participation in a Multiemployer Plan (*Updated April 19, 2010*)	E		F		
Investment Properties (*Updated April 1, 2010*)		E			F
Disclosure Framework (*Updated May 21, 2010*)			DP		

	2010			2011	
FASB EMERGING ISSUES TASK FORCE PROJECTS:	**2Q**	**3Q**	**4Q**	**1H**	**2H**
Health Care Entities: Presentation of Insurance Claims and Related Insurance Recoveries (09-K) (*Exposure Document issued 04/16/10*)	C	F			
Health Care Entities: Measuring Charity Care for Disclosure (09-L) (*Exposure Document issued 04/16/10*)	C	F			
Accounting for Costs Associated with Acquiring or Renewing Insurance Contracts (09-G)		F			
Health Care Entities: Revenue Recognition (09-H)		E	F		
How the Carrying Amount of a Reporting Unit Should Be Determined When Performing Step 1 of the Goodwill Impairment Test (10-A)		E	F		
Accounting for Multiple Foreign Currency Exchange Rates (10-B)		E	F		
Reporting of Participant Loans in Employee Benefit Plan Financial Statements (10-C)					
Accounting for Certain Fees Associated with Recently Enacted Health Care Legislation (10-D)					
Debtor's Accounting for Real Estate Subject to a Nonrecourse Mortgage in Default Prior to Forfeiture (10-E)					

Other Technical Activities

XBRL *(Updated October 2, 2009)*

Codes:

C – Comment Deadline
DP – Discussion Paper
E – Exposure Draft
F – Final Document
R – Roundtable Discussion

Report to the Congressional Oversight Panel Regarding Fair Value of Certain Securities and Warrants Acquired by the Treasury under TARP[1]

IN OCTOBER 2008, the U.S. Congress passed the Emergency Economic Stabilization Act (EESA), which included the Troubled Asset Relief Program (TARP). Under TARP, the U.S. government had a mandate to purchase equity securities that had lost their market liquidity due to uncertain value. Through the program, the government could provide funds to companies and in return receive warrants that gave the government the right to buy stock at a predetermined price. To help determined that price, a newly formed Congressional Oversight Panel for Economic Stabilization asked Duff & Phelps, a valuation firm, to determine a fair value.[2] By mid-2010, most TARP transactions had been unwound (see addendum to this appendix). Nonetheless, the Duff & Phelps report remains a valuation classic.

The following text summarizes the Duff & Phelps report, including its profile of Berkshire Hathaway's investment in Goldman Sachs. Note: The

(With an addendum from the Office of the Special Inspector General for the Troubled Asset Relief Program—SIGTARP)

Securities and Exchange Commission voted three to two along partisan lines to bring enforcement actions against Goldman Sachs for alleged violations of disclosure rules in a 2007 transaction involving mortgage-backed securities. On July 20, 2010, U.S. District Judge Barbara Jones in Manhattan approved a settlement between the SEC and Goldman Sachs in which Goldman Sachs agreed to pay $550 million in fines and penalties, the "largest penalty ever assessed against a financial services firm in the history of the SEC." Goldman acknowledged that "it was a mistake" to withhold disclosure and expressed regret for the error.[3]

A. Introduction

Duff & Phelps has been engaged by the Congressional Oversight Panel for Economic Stabilization to estimate the Fair Market Value of certain preferred stock securities and warrants of the Purchase Program Participants acquired by the Treasury through various TARP programs under the EESA.

Duff & Phelps is a leading provider of independent financial advisory and investment banking services. Our business focuses on providing independent valuation analysis to a broad array of financial and non-financial clients. Duff & Phelps has no ownership interest in the debt or equity securities of any of the nine Purchase Program Participants. Duff & Phelps has from time to time been engaged to provide valuation and investment banking services to certain of the Purchase Program Participants (unrelated to the Subject Investments), none of which has had a material impact on the financial results of Duff & Phelps. . . .

B. Engagement Overview and Procedures

Engagement Overview

Duff & Phelps has been engaged by the Congressional Oversight Panel for Economic Stabilization to estimate the Fair Market Value of the Subject Investments as of their respective valuation dates (the date following their respective public announcement dates):

Valuation Investment TARP Purchase Program
Participant **(followed by date/amount in billions/program)**

American International Group, Inc. 11/10/08 $40.0 SSFI
Bank of America Corporation 10/14/08 $15.0 CPP

Citigroup Inc. 10/14/08 $25.0 CPP
Citigroup Inc. 11/24/08 $20.0 TIP
The Goldman Sachs Group, Inc. 10/14/08 $10.0 CPP
JPMorgan Chase & Co. 10/14/08 $25.0 CPP
Morgan Stanley 10/14/08 $10.0 CPP
The PNC Financial Services Group 10/24/08 $7.6 CPP
U.S. Bancorp 11/3/08 $6.6 CPP
Wells Fargo & Company 10/14/08 $25.0 CPP
Total $184.2

For purposes of our analysis, Fair Market Value is defined as the price at which property would change hands between a willing buyer and a willing seller when neither is acting under compulsion and when both have reasonable knowledge of the relevant facts. As such, our analysis attempts to address the question, "What price would a third party pay for the Subject Investments, given their terms, on their respective valuation dates?" Our analysis does not address what terms or price the Treasury should have or could have accepted, nor is it intended to evaluate policy objectives.

Procedures

All information utilized and considered by Duff & Phelps in its analysis for this report was obtained from public sources. The procedures undertaken to estimate the range of Fair Market Values for the Subject Investments included, but was not limited to, the following:

1. Analysis of the conditions in and the outlook for the financial services industry (as of the respective valuation dates);
2. Analysis of economic, governmental and investment data;
3. Analysis of the history, current operations and outlook of the Purchase Program Participants;
4. Analysis of publicly available data concerning both the Purchase Program Participants and the Subject Investments;
5. Consideration of appropriate valuation methodologies for the Subject Investments (see Section IV, Valuation Methodologies);
6. Development of models appropriate for each of the valuation methodologies relied upon in our analysis;

7. Review of the Securities Purchase Agreement–Standard Terms, form of Warrant and form of Certificate of Designations used for the Subject Investments; and

8. Analysis of other facts and data we deemed relevant to arrive at a range of Fair Market Values for the Subject Investments.

C. Valuation Methodologies Overview

The scope of Duff & Phelps' engagement is to estimate the Fair Market Value of the TARP Preferred Stock and the TARP Warrants as of the valuation dates for the respective Subject Investments. Since the TARP Preferred Stock and the TARP Warrants are not publicly traded, our fundamental approach to valuing these securities is to use data obtained from the public debt, equity and derivatives markets to estimate certain parameters, such as discount rates, volatility and default assumptions. All of the Purchase Program Participants have common stock that is publicly traded, and most of the Purchase Program Participants have debt and preferred securities that are publicly traded . . . In addition, CDSs for all but one of the Purchase Program Participants (PNC) are also publicly Traded. . . .

Most issuers, investors and valuation practitioners believe that security prices determined in the financial markets provide the best indications of economic value. The turmoil in the financial markets leading to the TARP (outlined in section II), however, has created some concern that transaction prices are not always reliable indicators of fair values. To mitigate this concern, we have: (i) used several different valuation approaches; (ii) analyzed numerous publicly traded debt and preferred stock securities; and (iii) analyzed certain major market transactions which occurred during the relevant time period. In no case, however, do we attempt to assess whether the observed prices are consistent with other conceptions of fundamental value.

TARP Preferred Stocks

We utilized three methodologies to assess the value of the TARP Preferred Stocks:

1. Discounted Cash Flow Analysis Using Market Yields ("Yield-Based DCF Approach")

The TARP Preferred Stocks are perpetual securities that are callable by the issuer after three years (earlier under certain conditions). Therefore, the holder of the TARP Preferred Stock (i) is long a perpetual security and (ii) is short (has sold or written) a call option on the perpetual security. In the Yield-Based DCF Approach, we valued each component by analyzing the observed yields on other publicly traded preferred and debt securities issued by the Purchase Program Participants. Therefore, this approach allows direct comparisons of the TARP Preferred Stocks with similar securities. We performed our valuation of the perpetual component of the TARP Preferred Stocks by discounting the contractual cash flows (dividends) at a discount rate that reflects the risk of each TARP Preferred Stock. The discount rate that we determined for each of the TARP Preferred Stocks is comprised of the 30-year CMT yield as of the valuation date plus a spread. We determined the appropriate spread from an analysis of the publicly traded preferred and debt securities of the Purchase Program Participants. As we stated above, the publicly traded preferred securities are generally callable by the issuers. The call option is negative from the holder's perspective because the issuer of the security can call the security away from the holder, and presumably would do so when it is economical for the issuer and uneconomical for the holder. Thus, the call option lowers the value of the security and raises its indicated yield. The spreads that we observe, therefore, reflect the existence of call options. The size of this effect depends on the terms of each security. We adjusted the observed spreads to remove the call option effect, resulting in what is termed an "option-adjusted spread." In addition, a key difference that we adjusted for is the cumulative nature of the TARP Preferred Stocks versus the noncumulative nature of most of the publicly traded preferred stocks. We valued the call option (which is a negative value to the holder of the TARP Preferred Stocks) using methodologies that we describe in greater detail [later].

2. Contingent Claims Analysis ("CCA Approach")

In CCA, a firm's securities can be modeled as derivative securities on its assets. In the simplest case, a firm has one debt instrument outstanding, which is zero coupon debt. Upon maturity, if the asset value exceeds the face value of debt, the residual value belongs to the equity holders. Therefore, the equity of the company can be valued as a call option on the assets of the company. The strike price of the option is the face value of the debt, and the maturity of the option equals the maturity of the debt.

CCA models can vary considerably in their complexity and implementation. In some cases, they are implemented using the Black-Scholes-Merton formula. This approach has several limitations. In particular, it assumes a fixed valuation term with no default prior to the end of that term. Alternative applications of CCA, for example, the work by Crosby and Bohn and Lucas and McDonald, employ Monte Carlo simulation. . . . This is a very flexible methodology that models behavior and tracks changes in value through simulated time. Our CCA valuation approach follows closely to that described by Lucas and McDonald.

3. Discounted Cash Flow Analysis Using Survival Probabilities Derived from CDS Spreads ("CDS-Based DCF Approach")

This approach is a DCF analysis using as its information base CDS rates. In this approach, the Fair Market Values of the TARP Preferred Stocks are estimated as the discounted sum of the adjusted cash flows. This valuation methodology utilizes CDS rates to estimate the adjustments to cash flows. These adjustments incorporate both the probability of default and the premium the market requires to bear default risk. Using CDS rates is attractive because the CDS market is highly liquid with readily available and reliable price data. CDSs are contracts in which the buyer makes periodic payments (premium) to the seller. In return, the seller pays an amount that makes the buyer whole (protection) if the underlying instrument defaults. The premium is usually expressed as a "spread," a percentage of the notional amount of the underlying instrument. Because the level of premium the CDS seller demands is a function of the risk of the underlying instrument, default probabilities can be implied by the level of CDS spreads observed in the market. See Appendix Volume III-C for a more complete discussion of the methodology. We apply this methodology to the TARP Preferred Stocks with two important adjustments. First, preferred stock is likely to experience a lower recovery rate than debt on its face value in an event of default. Therefore, we have assumed a 0 percent recovery rate. Second, preferred stock can suffer a loss without an event of default if the company suspends dividends. To account for this possibility, we increased the CDS spreads.

We are not aware of a specific way to determine the amount by which a preferred spread should differ from a bond spread. Therefore, we calculated the estimated spread adjustment that would be necessary to produce values consistent with the results of our two other valuation methodologies. Thus, we did not utilize the CDS-Based DCF

Approach to determine independent valuations; instead, we utilized it to assess the reasonableness of the valuation results from the other two methodologies.

Market Transactions

There were a number of private sector investments in U.S. financial institutions as well as transactions involving investments in non-U.S. financial institutions by private investors and governments of other countries during the period from June 2007 to October 2008. Several of the transactions involving U.S. financial institutions included certain Purchase Program Participants. These transactions are summarized in **Exhibit D.1**.

Exhibit D.1 Market Transactions

Company/Investor	Date	Value (millions)	Securities
Countrywide/Bank of America	8/22/07	$2,000	Convertible preferred stock
Fannie Mae/ Institutional Investors	9/25/07	$1,000	Preferred stock
Washington Mutual/ Institutional Investors	10/25/07	$1,000	Preferred stock
Citigroup/ADIA	11/26/07	$7,500	Common stock and trust preferred stock
Morgan Stanley/ China Investment Corporation	12/19/07	$5,579	Common stock and trust preferred stock
Citigroup, Inc./ Government of Singapore Investment Corporation, Kuwait Investment Authority and others	1/15/08	£12,500	Convertible preferred stock
Merrill Lynch/Kuwait Investment Authority, Mizuho Corporate Bank, and others	1/15/08	$6,600	Convertible preferred stock
Washington Mutual/ TPG and others	4/7/08	$7,200	Common stock, preferred stock and warrants

(Continued)

(Continued)

Company/Investor	Date	Value (millions)	Securities
Wachovia/ Institutional Investors	4/14/08	$7,000	Common stock and convertible preferred stock
National City/Corsair Capital LLC, TPG-Axon Capital Management, L.P., and others	4/20/08	$7,000	Common stock, preferred stock and warrants
CIT/Institutional Investors	4/21/08	£1,500	Common stock and convertible preferred stock
Goldman Sachs/ Berkshire Hathaway	9/23/08	$5,000	Preferred stock and warrants
Morgan Stanley/MUFG	9/29/08	$9,000	Convertible and non-convertible preferred stock
Royal Bank of Scotland plc/U.K. Government and existing shareholders	10/13/08	£20,000	Ordinary shares and preference shares
Lloyds TSB Group plc/ U.K. Government and existing shareholders	10/13/08	£5,500	Ordinary shares and preference shares
HBOS plc/U.K. Government and existing shareholders	10/13/08	£11,500	Ordinary shares and preference shares
Barclays/Qatar Holding and Abu Dhabi	10/31/08	£7,050	Mandatorily convertible notes, reserve capital instruments and warrants

Source: Capital IQ.

Duff & Phelps analyzed these transactions in the context of our overall valuation analysis of the TARP Preferred Stocks and TARP Warrants. While analyzing comparable transactions can often provide useful valuation insights, we believe that in the case of the TARP Preferred Stocks and TARP Warrants there are certain limitations in the comparability of such transactions that should be noted. Specifically, with respect to the investments in U.S. financial institutions, comparability is limited since (i) they were completed before the adoption of the EESA on October 3, 2008, when the financial crisis was still developing and (ii) with the exception of the Goldman-Berkshire Hathaway and Morgan Stanley-MUFG transactions, they were completed well before October 2008, when the financial crisis became most serious and the Treasury and other governments took action. With respect to the investments in non-U.S. financial institutions, comparability is limited because the transactions resulted from government intervention, not arm's-length negotiations (other than the Barclays transaction).

Key Reference Transactions

The three transactions that we believe to be most relevant for purposes of our analysis are Goldman-Berkshire Hathaway, Morgan Stanley-MUFG, and Barclays-Qatar Holding and Abu Dhabi. The first two of these involved Purchase Program Participants, and all three of them occurred in the fall of 2008, after Lehman filed for bankruptcy and near the time of the initial announcements regarding the TARP investments. We specifically analyzed these transactions in conjunction with our review of data obtained from the public debt, equity and derivatives markets. The purpose of this comparative analysis is to understand the difference between observed market prices and yields for publicly traded debt and preferred securities of the Purchase Program Participants versus the price paid by investors in these three private transactions. Based on our analysis of these three transactions, we believe Berkshire Hathaway and Qatar and Abu Dhabi negotiated prices that reflect significant discounts to prices suggested by publicly traded securities (for reasons discussed below); based on a similar analysis, we believe MUFG's investment in Morgan Stanley was priced near prices suggested by publicly traded securities. Given the limited number of similar sized relevant transactions, and the fact that in two of these three transactions the investors negotiated a premium price, it is our judgment that utilizing data obtained from the public debt, equity and derivatives markets is more appropriate for purposes of our valuation analysis. . . .

Goldman-Berkshire Hathaway

We estimated the value of Berkshire Hathaway's investment in Goldman, after application of appropriate discounts due to reduced marketability, to be at a 108 to 112 percent premium to the face value of the investment at the time the transaction was announced. We believe that the premium that Berkshire Hathaway was able to obtain is explained by the intangible benefit associated with Mr. Buffett. Our view is that Berkshire Hathaway has a history of making investments at better-than-market pricing. For example, we note that on October 2, 2008, Berkshire Hathaway announced a $3 billion investment in GE. The investment in GE also included preferred stock and warrants on virtually the same terms as the Berkshire Hathaway investment in Goldman (notably, 10% dividend rate and warrants for 100% of initial investment). Since market yields for GE debt and preferred securities were also well below 10 percent on October 2, 2008, we believe Berkshire Hathaway's investment in GE was also priced at a discount to a public market price. We believe that Berkshire Hathaway is able to achieve terms that are unavailable to other private investors because of Mr. Buffett's history and reputation in the capital markets. In effect, Berkshire Hathaway is offering more than just capital; it is also selling the "Buffett" name as imprimatur on the viability of the entity receiving Buffett capital.

Barclays-Qatar Holding and Abu Dhabi

We estimated the value of Qatar's and Abu Dhabi's investment in Barclays, after application of appropriate discounts due to reduced marketability, to be at a 122 to 125 percent premium to the face value of the investment at the time the transaction was announced. We believe that the premium that Qatar and Abu Dhabi were able to obtain is explained, in part, by the intangible benefit of remaining independent of government ownership. At the time of Qatar's and Abu Dhabi's investment in Barclay's, the U.K. government agreed to make available to eligible U.K. banks, new capital in the form of preferred shares and common stock. The rate offered on the preferred shares was 12 percent until five years after issue, at which time the rate would reset quarterly to three-month LIBOR plus 7.0 percent. Regarding the common stock, the U.K. government would agree to backstop a new common stock offering to the participating bank's existing shareholders. Thus, the U.K. government would purchase any common shares not purchased by the participating bank's shareholders. In spite of the cheaper capital available from the U.K. government, Barclays proceeded to raise more expensive private capital so it could remain independent of government ownership.

Morgan Stanley-MUFG

We utilized the same OAY to analyze the MUFG investment in Morgan Stanley as we used to value to the TARP investment in Morgan Stanley. Based on this analysis and after application of appropriate discounts

due to reduced marketability, we estimated the value of MUFG's investment to be at a nominal discount to the face value of the investment
at the time the transaction was announced (88% to 94% of face value).

TARP Warrants

For the valuation of the TARP Warrants, we utilized an options pricing
approach implemented with a Monte Carlo simulation, which readily
accommodates time-varying interest rates and volatilities and incorporates adjustments to value to account for the issuer's ability to cancel
half of the warrants through a "Qualifying Equity Offering." Thus, our
options pricing model has the following embedded features:

1. American-style option;
2. Time varying volatility;
3. Time varying risk-free rate;
4. Dilution adjustment;
5. Dividend yield on common stock; and
6. Contingent cancellation of 50 percent of the TARP Warrants.

Reduced Marketability of the TARP Preferred Stocks and TARP Warrants

Our baseline valuations of the Subject Investments (using the methodologies summarized above) treat the TARP Preferred Stocks and the
TARP Warrants as if they were readily marketable (as of the valuation
dates). This follows directly from our fundamental valuation approach,
which is based on the pricing of publicly traded securities. We believe
that a hypothetical buyer of the Treasury's entire position in each of
the TARP Preferred Stocks and TARP Warrants would discount those
values to account for the reduced marketability of such large positions.
Thus, we applied a discount due to reduced marketability for the TARP
Preferred Stocks and TARP Warrants. The amount of the discounts
applied ranged from 5 to 10 percent for the TARP Preferred Stocks and
5 to 20 percent for the TARP Warrants.

D. Summary of Findings

The aggregate face amount of the 10 Subject Investments analyzed in
this report totals $184 billion. As summarized in the following table, we

estimate the value of these investments (as of their respective valuation dates) to be in the range of $112 billion to $132 billion in the aggregate, which represents approximately 61 to 71 percent of the face value of the investments. The range of value for each Subject Investment is the result of the low and high values derived from the Yield-Based DCF Approach and the CCA Approach previously described [in sections 1 and 2 above]. See **Exhibit D.2.**

Exhibit D.2 Valuation Summary (in billions, as of the respective valuation dates)

Purchase Program Participant	Valuation Date	Investment Amount	Total Estimated Value of Preferred and Warrants			Total Estimated Value of Preferred and Warrants as Percent of Face Value		
			Low		High	Low		High
American International Group, Inc.	11/10/08	$ 40.0	$ 14.2	to	$15.4	36%	to	38%
Bank of America Corporation	10/14/08	$ 15.0	$ 11.6	to	$13.3	77%	to	89%
Citigroup Inc.	10/14/08	$ 25.0	$ 14.2	to	$ 16.8	57%	to	67%
Citigroup Inc.	11/24/08	$ 20.0	$ 8.3	to	$ 11.7	41%	to	59%
The Goldman Sachs Group, Inc.	10/14/08	$ 10.0	$ 6.8	to	$ 8.2	68%	to	82%
JPMorgan Chase & Co.	10/14/08	$ 25.0	$ 19.0	to	$ 22.2	76%	to	89%
Morgan Stanley	10/14/08	$ 10.0	$ 4.7	to	$ 6.8	47%	to	68%
The PNC Financial Services Group	10/24/08	$ 7.6	$ 5.2	to	$ 5.8	69%	to	77%
U.S. Bancorp	11/3/08	$ 6.6	$ 5.9	to	$ 6.7	89%	to	102%
Wells Fargo & Company	10/14/08	$ 25.0	$ 21.7	to	$ 24.6	87%	to	99%
Total		**$184.2**	**$111.7**	**to**	**$131.6**	**61%**	**to**	**71%**

Note: All values are after applicable discounts due to reduced marketability.

E. Assumptions, Qualifications and Limiting Conditions

1. The information utilized in preparing this presentation was obtained from a wide array of public sources. No representation or warranty, expressed or implied, is made as to the accuracy or completeness of such information and nothing contained herein is, or shall be relied upon as, a representation, whether as to the past or the future. Duff & Phelps did not attempt to independently verify such information and we have relied upon the accuracy and completeness of all the information reviewed by us and have assumed such accuracy and completeness for purposes of rendering this report. Furthermore, Duff & Phelps has assumed that no other assets or liabilities exist for the Purchase Program Participants beyond those identified in public filings. We have also assumed that there has been no material change in the assets, financial condition, results of operations, business or prospects of the Purchase Program Participants since the date of the then-most recently publicly available financial statements of each of such Purchase Program Participant available at or prior to the valuation dates for the respective Subject Investments.

2. Our valuation analysis for the Subject Investments are based upon Duff & Phelps' independent assessment of general economic, financial and market conditions as they existed and could be evaluated by Duff & Phelps as of the valuation dates for the respective Subject Investments. Events occurring after the valuation dates for the respective Subject Investments could materially affect our analysis and value ranges. We have not undertaken, and we have no obligation, to update, revise or reaffirm this report or otherwise comment upon events occurring after the valuation dates for the respective Subject Investments. We are expressing no opinion herein as to the prices at which any of the securities of any of the Purchase Program Participants may trade at any time.

3. This report does not evaluate, value or opine on the underlying business or policy decision of the Treasury to make investments in any of the Subject Investments. The Treasury may have taken into account non-financial or other factors unrelated to the specific financial analysis performed by Duff & Phelps. This report does not attempt to include the value, if any, of such non-financial or

other factors in estimating the ranges of Fair Market Values of the Subject Investments.

4. No selected company, selected security or selected transaction used in our analysis is exactly comparable to the Purchase Program Participants or the Subject Investments.

5. This report or any results of Duff & Phelps' services shall not constitute a solvency opinion, fairness opinion or credit rating and may not be relied upon by you or any other party as such. Duff & Phelps did not independently evaluate any of the Purchase Program Participants' solvency or make an independent evaluation, appraisal or physical inspection of any specific assets, the collateral securing assets or the liabilities (contingent or otherwise) of the Purchase Program Participants or any of their respective subsidiaries, nor have we been furnished with any such evaluations or appraisals of any of the Purchase Program Participants' specific assets or liabilities (contingent or otherwise).

6. Duff & Phelps did not independently investigate any legal or regulatory matters involving any of the Purchase Program Participants.

7. We have assumed that public markets are efficient in the sense that all market participants receive and act on all relevant information as soon as it becomes available. Additionally, we have assumed that an investor in the Subject Investments would exhibit value-maximizing behavior.

8. We recognize there is diversity in how certain firms may apply FAS 157: Fair Value Measurement for financial reporting and we have made no determinations with regard to any of the Purchase Program Participants' methodologies or disclosures.

9. By its very nature, valuation work cannot be regarded as an exact science and the conclusions in many cases will of necessity be subjective and dependent on the exercise of individual judgment.

10. Duff & Phelps has not been requested to, and did not (a) conduct any discussions with the management of the Purchase Program Participants (b) negotiate the terms of the Subject Investments or (c) advise the Treasury, the Purchase Program Participants or any other party with respect to alternatives to the Subject Investments.

11. Duff & Phelps' report (a) does not address the merits of the underlying decision by the Treasury to enter into the Subject Investments and (b) does not create a fiduciary duty on Duff & Phelps' part to any party.

The analysis and conclusions presented in this report apply to this engagement only and may not be used out of the context presented herein. This report is valid only for the effective date specified herein and only for the purpose specified herein. This report may not be used for any purpose by any person other than the Congressional Oversight Panel for Economic Stabilization in its evaluations and recommendations regarding the Treasuries investments in the Subject Investments.

Addendum: Assessing Treasury's Process to Sell Warrants Received from TARP Recipients

Why SIGTARP Did This Study

The Emergency Economic Stabilization Act of 2008 ("EESA") mandated that the Department of Treasury ("Treasury") receive warrants or debt instruments when it invests in troubled assets under the Troubled Asset Relief Program ("TARP"). For public [sic] held institutions, the warrants provide Treasury the right, at its option, to purchase shares of common stock at a predetermined price. As recipient institutions repay their TARP investments, Treasury sells the warrants, either directly to the recipient institution at a negotiated price or via public auction.

Pricing the warrants is not straightforward, however, because there is limited market information concerning warrants of this duration. Treasury thus developed an approach to estimate fair market value in order to assess offers from institutions seeking to repurchase the warrants.

What SIGTARP Found

Once a publicly traded bank pays back its TARP investment, Treasury undertakes a process for the sale of the bank's warrants, either directly back to the bank through negotiation or to third parties through an auction. If a bank decides to repurchase its warrants, Treasury assesses the bank's bid after arriving at a "composite" estimated value for the warrants that references market quotes, financial modeling valuations, and third-party estimates. Treasury's Warrant Committee recommends whether to accept the offer, and the Assistant Secretary for Financial Stability makes the final decision. If a price cannot be negotiated, the warrants are auctioned publicly.

To its credit, Treasury has generally succeeded in negotiating prices from recipients for the warrants at or above its [sic] estimated composite value. Of the 33 public company warrant repurchases analyzed, 20 of the final negotiated prices were at or above Treasury's composite value, and nine of the final negotiated prices were just under the composite value [generally between 90–99 percent of composite value [4]]. The four remaining transactions included the first two completed (during which time Treasury was operating under a governing statute that limited how long Treasury had to negotiate and before Treasury had its valuation methodology worked out), and two for warrants in small institutions that received less than $100 million in TARP funds (for which valuation is difficult because of less liquidity in the bank's stock). Treasury has over time been more consistent in obtaining negotiated prices at or above its estimated composite value. In total, for all warrant transactions (repurchases and auctions) through March 19, 2010, Treasury received $5.63 billion in proceeds from warrant sales.[5]

Notes

1. This appendix is reprinted from the executive summary of Duff & Phelps, *Valuation Report: Congressional Oversight Panel*, February 4, 2009, http://cop.senate.gov/documents/cop-020609-report-dpvaluation.pdf.
2. Duff & Phelps the valuation company is no longer affiliated with the Duff & Phelps securities rating service, which is now part of Fitch.
3. Patricia Hurtado and Christine Harper, "SEC Settlement with Goldman Sachs for $550 Million Approved by U.S. Judge," Bloomberg.com, July 21, 2010. www.bloomberg.com/news/2010-07-20/goldman-sachs-settlement-with-sec-for-550-million-approved-by-u-s-judge.html.
4. Explanation derived from Statement of Kevin R. Puvalowski, Deputy Inspector General for the Troubled Asset Relief Program Before the House Committee on Financial Services, May 11, 2020. http://www.sigtarp.gov/reports/testimony/2010/Testimony%20Before%20the%20House%20Committee%20on%20Financial%20Services%20Subcommittee%20on%20Oversight%20and%20Investigations%205_11_10%20.pdf.
5. *Assessing Treasury's Process to Sell Warrants Received from TARP Recipients*, Office of the Special Inspector General for the Troubled Asset Relief Program, SIGTARP-10-006, May 2010. http://www.sigtarp.gov/reports/audit/2010/Assessing%20Treasury's%20Process%20to%20Sell%20Warrants%20Received%20From%20TARP%20Recipients_May_11_2010.pdf.

The Use of Mathematics in Finance

CORPORATE VALUATION FOR PORTFOLIO investment requires the director or indirect use of mathematics. As mathematician Gilbert Strang has noted, "The purpose of mathematics is to understand and explain patterns"[1]—and what could be more important for valuation? Analysts typically use a calculator with net present value, internal rate of return, yield to maturity, and natural logarithm and exponential functions.[2] But that is just the beginning. Value-minded investors need to understand how to *think* mathematically as well. We offer this primer on financial math for that purpose.

Types of Mathematics Used in Corporate Valuation

Types of math used in finance include *arithmetic, algebra*, and *calculus*. Corporate valuation also requires knowledge of *statistics*. By contrast, some types of math are less critical to finance, namely geometry (study of planes) or trigonometry (the study of how the sides and angles of a triangle are related to each other).

Arithmetic

Obviously addition and subtraction are most fundamental to valuation, as they form the basis for the financial statements for company, through the discipline known as accounting:

➤ The income statement tells us that revenues minus expenses equals net income (or net loss), a key valuation formula.

➤ The balance sheet tells us that assets equal liabilities plus equity, another key formula.

➤ Finally, the cash flow statement shows cash received from sales of goods and services minus cash paid for operating goods and services.

Multiplication and division are also critical. Currency amounts from financial statements can be combined with other currency amounts to create ratios through multiplication or division. For example, earnings amounts can be analyzed through earnings per share or price/earnings ratios.

Several kinds of math are required for professional valuation beyond addition, subtraction, and multiplication.

Algebra

Algebra (from the Arabic *jabara*, "to set," or to consolidate) shows the relations of elements in equations, and sets ground rules for moving elements from one side of an equation to another, or for canceling the equal terms that lie on respective sides of an equation.

The following three calculations (adapted with permission from a popular college textbook) show how to use algebra in finance.

Simple Algebraic Formulas

You can use algebra to calculates a prospective *equity premium*.

One approach would be to focus on dividends. The Gordon Growth Model (developed by Myron J. Gordon[3]) says

$$P = D/(k - g)$$

where

P = Stock price
D = Dividend dollars
k = Expected return
g = Growth rate

This formula can rearranged to solve for the expected return:

$$K = (D/P) + g$$

Another approach would be to focus on earnings, such as a one-year forward P/E multiple of the S&P500 index.[4]

Replacing D with earnings per share (E) × Payout $(1 - $ Retention rate), is as follows:

$$P = E (1-R)/k - (k - R)$$

If you solve for the expected return, the formula as

$$K = E/P$$

This is also the earnings yield, or 1/the P/E ratio.

You can also use algebra to calculate *equivalent forward or "trailing valuation" multiples* from any given multiple and parameters values characterizing the earnings of the firm.[5]

Simple algebra also enables you to compute the *debt capacity* of a company for a given period of amortization of senior debt principal under assumptions about various factors such as sales growth; earnings before interest, taxes, depreciation and amortization (EBITDA); sales margins; capital expenditures; changes in working capital, proportions of senior and subordinated debt; and interest rates.

The Algebra of Valuing Bid Prices

In a problem posed on its web site, IBM encourages its employees and customers to think mathematically.

Ponder This Challenge: S has a good, G, which he is considering selling to B. The values of G to S and B are independent uniformly distributed random variables between 0,1. S and B know this and know their own valuations but not the valuation of the other party.

1. Suppose B makes a single offer, which S accepts or rejects depending on whether or not the offer exceeds the value S places on the item. What should B offer to maximize his expected gain (the difference when a sale occurs between B's valuation of G and the sales price, 0 when no sale occurs) as a function of B's valuation of G? What is B's expected gain? What is S's?

2. Suppose there are two buyers B1, B2 (each with a valuation independently uniformly distributed between 0 and 1). Suppose each makes a single bid for G and S accepts the larger if and only if it

exceeds S's valuation. Find a bidding strategy for B1 and B2 that is optimal in that if one adopts it the other can do no better than to adopt it also. What will be the expected gains of B1, B2, and S?

Clarifications: Give the expected gains as an overall average, not as a function of the buyer's or seller's valuation. The seller's gain is the excess of the sales price over the seller's valuation (or 0 if no sale occurs). In part 2, each buyer bids without knowing the other buyer's bid or valuation. The solution to this problem, along with commentary for investors, appears in the endnotes.[6]

Calculus

Calculus is an activity of mathematics, based on algebra and geometry. It is built around two ideas, both concerned with limits.

> ➤ Integral focuses on accumulation of two-dimensional quantities in space, pictured as clusters or lines.
> ➤ Differential calculus is concerned with the rate of change of quantities.

Both are used in finance. Cash flow forecasts, for example, tend to use integral calculus while option pricing uses differential calculus.

Differential Equations

Differential calculus uses equations with an independent variable and a dependent variable. These equations help us solve the relationships between rates of change of continuously varying quantities—obviously a useful skill for corporate valuation.

In general, a differential equation gives a relationship between a function and its derivatives. To solve a differential equation means to find a function (or functions) whose derivatives obey the specified relationship.

Differential equations provide the medium for the interaction between mathematics (especially *calculus*) and various branches of science and engineering.

Most finance problems are expressed as a *partial differential equation*— that is, as an equation that involves functions of two or more variables and some of their partial derivatives.

One partial differential equation is the one for net present value, which calculates the difference between the present value of cash inflows and the present value of cash outflows.[7]

Here is the formula:

$$NPV = \sum_{t=1}^{T} \frac{C_t}{(1 + r)^t} - C_o$$

where

NPV = the net present value
C = cash
T and t = times
r = returns

and the Greek capital letter sigma Σ means summation.

The famous Black-Scholes formula developed by Fischer Black and Myron Scholes for valuing options is a partial differential equation:

$$C = SN(d_1) - ke^{(-rt)}N(d_2)$$

where

C = theoretical call premium
S = current stock price
t = time until option expiration
k = option striking price
r = risk-free interest rate
N = cumulative standard normal distribution
E = exponential term (2.7183)
d_1 = ln(s/k) + $(r + S^2/2)$ t/(s $\sqrt{t}$)
d_2 = d_{1_-}(s $\sqrt{t}$)
s = standard deviation of stock price
ln = natural logarithm

Logarithms

A logarithm is an exponent that defines to what power a base must be raised in order the give x, called the antilogarithm. Basically, a logarithm is a shortcut. Just as multiplication is a shortcut for addition (3 × 5 means 5 + 5 + 5); exponents are a shortcut for multiplication (4^3 means

$4 \times 4 \times 4$), and logarithms are a shortcut for exponents ($10^2 = 100$). A logarithm is the exponent or power to which a stated number, called the base, is raised to yield a specific number. So the logarithm of 100 to the base 10 is 2. This is written: $\log_{10} 100 = 2$. This kind of function is use to calculate how long it will take for the interest paid on a bank loan to reach a certain amount.

Statistics

Statistics is a science concerned with uncertainty. It applies mathematical techniques to collect and interpret quantitative data, using probability theory to estimate population parameters. Statistical methods may be parametric (setting parameters) or nonparametric (not setting parameters).

Choosing between the two approaches is important, and also controversial—especially when it comes to data that are highly dispersed, or, to use more graphic language "fat-tailed."[8] For example, the non-normal nature of daily stock returns has prompted some to use nonparametric statistics, but at least one financial economist has suggested that it would be better to set parameters on the analysis.[9]

Conversely, Nassim Nicholas Taleb, author of *The Black Swan*, has criticized uncritical use of "commoditized" metrics such as "standard deviation," "Sharpe ratio," "mean-variance," and so on in "fat-tailed" (statistically dispersed) domains where these terms have little practical meaning.[10]

Dispersion (Range, Variance, and Standard Deviation)

One important part of valuation is calculating the typical price paid for a company of a particular size in a particular industry. But this is more than figuring out the mean (average). While knowing the mean value of company prices in a particular set of data, it can also be informative to know how the data are spread out, or dispersed about the mean.[11]

➤ *Range.* This is the difference between the largest value and the smallest value in the data set. Range is not always reliable as a measure of dispersion since it is based on only two values in the set.

➤ *Mean absolute deviation.* This is the mean (average) of the absolute value of the difference between the individual values in the data set and the mean. The method tries to measure the average distances between the values in the data set and the mean.

$$\text{Population MAD} = \frac{1}{n} \sum_{i=1}^{n} |x_i - \bar{x}|$$

$$\text{Sample MAD} = \frac{1}{n-1} \sum_{i=1}^{n} |x_i - \bar{x}|$$

➤ *Variance.* This is measure of the average distance between each of a set of data points and their mean value. It is equal to the sum of the squares of the deviation from the mean value. To find variance for a set of data:
  ➤ Subtract the mean, $\bar{x}$, from each of the values in the data set, x_i.
  ➤ Square the result.
  ➤ Add all of these squares.
  ➤ Divide by the number of values in the data set.

$$\text{Population variance} = (\sigma x)^2 = \frac{1}{n} \sum_{i=1}^{n} (x_i - \bar{x})$$

$$\text{Sample variance} = (Sx)^2 = \frac{1}{n-1} \sum_{i=1}^{n} (x_i - \bar{x})^2$$

Standard deviation is the square root of the variance. The formulas are:

$$\text{Population standard deviation} = \sigma x = \sqrt{\frac{1}{n} \sum_{i=1}^{n} (x_i - \bar{x})^2}$$

$$\text{Sample standard deviation} = Sx = \sqrt{\frac{1}{n-1} \sum_{i=1}^{n} (x_i - \bar{x})^2}$$

Probability

The simple definition of probability is the ratio of the number of favorable outcomes to the total number of possible outcomes. In finance, it is more common to look for conditional probability. Calculating probability, especially conditional probability, requires information.

Applications of probability theory in finance include:

➤ Calculating probability of cash flow under most likely scenario.
➤ Calculating probability of cash flow under various scenarios weighted for probability.[12]
➤ Calculating probability of cash flow using simulations (e.g., Monte Carlo).

Binomial Distribution of Probability

If an event can have just two outcomes—success or failure—and if the possibilities of success are independent and constant, the distribution of probabilities (how chances of success will play out) is called binomial distribution.

Example of the use of binomial distribution in valuation:

The binomial options pricing model is a way to value options. It calculates varying price over time of the underlying instrument during a discrete time period (vesting). Option valuation is then computed (assuming risk neutrality) over the life of the option, as the price of the underlying instrument evolves.

Univariate Analysis

Descriptive statistics describe and summarize data. Univariate descriptive statistics describe individual variables. This approach explores each variable in a data set, separately. It looks at the range of values, as well as the central tendency of the values. It describes the pattern of response to the variable. It describes each variable on its own.

To visualize a distribution of a univariate data set, an investor can use a histogram (pictured as a bar chart, with the bars showing certain vs. uncertain data). This graphically summarizes the distribution of a univariate data set, showing:

1. Center (i.e., the location) of the data
2. Spread (i.e., the scale) of the data
3. Skewedness of the data

4. Presence of outliers
5. Presence of multiple modes in the data

These features provide strong indications of the proper distributional model for the data.

Histograms

When valuing the securities of a company, it is helpful to have a sense of the variance of its value. Histograms are useful for this. They are available in most general-purpose statistical software programs. They are also supported in most general-purpose charting, spreadsheet, and business graphics programs. The Moving Average Convergence Divergence (MACD) is used in technical analysis to gauge the strength of an asset's momentum. An increasing MACD histogram signals an increase in upward momentum, while a decreasing histogram is used to signal downward momentum. (See Chapter 5.)

Geometry and Trigonometry

Geometry is used for technical analysis. The charts in Chapter 5 demonstrate all the shapes that the technical analysts may detect.

As for trigonometry, some chartists (such as John Elher, who has a mesa sine wave theory) require use of a sine, which relates to a triangle's trigonometric functions. In order to define those functions for the angle A, start with an arbitrary right triangle that contains the angle A:

We use the following names for the sides of the triangle:

➤ The *hypotenuse* is the side opposite the right angle, in this case c.
➤ The *opposite side* is the side opposite to the angle we are interested in, in this case a.
➤ The *adjacent side* is the side that is a leg of the angle, but not the hypotenuse, in this case b.

Then,

➤ The *sine* of an angle is the ratio of the length of the opposite side to the length of the hypotenuse. In our case $\sin(A) = \text{opp/hyp} = a/c$.

Conclusion

Clearly mathematics is a useful tool for any investor who wants to determine a value for a corporation's securities. We hope that this appendix is useful in helping you "think mathematically" about valuation.

Symbols Used in Financial Mathematics[13]

The following list of symbols is from International Standards Organization (ISO) ISO 80000-2.

Mathematical Logic

Sign	Example	Name	Meaning and Verbal Equivalent	Remarks
$\wedge$	$p \wedge q$	Conjunction sign	p and q	
$\vee$	$p \vee q$	Disjunction sign	p or q (or both)	
$\neg$	$\neg p$	Negation sign	Negation of p; not p; non p	
$\rightarrow$	$p \rightarrow q$	Implication sign	If p then q; p implies q	Can also be written as $q \Leftarrow p$.

Sets

Sign	Example	Meaning and Verbal Equivalent	Remarks
$\in$	$x \in A$	x belongs to A; x is an element of the set A.	$A \ni x$ has the same meaning as $x \in A$.
$\notin$	$x \notin A$	x does not belongs to A; x is not an element of the set A.	The negation stroke can also be vertical.
$\ni$	$A \ni x$	The set A contains x (as an element).	Same meaning as $x \in A$.
$\not\ni$	$A \not\ni x$	The set A does not contain x (as an element).	Same meaning as $x \notin A$.
$\{\ \}$	$\{x_1, x_2, \ldots, x_n\}$	Set with elements $x_1, x_2, \ldots, x_n$.	Also $\{x_i : i \in I\}$, where I denotes a set of indices.

Sign	Example	Meaning and Verbal Equivalent	Remarks
$\{ \mid \}$	$\{x \in A \mid p(x)\}$	Set of those elements of A for which the proposition $p(x)$ is true.	Example: $\{x \in \mathbb{R} \mid x > 5\}$. The $\in A$ can be dropped where this set is clear from the context.
card	card(A)	Number of elements in A; cardinal of A.	
$\emptyset$		The empty set	
$\mathbb{N}$		The set of natural numbers; the set of positive integers and zero	$\mathbb{N} = \{0, 1, 2, 3, \ldots\}$ Exclusion of zero is denoted by an asterisk: $\mathbb{N}^\circ = \{0, 1, 2, 3, \ldots\}$ $\mathbb{N}_k = \{0, 1, 2, 3, \ldots, k-1\}$
$\mathbb{Z}$		The set of integers	$\mathbb{Z} = \{\ldots, -3, -2, -1, 0, 1, 2, 3, \ldots\}$ $\mathbb{Z}^\circ = \mathbb{Z}\backslash\{0\} = \{\ldots, -3, -2, -1, 1, 2, 3, \ldots\}$
$\mathbb{Q}$		The set of rational numbers	$\mathbb{Q}^\circ = \mathbb{Q} \backslash \{0\}$
$\mathbb{R}$		The set of real numbers	$\mathbb{R}^\circ = \mathbb{R} \backslash \{0\}$
$\mathbb{C}$		The set of complex numbers	$\mathbb{C}^\circ = \mathbb{C} \backslash \{0\}$
[,]	$[a,b]$	Closed interval in $\mathbb{R}$ from a (included) to b (included)	$[a,b] = \{x \in \mathbb{R} \mid a \le x \le b\}$
],] (,]	$]a,b]$ $(a,b]$	Left half-open interval in $\mathbb{R}$ from a (excluded) to b (included)	$]a,b] = \{x \in \mathbb{R} \mid a \le x \le b\}$
[,[[,)	$[a,b[$ $[a,b)$	Right half-open interval in $\mathbb{R}$ from a (included) to b (excluded)	$[a,b[= \{x \in \mathbb{R} \mid a \le x \le b\}$
],[(,)	$]a,b[$ (a,b)	Open interval in $\mathbb{R}$ from a (excluded) to b (excluded)	$]a,b[= \{x \in \mathbb{R} \mid a < x < b\}$
$\subseteq$	$B \subseteq A$	B is included in A; B is a subset of A.	Every element of B belongs to A. $\subset$ is also used.

(Continued)

(Continued)

Sign	Example	Meaning and Verbal Equivalent	Remarks
$\subset$	$B \subset A$	B is properly included in A; B is a proper subset of A.	Every element of B belongs to A, but B is not equal to A. If $\subset$ is used for "included", then $\subseteq$ should be used for "properly included".
$\not\subseteq$	$C \not\subseteq A$	C is not included in A; C is not a subset of A.	$\not\subset$ is also used.
$\supseteq$	$A \supseteq B$	A includes B (as subset).	A contains every element of B. $\supset$ is also used. $B \subseteq A$ means the same as $A \supseteq B$.
$\supset$	$A \supset B$.	A includes B properly.	A contains every element of B, but A is not equal to B. If $\supset$ is used for "includes", then $\supseteq$ should be used for "includes properly."
$\not\supseteq$	$A \not\supseteq C$	A does not include C (as subset).	$\not\supset$ is also used. $A \not\supseteq C$ means the same as $C \not\subseteq A$.
$\cup$	$A \cup B$	Union of A and B	The set of elements which belong to A or to B or to both A and B. $A \cup B = \{x \mid x \in A \lor x \in B\}$
$\cup$	$\bigcup_{i=1}^{n} A_i$	Union of a collection of sets	$\bigcap_{i=1}^{n} A_i = A_1 \cap A_2 \cap \ldots \cap A_n$, the set of elements belonging to at least one of the sets $A_1, \ldots, A_n$. $\bigcup_{i=1}^{n}$ and $\bigcup_{i \in I}$ are also used, where I denotes a set of indices.
$\cap$	$A \cap B$	Intersection of A and B	The set of elements that belong to both A and B, $A \cap B = \{x \mid x \in A \land x \in B\}$
$\cap$	$\bigcap_{i=1}^{n} A_i$	Intersection of a collection of sets	$\bigcap_{i=1}^{n} A_i = A_1 \cap A_1 \cap A_2 \cap \ldots \cap A_n$, the set of elements belonging to all sets $A_1, \ldots, A_n$. $\bigcap_{i=1}^{n}$ and $\bigcap_{i \in I}$ are also used, where I denotes a set of indices.

Sign	Example	Meaning and Verbal Equivalent	Remarks
\	$A \setminus B$	Difference between A and B; A minus B	The set of elements which belong to A but not to B. $A \setminus B = \{x \mid x \in A \wedge x \notin B\}$ $A - B$ should not be used.
$\complement$	$\complement_A B$	Complement of subset B of A	The set of those elements of A which do not belong to the subset B. The symbol A is often omitted if the set A is clear from context. Also $\complement_A B = A \setminus B$.
$(,)$	(a, b)	Ordered pair a, b; couple a, b	$(a, b) = (c, d)$ if and only if $a = c$ and $b = d$. $\langle a, b \rangle$ is also used.
$(,\ldots,)$	$(a_1, a_2, \ldots, a_n)$	Ordered n-tuple	$\langle a_1, a_2, \ldots, a_n \rangle$ is also used.
$\times$	$A \times B$	Cartesian product of A and B	The set of ordered pairs (a, b) such that $a \in A$ and $b \in B$. $A \times B = \{(a,b) \mid a \in A \wedge b \in B\}$ $A \times A \times \ldots \times A$ is denoted by A^n, where n is the number of factors in the product.
Δ	Δ_A	Set of pairs (a, a) $\in A \times A$ where a $\in A$; diagonal of the set $A \times A$.	$\Delta_A = \{(a, a) \mid a \in A\}$ id_A is also used.

Miscellaneous Signs and Symbols

Sign	Example	Meaning and Verbal Equivalent	Remarks
$\underset{\mathrm{def}}{=}$	$a \underset{\mathrm{def}}{=} b$	a is defined as b.	$\underset{\mathrm{def}}{=}$ is used when a is by definition equal to b.
$=$	$a = b$	a equals b.	$\equiv$ may be used to emphasize that a particular equality is an identity.
$\neq$	$a \neq b$	a is not equal to b.	$a \not\equiv b$ may be used to emphasize that a is not identically equal to b.
$\underset{\mathrm{def}}{=}$	$a \underset{\mathrm{def}}{=} b$	a is by definition equal to b.	:= is also used

(Continued)

(Continued)

Sign	Example	Meaning and verbal Equivalent	Remarks
$\triangleq$	$a \triangleq b$	a corresponds to b.	On a $1{:}10^6$ map: 1 cm $\triangleq 10$ km.
$\approx$	$a \approx b$	a is approximately equal to b.	The symbol $\simeq$ is reserved for "is asymptotically equal to."
$\sim$ $\propto$	$a \sim b$ $a \propto b$	a is proportional to b.	
$<$	$a < b$	a is less than b.	
$>$	$a > b$	a is greater than b.	
$\leq$	$a \leq b$	a is less than or equal to b.	The symbol $\leqq$ is also used.
$\geq$	$a \geq b$	a is greater than or equal to b.	The symbol $\geqq$ is also used.
$\ll$	$a \ll b$	a is much less than b.	
$\gg$	$a \gg b$	a is much greater than b.	
∞		Infinity	
() [] {} $\langle\rangle$	$(a + b)c$ $[a + b]c$ $\{a + b\}c$ $\langle a + b \rangle c$	$ac + b$, parentheses $ac + bc$, square brackets $ac + bc$, braces $ac + bc$, angle brackets	In ordinary algebra, the sequence of (), [], {}, $\langle\rangle$ in order of nesting is not standardized. Special uses are made of (), [], {}, $\langle\rangle$ in particular fields.
$\parallel$	AB $\parallel$ CD	The line AB is parallel to the line CD.	
$\perp$	AB$\perp$CD	The line AB is perpendicular to the line CD.	

Operations

Sign	Example	Meaning and verbal Equivalent	Remarks
$+$	$a + b$	a plus b	
$-$	$a - b$	a minus b	
$\pm$	$a \pm b$	a plus or minus b	
$\pm$	$a \pm b$	a minus or plus b	$-(a \pm b) = -a < b$
. . .	. . .	. . .	. . .

Functions

Example	Meaning and Verbal Equivalent	Remarks
f	Function f	. . .
. . .	. . .	. . .
⋮		

Exponential and Logarithmic Functions

Example	Meaning and Verbal Equivalent	Remarks
a^x	Exponential to the base a of x	. . .
e	Base of natural logarithms	$e = 2.718\ 281\ 8. . .$
. . .	. . .	. . .
⋮		

Circular and Hyperbolic Functions

Example	Meaning and Verbal Equivalent	Remarks
Π	Ratio of the circumference of a circle to its diameter	$n = 3.141\ 592\ 6. . .$
. . .	. . .	. . .
⋮		

Coordinate Systems

Coordinates	Position Vector and Its Differential	Name of Coordinate System	Remarks
x, y, z	. . .	Cartesian	. . .
ρ, φ, z	. . .	cylindrical	. . .
r, θ, φ	. . .	spherical	. . .

Vectors and Tensors

Example	Meaning and Verbal Equivalent	Remarks
a $\vec{a}$	Vector a	Instead of boldface, vectors can also be indicated by an arrow above the letter symbol. Any vector a can be multiplied by a number k, i.e., ka.
. . .	. . .	. . .
⋮		

Notes

1. Gilbert Strang, *Calculus* (Wellesley, Mass.: Wellesley-Cambridge Press, 1991).

2. See Ian Giddy, "Foundations of Finance." http://pages.stern.nyu.edu/~igiddy/finance.htm.

3. See Professor Myron J.Gordon's home page at http://www.rotman.utoronto.ca/~gordon/.

4. Additional inputs required are: five-year consensus growth rate of earnings, the long-term growth rate of earnings, present and long-term payout ratios, and the annually compound yield on the 10-year government bond benchmark. The prospective equity premium is defined as the difference between the rate required by investors on a market portfolio and the long-term government yield. The required return on equity is the rate that equates the present value of the future dividends of the market portfolio to the value of the portfolio. This description of the use of algebra in valuation is based on a discussion in Enrique R. Arzac, *Valuation for Mergers, Buyouts, and Restructuring* (New York: John Wiley & Sons, 2004), www.rafspage.de/valuation. "The mathematical requirement (of his book) is limited to basic algebra exception of a few sections on option pricing applications that use calculus notation."

5. This approach permits calculating a different multiple from a known multiple, checking a given multiple against another known multiple, and adjusting comparable multiples for different debt ratios and growth rates. In each case the corresponding common-size income statements (for $100 revenues) are calculated to facilitate interpretation of the results. It also decomposes multiples into their no-growth value and the franchise and growth factors. See note 11 for source.

6. IBM, "Ponder This," March 2008, http://domino.research.ibm.com/Comm/wwwr_ponder.nsf/solutions/March2008.html. The solution is as follows:

    1. Suppose B's valuation of G is p then B should offer S $p/2$. For suppose B offers x, then S will accept whenever S's valuation is less than x which will happen a fraction x of the time. When S accepts B's gain is $p - x$ so B's expected gain is $x \times (p - x)$. Elementary calculus shows this is maximized for $x=p/2$ as claimed.

        B's expected gain is integral(0 to 1) $\{p \times p/4\} = 1/12 = .0833 +$
        S's expected gain is integral(0 to 1) $\{(p \times p/8\} = 1/24 = .0416+$

    2. We claim B1 and B2 should offer $2^*p/3$ where p is the value they place on G. For suppose B1 adopts this strategy and B2 places value p on G. Suppose B2 offers x. Assume first $x < 2/3$. Then this will be the highest

bid whenever B1's valuation is less than $(3/2) \times x$ and will be accepted whenever S's valuation is less than x. So B2's expected gain is $x \times (1.5 \times x) \times (p - x)$. Again elementary calculus shows this is maximized for $x = (2/3) \times p$. Assume next $x > 2/3$. Then this will always be the highest bid so B2's expected gain is $x^{\circ}(p - x)$. This is decreasing for $x > 2/3$ (since it is decreasing for $x > p/2$ and $p/2 < 1/2$). So there is no reason to bid more than 2/3. Therefore the optimal strategy is to bid $2 \times p/3$. If either bidder adopts this strategy the other bidder does best to adopt it also.

7. See David Vyncke, Marc Goovaerts, and Jan Dhaene, "Convex Upper and Lower Bounds for Present Value Functions," *Applied Stochastic Models in Business and Industry* 17 (2001): 149–164, http://papers.ssrn.com/sol3/papers.cfm?abstract_id=884471. The authors present a methodology for approximating the distribution function of the net present value of a series of cash flows, when the discounting is presented by a stochastic differential equation.abstract.

8. Erich L. Lehmann, "Parametric Versus Nonparametrics: Two Alternative Methodologies, *Journal of Non-Parametric Statistics* 21, no. 4 (May 2009): 397–405.

9. Glenn V. Henderson Jr., "Using Daily Stock Returns in Event Studies and the Choice of Parametric versus Nonparametric Test Statistics," *Quarterly Journal of Business and Economics* 29 (1990): 70–85.

10. Nassim Nicholas Taleb, "Black Swans and the Domains of Statistics," *The American Statistician* 61, no. 3 (August 2007): 581–592, http://www.fooled-byrandomness.com/TAS.pdf.

11. The formulas and pictures are from Donna Roberts, "Measures of Dispersion," *Algebra 2 Trig*, http://www.regentsprep.org/Regents/math/algtrig/ATS1/Dispersion.htm.

12. For a good discussion, see Aswath Damodaran, "Probabalistic Approaches: Scenario Analysis, Decision Trees, and Simulations," http://pages.stern.nyu.edu/~adamodar/.

13. These symbols are selected from International Standards Organization, *Quantities and Units, Part 2: Mathematical Signs and Symbols to be Used in the Natural Sciences and Technology*, 1st. ed. (ISO 80000-2:2009, December 2009), sections 4 through 7, pp. 3–9.

The Modigliani-
Miller Theorems

UP TO THE MIDDLE of the 1950s, the literature of corporate finance consisted mainly of descriptions of methods and institutions.[1] Theoretical analysis was rare. It was not until Franco Modigliani and Merton Miller, in 1958, presented their now-famous theorem, and at about the same time James Tobin (Nobel Prize 1981) and others started to develop the theory of portfolio selection, that a scientific theory emerged concerning the connection between financial market characteristics and the financing of investments, debts, taxes, etc. Once established, this theory developed very rapidly.

The first Modigliani-Miller theorem concerns the question of how the market value of a firm is affected by the volume and structure of its debts. The central proposition of the theorem gives a clear answer to this question: neither the volume nor the structure of the debts affects the value of the firm—provided that the financial markets work perfectly, that there are no taxes, and that there are no bankruptcy costs.

Modigliani and Miller define the value of a firm as the sum of the market value of the equity stock and the market value of its debts. Their theorem states that this value is equal to the discounted value of the flow of its expected future returns, before interest, provided that the return on investment in shares of firms in the same risk class is used as the discount factor. This implies that the value is completely determined by this discount factor and by the return on existing assets, and is independent of how these assets have been financed. It further implies that average capital cost is independent of the volume and structure of the debts and equal to the expected return on investment in shares of firms in the same risk class.

In a later paper, Modigliani and Miller formulated another theorem stating that, for a given investment policy, the value of a firm is also independent of its dividend policy. A dividend increase, for instance, certainly increases shareholders' incomes, but this is neutralized by a corresponding reduction in share value.

The two Modigliani-Miller theorems hold good, irrespective of individual differences between shareholders' valuations of risk, leverage effects, durability of loans, etc. The logic of the theorems rests, in fact, on the assumption of perfect markets, namely that a shareholder can always, through his own borrowing or lending, compose his asset portfolio as he sees fit, and that he can, without costs, give it the composition he desires with respect to risk, leverage, etc. If for instance the risk level of a firm's assets is increased, the shareholders can neutralize this by lowering the risk of other assets in their portfolios.

The Modigliani-Miller theorems have had important implications for the theory of investment decisions. One is that such decisions can be separated from the corresponding financial decision. Another implication is that the rational criterion for investment decisions is a maximization of the market value of the firm, and a third is that the rational concept of capital cost refers to total cost, and should be measured as the rate of return on capital invested in shares of firms in the same risk class.

The Modigliani-Miller theorems represent a decisive breakthrough for the theory of corporate finance, and have had a great impact on later research in this area. Thus the scientific value of the authors' work is by no means limited to the formulation of the theorems, but refers to a great extent also to the introduction of a new method of analysis within the discipline of corporate finance. While the idea of treating financial decisions as a market allocation problem is perhaps not completely new, it was Modigliani and Miller who first used it for stringent analysis, thereby laying down guidelines for further research in this area.

Modigliani-Miller Propositions*[2]

M-M Proposition 1

In competitive, transaction costless, information efficient markets, with no taxes, the market value of the firm (i.e., market value of all of its securities) is independent of the firm's capital structure. That is, $V_U = V_L$; see definition below).

The proof of this proposition is based on the following arbitrage property of perfect markets.

Arbitrage Property

Two identical assets must have the same market price. Two assets are identical if either can be converted into the other.

Logic of M-M Proof: Let firm U be an unlevered firm and let firm L be an identical firm if levered (or be the same firm if levered); U and L differ only in that L is levered. V_U is the market value of firm U (therefore V_U is also the market value of the equity of firm U since it is unleveraged; E_L and D_L are the market values, respectively, of the equity and debt of firm L, and firm value $V_L = E_L + D_L$.

Compare buying percent P of firm L with the following: buying percent P of the equity (shares) of firm U *plus* personal borrowing of amount $P\,D_L$ *(using the shares of firm U as collateral)*. **Exhibit F.1** shows that the incomes of the two "strategies" are identical.

Exhibit F.1 Convert U into L Using [2]

Strategy	Net Investment of the Strategy	Income
1. Buy percent P of equity of firm L	$P\,E_L$	P [Profit − Interest]
2. Buy percent P of equity of firm U and borrow amount $[P\,D_L]$	$P\,V_U - P\,D_L$	P Profit − P Interest = $= P$ [Profit − Interest]

Since we can use strategy 2 to create the stock under strategy 1, strategy 2 must be at least as good as strategy 1, and therefore we must be willing to pay at least as much for strategy 2 as for strategy 1. That is,

$$P\,V_U - P\,D_L \geq P\,E_L,$$

which implies that

$$V_U \geq E_L + D_L = V_L \tag{F.1}$$

Now we will show that we can convert L into U. Compare two strategies: $1'$ Buy P percent of firm U; $2'$ Buy P percent of the shares of firm L, and buy percent P of the debt of firm L. **Exhibit F.2** shows that the incomes of the two strategies are identical.

Exhibit F.2 Convert L into U using Strategy $2'$

Strategy	Net Investment of the Strategy	Income
$1'$. Buy percent P of firm U equity	$P\,V_U$	P Profit
$2'$. Buy percent P of firm L debt and percent P of firm L equity	$P\,D_L + P\,E_L = P\,V_L$	P [Profit − Interest] + P Interest = P Profit

Since we can use strategy $2'$ to create the stock under strategy $1'$, strategy $2'$ must be at least as good as strategy $1'$, and, therefore, we must be willing to pay at least as much for strategy $2'$ as for strategy $1'$. That is,

$$P\,V_L \geq P\,V_U$$

which implies that

$$V_L \geq V_U \qquad\qquad (\text{F.2})$$

The only way for M-M Proposition 1 and M-M Proposition 2 to hold is for

$$V_U = V_L \qquad\qquad (\text{F.3})$$

which is M-M Proposition 1.

Assume that M-M Proposition 1 holds. Then we will see that the same investment is required to generate the same income whether or not the firm is levered. One share of the levered firm generates the same income as two shares of the unlevered firm with personal borrowing of $10.

One share of the levered firm:

$$\text{Investment} = \text{Cost of one share of } L = \$10$$

Income is one of: $0, $1, $2, or $3. Two shares of the unlevered firm with borrowing of $10:

$$\text{Investment} = \text{Cost of two shares of } U -$$
$$\text{Amount borrowed} = \$20 - \$10 = \$10$$

$$\text{Income} = \text{Firm income on two share} - \text{Interest}$$
$$\text{on personal debt} = \text{one of: } \$0, \$1, \$2, \text{ or } \$3$$

M-M Proposition 2

In competitive, transaction costless, information efficient markets, with corporate tax-deductibility of interest, the market value of the firm (i.e., market value of all of its securities) equals:

$$V_L = V_U + T D_L$$

where V_L is the value of the firm if it has debt, V_U is the value of the firm if it has no debt, T is the corporate tax savings per dollar of debt, and D_L is the market value of the firm's debt.

In the above relationship, T is equal to the firm's tax rate if all debt interest is tax deductible. However, if some or all of the interest is not tax deductible, T is not the marginal tax rate. For example, if 80 percent of the interest were tax deductible and the corporate tax rate were 34 percent, then, in the above equations, $T = .8 \times .34 = .272$.

The proof for the M-M Proposition 2 is similar to the proof with no taxes and so will not be shown here.

To illustrate, suppose that Royal Corporation is all-equity financed and worth $400 million ($V_U$ = $400 million). It plans to change its financial structure (but not its assets) by borrowing $100 million and using the $100 million for a share repurchase. Royal's tax rate is 34 percent and all of the interest on its debt is tax deductible. Proposition 2 states that it can expect its new value to be:

$$\begin{aligned}
V_L &= V_U + T D_L \\
&= \$\,400{,}000{,}000 + 34\,(\$100{,}000{,}000) \\
&= \$\,434{,}000{,}000
\end{aligned}$$

Notes

1. This section is based on Nobel Foundation, "Press Release," October 15, 1985, http://nobelprize.org/nobel_prizes/economics/laureates/1985/press.html, accompanying the award of the 1985 Nobel Prize in Economics to Franco Modigliani. (Merton Miller won the prize in 1990.)
2. This section is excerpted from Richard Brealey, Stewart Myers, and Franklin Allen, Chapter 17, "Understanding Options" in *Principles of Corporate Finance* (New York: McGraw-Hill, 2008).

Uniform Standards of Professional Appraisal Practice (USPAP)[1]

The *Uniform Standards of Professional Appraisal Practice* (USPAP) are the generally accepted standards for professional appraisal practice in North America. USPAP contains standards for all types of appraisal services. Standards are included for real estate, personal property, business, and mass appraisal.

Standard 9: Business Appraisal, Development

In developing an appraisal of an interest in a business enterprise or intangible asset, an appraiser must identify the problem to be solved, determine the scope of work necessary to solve the problem, and correctly complete the research and analyses necessary to produce a credible appraisal.

> *Comment: STANDARD 9 is directed toward the substantive aspects of developing a credible appraisal of an interest in a business enterprise or intangible asset.*

Standards Rule 9–1

In developing an appraisal of an interest in a business enterprise or intangible asset, an appraiser must:

(a) be aware of, understand, and correctly employ those recognized approaches, methods and procedures that are necessary to produce a credible appraisal;

Comment: Changes and developments in the economy and in investment theory have a substantial impact on the business and intangible asset appraisal profession. Important changes in the financial arena, securities regulation, financial reporting requirements, and law may result in corresponding changes in appraisal theory and practice.

(b) not commit a substantial error of omission or commission that significantly affects an appraisal; and

Comment: An appraiser must use sufficient care to avoid errors that would significantly affect his or her opinions and conclusions. Diligence is required to identify and analyze the factors, conditions, data, and other information that would have a significant effect on the credibility of the assignment results.

(c) not render appraisal services in a careless or negligent manner, such as by making a series of errors that, although individually might not significantly affect the results of an appraisal, in the aggregate affect the credibility of those results.

Comment: Perfection is impossible to attain, and competence does not require perfection. However, an appraiser must not render appraisal services in a careless or negligent manner. This Standards Rule requires an appraiser to use due diligence and due care.

Standards Rule 9–2

In developing an appraisal of an interest in a business enterprise or intangible asset, an appraiser must:

(a) identify the client and other intended users; (note 110)
(b) identify the intended use of the appraiser's opinions and conclusions; (note 111)

Comment: An appraiser must not allow the intended use of an assignment or a client's objectives to cause the assignment results to be biased.

(c) identify the standard (type) and definition of value and the premise of value;
(d) identify the effective date of the appraisal;
(e) identify the characteristics of the subject property that are relevant to the standard (type) and definition of value and intended use of the appraisal, including:

(i)   the subject business enterprise or intangible asset, if applicable;

(ii)   the interest in the business enterprise, equity, asset, or liability to be valued;

Comment: The interest to be valued may represent all owner- ship rights or a subset of those rights, such as a specific right to use the asset.

(iii)   all buy-sell and option agreements, investment letter stock restrictions, restrictive corporate charter or partnership agree- ment clauses, and similar features or factors that may have an influence on value;

(iv)   the extent to which the interest contains elements of owner- ship control; and

Comment: The elements of control in a given situation may be affected by law, distribution of ownership interests, contractual rela- tionships, and many other factors.

(v)   the extent to which the interest is marketable and/or liquid;

Comment on (i)–(v): An appraiser must identify the attributes of the interest being appraised, including the rights and benefits of ownership.

The information used by an appraiser to identify the property characteristics must be from sources the appraiser reasonably believes are reliable.

(f)   identify any extraordinary assumptions necessary in the assignment;

Comment: An extraordinary assumption may be used in an assignment only if:

° it is required to properly develop credible opinions and conclusions;

° the appraiser has a reasonable basis for the extraordinary assumption;

° use of the extraordinary assumption results in a credible anal- ysis; and

° the appraiser complies with the disclosure requirements set forth in USPAP for extraordinary assumptions.

(g)   identify any hypothetical conditions necessary in the assignment; and

Comment: A hypothetical condition may be used in an assignment only if:

° use of the hypothetical condition is clearly required for legal purposes, for purposes of reasonable analysis, or for purposes of comparison;

  *use of the hypothetical condition results in a credible analysis; and

  *the appraiser complies with the disclosure requirements set forth in USPAP for hypothetical conditions.

(h) determine the scope of work necessary to produce credible assignment results in accordance with the SCOPE OF WORK RULE.

Standards Rule 9–3

In developing an appraisal of an equity interest in a business enterprise with the ability to cause liquidation, an appraiser must investigate the possibility that the business enterprise may have a higher value by liquidation of all or part of the enterprise than by continued operation as is. If liquidation of all or part of the enterprise is the indicated premise of value, an appraisal of any real property or personal property to be liquidated may be appropriate.

 Comment: This Standards Rule requires the appraiser to recognize that continued operation of a business is not always the best premise of value because liquidation of all or part of the enterprise may result in a higher value. However, this typically applies only when the business equity being appraised is in a position to cause liquidation. If liquidation of all or part of the enterprise is the appropriate premise of value, the scope of work may include an appraisal of real property or tangible personal property. If so, competency in real property appraisal (STANDARD 7) or tangible personal property appraisal (STANDARD 7) is required.

Standards Rule 9–4

In developing an appraisal of an interest in a business enterprise or intangible asset, an appraiser must collect and analyze all information necessary for credible assignment results.

(a) An appraiser must develop value opinion(s) and conclusion(s) by use of one or more approaches that are necessary for credible assignment results.

(b) An appraiser must, when necessary for credible assignment results, analyze the effect on value, if any, of:

(i)   the nature and history of the business enterprise or intangible asset;

(ii) financial and economic conditions affecting the business enterprise or intangible asset, its industry, and the general economy;

(iii) past results, current operations, and future prospects of the business enterprise;

(iv) past sales of capital stock or other ownership interests in the business enterprise or intangible asset being appraised;

(v)   sales of capital stock or other ownership interests in similar business enterprises;

(vi) prices, terms, and conditions affecting past sales of similar ownership interests in the asset being appraised or a similar asset; and

(vii) economic benefit of tangible and intangible assets.

Comment on (i)–(vii): This Standards Rule directs the appraiser to study the prospective and retrospective aspects of the business enterprise and to study it in terms of the economic and industry environment within which it operates.

(c) An appraiser must, when necessary for credible assignment results, analyze the effect on value, if any, of buy-sell and option agreements, investment letter stock restrictions, restrictive corporate charter or partnership agreement clauses, and similar features or factors that may influence value.

(d) An appraiser must, when necessary for credible assignment results, analyze the effect on value, if any, of the extent to which the interest appraised contains elements of ownership control and is marketable and/or liquid.

Comment: An appraiser must analyze factors such as holding period, interim benefits, and the difficulty and cost of marketing the subject interest.

Equity interests in a business enterprise are not necessarily worth the pro rata share of the business enterprise interest value as a whole. Also, the value of the business enterprise is not necessarily a direct mathematical extension of the value of the fractional interests. The degree of control, marketability and/or liquidity or lack thereof depends on a broad variety of facts and circumstances that must be analyzed when applicable.

Standards Rule 9–5

In developing an appraisal of an interest in a business enterprise or intangible asset, an appraiser must:

(a) reconcile the quality and quantity of data available and analyzed within the approaches, methods, and procedures used; and

(b) reconcile the applicability and relevance of the approaches, methods and procedures used to arrive at the value conclusion(s).

Comment: The value conclusion is the result of the appraiser's judgment and not necessarily the result of a mathematical process.

Note

1. This appendix is excerpted with permission from the Uniform Standards of Professional Appraisal Practice, 2010–2011 Edition. As a framework for the following standards, there are additional standards pertaining to ethics and competency. Standards 1 through 8 pertain to real property. All these additional standards, as well as the selected text, may be viewed at http://www.uspap.org/2010USPAP/index.htm.

Global Industry Classification Standard (GICS) Sectors and Industry Groups

THE GLOBAL INDUSTRY Classification Standard (GICS) was developed by MSCI, a provider of global indexes, and Standard & Poor's, a financial data and investment services company and a provider of global equity indexes.

The GICS classifications, based on discussions with asset owners, portfolio managers, and investment analysts around the world, are designed to respond to the global financial community's need for an accurate, complete, and standard industry definition.

The broadest categories of the GICS structure have 10 sectors (two digits) and 24 industry groups (four digits). In addition, but not included here, the GICS has 68 industries and 154 subindustries.

Sectors

10	Energy
15	Materials
20	Industrials
25	Consumer Discretionary
30	Consumer Staples
35	Healthcare
40	Financials
45	Information Technology
50	Telecommunications Services
55	Utilities

Industry Groups

1010	Energy
1510	Materials
2010	Capital Goods
2020	Commercial and Professional Services
2030	Transportation
2510	Automobiles and Components
2520	Consumer Durables and Apparel
2530	Consumer Services
2540	Media
2550	Retailing
3010	Food and Staples Retailing
2020	Food, Beverage, and Tobacco
3030	Household and Personal Products
3510	Healthcare Equipment and Services
3520	Pharmaceuticals, Biotechnology, and Life Sciences
4010	Banks
4020	Diversified Financials
4030	Insurance
4040	Real Estate
4510	Software and Services
4520	Technology Hardware and Equipment
4530	Semiconductors and Semiconductor Equipment
5010	Telecommunication Services
5510	Utilities

Damodaran Spreadsheets for Valuation[1]

PROFESSOR ASWATH DAMODARAN, Professor of Finance and David Margolis Teaching Fellow at the Stern School of Business at New York University, and eminent valuation author, has collected a great number of spreadsheets. He lists them on his web site as follows:

1. *Corporate finance spreadsheets* are most useful for conventional corporate financial analysis. They include spreadsheets to analyze a project's cash flows and viability, a company's risk profile, its optimal capital structure and debt type, and whether it is paying out what it can afford to in dividends (http://pages.stern.nyu.edu/~adamodar/ New_Home_Page/spreadsh.htm#cf).

2. *Valuation inputs spreadsheets* enable analysts to:
   a. Estimate the right discount rate to use for your firm, starting with the risk premium in your cost of equity and concluding with the cost of capital for your firm.
   b. Convert R&D and operating leases into capitalized assets.
   c. Estimate the right capital expenditures and diagnose the terminal value assumptions to see if they are reasonable (http://pages.stern .nyu.edu/~adamodar/New_Home_Page/spreadsh.htm#valinputs).

3. *Valuation model reconciliation* reconciles different DCF approaches: free cash flow to equity (FCFE) versus dividend discount model, FCFE versus free cash flow to the firm (FCFF) model, economic value added versus cost of capital, and net debt versus gross debt approaches (http://pages.stern.nyu.edu/~adamodar/New_Home_ Page/spreadsh.htm#valreconcile).

4. *Big picture valuation spreadsheets* require a large number of inputs, but they are flexible enough to enable valuation of any company. The analyst must decide whether to use a dividend, FCFE, or FCFF model spreadsheet (http://pages.stern.nyu.edu/~adamodar/ New_Home_Page/spreadsh.htm#ginzumodels). To help selection, try the "choosing the right model" spreadsheet first (http://www .stern.nyu.edu/~adamodar/pc/model.xls).

5. *Focused valuation spreadsheets* are useful for analysts who have chosen a particular model, such as stable growth dividend discount, two-stage FCFE, and the like (http://pages.stern.nyu.edu/~adamodar/ New_Home_Page/spreadsh.htm#valmodels).

6. *Situation-specific spreadsheets* are available for special circumstances, including:

   a. *Financial services firms.* Though dividend discount models tend to be the weapon of choice for many, here is an excess equity return model (http://pages.stern.nyu.edu/~adamodar/New_Home_Page/ spreadsh.htm#finsvc).

   b. *Troubled firms.* This includes an earnings normalizer spreadsheet, a generic valuation model for valuing a firm as a going concern, and a spreadsheet that helps the analyst estimate the probability that a troubled firm will not survive (http://pages .stern.nyu.edu/~adamodar/New_Home_Page/spreadsh.htm# troubledfirms).

   c. *Private companies.* Here are spreadsheets for adjusting discount rates and estimating illiquidity discounts for private companies (http://pages.stern.nyu.edu/~adamodar/New_Home_Page/ spreadsh.htm#pvtfirms).

   d. *Young and high-growth firms.* Here is a revenue growth estimator as well as a generic valuation model for high-growth firms in this section (http://pages.stern.nyu.edu/~adamodar/New_ Home_Page/spreadsh.htm#higrowthfirms).

7. *Multiples.* These spreadsheets enable an analyst to estimate equity as well as firm value multiples, based on fundamentals (http://pages.stern .nyu.edu/~adamodar/New_Home_Page/spreadsh.htm#multiples).

8. *Valuation in acquisitions.* These spreadsheets help an analyst value synergy in an acquisition and analyze a leveraged buyout (http:// pages.stern.nyu.edu/~adamodar/New_Home_Page/spreadsh .htm#acqvaln).

9. *Valuation in other assets.* Here is a model for valuing income-generating real estate (http://pages.stern.nyu.edu/~adamodar/New_Home_Page/spreadsh.htm#otherassets).

10. *Value enhancement spreadsheets.* In this section, a spreadsheet reconciles EVA and DCF valuation, a model for estimating CFROI and a DCF version of a value enhancement spreadsheet (http://pages.stern.nyu.edu/~adamodar/New_Home_Page/spreadsh.htm#valueenh).

11. *Basic option pricing models.* Here are Black-Scholes models for valuing short-term options, long-term options, and options that result in the dilution of stock (such as warrants). In addition, this section has spreadsheets that convert Black-Scholes inputs into binomial model inputs and use the binomial model to value options (http://pages.stern.nyu.edu/~adamodar/New_Home_Page/spreadsh .htm#basicoption).

12. *Real option models in corporate finance.* This section features three basic real option models: the option to delay, the option to expand, and the option to abandon. In addition, the value of financial flexibility is considered as an option (http://pages.stern.nyu.edu/~adamodar/New_Home_Page/spreadsh.htm#optincf).

13. *Real option models in valuation.* This section contains models to value both a patent (and a firm owning a patent) as an option, natural resource firms and equity in deeply troubled firms (http:// pages.stern.nyu.edu/~adamodar/New_Home_Page/spreadsh .htm#optinval).

Professor Damodaran adds, "These spreadsheet programs are written in Microsoft Excel and are not copy protected. Download them and feel free to modify them to your own specifications. I do have video guides available for some of the most accessed spreadsheets. I hope they are useful." The authors are grateful for his generosity in sharing these helpful tools.

Note

1. This appendix was summarized from Aswath Damodaran, *Damodaran Online*, http://pages.stern.nyu.edu/~adamodar/ with Professor Damodaran's kind permission. Professor Damodaran is the author of several valuation books, including *Damodaran on Valuation: Security Analysis for Investments*, 2nd ed. (Hoboken, N.J.: John Wiley & Sons, 2006), which is listed in this book as recommended reading.

Monte Carlo Simulation for Security Investments

THE DUFF & PHELPS February 2009 *Valuation Report* to the Congressional Oversight Panel (see Appendix D) included a section on Monte Carlo simulation in a technical appendix.[1] The first three paragraphs of Appendix J are taken from that section of the Duff & Phelps report. The remainder of this appendix reports on a text run by the authors.

Monte Carlo simulation was developed by scientists working on the Manhattan Project in the 1940s. The essence of the idea is to repeat a process many times, observe the outcome, and use that information to calculate the answer sought. Consider this simple example. A person wants to know what the odds are for each value for the sum of the throw of two dice. This is a relatively simple problem to solve using basic logic. Now, suppose someone wishes to know the probability of getting a sum of 33 on the throw of 10 dice. Simple logic will not suffice, and deriving a solution to this problem will be very challenging. It is feasible and relatively simple, however, to have a computer "throw" 10 dice a large number of times and record the outcomes. This produces a Monte Carlo simulation estimate of the true probability of the sum being 33. The larger the number of times the computer throws the dice, the more accurate the estimate is.

Monte Carlo simulation can be used to value derivatives. In the simplest case, you can simulate a common stock price and use the values produced to replicate the results of the Black-Scholes-Merton formula. Of course, the purpose is to use the method to answer more complex questions. This report uses Monte Carlo simulation in two ways. First, value the warrants using volatility and interest rates that vary over time because this is a more accurate representation of reality. Monte Carlo simulation also allows us to model conditions under which refinancing would cancel one-half of the warrants. Second, Monte Carlo simulation is used to model the evolution of the value of the assets of the subject companies over time in contingent claims analysis (CCA), which has a significant number of complexities that require simulation.

A lattice of values for the underlying random variable can be used to calculate derivative values. A lattice is akin to a simulation with the exception that in each interval of time the underlying variable can move to only one of two values, given its current value. The price lattice in **Exhibit J.1**, which is a representation of the price movements of a common stock over a six-week period, illustrates this point. The stock price starts at 100, and at the end of the first week can be either 102.83 or 97.28. In this model the probability of each is 0.5. If the price moves to 102.83 at the end of the first week, then at the end of the second week, it can be either 105.74 or 100.04. The lattice summarizes the distribution of the stock price at the end of six weeks in terms of the seven prices shown with their associated probabilities. For example, the probability of the

Exhibit J.1 Price Lattice Illustration: Price Movements of a Common Stock over a Six-Week Period

Week							Probability
0	1	2	3	4	5	6	
						118.24%	1.6%
					114.99%		
				111.82%		111.86%	9.4%
			108.74%		108.78%		
		105.74%		105.79%		105.83%	23.4%
	102.83%		102.87%		102.91%		
100.00%		100.04%		100.08%		100.12%	31.3%
	97.28%		97.32%		97.36%		
		94.64%		94.68%		94.71%	23.4%
			92.07%		92.10%		
				89.57%		89.60%	9.4%
					87.13%		
						84.77%	1.6%
						Total	100%

Source: Duff & Phelps, Appendix: Volume III – Technical Appendix, p. III-2. (See endnote 1.)

price being 105.83 is 23.4 percent. The more steps there are in a lattice, the more accurately it models the movements of the stock price, which obviously can assume more than just seven prices. Lattices are useful for valuing derivatives when there are call provisions.

Volatility and Time Horizon Exercise

The following paragraphs describe how the coauthors of this book used the suggested Monte Carlo simulation exercises at *MoneyChimp*.[2]

➤ The volatility of an investment is measured by the standard deviation on the rate of return.
➤ We chose an investment with a specified return and volatility, and the graph produced a bell curve of possible outcomes.
➤ An area called the "negative return zone" was proportional to the probability that we would *lose* money on our investment.

Here are some things we tried:

➤ We set the time horizon to five years and compared the results for the stocks and bonds portfolios. We found that the stocks graph lay to the right of the bonds graph, as you'd expect (the expected return is higher) but the so-called danger zone for stocks was also larger. This is the classic risk-reward trade-off. If two identical groups of people invested in portfolios like these, the average gain of the stocks group would be greater than that of the bonds group, but the stocks group would have a larger number of investors who actually *lost* money.
➤ Then we tried the stocks portfolio with different time horizons. We found that the danger zone decreased as the time horizon grew. Conventional investing wisdom says that volatile (high-risk/potentially high-return) investments are more appropriate for long-term than for short-term investments, and the resulting graph proved the point.
➤ Next we tried stocks with a time horizon of one year. Now the graph lost its bell curve. Over this short a time frame, the stock market was really random, more like a game of chance than an investment.

Notes

1. Duff & Phelps, *Appendix: Volume III - Technical Appendix*, February 4, 2009, http://cop.senate.gov/documents/cop-020609-report-dpvaluation-app03.pdf.

2. "Volatility and Your Time Horizon," MoneyChimp.com, http://www .moneychimp.com/articles/risk/longterm.htm. In our Monte Carlo simulation, we calculated many possible outcomes, to show both the return we expected and the risk that we would not achieve it.

Antivaluation! Human Valuation and Investment Foibles

BEFORE VALUING A company, investors need to evaluate *themselves*. Are they avoiding tricks of mind that compromise investment choices? To avoid faulty reasoning, it is a good idea to check for valuation bias and fallacy.

Slanted or illogical thinking can undo all the good that objective, reasoned valuation can accomplish. Indeed, one reason investors use indexes for stock choices and algorithms for trading moves is to restrain human impulses.

But rather than avoid their personal natures, perhaps investors can improve and use them. So to that end, here is an alphabetical list of investment foibles (some biases, some fallacies) to avoid.[1]

Some Common Biases in Valuation Choices

Countless biases can affect valuation and investment choices. In fact, an entire field, called "behavioral finance," is devoted to biases. The following representative baker's dozen may raise readers' awareness. Investors don't have to know what all the fallacies are; they simply need to be prepared to check their independence.

➤ *Anchoring.* Investors become focused on price points that influence their decisions and may ignore valuation findings. If an investor buys a stock at $80, and it falls to $60 because the fundamentals have changed irrevocably—for example, the government has passed a law severely restricting sale of a key product—the investor may be reluctant to sell under the anchor of $80.

    Valuation tip: Don't get fixated on any one benchmark for your valuation work.

➤ *Attribution bias*. Past successes tend to generate overconfidence. People take too much credit for successes and too little blame for failures; they attribute successes to their own prowess but failures to forces beyond their control.[2]

    Valuation tip: Don't assume that, because a company has done well in the past, it will do well in the future; differentiate between the root causes of success and flukes. (See the discussion of earnings quality in Chapter 3.)

➤ *Cognitive dissonance* refers to a state of mind in which contradictory ideas and/or actions coexist. This is a very broad and well-known term and needs no special references here.

    Valuation tip: Make sure your valuation decisions match your valuation findings.

➤ *Confirmatory bias*. People have a tendency to overweigh data confirming prior beliefs while dismissing data contradicting prior beliefs.

    Valuation tip: When you select formulas or variables for valuation, be willing to go against the grain of your own past approaches. Don't pick only the indicators that make your investment choice look good.

➤ *Conformity* causes people to change their behavior as a result of pressure from others.[3]

    Valuation tip: Don't pick a particular valuation approach, or adjust a value within that approach, just because others are doing so.

➤ *Control illusion*. Many suffer from the false belief that they have control over something uncontrollable. Conformists are likely to rationalize, so see Rationalization.

    Valuation tip: When creating a valuation formula, remember to factor in uncertainty.

➤ *Denial*. People in hazardous conditions sometimes believe what they want to believe and ignore other evidence. In one study, researchers found that workers in hazardous industries convince themselves that the industry where they were working is safe. When asked if they would propose safety equipment, they said no.[4]

Valuation tip: Don't minimize negative findings.

➤ *Disposition effect*. When an investor overvalues a company and refuses to sell its stock even thought its pricing is steadily declining, this irrational behavior is called the *disposition effect*.[5]

Valuation tip: If a company's securities keep losing value, recheck your valuation assumptions (e.g., strength of earnings, discount rate for future cash flow, etc.) and consider downgrading them.

➤ *Emotional attachment*. Sometimes emotional attachment to an investment position masquerades as the exercise of discretionary judgment. One study showed that investors who fared best during a recent market downturn had restrictive rules that prevented them from holding on to stocks (for emotional or other motives) that did not meet the criteria.[6]

Valuation tip: If you find that your gut instinct always results in faulty valuation (and hence faulty investment choices), try using and sticking to stricter criteria.

➤ *Group thinking*. Different answers given by individuals converge to a single answer when the individuals are in a group.[7] Also, individuals sometimes give wrong answers in order to conform to group norms.[8]

Valuation tip: When valuing company worth, keep marching to the beat of your own drum.

➤ *Optimism*. People are generally optimistic. In one study, undergraduates were asked to relate how likely various life events were to happen to them. The result: students systematically thought that good events were likely to happen to them while bad events were more likely to happen to other students.[9]

Valuation tip: When you like an industry or company, be especially careful not to minimize weak areas and downsides.

➤ *Rationalization*. Cognitive dissonance causes people to rationalize actions that differ from their own preferences.[10] Conformists are more likely to rationalize, so see *Conformity*.

Valuation tip: If you find yourself making too many exceptions to your valuation rules, check your motives.

➤ *Self-serving biases.* People reach conclusions about reality (including their own skills) that favor them.[11]

    Valuation tip: As you set a value, ask yourself, what's in it for me? If there *is* something in it for you, make an adjustment to eliminate the bias.

Some Common Fallacies in Valuation Reasoning

These biases pertain to behavior based in emotions. Some investors might think that they can overcome these biases through logic, which can be defined as moving from one or more true statements to additional true statements through valid induction, deduction, or inference. The problem is that it is possible to move from one set of statements to others in ways that only appear to be logical but that are, in fact, wrong— that is, based on fallacies.

Fallacies of logic often bolster unconscious bias. So, to counteract bias, identify and eliminate fallacies. A number of logicians have tried to list fallacies.[12] The following list, based in part on longer lists developed by expert David Straker, offers a way to categorize some common fallacies.[13]

➤ *Causal fallacies.* When we assume, imply, or state that something caused something else, but it is not true.

➤ *Tautology.* A is B, therefore A is B.

➤ *False cause.* A causes B (but no proof).

Example of Fallacious Reasoning about Valuation

Following a 1 percent rise in interest rates in the fourth quarter of last year, Company X's earnings dropped by 1 percent. The Federal Reserve Bank has just announced that it will be raising interest rates again, so look for another drop in Company X earnings (a causal post hoc type of fallacy).

➤ *False effect.* A is assumed to cause B. B is proven wrong, so A is wrong.

➤ *Post hoc.* X follows Y. Therefore X is caused by Y.

➤ *Deductive fallacies.* Incorrectly going from general to specific rules. Y is used to explain X. But X does not fall under Y. Common forms include *accident* and *division* (see next section).

➤ *Distraction fallacies.* Moving attention away from the real argument, such as using a red herring (false issue) or straw man (false opponent) or poisoning the well (discrediting the opponent).

➤ *Inductive fallacies.* Incorrectly going from specifics to general rules. Inductive reasoning uses a move from specific instances to general rules. Inductive (or "generalization") fallacies fail because they break the rules of this form of reasoning. They include fallacies of *composition* (generalizing from a few to the whole set), false analogies (X has property Y; Z is like X; so Z has property Y) and an unfounded generalization (generalizing from too small a sample).

➤ *Nonsequitur fallacies.* When one argument does not follow from the other. Non sequiturs happen when we affirm the consequent (if A, then B. B is true; so A is true) or deny the antecedent (if A, then B; A is false, so B is false).

➤ *Syllogistic fallacies.* Aristotle defines a syllogism as a "discourse in which, certain things having been supposed, something different from the things results because these things are so." In a fallacy, these things are *not* so! Some common syllogistic fallacies are:

  ➤ *Four terms.* Syllogisms must concatenate, and as such, work in threes. The following statement breaks that rule: A is B; all C is D; so all A is D.

  ➤ *Illicit major.* All X is Y. No P (which is a subset of Y) is X. Therefore no P is Y.

  ➤ *Illicit minor.* All X are Y; all X are P; therefore all P are Y.

Aristotle's 13 Fallacies

Fallacies of Speech

1. *Accent.* Emphasizing something too much.
2. *Amphiboly.* Ambiguous grammatical structure.
3. *Equivocation.* Misleading use of a term with more than one meaning.

4. *Composition*. Claiming that what is true of the parts is true for the whole.
5. *Division*. Claiming what is true for the whole is true for the part.
6. *Figure of speech*. Through homonym, shifting the meaning of a word from the figural to the literal during the same argument.

Fallacies of Reasoning

1. *Accident*. Applying what is meant to be a general rule of thumb with exceptions to a case where it does not apply.
2. *Affirming the consequent*. If P, then Q; Q, therefore P. This is false. Even if P causes Q, Q does not necessarily cause P.
3. *"Based on this."* Taking an attribute that belongs in one area and assuming that it can be applied to a wider area.
4. *Ignorance of refutation*. Missing the whole point. Someone makes an argument that could lead to a valid conclusion, but the stated conclusion is something else. (A set of statements leads to conclusion X. Yet conclusion Y is drawn.)
5. *Begging the question*. Not answering the question asked.
6. *False cause*. Incorrectly attributing cause.
7. *Many questions*. Combining unrelated questions. A is an attribute of B; so A is an attribute of C.

Notes

1. In addition to sources cited in these endnotes, we found the following: John Allen Paulos, "Cognitive Dissonance," in *A Mathematician Plays the Stock Market* (New York: Basic Books, 2003), http://www.efmoody.com/planning/cd.html.
2. S. Gervais and T. Odean. "Learning to Be Confident," *The Society for Financial Studies* 14 (2001): 1–27.
3. A. Nir, "A Behavioral Model of Consumption Patterns: The Effects of Cognitive Dissonance and Conformity," Research Paper, Tilburg University, Center for Economic Research, 2004, http://ideas.repec.org/p/dgr/kubcen/200448.html.
4. See G. Akerlof and W. T. Dickens, "The Economic Consequences of cognitive Dissonance," *American Economic Review* 72 (1982): 307–319.
5. Daniel Kahneman, "On Humans and Decision Making," *Journal of Financial Planning* 17 (August 2004): 10–13.

6. Christophe Faugere, Hany A. Shawky, and David M. Smith, "How to Get out of Stock," *The Journal of Portfolio Management* 30 (Spring 2004): 95–105.

7. M. Sherif, *The Psychology of Social Norms* (New York: Harper, 1936).

8. S. E. Asch, " Effects of Group Pressure upon the Modification and Distortion of Judgment," in *Groups, Leadership, and Men*, edited by H. Guetzkow. (Pittsburgh: Carnegie Press, 1951). *Note*: re giving wrong answers on purposed to conform.

9. Margaret W. Matlin, "Pollyanna Principle," in *Cognitive Illusions: A Handbook on Fallacies and Biases in Thinking, Judgement and Memory*, edited by Rüdiger Pohl (London: Psychology Press, 2004).

10. A. Nir, "A Behavioral Model of Consumption Patterns: The Effects of Cognitive Dissonance and Conformity," Research Paper, Tilburg University, Center for Economic Research 2004.

11. R. Libby and M. G. Lipe, "Incentives, Effort and the Cognitive Processes Involved in Accounting-Related Judgments," *Journal of Accounting Research* 30 (1992): 249–273. See also Joyce Ehrlinger, Kerri Johnson, Matthew Banner, David Dunning, and Justin Kruger, "Why the Unskilled Are Unaware: Further Explorations of (Absent) Self-Insight among the Incompetent," *Organizational Behavior and Human Decision Processes* 105 (January 2008): 98–121.

12. A list of 49 fallacies appears at David Straker, "Fallacies: alphabetic list (unique)." ChangingMinds.org, http://changingminds.org/disciplines/argument/fallacies/fallacies_unique.htm. Dr. Michael C. Labossiere lists 42 at "Fallacies," *The Nizkor Project*, http://www.nizkor.org/features/fallacies/. For a shorter top 20 list, see "Top 20 Logical Fallacies," *The Skeptics Guide to the Universe*, http://www.theskepticsguide.org/resources/logicalfallacies.aspx.

13. David Straker, "Fallacies," ChangingMinds.org, http://changingminds.org/disciplines/argument/fallacies/fallacies.htm.

Fair Value Measurement of Derivatives Contracts[1]

IN SEPTEMBER 2006, the Financial Accounting Standards Board (FASB) issued SFAS 157, *Fair Value Measurement*, a sleepy title to an accounting standard that had (and still has) huge implications for companies with balance sheets largely composed of financial instruments.[2] According to this standard, if a company holds financial assets or liabilities that are not exchange traded, it would mark to market those instruments at the *exit price*—defined as, what would a willing buyer pay for this?

Before this standard, the fair value definition was determined between a willing buyer and a willing seller. In the derivatives world, the midpoint between the bid and ask spread would suffice, and it did so for many years. In FAS 157, the FASB told corporations to mark to market derivatives contracts and other securities to the bid.

The new paradigm couldn't have happened at a worse time. Never did the FASB contemplate an economic environment market with an absence of willing buyers. As a result, companies wrote larger than expected mark-to-market losses on financial instruments that were worth less (if not worthless) simply because of the absence of buyers in the market on which to fairly estimate the bid amount. Counterparties providing estimated pricing needed to be willing to buy at the estimated level.

After two quarters of U.S. companies' posting mark-to-market losses that were blamed on SFAS 157, the FASB chairman clarified—in FAS 157–4—that discounted cash flows may be used as a reliable measure that conformed to the terms of U.S. GAAP.[3] But SFAS 157–4 did not eliminate fair value measurement. Although the financial instrument may be generating cash flows as expected, market conditions external to the company still ultimately determine the fair value measure.

Today, SFAS 157–4 is a cornerstone of valuation, under Codification Topic 820, Fair Value Measurements and Disclosures.

Notes

1. This appendix was prepared by Marti Tirinnanzi, principal examination specialist, Office of Market Risk, Federal Housing Finance Agency.
2. For the current standard, see Topic ASC 820 Codification Topic 820, Fair Value Measurements and Disclosures at fasb.org. (Registration is required.)
3. FASB, "Determining Fair Value When the Volume and Level of Activity for the Asset or Liability Have Significantly Decreased and Identifying Transactions That Are Not Orderly," April 9, 2009. http://www.fasb.org/cs/ ContentServer?c=Pronouncement_C&pagename=FASB%2FPronounce ment_C%2FStatusPage&cid=1176154735524.

APPENDIX M

Final Report of the Advisory Committee on Improvements to Financial Reporting to the United States Securities and Exchange Commission[1]

IN THIS FINAL REPORT, the Committee makes recommendations on 1. Substantive Complexity; 2. Standard Setting Process; 3. Audit Process; and 4. Delivering Financial Information. This appendix excerpts summaries of these sections.

1. Substantive Complexity

Recommendation 1.1

Avoidable complexity caused by the mixed attribute model should be reduced in the following respects:

> *Measurement framework*—The SEC should recommend that the FASB be judicious in issuing new standards and interpretations that expand the use of fair value in areas where it is not already required until:
>> The FASB completes a measurement framework to systematically assign measurement attributes to different types of business activities.

➤ The SEC, the FASB, and other regulators and standards-setters develop and implement a plan to strengthen the infrastructure that supports fair value reporting.
➤ *Financial statement presentation*—The SEC should recommend that the FASB consider the merits of:
  ➤ Assigning a single measurement attribute within each business activity to the maximum extent feasible, which is consistent across the financial statements.
  ➤ Aggregating financial statements by meaningful categories of business activities, such as the operating, investing, and financing sections.
  ➤ Developing a practical means for reconciling the statements of income and cash flows by major classes of measurement attributes.

Recommendation 1.2

The SEC and the FASB should work together to develop a disclosure framework to:

➤ Integrate existing SEC and FASB disclosure requirements into a cohesive whole to ensure meaningful communication and logical presentation of disclosures, based on consistent objectives and principles. This would eliminate redundancies and provide a single source of disclosure guidance across all financial reporting standards.
➤ Require disclosure of the principal assumptions, estimates, and sensitivity analyses that may impact a company's business, as well as a qualitative discussion of the key risks and uncertainties that could significantly change these amounts over time. This would encompass transactions recognized and measured in the financial statements, as well as events and uncertainties that are not recorded.

Recommendation 1.3

The SEC and FASB should also establish a process of coordination for the Commission and the FASB to regularly assess the continued relevance of disclosure guidance in both bodies of literature, particularly as new FASB standards are issued. Existing guidance should be updated or removed, as appropriate.

Recommendation 1.4

Recognition guidance in U.S. GAAP should be based on a presumption that bright lines should not exist. As such, the SEC should recommend that the recognition guidance in new projects undertaken jointly or separately by the FASB avoid the use of bright lines, in favor of proportionate recognition. Where proportionate recognition is not feasible or applicable, the FASB should provide qualitative factors in its recognition guidance. Finally, enhanced disclosure should be used as a supplement or alternative to the two approaches above. Any new projects should also include the elimination of existing bright lines in the recognition guidance of relevant areas to the extent feasible as a specific objective of those projects, in favor of the two approaches above.

Recommendation 1.5

Constituents should be better trained to consider the economic substance and business purpose of transactions in determining the appropriate accounting, rather than relying on mechanical compliance with rules. As such, the SEC should undertake efforts to, and also recommend that the FASB, academics, and professional organizations, better educate students, investors, preparers, auditors, and regulators in this respect.

Recommendation 1.6

U.S. GAAP should be presumptively based on business activities, rather than industries. As such, the SEC should recommend that any new projects undertaken jointly or separately by the FASB be scoped on the basis of business activities, except in rare circumstances. Any new projects should include the elimination of existing industry-specific guidance—particularly that which conflicts with generalized U.S. GAAP—in relevant areas as a specific objective of those projects, except in rare circumstances. Considering the pace of convergence efforts, the SEC should also recommend that in conjunction with its current codification project, the FASB add a project to its agenda to eliminate existing industry-specific guidance which conflicts with generalized U.S. GAAP, except in rare circumstances.

Recommendation 1.7

U.S. GAAP should be based on a presumption that formally promulgated alternative accounting policies should not exist. As such, the SEC should recommend that any new projects undertaken jointly or separately by the FASB not provide additional optionality, except in rare circumstances. Any new projects should also include the elimination of existing alternative accounting policies in relevant areas as a specific objective of those projects, except in rare circumstances.

Recommendation 1.8

U.S. GAAP should be scoped with sufficient precision to minimize the use of scope exceptions. As such, the SEC should recommend that any new projects undertaken jointly or separately by the FASB be carefully scoped to minimize the use of exceptions. Any new projects should also seek to refine the scope of existing standards in relevant areas as a specific objective of those projects to minimize existing scope exceptions.

Recommendation 1.9

U.S. GAAP should be based on a presumption that similar activities should be accounted for in a similar manner. As such, the SEC should recommend that any new projects undertaken jointly or separately by the FASB should not create additional competing models, except in rare circumstances. Any new projects should also include the elimination of competing models in relevant areas as a specific objective of those projects, except in rare circumstances.

4. Delivering Financial Information

Recommendation 4.1

The SEC should, over the long-term, mandate the filing of interactive data-tagged financial statements after the satisfaction of certain preconditions relating to: (1) successful XBRL U.S. GAAP Taxonomy testing, (2) the capacity of reporting companies to file interactive data-tagged financial statements using the new XBRL U.S. GAAP Taxonomy on the SEC's EDGAR system, and (3) the ability of the EDGAR system to provide an accurately rendered version of all such tagged information. The SEC should phase in interactive data-tagged financial statements as follows:

➤ The largest 500 domestic public reporting companies based on unaffiliated market capitalization (public float) should be required to furnish to the SEC, as is the case in the voluntary program today, a document prepared separately from the reporting companies' financial statements that are filed as part of their periodic Exchange Act reports. This document would contain the following:

➤ Interactive data-tagged face of the financial statements.

➤ Block-tagged footnotes to the financial statements.

➤ Domestic large accelerated filers (as defined in SEC rules, which would include the initial 500 domestic public reporting companies) should be added to the category of companies, beginning one year after the start of the first phase, required to furnish interactive data-tagged financial statements to the SEC. Once the preconditions noted above have been satisfied and the second phase-in period has been implemented, the SEC should evaluate whether and when to move from furnishing to the SEC interactive data-tagged financial statements to the official filing of such financial statements with the SEC for the domestic large accelerated filers, as well as the inclusion of all other reporting companies, as part of a company's Exchange Act periodic reports.

Recommendation 4.2

The SEC should issue a new comprehensive interpretive release regarding the use of corporate web sites for disclosures of corporate information, which addresses issues such as liability for information presented in a summary format, treatment of hyperlinked information from within or outside a company's web site, treatment of non-GAAP financial disclosures and GAAP reconciliations, and clarification of the public availability of information disclosed on a reporting company's web site.

Industry participants, including investors, should coordinate among themselves to develop uniform best practices on uses of corporate web sites for delivering corporate information to investors and the market.

Recommendation 4.3

The SEC should encourage private-sector initiatives targeted at best practice development of company use of KPIs in their business reports. The SEC should encourage private sector dialogue, involving preparers, investors (including analysts), and other interested industry participants, such as consortia that have long supported KPI-like concepts, to generate understandable, consistent, relevant, and comparable KPIs on relevant activity and, as appropriate, industry specific, bases. The SEC also should encourage companies to provide, explain, and consistently disclose period-to-period company-specific KPIs. The SEC should consider reiterating and expanding its interpretive guidance regarding disclosures of KPIs in management's discussion and analysis (MD&A) and other company disclosures.

Recommendation 4.4

Industry groups, including the National Investor Relations Institute, Financial Executives International, and the CFA Institute, should update their best practices for earnings releases. Such updated best practices guidance should cover, among other matters, the type of information that should be provided in earnings releases and the need for investors to receive information that is consistent from quarter to quarter, with an explanation of any changes in disclosures from quarter to quarter. Further, the best practices guidance should consider recommending that companies include in their earnings releases their condensed financial statements (including income statement, balance sheet, and cash flows); locate GAAP reconciliations in close proximity to any non-GAAP financial measures presented; and provide more industry- and company-specific key performance indicators [KPIs].

The SEC should consider reiterating its view that web site disclosures regarding GAAP reconciliations for non-GAAP financial measures presented in connection with earnings calls be available on such sites for at least 12 months.

Recommendation 4.5

The SEC should mandate the inclusion of an executive summary in the forepart of a reporting company's filed annual report on Form 10-K that will provide a roadmap to the fuller discussion in the report. In filed quarterly reports on Form 10-Q, the executive summary should provide material updates to the executive summaries in the annual or prior quarterly reports. The executive summary should provide summary information, in plain English, in a narrative and perhaps tabular format of the most important information about a reporting company's business, financial condition, and operations, and provide the context for the disclosures contained in the annual report.

As with the MD&A, the executive summary should be a concise and balanced discussion that identifies the most important themes or other significant matters with which management is primarily concerned. The executive summary should be required to use a layered approach that would present information in a manner that emphasizes the most important information about the reporting company and include cross-references to the location of the fuller discussion in the annual report.

To the extent a similar summary may otherwise be included or useful elsewhere in the report, such as in MD&A, the subsequent section would not need to replicate the discussion, but instead could cross-reference such executive summary. The summary should include page number references to more detailed information contained in the document (which, if the report is provided electronically, could be hyperlinks). The executive summary should be required for all filers, although we believe that the best approach would be to start with executive summaries for large companies and then gradually phase-in executive summaries for smaller public companies.

Note

1. Excerpted from Advisory Committee on Improvements to Financial Reporting, U.S. Securities and Exchange Commission, *Final Report of the Advisory Committee on Improvements to Financial Reporting to the United States Securities and Exchange Commission*, August 1, 2008, http://www.sec.gov/about/offices/oca/acifr/acifr-finalreport.pdf.

Valuing Values[1]

As you look at the value of an enterprise designed to make money, it may seem odd that its full value is not necessarily expressed by its bottom line, assets, or cash flow. Companies generate not just economic wealth; they generate social, technological, environmental, and other noneconomic impacts as well. In fact, wealth is not even the foundation of a value of a company; rather the value of a company lies in how its products and services add value to human existence, thereby creating wealth.

In recent years, a growing movement has sought to monetize and quantify these noneconomic impacts, opening up whole new ways to look at the value of an enterprise. This is not to say that philanthropy is the full measure of its social impact either. In fact, many business leaders would say it's just the tip of the iceberg. Companies contribute roughly $20 billion in philanthropy to local communities. By comparison, they invest over $1 trillion in employee benefits, generate over 150 million jobs in the United States and millions more around the world, and produce 85 percent of the products and services that support everyday life. This doesn't even take into account their interconnectedness with vendors and customers around the world. In short, our concept of the value of commercial enterprises is very underweighted if we focus on just traditional financial indicators.

The following discussion will provide a brief typology of issues affecting the social value of business.

Exhibit N.1 Value Pyramid

The Methodological Challenge

Social impacts come in many different incarnations. For example, suppose someone asked how your company reduces poverty—a top-tier social priority. You could argue that it does so by generating employment, lowering prices and increasing access to a product or service, through its philanthropic contributions to local charities, and because of the business your company provides to all of the vendors in your supply chain and the business your vendors provide to their supply chains, and so on.

Issues like time, populations served, and intensity of engagement affect social impact (see **Exhibit N.2**). Some people value intense engagements with a few people (i.e., hiring and retaining a few ex-offenders), while others favor breadth and outreach (support for a public service campaign on a cable channel). Some people favor immediacy: How much can we reduce violent crime in six months? Others favor endurance: How long can we keep violent crime at historically low levels? The individual business doesn't necessarily have the time or the means to calculate how its activities either depend on these social impacts or affect them.

Beyond questions of breadth or depth, endurance or immediacy, there are questions of aspect: Is education more important than health care or health care more important than the environment? How do you prioritize among various social needs?

There is a flip-side to this question, which is how to quantify the non-economic costs of an enterprise. Economists have labeled these costs "externalities," and they point to things like the effluent produced by a manufacturing process that pollutes a river stream as an example of this kind of cost. The firm does not pay the full cost of cleaning up

Exhibit N.2 Factors Influencing Social Impact

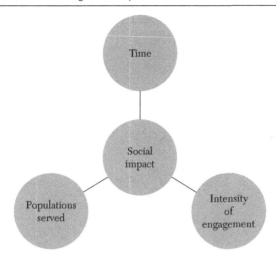

the pollution, nor is the cost fully priced into the products that it sells. There is a social impact that is externalized, or borne not by the firm, but by the surrounding community. These externalities can be difficult to quantify as well. What percentage of a stream's biological degradation can be directly attributed to any single source along a stream bank? The blending of public, private, and natural space complicates attribution and responsibility for externalities.

Economic Value and Social Value

Despite these methodological difficulties for the time being, let's say that we can bundle them into something we can collectively label as a firm's social value or, as Jed Emerson argues, the noneconomic portion of its "blended value." Emerson and others argue that a firm's total value is inextricably linked to all of its economic, political, social, and environmental impacts, and the sum total of these positive and negative contributions is its blended or total value (see **Exhibit N.3**).

This assumption lends itself to a simple way to segment four different questions of value:

➤ What is the economic value of its economic impacts, EV(EI)?
➤ What is the economic value of its social impacts, EV(SI)?

Exhibit N.3 Total Impact of a Corporation

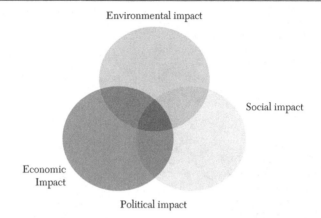

➤ What is the social value of its economic impacts, SV(EI)?
➤ What is the social value of a firm's social impacts, SV(SI)?

The EV(EI) is captured through balance sheets, income statements, cash flows, and P/E ratios.

As for the EV(SI) of the enterprise, Boston College's Center for Corporate Citizenship has labeled this the "business case" for corporate social responsibility and has grouped it into the following categories:

➤ Reputation
➤ License to operate
➤ Talent attraction, morale, and retention
➤ Operational efficiency
➤ Future business opportunities
➤ Sustainability

Reputation can be measured in terms of goodwill on the balance sheet, but it is also something deeper and more elusive to quantify. It can also be embedded in the value of the firm's brand, its marketing budget, its relationships with its customers (customer turnover), and its market share.

Johnson & Johnson (J&J) faced a terrible crisis when its product Tylenol was tampered with in 1982 and seven people died as a result of the poisoned medicine. Its enterprise value could have gone to zero, as Enron's did in 2002, but instead, the company actually saved the brand and increased market share. It is extremely doubtful that this kind of tragedy or brand strength was priced into the stock before the crisis, and yet there is no doubt that J&J's reputation played a crucial role in its survival.

Another major economic driver of corporate social responsibility (CSR) is what is called "license to operate," a shorthand way of describing the permissions or obstructions that a community imposes on a company to do business within its jurisdiction. CSR can help companies overcome NIMBY ("not in my backyard") opposition to site selections. It can help companies gain access to tax credits, subsidies, and other emoluments. It can reduce regulatory burdens and open channels of communication. Companies as varied as Walt Disney and Fairmount Minerals incorporate license to operate issues in their strategic planning. Metrics to consider on this score might include days from site selection to groundbreaking, community recruitment solicitations (how many times does your company get invited to come invest in a new community?), and comparative regulatory burdens.

Talent attraction, morale, and retention are other huge drivers of CSR practices. Companies like KPMG and Wegmans view their human talent as key differentiators. In this regard, attracting and retaining employees is a fundamental motivator for what they do. Companies with high social impact often find that employees give them a "home team" discount.

Operational efficiency has been a particularly pleasant outcome of some of the environmental stewardship practices implemented in many companies. UPS, for example, has reduced its fuel consumption. Many hotels have reduced water consumption and energy costs. Supermarkets have reduced paper and plastic costs by encouraging consumers to shift to reusable bags.

Future business opportunities can open up as a result of social concerns. Verizon had engaged with handicapped and elderly populations for many years, and as a product of its research, it found that some people had difficulties with phones with small keypads. When it developed a new phone with a larger dial pad, it developed a whole new product line.

There is also a gray area between philanthropy and social investment where sustainability practices also lie. Moving has often been cited as one of the top ten most stressful occurrences in an individual's life, and similar traumas arise when a firm decides to relocate. However, firms can and do relocate to take advantage of better tax structures, to be closer to customers, or to have access to better infrastructure, resources, or human talent.

This is why many community relations managers focus on improving their local communities as much as possible to sustain the capacity of their firm to continue to operate in their current location. It is very difficult to fully quantify the economic value of a vice president getting involved in a local school board or supporting a local symphony or arts program, but these activities contribute to the attractiveness of a community. Companies like SAS Institute and Google invest in chefs, day care centers, natural park and campus settings not just as whims, but because they contribute to the business environment.

Potential ways for pricing this kind of activity might include pricing the cost-benefit of relocating to other communities, employee recruitment, retention and benefit costs, the attraction of other companies and organizations to the community (expansion of local market opportunities), and quality-of-life metrics.

Just as companies are looking at the economic value of their social impacts, they are also beginning to take stock of the social impacts of their economic activities SV(EI). It doesn't cost Tastykake much one way or the other to maintain its headquarters in downtown Philadelphia, but by doing so it helps to anchor a neighborhood and prevent community disruption.

Many corporate foundation and corporate social responsibility managers struggle mightily with the question of valuing a firm's social impacts. As Cathy Clark and the team at the Research Initiative on Social Entrepreneurship (RISE) have documented, companies tend to track their inputs (number of hours volunteered or dollars given to charity) and their outputs (number of homes built with Habitat for Humanity for example), but things tend to break down when they try to evaluate the outcomes and their specific impact on the outcome of their social contributions (see **Exhibit N.4**).

This has to do with the complexity of variables associated with social projects. Do you think the food kitchen that increases the number of people it feeds is doing a better job than the food kitchen that reduces the number of people it feeds because it has helped some of its former clients gain self-sustaining employment?

Exhibit N.4 Relationship of Social Contributions to Effect on Enterprise

Case	Issue	Solution	Economic Value	Social Impact
AmCham Jamaica	Murder rate affecting tourism	Import Community Safety Best Practices from the United States and create public-private partnership with the Jamaican government	Better tourism image, less business risk	Reduce crime, improve community livability
Pfizer	HIV/AIDS in Africa	Distribution of Diflucan	Transmission knowledge/ delivery network	Better access to medical treatment
Manhattan Chamber	9-11 response	Small loans to small businesses	Keep small business base from going under south of 14th	Reduce neighborhood disruption, help to begin the healing process
Texaco	Artistic support	Sponsor the Metropolitan Opera	Brand, reputation	Enrich the cultural life of New York

Also, the ability to compare the value of an education program to a health care program is very contextual. When people are dying of HIV/AIDS, health may be paramount. When disease is relatively under control but literacy and skills capacity are low, education may be more vital. Which is a more important social impact: building a playground for all of the kids in a neighborhood or building a house for a single poor family?

The conventions don't currently exist, but companies are increasingly asking how to compare different social programs in different industries (food kitchens versus homeless shelters), how to evaluate different social programs in the same industry (food kitchen A versus food kitchen B), and how to evaluate the progress of the same social program over time (food kitchen A's social impact in 2008 versus 2009) In other words, how do you compare apples to oranges, apples to apples, and the apple over time? In this regard, a comparison with financial tools might be edifying.

Financial Investing vs. Social Investing Tools

The starkest contrast in investing tools exists between the tools available for investors seeking to capture the economic value of economic impacts and for investors seeking to capture the social value of social impacts.

As you can see in **Exhibit N.5**, there is no clear oversight agency for social reporting, no generally accepted accounting principles (GAAP) or accounting standards for social auditors, no generally accepted value statements, no generalized public update system like the stock ticker or the daily stock pages in major metropolitan newspapers, no consensus on currency, and no common standard on investor payback.

Nonprofit organizations have to file a Form 990 with the (Internal Revenue Service (IRS), which is basically a modified income statement. They have to list their top social programs, but their assessment of their progress is purely qualitative. There is nothing like the investigative resources of the U.S. Securities and Exchange Commission (SEC) or the rigorous accounting and reporting of GAAP and Financial Accounting Standards Board (FASB) support for social investors.

Exhibit N.5 Oversight Agencies and Social Reporting

Evaluation Support Systems	Financial Investor Support Infrastructure Measuring EV(EI)	Social Investor/ Philanthropy Support Infrastructure Measuring SV(SI)
Oversight agency	SEC	Part of the IRS
Accounting principles	GAAP	No generally accepted principles
Accounting standards	FASB	Does not exist for social value—use modified EV metrics
Value statements	Cash flow, balance sheet, income statement	990 (modified income statement—doesn't capture social outcomes)
Public update frequency	Daily (financial pages, stock tickers)	Does not exist
Currency	Dollars	Time, resource capacity, education, health, etc.
Investor payback	Return on investment	No common standard

Companies can deduct up to 10 percent of their pretax income for charitable contributions in some circumstances, but again, the cost-benefit of these contributions and their social efficacy is almost purely qualitative.

Likewise, nonprofit practices aren't grouped around Standard Industrial Classification (SIC) codes, despite the fact that there are now more than 1.5 million 501c3 nonprofit organizations in the United States.

This is not to say that there are not resources for companies interested in social investing. Organizations like the Foundation Center, Guidestar, and Charity Navigator provide information about nonprofit programs, and they provide assessments of their productivity.

However, even some of these services are confusing. Can you imagine buying a box of cereal with two prices broken out, one for the product and the other for the overhead associated with the box of cereal? Yet this is one way that nonprofits evaluate their efficiency, as though their accounting, administrative, and marketing efforts were somehow not integral to accomplishing their mission.

Cathy Clark and her team have begun to codify a different approach to capturing social impact. They argue that there are three general groups of metrics: (1) process methods that measure the efficiency and effectiveness of operations, (2) impact methods that relate to outputs and outcomes, and (3) monetization methods that seek to translate these social contributions into dollar values.

Whereas Guidestar and Charity Navigator may be particularly helpful in assisting investors in analyzing the efficiency and effectiveness of operations, impact and monetization are more problematic.

One of the most promising areas for evaluating impact is to benchmark social practices between communities. For example, as the number of major hurricanes making landfall has grown to become statistically significant in the modern era, the average is converging around a category 2, displacing 100,000 people for one week and causing 50 casualties or less. There are outliers like Hurricane Katrina, but as the sample becomes more statistically significant, it's going to be increasingly easier for managers to evaluate aid provider performance against the mean.

This is also driving the effort to collect data on school performance. Data mining now allows education investors to analyze performance by subject (math, science, reading, etc.), by income level, by race, ethnicity, and gender, and so forth, which enables investors to identify gaps that they want to address.

Cross-sector comparison is much more problematic. How do you compare contributions for tuberculosis to funding a scholarship? This is why the community chest and community foundation movement developed, which has grown into the United Way movement, and why many companies have set up open-ended employee volunteer and philanthropic programs with the help of agencies like Volunteer Match and The JK Group. The priorities that people place on different social programs are fluid, and they like to have a portfolio of projects that they can support. Sometimes health care issues are at the top of the list, sometimes environmental issues are, and sometimes education and poverty reduction can take pride of place. Companies don't necessarily want to be in the position of picking winners and losers, and in a sense they feel that if they are to engage with their local communities holistically, they need to be able to offer their employees the opportunity to engage in a wide array of them. (See **Exhibit N.6**.)

This still doesn't keep companies from trying to monetize their social contributions. A group of Minnesota companies came up with the idea of contributing 5 percent of pretax profits to community improvements. Target contributes over $2 million per week to charity. Salesforce.com funded the Salesforce.com Foundation with stock from the company. The industry average varies between 1 and 2 percent of pretax profits.[2]

Exhibit N.6 Financial versus Social Investor Support

	Financial Investor Support	Social Investor Support
Cross-sector comparisons	P/E, PEG, ROI	Grant levels, tax rebates
Industry comparisons	Same-store sales (retail), R&D pipeline (pharmaceutical), etc.	Recidivism rates (ex-offenders), tests (academic programs), vaccination rates (health), etc.
Entry decision	Stock purchase	Grant or sponsorship
Research firms	Lehman, Value Line, The Motley Fool	Guidestar, Charity Navigator
Brokers	Schwab, Merrill Lynch, T. Rowe Price	United Way, USA Freedom Corps
Exit Decision	Sell stocks	Cease grants/sponsorships

In this regard, the lack of tools for evaluating the economic value of social impacts is particularly acute. Some of the issues that are ripe for current and future study include:

➤ What is the economic impact of improving community safety? The Business Civic Leadership Center (BCLC) of the U.S. Chamber of Commerce has collected anecdotal evidence that community safety contributes significantly to small business investment, particularly in distressed communities.

➤ What is the economic impact of improved schools? Companies like PNC Financial Services and GlaxoSmithKline point to evidence that early childhood education and grade school career mentoring can have a significant impact on future employment success. Will every student that they support contribute directly to their own firm's profitability? Likely not, but CSR managers in both firms believe there will be operational benefits down the road. They consider themselves social investors, not just philanthropists.

➤ What is the economic impact of reducing the impact and duration of displacement from disasters? BCLC estimates that disasters now cause $38 billion a year in lost productivity to the United States. What any individual business does to contribute to disaster assistance may not be strictly economic, but there is an economic benefit to helping customers and vendors recover.

The more accurately that the economic impacts of social issues are known, the better firms will be able to price their social engagement and move away from strictly qualitative rules of thumb.

Significant progress has been made in developing architecture to capture the social value of economic impacts. In this regard, the Global Reporting Initiative has set up a template that over 1,000 organizations use to report on their activities. The impacts captured are focused on externalities such as environmental impact, workforce impact, human rights, community impacts, indigenous peoples, cultural sensitivity, and poverty alleviation.

Whereas in 1999 fewer than twenty Fortune 500 companies produced CSR reports, now a majority of the Fortune 1000 produce them, including companies like General Electric, UPS, and ExxonMobil.

A cottage industry of consultants and specialists has grown up around the effort to capture the social impacts of economic activities, including Business for Social Responsibility, AccountAbility, Sustainability, and Brody Weiser Burns, among others.

These efforts are having a financial impact as companies like KLD Research & Analytics and the Calvert Group use these metrics to decide which companies they invest in. As a percentage of the overall investor pool, socially responsible investors (SRIs, as they title themselves) are a small minority, accounting for $2.1 trillion of the $17 trillion capital pool surveyed by Jed Emerson and his team in 2003.[3] However, they have been growing increasingly more mainstream, as both the Dow Jones & Company and Financial Times have set up sustainability indexes: the Dow Jones Sustainability Index and FTSE4Good.

Again, the challenge for corporate directors is that SRI funds are highly fragmented and may have significantly divergent interests. Historically, they grew out of the desire of church funds' desire not to purchase so-called sin stocks like tobacco-, gambling-, or military-related ventures. Now there are funds targeted at environmental performance, against Burma, for distressed communities, against Cuba, for Cuba, and so on.

Corporate directors also have to recognize that not all SRI funds are primarily focused on securing optimal economic returns, but would rather sacrifice some financial return to meet their political or social objective. In recent years, companies have had to contend with a number of stakeholder resolutions around political objectives. Companies are having to distinguish between social issues that materially affect the economic future of the firm and those that serve as a distraction and reduce the future competitiveness of the firm. The problem is that they may have investors with different views about those distinctions. However, there aren't good systems established yet to monitor the economic responsibility of these SRI funds.

Engaging with investors who seek socially and economically "balanced" returns requires significant balanced judgment on the part of corporate directors.

Valuing Values

It is difficult in this brief sketch to map out all of the intricacies associated with trying to capture the total or blended value of a firm. However, corporate directors can see the value of values in a number of financial and operational metrics. These include:

➤ Intangible assets
➤ Goodwill
➤ Bad debt allowance
➤ Shrinkage
➤ Brand value
➤ Return/employee
➤ Length of accounts receivable
➤ Selling, general, and administrative expenses
➤ Lawsuits
➤ Not in my backyard (NIMBY)–related issues
➤ Employee recruitment costs
➤ Employee retention costs

On the other hand, corporate directors may want to keep an eye on social and environmental indicators such as:

➤ The firm's contribution to community quality of life, schools, environment, health care, poverty reduction, job and business creation
➤ Environmental outputs—emissions, carbon, waste, consumption
➤ Wages and benefits compared to employee peer groups
➤ Civic engagement (participation on nonprofit boards, volunteerism, donations, etc.)

But the value of values may lie in that hardest-to-quantify aspect: the ethical culture of the firm. Business is based on transactions. Successful businesses generate repeated transactions, and repeated transactions lead to relationships. Customers trust good businesses to deliver on their brand promise and provide quality goods and services. Employees trust that their employers will look out for their interests. Investors trust that the information they receive is credible, material, significant, and relevant. This is why surveys—including the survey coproduced by the BCLC and Boston College's Center for Corporate Citizenship—consistently show why business managers rate operating ethically above making a short-term profit. Without trust, businesses don't have any business, as amply demonstrated by Enron, Arthur

Andersen, WorldCom, Global Crossing, and a host of other inglorious examples of business scandal and chicanery. The value of values is that they enable businesses to build relationships with their customers, employees, investors, and the local communities that enable them to do business for the long term.

Notes

1. By Stephen Jordan, senior vice president and executive director, Business Civic Leadership Center, U.S. Chamber of Commerce, Washington, D.C. http://www.uschamber.com/bclc.
2. These corporate contribution figures are subject to change, and the most up-to-date figures can usually be found on the Web sites of most major companies. Also, at the time of writing, the Committee to Encourage Corporate Philanthropy, the Chronicle of Philanthropy, the Conference Board, and Giving USA all produce relevant information on this subject.
3. Jed Emerson and Sheila Bonini, "The Blended Value Map: Tracking the Intersects and Opportunities of Economic, Social and Environmental Value Creation," Blendedvalue.org, October 23, 2003, p. 28, http://www.blendedvalue.org/media/pdf-bv-map.pdf.

XBRL Guidance

What Is XBRL?[1]

XBRL is a language for the electronic communication of business and financial data that is revolutionizing business reporting around the world. It provides major benefits in the preparation, analysis, and communication of business information. It offers cost savings, greater efficiency, and improved accuracy and reliability to all those involved in supplying or using financial data.

XBRL stands for eXtensible *B*usiness *R*eporting *L*anguage. It is one of a family of XML[2] languages that is becoming a standard means of communicating information between businesses and on the Internet.

XBRL is being developed by an international nonprofit consortium of approximately 450 major companies, organizations and government agencies. It is an open standard, free of license fees. It is already being put to practical use in a number of countries and implementations of XBRL are growing rapidly around the world. . . .

The idea behind XBRL, eXtensible Business Reporting Language, is simple. Instead of treating financial information as a block of text—as in a standard Internet page or a printed document—it provides an identifying tag for each individual item of data. This is computer readable. For example, company net profit has its own unique tag.

The introduction of XBRL tags enables automated processing of business information by computer software, cutting out laborious and costly processes of manual re-entry and comparison. Computers can treat XBRL data "intelligently": they can recognize the information in an XBRL document, select it, analyze it, store it, exchange it with other computers and present it automatically in a variety of ways for users. XBRL greatly increases the speed of handling of financial data, reduces the chance of error and permits automatic checking of information.

Companies can use XBRL to save costs and streamline their processes for collecting and reporting financial information. Consumers of financial data, including investors, analysts, financial institutions, and regulators, can receive, find, compare, and analyze data much more rapidly and efficiently if it is in XBRL format.

XBRL can handle data in different languages and accounting standards. It can flexibly be adapted to meet different requirements and uses. Data can be transformed into XBRL by suitable mapping tools or data can be generated in XBRL by appropriate software.

How Can Investors in Companies Using U.S. GAAP Locate and Use XBRL Information?[3]

On January 30, 2009, the SEC adopted rules that would require companies to provide to the SEC financial statements in XBRL format, as well as posting to corporate web sites (if companies maintain web sites). These rules, which apply to domestic and foreign companies using U.S. GAAP and to foreign private issuers using International Financial Reporting Standards (IFRS) as issued by the International Accounting Standards Board (IASB) were are effective April 13, 2009.[4]

The XBRL data is required, as an exhibit, with a company's annual and quarterly reports, transition reports, and Securities Act registration statements as well as reports on Form 8-K or Form 6-K that contain revised or updated financial statements. The tagged disclosures will include companies' primary financial statements (including balance sheet, income statement, statement of comprehensive income, statement of cash flows and statement of owners' equity), footnote disclosures, and financial statement schedules. The disclosure in XBRL format must be submitted as an exhibit along with the traditional electronic filing formats in ASCII or HTML. (See **Exhibit O.1**.)

Exhibit 0.1 Table for XBRL

	S-1	S-3	S-4[1]	S-8	S-11	F-1	F-3	F-4[1]	10	8-K[2]	10-D	10-Q	10-K
(1) Underwriting agreement	X	X	X	—	X	X	X	X	—	X	—	—	—
(2) Plan of acquisition, reorganization, arrangement, liquidation, or succession	X	X	X	—	X	X	X	X	X	X	—	X	X
(3) (i) Articles of incorporation	X	—	X	—	X	X	—	X	X	X	X	X	X
(ii) Bylaws	X	—	X	—	X	X	—	X	X	X	X	X	X
(4) Instruments defining the rights of security holders, including indentures	X	X	X	X	X	X	X	X	X	X	X	X	X
(5) Opinion re legality	X	X	X	X	X	X	X	X	—	—	—	—	—
(6) [Reserved]	N/A	N/A	N/A	N/A	N/A	N/A	N/A	N/A	N/A	N/A	N/A	N/A	N/A
(7) Correspondence from an independent accountant regarding nonreliance on a previously issued audit report or completed interim review	—	—	—	—	—	—	—	—	—	X	—	—	—
(8) Opinion re tax matters	X	X	X	—	X	X	X	X	—	—	—	—	—

(*Continued*)

Exhibit 0.1 Table for XBRL (*Continued*)

	S-1	S-3	S-4I	S-8	S-11	F-1	F-3	F-4I	10	8-K2	10-D	10-Q	10-K
(9) Voting trust agreement	X	—	X	—	X	X	—	X	X	—	—	—	X
(10) Material contracts	X	—	X	—	X	X	—	X	X	—	X	X	X
(11) Statement re computation of per share earnings	X	—	X	—	X	X	—	X	X	—	—	X	X
(12) Statements re computation of ratios	X	X	X	—	X	X	—	X	X	—	—	—	X
(13) Annual report to security holders, Form 10-Q or quarterly report to security holders	—	—	X	—	—	—	—	—	—	—	—	—	X
(14) Code of Ethics				X	X	X	X		—			X	
(15) Letter re unaudited interim financial information	X	X	X	X	X	X	X	X	—	—	—	X	—
(16) Letter re change in certifying accountant	X	—	X	—	X	—	—	—	X	X	—	—	X
(17) Correspondence on departure of director	—	—	—	—	—	—	—	—	—	X	—	—	—
(18) Letter re change in accounting principles	—	—	—	—	—	—	—	—	—	—	—	X	X

Exhibit 0.1 Table for XBRL (*Continued*)

	S-1	S-3	S-4	S-8	S-11	F-1	F-3	F-4	10	8-K2	10-D	10-Q	10-K
(19) Report furnished to security holders	—	—	—	—	—	—	—	—	—	—	—	X	—
(20) Other documents or statements to security holders	—	—	—	—	—	—	—	—	—	X	—	—	—
(21) Subsidiaries of the registrant	X	—	X	—	X	X	—	X	X	—	—	—	X
(22) Published report regarding matters submitted to vote of security holders	—	—	—	—	—	—	—	—	—	—	X	X	X
(23) Consents of experts and counsel	X	X	X	X	X	X	X	X	—	X5	X5	X5	X5
(24) Power of attorney	X	X	X	X	X	X	X	X	X	X	—	X	X
(25) Statement of eligibility of trustee	X	X	X	—	—	X	X	X	—	—	—	—	—
(26) Invitation for competitive bids	X	X	X	—	—	X	X	X	—	—	—	—	—
(27) through (30) reserved													

Source: U.S. Securities and Exchange Commission Securities Act Forms and Exchange Act Forms, at U.S. SEC "17 CFR Parts 229, 230, 239, 240 and 249: Interactive Data to Improve Financial Reporting," § 229.601 (Item 601) Exhibits, pp. 160–161. http://www.sec.giv/rules/final/2009/33–9002.pdf.

Notes

1. The authors formed this appendix from several authoritative sources, including materials in the public domain from the Securities and Exchange Commission. The first seven paragraphs (the definition of XBRL) are adapted from "What is XBRL" from XBRL International, http://www.xbrl .org/Home, at http://xbrl.org/frontend.aspx?clk=LK&val=20. The remaining sections of this appendix are sourced as noted below in notes 3 and 4.
2. XML stands for extensible markup language.
3. From the American Institute of Certified Public Accountants." SEC Rules for Reporting Financial Statements in XBRL Format." http://www.aicpa .org/interestareas/accountingandauditing/resources/xbrl/pages/secrules-forreportingfinancialstatementsinxbrlformat.aspx?action=print.
4. U.S. SEC, "17 CFR Parts 229, 230, 232, 239, 240 and 249: Interactive Data to Improve Financial Reporting." http://www.sec.gov/rules/final/2009/ 33-9002.pdf.

Pension Fund Valuation Guidance

INTERNATIONAL ACCOUNTING STANDARDS determine how companies report the value of their pension fund assets. The International Financial Reporting Standards (IFRS) encourage (and may soon require) companies to include on the company balance sheet the value of *total future obligations* regarding employees' pension entitlements.

Before the end of 2004, under International Accounting Standard (IAS) 19, companies routinely *amortized* this obligation, spreading it out over time. Whenever an obligation would fall due (that is, whenever a retiree got a check), this obligation was recognized as a liability. Otherwise, it was not so recognized.

On December 16, 2004, however, the International Accounting Standards Board (IASB) issued an amendment to IAS 19, *Employee Benefits*. The IASB decided to allow the option of recognizing actuarial gains and losses *in full* in the period in which they occur, outside profit or loss, in a *statement of recognized income and expense*. (This option is similar to the requirements of the UK standard, FRS 17, *Retirement Benefits*.[1])

Until then, IAS 19 had required actuarial gains and losses (i.e., unexpected changes in value of the benefit plan) to be recognized in profit or loss (income statement), *either* in the period in which they occur *or* spread over the service lives of the employees. As mentioned, many entities chose to spread the gains and losses. Under the amendment, entities that were spreading the gains and losses were free change to that approach to a lump sum approach. And the amendment allowed companies that were already showing the surplus or deficit in full under

FRS 17 to continue with their present policy (but not to switch over to amortization). These amendments to FRS 17 were trying to nudge companies toward reporting the amounts in one lump sum. The December 2004 amendment also (1) specifies how group entities should account for defined benefit group plans in their separate or individual financial statements and (2) requires entities to give additional disclosures.

Also in the December 2004 amendments, the IASB confirmed its ongoing work on postemployment benefits, looking at fundamental aspects of measurement and recognition. Then, in April 2009, the IASB staff recommended that the board confirm its preliminary view that entities should recognize all changes in the value of plan assets and in the postemployment benefit obligation in the financial statements in the period in which they occur.[2] Here is an excerpt from the IASB release on this subject, from April 2010:

IASB Press Release
29 April 2010

IASB proposes improvements to defined benefit pensions accounting

The International Accounting Standards Board (IASB) today published for public comment an exposure draft of proposed amendments to IAS 19 *Employee Benefits*.

The proposals would amend the accounting for defined benefit plans through which some employers provide long-term employee benefits, such as pensions and post-employment medical care. In defined benefit plans, employers bear the risk of increases in costs and of possible poor investment performance.

The amendments would address deficiencies in IAS 19 by requiring entities:

➤ to account immediately for all estimated changes in the cost of providing these benefits and all changes in the value of plan assets (often referred to as removal of the 'corridor' method);

➤ to use a new presentation approach that would clearly distinguish between different components of the cost of these benefits; and

➤ to disclose clearer information about the risks arising from defined benefit plans.

The proposals have been developed following a rigorous and comprehensive due process. A discussion paper *Preliminary Views on Amendments to IAS 19* was published for public comment in 2008 with 150 comment letters received. The Board then met on 13 occasions to consider the responses and further refine the proposals, seeking input from a broad range of interested parties (including the IASB's Employee Benefits Working Group). The Board and staff will undertake further outreach during the comment period to ensure that the views of all interested parties are taken in to consideration.

Introducing the exposure draft, Sir David Tweedie, chairman of the IASB, said:

> IAS 19 was inherited from our predecessor body and an overhaul of pensions accounting is long overdue. The proposals, if adopted, will significantly improve the transparency and comparability of pension obligations.
>
> *(page 2)*

We now seek input from interested parties in order to refine the proposals further, with the aim of publishing a final standard in 2011.

The exposure draft *Defined Benefit Plans* is open for comment until September 6, 2010. It can be accessed via the "Comment on a proposal" section on www .iasb.org from today.

An IASB "Snapshot," a high-level summary of the proposals, is available to download free of charge from the IASB web site: http://go.iasb.org/pensions.

Notes

1. Experts cited by *Financial Times* expressed concern over the iBoxx AA 15-year-plus bond index, a traditional benchmark used by pension funds, and they predict a dispersion of discount rates. This, in turn, will lead to problems in comparing one pension fund's liabilities against another's. See Norman Cohen and Jennifer Hughes, "Call for Change in Pension Deficit Reporting." *Financial Times*, December 31, 2008.
2. IASB, "IASB Meeting Staff Paper: Recognition of Changes in Defined Benefit Obligations and in Plan Assets," April 2009, http://www.iasb .org/NR/rdonlyres/1A583703-BD94-4203-A4C8-56414B82393B/0/PEB-0904b03Aobs.pdf.

Stock Indexes

BY ANALYZING A COMPANY well and by remaining active in the company's governance, an investor can achieve sustained and significantly positive returns from an equity investment, compared to the market as a whole or a representative index.

At the same time, for the purposes of portfolio investment, it is a good idea to invest in one or more indexes, whether via a mutual fund or, for the professional, via an exchange-traded fund. We need to hedge against the bet that our own analysis is sound.

An index is a representative selection of stocks that captures a market as a whole, whether globally or nationally. A growing number of indexes have a theme or flavor, such as social responsibility, but in our view these are not really indexes—not really random walks through Wall Street; they are really special-purpose funds. Here are some of the more widely used indexes:[1]

➤ Amex Composite
➤ Dow Jones Industrial Average
➤ FTSE NASDAQ 500
➤ Morningstar
➤ MSCI World
➤ NASAQ 100
➤ NASDAQ Composite
➤ NYSE Composite
➤ Russell 3000
➤ S&P 500

➤ S&P Mid-Cap
➤ Vanguard 500
➤ Wilshire 5000

Note

1. This list is adapted from Nasdaq, "Stock Market Indices," http://quotes .nasdaq.com/aspx/marketindices.aspx.

U.S. Business Cycle Expansions and Contractions

Business Cycle Reference Dates		Duration in Months			
Peak	Trough	Contraction	Expansion	Cycle	
Quarterly dates are in parentheses		*Peak to Trough*	*Previous trough to this peak*	*Trough from Previous Trough*	*Peak from Previous Peak*
	December 1854 (IV)	—	—	—	—
June 1857 (II)	December 1858 (IV)	18	30	48	—
October 1860 (III)	June 1861 (III)	8	22	30	40
April 1865 (I)	December 1867 (I)	32	46	78	54
June 1869 (II)	December 1870 (IV)	18	18	36	50
October 1873 (III)	March 1879 (I)	65	34	99	52
March 1882 (I)	May 1885 (II)	38	36	74	101
March 1887 (II)	April 1888 (I)	13	22	35	60
July 1890 (III)	May 1891 (II)	10	27	37	40
January 1893 (I)	June 1894 (II)	17	20	37	30

(Continued)

(Continued)

December 1895 (IV)	June 1897 (II)	18	18	36	35
June 1899 (III)	December 1900 (IV)	18	24	42	42
September 1902 (IV)	August 1904 (III)	23	21	44	39
May 1907 (II)	June 1908 (II)	13	33	46	56
January 1910 (I)	January 1912 (IV)	24	19	43	32
January 1913 (I)	December 1914 (IV)	23	12	35	36
August 1918 (III)	March 1919 (I)	7	44	51	67
January 1920 (I)	July 1921 (III)	18	10	28	17
May 1923 (II)	July 1924 (III)	14	22	36	40
October 1926 (III)	November 1927 (IV)	13	27	40	41
August 1929 (III)	March 1933 (I)	43	21	64	34
May 1937 (II)	June 1938 (II)	13	50	63	93
February 1945 (I)	October 1945 (IV)	8	80	88	93
November 1948 (IV)	October 1949 (IV)	11	37	48	45
July 1953 (II)	May 1954 (II)	10	45	55	56
August 1957 (III)	April 1958 (II)	8	39	47	49
April 1960 (II)	February 1961 (I)	10	24	34	32
December 1969 (IV)	November 1970 (IV)	11	106	117	116
November 1973 (IV)	March 1975 (I)	16	36	52	47
January 1980 (I)	July 1980 (III)	6	58	64	74
July 1981(III)	November 1982 (IV)	16	12	28	18

July 1990 (III)	March 1991(I)	8	92	100	108
March 2001 (I)	November 2001 (IV)	8	120	128	128
December 2007 (IV)			73		81
Average, all cycles:					
1854–2001 (32 cycles)		17	38	55	56[a]
1854–1919 (16 cycles)		22	27	48	49[b]
1919–1945 (6 cycles)		18	35	53	53
1945–2001 (10 cycles)		10	57	67	67

Notes: Contractions (recessions) start at the peak of a business cycle and end at the trough.
[a]31 cycles.
[b]15 cycles.
Source: National Bureau of Economic Research, Inc. "US Business Cycle Expansions and Contractions," http://www.nber.org/cycles/cyclesmain.html.

The determination that the last expansion ended in December 2007 is the most recent decision of the Business Cycle Dating Committee of the National Bureau of Economic Research (NBER). The NBER does not define a recession in terms of two consecutive quarters of decline in real GDP. Rather, a recession is a significant decline in economic activity spread across the economy, lasting more than a few months, normally visible in real GDP, real income, employment, industrial production, and wholesale-retail sales. For more information, see the latest announcement from the NBER's Business Cycle Dating Committee, available from http://www.nber.org/cycles/cyclesmania.html.

Wisdom from Norway

Two Speeches from a Norwegian State Pension Plan Inspire a Long-Term View

From Oil to Equities: Knut N. Kjær[1]

The Government Pension Fund–Global is a unique instrument for diversifying government wealth and transforming income from temporary petroleum resources into a permanent flow of investment income. Financial theory offers a useful framework for both assessing the strategic future composition of wealth and for organizing the operational implementation of management.

What can really benefit future generations is that Norway succeeds in continuing the transformation/diversification of wealth into foreign financial assets. This increases the expected return and reduces the overall risk associated with the assets. There are very good reasons for increasing the allocation to equities, but this requires that we are able to adhere to the strategy under shifting market conditions.

As a financial investor, Norway earns the return provided by broad investment portfolios in the market. In this part of management there are substantial economies of scale, and under the present framework Norges Bank[2] can handle a considerably larger volume of capital. What is demanding is that active management must also consistently generate added value. This activity is talent-based. In this respect, we are a global operator constantly searching for talents. We are less concerned about whether they are employed by external managements companies or whether they are employees of NBIM [Norges Bank Investment Management].

A challenge that I could also have discussed at length is our task of acting as a demanding owner vis-à-vis the more than 3,000 companies in which we have an equity stake. So far this year, for example, we have voted on 23,363 issues in 2,189 companies. We have high ambitions with regard to playing a leading role internationally in fostering corporate governance and we are subject to a demanding requirement from the Ministry of Finance to take particular account of an investment horizon that spans many generations ahead. This implies imposing ethical requirements on companies.[3]

Investing for the Long Term: Governor Svein Gjedrem[4]

The oil age in Norway has spanned some 40 years, and it appears that it will continue for years ahead.

The idea of a fund arose in the early 1980s. Up to 1995, all government revenues were used for investment in the petroleum sector and to cover budget deficits during the recession around 1990. . . .

The accumulation of capital in the Government Pension Fund–Global reflects the depletion of a nonrenewable resource, which is exchanged for financial assets through the Fund's investments (see **Exhibit S.1.**). Sound returns on these investments will help us cope with future financial commitments linked to an aging population.

Exhibit S.1 Market Value of the Government Pension Fund–Global (billions NOK[5])

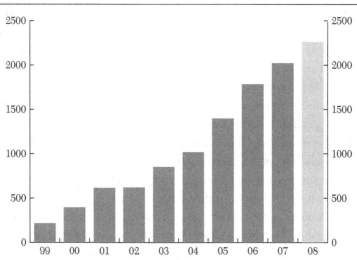

But at the same time as the wave of an aging population flows toward us with its demand for public services and increased consumption, we also should ask if investments in Norway could be an alternative to those we make in international financial markets. And clearly, a good argument could be made for investing more in schools, universities, and research to develop our human capital. But that should be possible in any case, given the increased spending the fiscal rule already allows for.

It could also be argued that we should invest more in our domestic infrastructure, for example roads and highways. This may be important for regional reasons. But on the margin, these investments are probably not adding very much to our economic growth. To illustrate this point, the net present value of road projects in the new 10-year national investment plan is estimated at some NOK 20 billion after positive effects on road safety and the environment have been taken into account.[6]

Among other important tasks in coming years and decades, the government would need return from financial assets to provide for future pensioners. We can probably expect that productivity and real wages will continue to grow in parallel, and future pensioners would most likely want to take part in that welfare gain. This may imply that government expenditures will increase more than the overall growth in the economy, as the number of pensioners is growing fast and the demand for healthcare also will be higher. Although real wages increase, it will not be easy to raise the tax level. Thus, the government will need return from financial assets to finance the increased expenditure for pensioners.

International capital markets have played a crucial role in allowing us to follow the strategy for extraction of petroleum. We drew heavily on borrowing opportunities abroad when the petroleum industry was being built up. We did the same in order to expand welfare schemes and to finance the countercyclical policy of the mid-1970s and the early 1990s. Over the last decade and a half, international capital markets have enabled us to convert national oil and gas resources into equities and bonds abroad in the Fund.

The implementation of our investment strategy is dependent on free capital movements. I would like to remind the audience that only some 25 to 30 years ago we had very rigorous capital restrictions ourselves. For instance, Norwegians could only purchase foreign equities through a fixed pool established in the 1960s (by using the so-called "security dollar" market), and foreigners' investments in Norwegian equities were strictly regulated and actually limited to NOK 50,000 per person until 1979. That ceiling was raised to NOK 1 million in 1979.

Experiences over the past year may cast doubt on the effectiveness and benefits of international capital markets. Nevertheless, history has seen a number of deep financial crises, and it is my belief that market conditions will also return to normal this time. I am confident that private entrepreneurship and public limited companies will continue to exist as the primary organizational bodies for commercial activities.

Owners and investors will also be needed in the years to come. But capitalism will have to adapt. After all, the willingness to trust the free play of market forces in finance has been seriously impaired.

International stock exchanges lost more of their value in 2008 than in any other single year in recent history. Absolute results, especially with regard to equities, were highly unusual. Many investors have suffered losses. As a result of this experience, required returns will be higher in the future. An investor such as the Government Pension Fund–Global will earn more in the long term because of wide fluctuations in equity values.

The Fund has a longer investment horizon than the vast majority of other market participants. The important question is therefore how sound today's investments will prove to be in the long term. The government now owns close to 1 percent of the global business sector. This represents real value that will provide a return reflecting both global economic growth and the risk related to fluctuations in equity prices.

Another virtue of the Fund is the strict division of labor between the Norwegian government as owner and Norges Bank as the manager. The bank has been given a clear mandate which regulates our responsibilities as the operational manager of the Fund.

The Fund has important distinguishing characteristics which form the basis for the investment strategy. The most important are its size and long-term investment horizon. Our potential to achieve results as an investor lies in turning these factors to the Fund's benefit through active strategies, and our most important advantage is the possibility of implementing these strategies at low cost.

Our owner expects added value from active ownership. It is important that large institutional investors such as Norges Bank exercise their rights as minority shareholders. In our dealings with companies, our legitimacy and influence depend on us being seen as a long-term investor pursuing financial interests.

It is clear to me that the quality of the investment management organization can only be ensured by pursuing excellence in all parts of the investment activities. To build an organization which aims to be average will only assure mediocrity.

The financial crisis revealed that many institutions based their strategies on short-term funding. When credit was no longer available, many business models collapsed. Heavy losses were passed on to owners and investors.

The situation for savings in the Fund is different. We have had to record losses on equity investments and active credit investments. However, the Fund has no traditional liability side and liquidity risk is low. The growing risks in the market did not force us to make changes that would have resulted in huge realized losses for our owners.

The final results of our strategies through the troubled waters of the financial crisis cannot be deduced from the quarterly results at the peak of the crisis. Actually, the Fund has spent the last few quarters increasing its ownership in companies worldwide. As for credit, values are not lost as long as borrowers fulfill their obligations. The Fund is prepared to retain ownership of its illiquid investments until they mature in a few years time. Moreover, unless the economic outlook goes from bad to considerably worse, the Fund will record a substantial excess return in years ahead from holding on to assets that the market has priced down due to a collapse in liquidity and fear. In fact, as the global economy seems to be stabilizing, this effect is already evident.

Let me conclude by underlining the topic of this conference: "Investing for the long run." The Fund is a long-term savings plan and capable of riding out large swings in the markets. This is the very foundation of the investment strategy. Our ability to adhere to this strategy in a critical phase—even if this should last for some time—is crucial if the Fund is to deliver the returns we expect in the longer term.

Epilogue

In a January 29, 2010, presentation, Yngve Slyngstad, CEO of Norges Bank Investment Management, struck a blow for active investment:

"Norges Bank cannot recommend a passive investment strategy which does not seek to achieve cost effective market exposure, insight into the underlying assets in which we are invested, or an understanding of the overall risk of our investments."

Slyngstad was responding to a December 1, 2009, report, *Evaluation of Active Management of the Norwegian Government Pension Fund–Global*, which recommended supplementing active investment with a more automated approach using "exotic betas" that would mimic investment activism.[7]

Slyngstad's simple statement at the end of a lengthy struggle to defend live investment is the investment equivalent of Martin Luther spiking his manifesto on the cathedral door.

Norge Bank has taken the hard road. It has analyzed transaction costs, the pluses and minuses of size, and the advantages and drawbacks of indices—and has come to the conclusion that large, long-term investors will need to be active.

We will refrain from reading too much into this carefully reasoned statement. However, it may not be too optimistic to say that inefficiencies are of the essence in securities markets, so opportunity, in the abstract, is abundant.

Robert A. G. Monks and Alexandra R. Lajoux, June 30, 2010.

Notes

1. "From oil to equities: Address by Knut N. Kjær, Executive Director of the Norwegian Pension Fund–Global, at the Norwegian Polytechnic Society on 2 November 2006," *Norges Bank*, http://www.norges-bank.no/templates /article____51952.aspx.
2. The central bank of Norway.
3. As of late 2009, the performance of this fund remained strong.
4. Excerpted from "Investing for the long run: Dinner speech by Governor Svein Gjedrem at The Norwegian Government Pension Fund's Investment

Strategy Summit, Oslo, 3 June 2009," *Norges Bank*, http://www.norges-bank.no/templates/article____74109.aspx.

5. Norwegian krone.

6. "National Transport Plan 2010–2019" (St.meld.nr.16 (2008–2009)).

7. Andrew Ang, William Goetzman, and Steven Schaefer, *Evaluation of Active Management of the Norwegian Government Pension Fund*–Global http://www.regjeringen.no/upload/FIN/Statens%20pensjonsfond/rapporter/AGS%20Report.pdf.

Recommended Reading on Corporate Securities Valuation

VALUING SECURITIES ISSUED by publicly traded companies takes time and hard-earned experience, but these 12 books can speed investors through the school of hard knocks. Some are classics written decades ago, but only the most recent edition or printing is listed. (The present book is included here in the humble hope that serious practitioners, teachers, and students of valuation will include it in their canon as well.)

Buffett, Warren E. *The Essays of Warren Buffet,* 2nd ed., edited by Lawrence A. Cunningham. New York: The Cunningham Group, 2008.

Damodaran, Aswath. *Damodaran on Valuation: Security Analysis for Investments,* 2nd ed. Hoboken, N.J.: John Wiley & Sons, 2006.

English, James. *Applied Equity Analysis: Stock Valuation Techniques for Wall Street Professionals.* New York: McGraw-Hill, 2001.

Graham, Benjamin, and David Dodd. *Security Analysis,* 6th ed. New York: McGraw-Hill, 2009.

Koller, Tim, Mark Goedhart, and David Wessels. *Valuation: Measuring and Managing the Value of Companies,* 4th ed. Hoboken, N.J.: John Wiley & Sons, 2005.

LeBaron, Dean, and Romesh Vaitilingam. *Treasury of Investment Wisdom.* Hoboken, N.J.: John Wiley & Sons, 2002.

Monks, Robert A. G., and Alexandra R. Lajoux. *Corporate Valuation for Portfolio Investments: Assets, Earnings, Cash Flow. Stock Price, Governance, and Special Situations.* Hoboken, N.J.: John Wiley & Sons, 2011.

Rappaport, Alfred, and Michael J. Mauboussin. *Expectations Investing: Reading Stock Prices for Better Returns.* Boston: Harvard Business School Press, 2001.

Rosenbaum, Joshua, and Joshua Pearl. *Investment Banking: Valuation, Leverage Buyouts, and Mergers & Acquisitions.* Hoboken, N.J.: John Wiley & Sons, 2009.

Soros, George. *The Alchemy of Finance.* Hoboken, N.J.: John Wiley & Sons, 2003.

Stowe, John D., Thomas R. Robinson, Gerald E. Pinto, and Dennis W. McCleavey. *Equity Asset Valuation.* Hoboken, N.J.: John Wiley & Sons, 2007.

Vause, Bob. *Guide to Analysing Companies,* 5th ed. (Economist Series). New York: Bloomberg Press, 2009.

Index